THE DECORATED TENEMENT

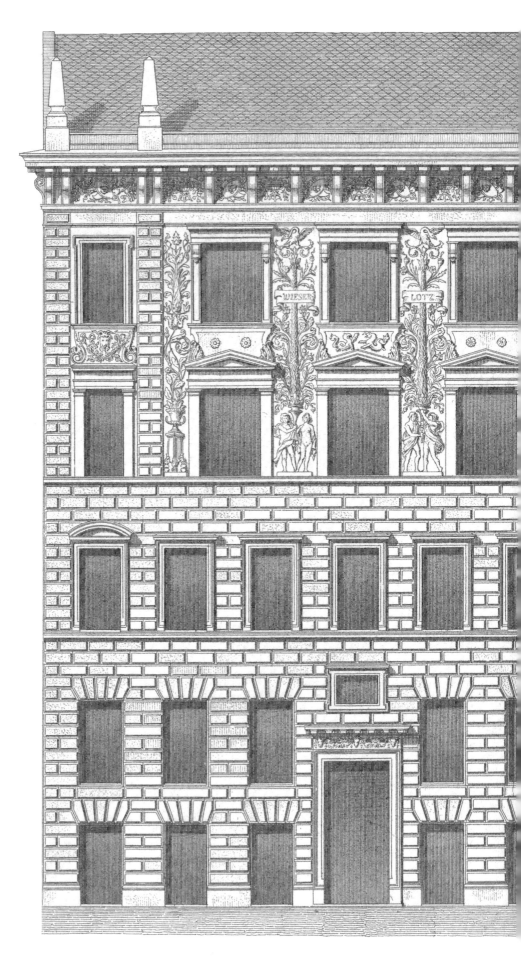

THE DECORATED TENEMENT

How Immigrant Builders and Architects Transformed the Slum in the Gilded Age

ZACHARY J. VIOLETTE

University of Minnesota Press

Minneapolis || London

Illustrations in this book were funded in part or in whole by a grant from the SAH/Mellon Author Awards of the Society of Architectural Historians.

Published by the University of Minnesota Press
111 Third Avenue South, Suite 290
Minneapolis, MN 55401-2520
http://www.upress.umn.edu

Printed in Canada on acid-free paper

The University of Minnesota is an equal-opportunity educator and employer.

25 24 23 22 21 20 19   10 9 8 7 6 5 4 3 2 1

Library of Congress Cataloging-in-Publication Data
Names: Violette, Zachary J., author.
Title: The decorated tenement : how immigrant builders and architects transformed the slum in the Gilded Age / Zachary J. Violette.
Description: Minneapolis : University of Minnesota Press, 2019. | Includes bibliographical references and index. | Identifiers: LCCN 2018045735 (print) | ISBN 978-1-5179-0412-8 (hc) | ISBN 978-1-5179-0413-5 (pb)
Subjects: LCSH: Tenement houses—United States—History—19th century. | Architecture and society—United States—History—19th century. | Immigrants—Housing—United States—History—19th century.
Classification: LCC NA7880 .V56 2019 (print) | DDC 728/.314097309034—dc23
LC record available at https://lccn.loc.gov/2018045735

Contents

∩∩∩∩∩∩∩∩∩∩∩∩∩∩∩

Situating the Decorated Tenement

∪∪∪∪∪∪∪∪∪∪∪∪∪∪∪

> What is to be said to the tenement population is to be said plainly, that flourishes are not wanted any more than they can be afforded.
>
> **Grosvenor Atterbury, 1906**

> I should think with a few modifications in the interests of the health, decency and cheerfulness of the inmates, his plan for a "model" tenement house might do very well for the indigent or the criminal.
>
> **Peter Herter, 1900**

At the dawn of the twentieth century, Harris Fine and Florence Van Cortlandt Bishop both set about improving the notorious housing conditions on the Lower East Side of New York, which throngs of immigrants were then making one of the most densely populated places on earth.[1] To do so, both built modern, six-story, white-brick tenements on the neighborhood's crowded streets. But the social distance between Fine, himself a recent immigrant, and Bishop, a wealthy widow from an old family, was far greater than the four blocks that separated their projects, at 303–305 Broome Street and 58 Hester Street, respectively. Fine's and Bishop's differing economic backgrounds, cultural frames of reference, and apparent attitudes toward tenement life informed sharply divergent approaches to their new buildings. The varying priorities reflected in the design of these tenements, and the many others like them, gave distinct visual and physical dimension to many of the class and cultural conflicts at the heart of the Gilded Age city.[2]

The housing Fine provided for his working-class and immigrant tenants was markedly better than anything such residents could have expected in this neighborhood even a generation earlier. A carpenter by trade, Fine had fled the pogroms of his native Russia in 1884. Living just a few blocks away from his Broome Street project, he responded to the preferences, tastes, and desires of his tenants, with whom he shared far more similarities than differences.[3] Therefore, his 1899 tenement had many features that until recently had been reserved for a much higher grade of housing, incorporating many advances in industrial production. For much of the nineteenth century, the urban working class had been terribly housed, often crowded into two-room units in hand-me-down buildings with few conveniences. But the five-room apartments at 303–305 Broome Street had designated formal dining rooms and parlors—cherished markers of gentility—as well as modern amenities, like kitchens with hot water boilers and dumbwaiter access, and full private bathrooms. Residents entered through a frescoed and mosaic-tiled lobby and ascended a marble-treaded stair. But most publicly and dramatically in a neighborhood long dismissed as a slum, the facade was exuberant with classical terra-cotta ornamentation in high relief, with a tall sheet-metal cornice stamped with gilded letters proudly announcing Fine's name (Plate 1).[4] The ornate facade was an important achievement, an exercise in visual equality in a culture that signaled social capital in large measure through such public displays. In doing so the architects, German-born Herman Hornberger and Charles Straub, were engaging with a deep tradition of such facades on the European continent. Hornberger and Straub specialized in tenement construction, designing hundreds of similar buildings for immigrant developers throughout the city's working-class neighborhoods. Having worked for over a decade to save the necessary capital, and borrowing the rest from immigrant bankers, Fine would eventually build at least a dozen new tenements on this model, including two entire block fronts on Broome Street (see Figure 3.23 and Plate 22). While he was rapidly reforming the housing conditions of his neighborhood, Fine's work was by no means philanthropy but a vibrant, indeed highly profitable immigrant enterprise deeply engaged with the culture of a growing enclave.

Bishop had other ideas about how to reform the tenement. If she even perceived the substantial social and material improvements represented by Fine's buildings, she probably dismissed them as a cheap sham or a distasteful sign of misplaced priorities. From a prominent and well-established New York family and the widow of socialite millionaire David Wolfe Bishop, she was heir to a great fortune made in hardware and real estate.[5] Thus, she may have shared the class, ethnic, and religious prejudices that caused many in her circle to view upwardly mobile new immigrants like Fine with suspicion or disdain. A longtime patron of the Catherine Street Mission with a genuine desire to ameliorate poor living conditions, she thought she could intervene more positively in the lives of the immigrant working class than the "skin builders" like Fine then making money in these neighborhoods.[6] She thought, however, that instead of being accommodated, her tenants' tastes and desires needed to be reformed and disciplined to more closely comport with what was expected by the American class hierarchy. So her 1901 tenement at 58 Hester Street was to be a model of good taste and proper living. While Bishop directed construction from her summer house in the

Berkshires in western Massachusetts, she turned to architect Ernest Flagg.[7] Famous for his skyscraper designs, the wealthy and well-connected architect was deeply interested in housing as a social issue. He declared that the tenements in which most New Yorkers lived were "evil," a frequently repeated and literally meant refrain informed by a widespread American aversion to multifamily housing. While he advocated a cure in the form of philanthropic housing, Flagg's notions were mostly theoretical; by 1901 only a handful of his model tenements had been built.[8] Indeed, many of his ideas sprang from a fundamental misunderstanding and mistrust of urban working-class culture. For example, fearful that tenants would take in boarders or manufacture goods in their homes—common and vital economic strategies that were anathema to middle-class notions of domesticity—Bishop and Flagg reverted to a two-room plan, long out of fashion except among reformers, to make either activity more unpleasant or impossible. Residents would have an open living room, larger than any single room in Fine's tenement, for eating, cooking, living, and work. The second room served as a bedroom. Distrustful that residents would use a bathtub for its intended purpose, the reformers eschewed the full bathrooms of Fine's building in favor of a water closet adjoining each living room. (This was still an advance over the shared toilets that had been standard in new tenements until a few years earlier.) But the most striking and immediately recognizable difference between Bishop's and Fine's buildings was the treatment of the facade. Gone was the terra-cotta finery, replaced by an austere but sanitary wall of glazed white brick (Figure I.1). Yet Bishop's building cost nearly

Figure I.1. Florence Van Cortlandt Bishop Tenement, 58 Hester Street, New York (1901). Ernest Flagg, architect. For plan, see Figure 7.8B. Designed by an important architect for a wealthy client and lauded as a philanthropic model, this tenement embodied elite reformers' class-infused notions of propriety. Compare to the nearby contemporaneous building in Plate 1. Photograph by Sean Litchfield.

30 percent more to build than Fine's, and residents could expect to pay similar, if not higher, rents for their rooms.[9]

Flagg's idea of a model tenement irked Peter Herter, an architect and builder born and educated in Germany, who along with his two brothers had been designing and building their own type of improved tenement in New York since the 1880s. Indeed, Fine's buildings owed much to Herter's model. An important but largely forgotten figure, throughout this book Herter will act as our guide to the lost world of the immigrant tenement builder and architect. In 1900 he excoriated the appearance and accommodations of Flagg's model tenement in the *Real Estate Record and Builders' Guide,* the city's leading building trades publication:

> I almost fear poor Mr. Flagg made a mistake, and instead of sending you a plan for a tenement house, he sent you a plan that was left over in his office for a poor house or a prison. I never designed a building of either class, but I should think with a few modifications in the interests of the health, decency and cheerfulness of the inmates, his plan for a "model" tenement house might do very well for the indigent or the criminal.[10]

Flagg's design was certainly not a mistake but clearly reflected his view of the purpose of the model tenement. Like the prison or the poorhouse, it was an institution of social reform and control, provided at limited profit (but charging market rent) through the philanthropy of genuinely concerned citizens to inculcate proper standards of living, taste, domesticity, work habits, and even morality among its inmates. To Herter, on the other hand, the tenement was a commercial product, efficiently produced but thoughtfully calibrated to meet, not reform, the desires, tastes, aspirations, and income of its residents and to profit its builder. "I have no hesitation in saying," Herter declared of Flagg, "that . . . he knows very little about tenement houses and the people who live in them, what they want, and what they will and will not pay for." The disdain Flagg and many other reformers had for the needs and tastes of most tenants led Herter to conclude that "the greatest enemies of the poor . . . have often been their public friends."[11]

The contrast between Bishop's austere tenement and Fine's elaborated one appeared frequently in the dense immigrant working-class neighborhoods of both New York and Boston. In the latter city, the North End buildings of the reform-minded Boston Cooperative Building Company, designed by prominent architects including Cabot & Chandler and Alexander W. Longfellow, were dour red-brick piles, following a well-established pattern.[12] Cabot & Chandler's 1887 building at Thatcher and Endicott Streets was perhaps the most dignified, meeting the intersection with an elegant curve (Figure I.2). Most of their other tenements were plain as a storage warehouse. Like Flagg, Cabot & Chandler employed a visual vocabulary of poverty, an austerity of appearance and accommodations that used architectural forms to reify traditional class differentiations. Not surprisingly then, their treatment of this corner paled in comparison to the elaborate display of sheet-metal covered oriels and terra-cotta ornament that appeared on Etta Lebowitch's building two blocks away at the intersection of Prince and Salem Streets (Plate 2). Built just a few years later by a Russian Jewish immigrant, and designed by Charles A. Halstrom, who was raised in a North End tenement by immigrant parents, the Lebowitch tenement leveraged the leveling and bettering influences of industrial production, transgressing well-established boundaries to soften the highly visible class differences that had long marked the housing and material culture of the working class.[13]

Reform-minded elites like Flagg, Bishop, Cabot & Chandler, and the backers of the Boston Cooperative Building Company have long played a prominent role in social and architectural historians' narrative on housing in the late nineteenth- and early twentieth-century city. This book, however, is different, decidedly shifting the focus away from the myriad housing reform movements and their representations. While intellectually and socially important and crucial for later developments such as urban planning and public housing, these movements produced a vanishingly small number of buildings and laws that changed the shape, if not the substance, of tenement construction in this period. Reform is therefore a highly problematic lens through which to understand a substantial portion of the urban landscape.

Instead, this book delves deeply into the object of that reform: buildings like those built by Fine and Lebowitch and designed by architects like Halstrom, Herter,

Figure I.2. Boston Cooperative Building Company Tenement, 13 Thatcher Street, Boston (1887). Cabot & Chandler, architects. This building meets its intersection with an elegant curve, but it still follows a well-established pattern of austere philanthropic tenements in Boston. Compare to the nearby building in Plate 2. Photograph by Sean Litchfield.

and Hornberger and Straub. These first-generation (and to a lesser extent second-generation) immigrant architects and builders were instrumental in shaping the working-class landscape of the late nineteenth- and early twentieth-century city, building housing on a much larger scale than the reformers. Indeed, the majority of the tenements in these cities were built by people like them in the period between the Civil War and World War I. And in this book I endeavor to meet them on their own terms, situating their buildings primarily in the context of working-class taste and living standards instead of outsiders' often hostile perceptions. In treating these buildings and those who created them as worthy of sustained and sympathetic attention, I hope to shed light on underappreciated aspects of this important historical moment, complicating monolithic notions of architectural taste and housing standards, and exploring the diversity of backgrounds and cultural positions of those responsible for the creation of housing and urban space in the Gilded Age city.

Indeed, while urban historians interested in real estate and immigration, most notably Jared Day and Donna Gabaccia, have demonstrated the important part immigrant developers played, these builders' contribution to the built form of the tenement and to the rapid remaking of the urban landscape has been poorly understood.[14] The form and appearance of the American tenement as they came to be understood were directly influenced by this era's patterns of cultural migration and widespread economic and social changes. The design of these buildings reflected much of the cross-cultural hybridity of the cosmopolitan American city in the early stages of industrial capitalism. But these new buildings also played an important role in the life of the immigrant working class. They helped mitigate the squalor of the antebellum slums with new, commodious, and, to many, attractive buildings, responsive to the desires of new populations there. And the social position of these builders and architects was key to this process. Knowing much more than housing reformers about tenements and the people who inhabited them, immigrant builders and architects were the driving force in a major rise in working-class living standards that occurred in the last years of the nineteenth century. Yet their role in shaping the urban landscape has been consistently ignored, if not maligned, in favor of a narrative that privileges elite interventions. This omission was largely an artifact of the suspicion and disdain with which the American city, and those who built it, has long been viewed.

The Tenement City

Like railroad lines, steam engines, factories, department stores, elevators, and skyscrapers, the tenement played a key part in the process of urbanization in nineteenth-century Boston and New York, an era of dramatic social, economic, and cultural change. Thus, it was treated with the same sort of ambivalence that greeted this rapid restructuring of American life, leading many to express unease with the consequences of modernity, urbanity, and industrial capitalism. The tenement, as a specialized building type, developed simultaneously with the formation of the American

working class.[15] As historian Elizabeth Blackmar has noted, the earliest manifestations of the tenement in the early part of the century were intimately tied to the rise of
wage labor and the concomitant breakdown of older systems of craft production and
apprenticeship, and the severing of relationships of interdependence. The housing crisis resulting from the Panic of 1837, occurring alongside rapid urban growth resulting
from internal improvements such as the Erie Canal, was the major impetus for the
development of the first tenements in New York.[16] The appearance of these buildings
in Boston during a slightly later period tracked similar changes, as both cities became
a place of interchange for people, goods, and ideas to and from the hinterlands. Into
this already dynamic environment, mass immigration after about 1845, first from
Ireland and Germany and after about 1880 from southern and eastern Europe, dramatically increased the scale of urban growth.[17]

The often-repeated population statistics give a sense of this dislocating change.
The population of Boston, whose social, demographic, and economic preeminence
dimmed in this period, still rose dramatically from just over eighteen thousand in
1790 to nearly three-quarters of a million by 1910. New York's economic and cultural
position solidified, with a population that skyrocketed from just over thirty-three
thousand to over four million in the same period. And both cities were focal points
of European immigration. At the turn of the twentieth century, New York and Boston
boasted the highest percentage of foreign-born inhabitants of all major American
cities.[18]

And these two cities, for reasons of geography and culture, were unusual among
their American counterparts for their reliance on dense multifamily housing to shelter these new crowds, a fact that led to frequent, and not always favorable, comparison
with Europe and each other.[19] As early as 1865, the tenement was a well-established
form in New York, which boasted over fifteen thousand such buildings, both purpose-
built and converted structures; thousands more could be found in Boston.[20] By the
turn of the twentieth century, half the residents of both cities were said to live in
tenements.[21]

These statistics bore on a fundamental tension in Gilded Age America between
those who believed multifamily housing was necessary and even desirable, and the
other half who considered it a threat to American ideals, especially when occupied by
the immigrant poor and working class.[22] Indeed, the rise of the tenement landscape
was far from neutral, but a site of struggle that bore upon key questions of American
self-conception. No physical object seemed to more fully represent the threat that
mass urbanization and immigration posed to cherished ideas of American culture
and society than the tenement. Redolent with associations with the struggles of the
Old World, incompatible with the apparent spaciousness of the North American continent, multifamily housing seemed to many well-established Americans an incomprehensibly foreign and perhaps even ominous institution to be avoided at all costs.
As one period observer noted bluntly in 1892, "Americans will not, as a rule, occupy
tenements."[23]

If the city was the economic engine of nineteenth-century industrial capitalism, and the tenement an important part of that growth, the rise of both was treated with ambivalence and mistrust. An abiding strain of American thought, often repeated but by no means universally held, located the spiritual and intellectual center of the nation in the middle landscape of the agricultural hinterland, or the seemingly open lands of the West.[24] To this view, the city itself, not to mention the tenement, was seen as a corrosive force on the American body politic. According to certain deeply ingrained ways of thinking, the ascendant city posed both a physical and a psychic threat to the nation, representing a locus of supposed sin and vice that signaled a loss of shared agrarian values.[25]

These fears were exacerbated not only by the internal flow of people and resources from the countryside to the city but also by mass immigration, as the cities became filled with millions of new residents whose ability to assimilate was contested. The landscape of unfamiliar language, religion, mores, and culture resulted in an undercurrent of xenophobia that would influence much of the thinking about the city. And the focal point of this fear was the coalescing, dense, almost exclusively working-class neighborhoods. While the core of these areas had long housed people of modest means, the new working-class landscape seemed to quickly engulf surrounding neighborhoods, impelling the movement of the middle class and elite farther from the city center.[26]

As the nineteenth century progressed, and the immigrant and working-class population continued to rise, overt class and cultural struggles became an increasingly common feature of American life. Much of this conflict played out over both physical and political control of urban space, with the tenement implicated in many of these squabbles. Part of the complex of responses to this was a retreat by many in the middle class to increasingly romantic notions of the home, ideally situated in a picturesque, rural landscape, as a haven from the apparent evils of the industrial city.[27] Indeed, the power of the landscape to rejuvenate was held by many as gospel in this period.[28] Due in part to the cost and difficulty of transportation, the picturesque suburban landscapes that were the purest manifestation of this phenomenon were not available to the vast majority of city dwellers of any class. Yet this ideal was in the background of much of the critique of urban form in this period. It also informed some of the largest civic improvements. The construction of major parks, such as the Frederick Law Olmsted–designed Central Park in New York and the Emerald Necklace and Franklin Park in Boston, were explicitly framed as a respite from the increasingly dense urban landscape.[29] Later movements succeeded in creating parks and playgrounds, such as Boston's Charlesbank and New York's Seward and Mulberry Bend Parks, within tenement neighborhoods instead of at the urban periphery.

The political power vacuum left by the movement of many in the middle and upper classes away from dense downtown wards gave rise to the development of machine politics, driven largely by working-class and immigrant voters. These "low ward politicians," as they were derisively called, sought to redirect the wealth of city coffers back to politically well-connected supporters in the tenement districts through patronage jobs and lavish spending on public works projects, enriching themselves through kickbacks and other forms of graft in the process.[30] An early and imperfect social welfare scheme, but seemingly lacking in high ideals and high morals, this system threatened cherished civic notions. The nexus in New York between the tenement and Tammany Hall was explicitly drawn, both in terms of residents and builders, and many in the genteel classes thought both were in dire need of reform.[31] Indeed, one prominent observer called the relationship between tenement builders and the New York Democratic Party "the most corrupt 'ring' that was every known in New York City."[32]

While machine politics offended the immediate political sensitivities of the bourgeoisie, the corruption of politics represented by the ward bosses was, to them, only the secondary public "evil" emanating from these neighborhoods. The greatest public threat, in the words of reformer and architect Marcus T. Reynolds, was the "danger of socialistic and anarchistic uprisings."[33] Indeed, the radical foment against industrial capitalism (as opposed to the genteel critique of its manifestations) was reaching a crescendo in the tenement districts.[34] From the Astor Place disturbances of the 1840s, to the Draft Riots of 1863, to the Tompkins Square riot and the rise of the militant labor movement starting in the 1870s, as well as later incidents, there seemed a growing trend of agitation from those who advocated for a radically different economic and political system, representing a fundamental threat to the power structure.[35] Indeed, the tenement itself seemed to breed these ideas. As a result, the near-collective living conditions, the tenants' apparent disinterest in the privately owned suburban home, the unfamiliar customs and sexual mores, the blurred boundaries between public and private space, the ease of mass public assembly, and the quick dissemination of ideas and information possible in close quarters all took on sinister political overtones.[36]

Finally, the contagion of these areas was more than political. With their poor access to sanitation and health care, repeated and virulent outbreaks of infectious diseases were centered on these neighborhoods throughout the nineteenth century. These contagions seemed a threat to more respectable parts of the city, not only due to their physical proximity but also through the clothing, cigars, and artificial flowers that were manufactured there. In this way both the production and consumption of material goods were directly linked to contagion, with the former seeming to have dire but often ill-defined consequences that seemed to corroborate moralists' claim about the inherent dangers of material progress.

As the specter of the tenement increasingly haunted well-established Americans with horrors real and imagined, these groups responded by placing increasingly onerous restrictions on numerous facets of immigrant working-class life, culture, and economic activity (Figure I.3). These social-control schemes included regulations on push carts, increasingly tough standards for sanitary food, control of entertainment through increasingly stringent public assembly laws, strict liquor control and eventually prohibition, regulation of sexual morality, as well as increasingly circum-scribed use of public streets and parks.[37] Eventually immigration was sharply cur-tailed through nativist policies in an attempt to neutralize the threat.[38]

Anti-tenement Reform

Among the most prominent and enduring of these social control measures was the housing reform movement that sought to eliminate the slums themselves. The physi-cal landscape of these places in the first three-quarters of the nineteenth century seemed to match their apparent social, political, and moral degeneracy. Almost en-tirely an ad-hoc landscape made up of older structures converted from other uses, these buildings were frequently ill suited to the intense occupancy to which they were put, and rapidly deteriorated under heavy occupancy and absentee landlord-ism (Figure I.4). The wretched conditions of these neighborhoods in the antebellum period would become iconic, devolving into visual and literary tropes that were well worn by the end of the century. The totalizing notion of these areas as "slums" would continue to shape outsider perceptions well into the twentieth century. While driven by abiding concerns over the physical manifestations of poverty, acceptance of these images was fed by the prevalent anti-urbanism and xenophobia of the period. These fears drove episodic, though often intense, interest in reform through housing laws and model tenements.[39] The contours of this movement have been the subject of con-siderable scholarly interest and are discussed at length elsewhere.[40] Yet it is impos-sible to fully understand the tenements of Boston and New York without reference to the housing reform movement.

Housing of the poorest members of society had been understood to be a public responsibility since the colonial period; however, calls for reform of the emergent slum districts did not come until the onset of Irish immigration, with calls to action beginning as early as 1843 in New York, and 1846 in Boston.[41] The earliest housing reformers concentrated on ameliorating the conditions of the first manifestations of the slum landscape and greeted the arrival, in large numbers by midcentury, of newly built tenements with ambivalence, sometimes seeing them as an improvement but more frequently casting them as a legitimization of already bad conditions. Most, however, shared the view that the tenement was fundamentally threatening. The re-form movement would gain traction at the end of the nineteenth century due in no small measure to the writings and photographs of journalist Jacob Riis, which played upon many well-established slum tropes. Throughout the long period of housing re-form, the efforts can be classed into two basic categories: building laws designed to regulate tenement construction, and the construction of new, "model" tenements that would embody their ideals about a moral environment for the poor and working class.

Regulations enacted at the city and state level in both places put increasing re-straints on what tenement builders were allowed to build, setting minimum standards for light, air circulation, and open space and increasing requirements for sanitary

Figure I.3. Udo Keppler, "The Tenement— A Menace to All" (1901). To many (including the creators of this illustration of a hypothetical New York building), the tenement was "not only an evil in itself" but a specter haunting both the rich and poor because it supposedly bred "vice, crime, and disease." *Puck Magazine*, March 20, 1901. Library of Congress Prints and Photographs Division.

THE TENEMENT—A MENACE TO ALL.

Not Only an Evil in Itself But the Vice, Crime and Disease it Breeds Invade the Homes of Rich and Poor Alike.

Dens of Death.

Figure I.4. "Dens of Death." A photograph from the 1870s of the deteriorated rear elevation of a row of Federal-era brick-fronted houses on Baxter Street in New York, hastily converted for multifamily occupancy. Early purpose-built tenements loom behind. Shortly after this picture was taken, an elaborate tenement designed by Peter Herter was built in the open space in the background (see Figure 5.3). These "dens of death" were demolished in the 1890s for Mulberry Bend Park (Figure E.4). From Jacob Riis, *The Battle with the Slum*, 21.

facilities. The earliest of these laws was enacted in New York in 1867. That state's 1901 tenement house law, with its generous requirements for light and sanitation, was the movement's central victory and the model for future housing laws nationwide, including similar rules adopted in Boston in 1908 and all of Massachusetts five years later. Many backers of these laws were explicit that their goal was to regulate the tenement out of existence. Indeed, their passage represented a triumph of the reformers' social agenda. Yet, in practical terms these laws typically codified innovations already provided in the best tenements, curbed the worst abuses, and presented design and planning challenges that were easily met by tenement architects. Thus, even the signal 1901 law changed little about the process by which most tenements were built, except to gradually discourage the most economically precarious builders on the smallest downtown lots.[42]

The model tenements, on the other hand, explicitly encoded reformers' tastes, prejudices, and worldviews. They were the subject of considerable attention when new, and have continued to dominate the discourse on the history of housing. Yet, these buildings had a negligible effect on the lives of most of the urban working class. Built in inconsequential numbers—hundreds as compared to the tens of thousands of commercially built tenements—they failed to gain traction among the residents they were intended to serve and were often economic failures. Like Ernest Flagg's building for Florence Van Cortlandt Bishop, they often represented a sharp disconnect between the priorities of their elite backers and the wants and needs of their working-class residents.

Drawn largely from the white, Protestant,[43] middle and upper classes, reformers generally believed that work toward social good was both a civic duty and a religious calling. Historian Jackson Lears has classified them as antimodernists: "Old-stock, Protestant, they were the moral and intellectual leaders of the American WASP bourgeoisie . . . who helped (sometimes unwittingly) to maintain dominant norms and values," through numerous social causes.[44] Many were from wealthy families and had connections to elite institutions; they sought to maintain or restore a social order that reproduced their considerable privilege. Their charity work, therefore, was conducted in a way that reinforced claims to power based on their perceived moral superiority and managerial prowess. An inherently conservative movement, nineteenth-century housing reform arose, according to political scientist Richard Foglesong, from "capital's need to maintain its position of hegemonic class leadership and stimulate worker acceptance of capitalism. It was not its economic needs directly but the political and ideological needs of capital that made limited housing reform possible."[45]

Many leaders of the housing reform movement were architects, Ernest Flagg, Grosvenor Atterbury, and Alexander W. Longfellow Jr. among them. Their training at elite architectural schools—Flagg and Longfellow studied at the École des Beaux-Arts in Paris, Atterbury at Yale and Columbia—and their close ties to the economic and social elite made them seemingly ideal figures to both identify and vanquish the "tenement house evil." Much of their work depended on the collection of statistics and other data, often published in voluminous and prodigiously illustrated volumes, which gave their work the air of pseudoscientific legitimacy. This was part of what historian Paul Boyer has called the era's "fetish for scientific objectivity," which played an important role in the "secularization of the urban moral-control movement."[46] In the case of housing, reformers tended to mystify the process of tenement construction. They invented stock characters like the heedless "skin builder" and the mindless "plan mill" in an attempt to frame the working-class builder and architect as pernicious and out of the ordinary, in need of radical intervention.

Steeped in the nineteenth-century theory of environmental determinism, housing reformers were, on the whole, convinced that the poverty, despair, and social ills witnessed in the slums were primarily caused by the physical environment of these districts.[47] When reformers said the tenements were "evil," they meant so literally. Not just physically immiserating, tenements were seen as a corrupting force threatening the spiritual salvation of those who lived in or even near them. Given a better environment, more in line with middle-class notions of propriety and respectability, reformers reasoned, the residents of these districts would be transformed into respectable citizens. This reasoning, of course, deflected blame for the problems of inequality from structural economic and social factors and onto inanimate objects and the poor themselves.[48] Following on this belief, they did little to challenge the status quo of widening economic and social disparity, leaving unchallenged the system of low wages, high land values and rents, and economic exploitation that formed the basis of the elite status of many of their reformers' circle. (Reformers later in the twentieth century, many more of whom were drawn from the working class, would have an increasingly nuanced understanding of these matters.) Instead, they leveraged their considerable political and economic power to insert themselves quite directly into the lives of tenement residents as managers, settlement-house workers, and building inspectors.[49]

Key to the tenement reform movement was a concern for not just social but aesthetic purity.[50] Reformers did not want to simply remake the housing conditions of the working class, they wanted to reform their tastes. To many, this was a matter of outsized importance. Representing a long-standing and deeply engrained puritanical strain of American culture, most reformers thought working-class material culture should be plain, modest, practical, and simple and that any deviation from this was a sign of wickedness. Indeed, this policing of consumption was integral to the project of redirecting blame for the conditions of the slum onto its residents and their supposed profligacy, and away from the structure of the economy itself.[51] By the end of the nineteenth century, purity, and the closely related notions of hygiene, was emphasized and sometimes even ascribed seemingly mystical qualities. Thus, the push for aesthetic purity was a constituent part of the crusade for moral and cultural purity on the part of housing reformers. Many of their model tenements, such as Flagg's building for Florence Van Cortlandt Bishop, were aggressively austere, with sanitary glazed white brick and few ornamental nooks and crannies to catch dirt. Sometimes the connection between aesthetic and physical purity was explicitly drawn, as in the militancy against wallpaper, a cherished means of affordable elaboration for many tenement parlors and dining rooms that reformers abhorred and sought to prohibit, because they thought it harbored dirt.

The Shanty and the Palace, or the Great Tenement Rebuilding

During the period of greatest reform interest in the slums, in the last two decades of the nineteenth century and first decade of the twentieth, these neighborhoods were rapidly being rebuilt with new, purposeful, dense tenements whose living standards, while they may not have met middle-class expectations (or subsequent ideals), were certainly in line with or improvements upon period working-class norms. While they could do little to change the fundamental nature of the urban real estate market, in an era when the needs and desires of the immigrant working class were routinely disdained or ignored, these buildings represented a vast physical, technological, and aesthetic advancement over what they replaced, though in many ways they were an incremental change compared to reformers' radically anti-tenement schemes. In 1899 the *New York Times,* usually a steady purveyor of slum stereotypes, remarked on the "gratifying and wonderful" transformation that had taken place in the Lower East Side in the previous decade. The district seemed "born anew," abounding everywhere with "substantial, and in some instances handsome new tenement houses, five and six stories tall" with quarters that were "comfortable and commodious."[52]

Yet, in general, these changes did little to modify the popular perception of the working-class landscape. Indeed, housing reformers often elided representation of such improvement, drawn to the rapidly disappearing areas that continued to re-inforce the older, static image of the slum. To the extent they acknowledged the new, purpose-built, improved tenements of the late nineteenth century, they were certain they had to be a cheap sham, a chimera little better than what they replaced. The media sensation surrounding the dramatic 1885 collapse of a block of tenements under construction, and the resulting manslaughter conviction of their German-immigrant builder, only helped to cement in the public's mind the view that these new buildings were "shaky," and their builders purely interested in profit and exploitation, even at the expense of public safety.

In some ways these new buildings were feared because of their generally good quality. They made these revitalized neighborhoods not only denser but an essentially permanent, vitally necessary, and, for many, even desirable feature of the landscape. Indeed, the *Times* extolled the great benefit the improved housing represented for the vast number of workers in the nearby Broadway garment lofts.[53] The squalid build-ings being destroyed were old, converted structures from which the last value was being extracted. They were, as such, impermanent by nature. Anti-tenement critics could take solace in the expectation that those buildings, as bad as they were, would soon be swept away for something more respectable. Many assumed commercial or industrial structures would soon rise in these neighborhoods as the adjoining central business districts expanded.[54] Instead, a solid fabric of new and commodious tenements took their place. The permanence and intentionality of these buildings (even if reformers insisted that they were flimsy) seemed to embody widespread fears that highly visible signs of social, cultural, and economic difference, instead of being a fleeting condition, were now an immutable feature of American urban life.[55] The often-reproduced images of models, created for the New York Charity Organization Society's 1900 Tenement House Exhibition, of a scrappy East Side block made over into a monolith of tall brick tenements seemed calculated to underscore this fear (Figure I.5).[56]

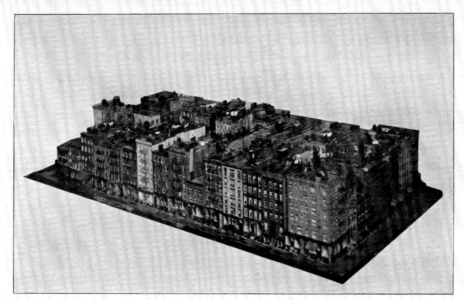

A Typical East Side Block.

As a Solid Block of Double-deckers, Lawful until now, would appear.

Figure I.5. A pair of often-reproduced images of models from the 1900 Charity Organization Society Tenement House Exhibit. The first model shows a "typical" East Side New York block, bounded by Chrystie, Forsyth, Canal, and Bayard Streets, with an essentially impermanent landscape of old, ad-hoc slums interspersed with newer tenements. The second model shows the same block fully rebuilt with new tenements. These models were calculated to highlight not only density but also the threateningly permanent nature of the new tenement landscape, as compared to the ad-hoc slum landscape it replaced. From Jacob Riis, *The Battle with the Slum*, 106.

The case for improved urban working-class housing seemed not just hopeless but undesirable to many in the American elite. A growing consensus was hostile to the very existence of the tenement, no matter how "reformed," and considered its eventual elimination, in favor of a cottage in the suburbs or countryside, to be the highest social good.[57] In fact, the increasing popularity of multifamily living, whether occupied by rich or poor, was to some a threat to cherished myths of American exceptionalism. But anti-tenement advocates often took on a peculiarly American sort of fanaticism in this regard.[58] They sometimes couched their argument in religious terms, seeing tenements as a treacherous deviation from a divinely inspired social order. William B. Patterson, a leader in the Methodist Episcopal church, was perhaps the most unabashed, suggesting with rhetorical flourish that the biblical murderer and city builder Cain himself was the originator of the tenement. Patterson plainly articulated an idea commonly held by many American Protestants: "The tenement is an impediment to God's plan for the home." No matter how decent, safe, or commodious such a building could be made, he insisted, "this basic fact will remain."[59] Journalist and reformer Jacob Riis basically agreed with this formulation. In perhaps his most fanatical statement, he proclaimed in 1889 (and repeated over the next decades) that "a shanty is better than a flat in a cheap tenement any day" (Figure I.6).[60]

That statement certainly would have seemed fanatical to a resident of one of the new tenements that were going up in the late 1880s or 1890s. These tenants had a whole host of things that many in the working class never had access to before: a kitchen with a range, a hot water boiler, and a sink with running water and sewer connection; a dumbwaiter easing the vertical lugging of goods and fuel; a flush toilet, albeit likely down the hall and shared with a number of other families; a separate parlor, wallpapered, with folding blinds, a faux-marble mantel, and fancy lambrequins, even if the room was rented out at night or doubled as a bedroom; gas lighting; maybe a dining room; a marble lobby with colored glass, painted frescoes, and tile floors; all

Figure I.6. Jacob Riis, "Shanty Town—Some of Its Last Remnants," New York (1896). Riis repeatedly declared that "a shanty is better than a flat in a cheap tenement any day," preferring the individual cottages of this upper Manhattan squatters camp to the modern tenements rising behind it, despite the far better accommodations in those buildings. Courtesy of Museum of the City of New York, 90.13.1.303.

in a building whose facade employed widely understood visual symbols of respect and propriety (Figure I.7). Just what, then, was better about a shanty? Maybe air and light, but privacy for sure: four walls and a roof for a single, private family was held up by Riis and his ilk as a sacred right. But it would come at the cost of cosmopolitanism, fashionability, even modernity itself. A shanty probably would not have been more comfortable, certainly not more technologically advanced, than a new tenement flat, even a cheap one.

But for many reformers in the nineteenth century, social control and spiritual elevation, not material progress, were the goal. As an embodiment of the agrarian, individualistic ideal of the worker and his Christian family in a detached cottage, the shanty would be philosophically better to those who considered the single-family home to be fundamental to the preservation of an orderly society that placed the Anglo-American elite at the top of the hierarchy.[61] Crucially, the reformers' disdain for the tenement was tied to Enlightenment-era English construction of self-identity, as well as the rise of a bourgeoisie who tended to construct that identity through their private home. As historian John Archer has noted, "The evolution of Anglo-American political and economic thought since the late seventeenth century has increasingly cast the self as obligated to establish its own place in the social and economic nexus, and free to succeed or fail in that quest." The house, always single-family, usually

Figure I.7. Tenements, Madison Street, New York, circa 1914. Folding blinds and mosaic lobby floors signaled interior accommodation, while lace curtains were evocative of tenants' domestic practices in these buildings, then a quarter century old. The ornamental facade was a commonly understood symbol of respect and propriety, even if the laundry hung from the front fire escape subverted that meaning. For a contemporary view of these buildings, see Plate 14. Courtesy of Milstein Division of United States History, Local History, and Genealogy, New York Public Library, Astor, Lenox, and Tilden Foundations.

freestanding, and ideally constructed to reflect the identity of the male head of household, was essential to that quest.[62]

Just as the idea of the freestanding, single-family home as fundamental to the American standard of living was crystalizing as a middle-class consensus, tenement builders were promoting something diametrically opposed, a housing type that was an urbane alternative, fully grounded in Old World ideals.[63] Hailing from a continental European background, many tenement builders, architects, and some tenants generally lacked the zealous faith in the regenerative goodness of the single-family home in the countryside. Instead their ideas of modernity and improvement represented a fuller embrace of industrial production that looked to more urban forms, such as the street facade of the palace, a common European building type that often expressed a communal—as opposed to individual—identity.[64] Starting from an equally valid yet fundamentally opposed point of view, indeed one perhaps more aligned with the realities of the modern city, these builders and many of their tenants did not have to reconcile themselves to the tenement, because urban multifamily living was not held as inherently problematic as it was in the emerging American consensus.[65] Yet the great imbalance of power between an entrenched elite and these newcomers meant that those controlling the discourse consistently framed the tenement as an inadequate, even un-American means of housing.

It is clear that many immigrant tenants preferred the stylish respectability of the elaborate new tenements to the puritanical, decorous visual austerity of the reformer's model. The design of those model buildings was rooted in the belief that they were at best provisional until more ideal types of housing could be provided in the suburbs. Backers thus had to manage their residents' preferences accordingly. As reformer Elgin Gould, president of the City and Suburban Homes Company, noted in 1896 of model tenements, "It is never advisable to make this class of building too attractive" lest workers who could afford to move to the suburbs be tempted to stay in the center city.[66] Indeed, the contrasting appearance of these buildings clearly informed prospective tenants' reaction to them. Riis noted a particularly telling example:

> The owners of a block of model tenements uptown had got their tenants comfortably settled, and were indulging in high hopes of their redemption under proper management, when a contractor ran up a row of "skin" tenements, shaky but fair to look at, with brown-stone trimmings and gewgaws. The result was to tempt a lot of the well-housed tenants away.[67]

Tenants showed little interest in being redeemed, of course, less so if that redemption meant being subjected to the high-handed moralism with which these paternalistic institutions were run, similar to the invasive "scientific" management they were increasingly subjected to at work.[68] At the most basic level, many bristled, consciously or not, at the notion that only austere forms were appropriate for people of their status. Gould complained bitterly about tenants' "prejudice against the appearance" of his model buildings, which they thought "looked too much like a barrack or public institution."[69] Tenants were indeed tempted away by the speculator's elaborate and palatial-looking tenements, employing familiar but previously inaccessible visual signs of their modernity, fashionability, and agency. Many of the same tenants also wore stylish but inexpensive ready-made clothes and bought elegant but affordable industrially made furniture. The skin builder's "trimmings and gewgaws" were indeed an essential part of this equation.[70] These flourishes were not only wanted, they could now be afforded, thanks to the processes of industrialization that had impelled many to the city in the first place. In the cosmopolitan city of the late nineteenth century, "shaky but fair to look at" won out against solid but oppressive in architecture as much as stylish but cheap won out against dowdy but practical in clothing.

Redeeming the "Skin Builder"

The improved, decorated tenements of late nineteenth- and early twentieth-century Boston and New York force us to confront the historical contingencies of the housing reform movement. The struggle for better housing against the all-too-real squalor of the antebellum slum was not the simple, pitched battle of the evil tenement builder against the altruistic reformer, as it has so often been portrayed. Many in both groups had an earnest desire to improve conditions, as well as a complicated range of other motives that were reflected in their design choices and their critique of those of others. Reformers had a genuine humanitarian concern to ameliorate truly wretched housing conditions. Yet their drive for social good was mixed with snobbery and opprobrium, sometimes informed by ethnic and class prejudices. Their often simplistic focus on physical conditions allowed them to dodge more difficult questions about the structure of the economy, the nature of capitalism, and their own culpability in perpetuating inequality. Often well-to-do and well-established, they projected their fear of a loss of social status onto these new and unfamiliar cultural forms and disdained their working-class tenants' priorities.

On the other hand, tenement builders were not uniformly rapacious but rationally embraced a necessary urban building form denigrated by others and demonstrated communal commitments in doing so. Their pride of ownership was reflected by the common practice of inscribing owners' names in gilded letters on building facades, as Harris Fine did on Broome Street. These builders and architects, largely drawn from the immigrant working or petty merchant class, exploited the housing market as a means of economic ascendency while harnessing its power to improve, however incrementally, the living standards and appearance of communities of which they were often members. Yet their eagerness to make a mark in an unfamiliar culture was constrained by the realities of the urban land market and combined with a profit motive that often seemed excessive in the face of grinding poverty.

A key preoccupation of urban social history, the motives of the Progressive Era reform movements, including housing reform, have been scrutinized by scholars for decades. But even the best of these have relied to some degree on the stereotyped image of the tenement and its builders promoted by reformers themselves. Many of the most important works on housing in New York, including studies by Richard Plunz and by Nicholas Dagen Bloom and Matthew Lasner, treat the speculatively built tenements of the nineteenth century as a step in an evolution toward the reform housing of the turn of the twentieth century and ultimately the public housing that followed it.[71] This is an important, if presentist, narrative, but not the only lens through which to view the tenement. Social and economic historians including Elizabeth Blackmar, Jared Day, and Donna Gabaccia have illuminated other important aspects of the tenement's construction and occupancy, situating them within the context of the real estate industry and the lived experience of immigrant groups. Additionally, a considerable number of works on the history of housing give the tenement chapter-length treatment, also usually in the context of elite experiments in, or social policy toward, affordable housing.[72] Yet, while there has been scattered interest in it, until now there has been no systematic survey of the architecture of the nineteenth-century speculative tenements that still make up a significant portion of the landscape of both cities.[73] This book aims to help fill that gap.

As compelling material evidence, the decorated tenement complicates the frequently asserted notion that the market for urban working-class housing in this period failed spectacularly and uniformly. Instead it created, for a while and within serious constraints, buildings that were responsive to the needs and desires of their residents.[74] In the era of laissez-faire capitalism, before the much-needed (if ultimately insufficient) twentieth-century interventions of subsidized and public housing and rent regulation, virtually all housing was provided by the private market, and tenants were at the mercy of its forces. These forces brought not only the hardship and inequality that necessitated the social safety net developed in the later period, but also increasing wealth leading to an unprecedented betterment in material standards and housing conditions for all classes. This notion that immigrants had some agency to control their material conditions follows the work of other scholars of working-class culture, particularly those attuned to the physical evidence of past lives. Historical archaeologist and urban historian Alan Mayne, for instance, has thoroughly exploded the slum stereotype.[75] In addition to Day and Gabaccia, Joseph Bigott, Oliver Zunz, and Margaret Garb have demonstrated the immigrant working class's participation in the market for their own housing, particularly in the industrial Midwest.[76] Thomas Hubka has demonstrated a substantial improvement in working-class housing standards, while Lizabeth Cohen, as well as archaeologists exploring the remains of Five Points, among others, have demonstrated the agency of the working class in negotiating the new material culture of the industrial city.[77]

But my goal here is by no means to defend the lightly regulated free market system under which this housing was built, whose horrors—participants' ability to improve their conditions within it notwithstanding—have been well documented. Instead, I want to demonstrate the cultural conflicts inherent in the built environment this system brought about, for better and for worse. The tenement does not need to be good, or even almost all right, by present standards for us to take these buildings seriously as works of design that encoded much more than just the oppression and inequalities of urban industrial capitalism. If we are to fully understand this period and the landscapes it created, we must not look just for the precedents for the important social innovations of the twentieth century but to what was truly most important in the nineteenth. And while the housing reform movement may have eventually led to real social progress, in this period its class and cultural myopias had the effect of stigmatizing—indeed quite literally demonizing—and perhaps stymieing those then effecting the most positive change in housing conditions for the greatest number of tenants. These new tenements were indeed desired by their tenants, offering at affordable rents housing of previously unimaginable quality in the city center, long before the government did. As Peter Herter noted in 1900, "the great bulk of our citizens live in tenement houses and the investor and builder must provide these." But the best of these, he feared, were being driven away as they increasingly found themselves "the object of sentimental crusades on the part of ignorant reformers."[78]

Yet, while we know much about these "ignorant" reformers and their representations, even the finest scholarly works on the tenement scarcely contain the name of a single tenement builder and only passing reference to the occasional architect, let alone much sense of their relationship to their community or architecture at large. While essential to rebuilding the tenement landscape, Peter Herter and his ilk have vanished almost entirely from the historical discourse. Instead, they have commonly been treated as the anonymous (and therefore easy to disdain) bogeymen of the "real estate speculator," the "construction industry," or the period term "skin builder." Reflecting the reformers' narrative, the variety and evolution that occurred within this landscape have seldom been treated as anything other than the product of the reform movement. Further, few works on the tenement illustrate specific examples, and then only in plans, nor do they discuss them in light of the particularities of their design and construction, the sort of attention that is routinely afforded more elite building types. This book, on the other hand, works to personalize and contextualize the Gilded Age tenement and those who built it, and to understand the cultural processes that resulted in its physical form.

The Decorated Tenement

Throughout this book I will use the term *decorated tenement* to describe the group of buildings that is the main focus of my attention.[79] In doing so I intend less to identify a building type than to describe an attitude and process, to separate those who went beyond the bare minimum in providing working-class housing from those who did not. To be precise, I use decorated tenement to mean a building built in a "slum" neighborhood for working-class, usually immigrant residents, whose facade is ornamented at least to the standard of more respectable architecture through the use of newly affordable, industrially made architectural material. This definition encompasses tens of thousands of buildings in Boston and New York, and more in other cities. Yet even the most banal stand in defiance of long-held beliefs about the slum landscape and of reformers' instance on simplicity, cleanliness, and restrained decorum.

The reader may find this book's focus on the aesthetics of tenements to be unexpected, perhaps even impertinent. While the internal arrangement of these buildings has received a fair amount of attention, the "mystery" of the elaborate facades has frequently been afforded only a sentence or phrase, at most a few derisive pages, if acknowledged at all.[80] The matter of facade treatment has seemed at first blush a matter too trivial for social and cultural historians, interested in living conditions, reform movements, public policy, and other such concerns.

But this persistent refusal to consider the tenement on anything other than strictly practical and utilitarian terms is grounded in fundamentally classist assumptions. These facades were rich with cultural meanings: through its use of elaborate forms, the decorated tenement appropriated signs of wealth and power, using symbols broadly associated with luxury in a situation that called for frugality. The symbolic language of nineteenth-century architecture had been recovered from historical sources by an intellectual elite who pressed it into service to do specific social and cultural work. Its appropriation by tenement builders was an important exercise in equality but also diminished the power of those symbols in the eyes of those who had previously employed them as their exclusive purview.[81] This ornament played an important role in the creation of meaning in a highly contested landscape. To fully evaluate these buildings, then, we must understand them not just in terms of housing standards but in terms of aesthetic standards as well. To ignore the aesthetic would be to reproduce the class chauvinism of the nineteenth century (and later) that held that, no matter what they wanted, practical improvements were the best the working class deserved.

The decorated tenements were unmistakable signs of improvement and even communal identity within iconic ethnic neighborhoods. This signaling, enacted through architectural ornament, was intimately tied to rising material standards. They represented an arena of conflict between the taste of newly arrived groups and well-established mainstream tastes. Influenced by the work of historian Lizabeth Cohen, numerous studies of working-class, particularly immigrant, material culture of this period have demonstrated a fondness for elaborate forms—mostly in terms of clothing and furnishing—often in ways that exceeded middle-class standards. The facade of the decorated tenement was the most durable manifestation of this phenomenon.[82]

Ornamented buildings are usually analyzed in terms of architectural style, a topic widely debated in the nineteenth-century age of eclecticism that has engaged architectural historians ever since. Yet, this academic categorization of historical forms has been highly problematic in the discussion of the tenement, whose architects tended to selectively and intentionally embrace and exaggerate certain features while ignoring others. Indeed, many of the most highly developed decorated tenements were quite idiosyncratic in the context of architecture of their moment. Many of these buildings did not fit neatly into well-established, monolithic style categories, where purity and significance were judged by the ability to produce examples familiar to the aesthetic frames of reference of the hegemonic culture. As a result, when noticed at all, well-developed examples of the decorated tenement have been routinely dismissed as "naive" or "unsophisticated," if not "crude" and "vulgar."[83] Yet, as chapter 3 will demonstrate, the decorated tenement's place within the nineteenth-century parade of styles was far from the most important evolution witnessed then.

Instead, the most important change was the rising visual standards promoted by some builders of working-class housing (Figure I.8). The fundamental question that tenement builders had to answer was not in what style to build but *how much* of the newly available ornament to use. Answering this question was far closer to the reality of how speculative buildings were historically designed and experienced, and illuminated much more about the outlook of a builder on his or her building and its perceived audience. The ability to create something like visual parity between tenements and more elite architecture was an important democratizing phenomenon. Yet this new egalitarianism of degree of ornament was far from universally welcomed, and this unfamiliar taste was frequently considered suspect, even vulgar, by highbrow critics. Degree of ornamentation, therefore, was a much more consequential choice for a builder than selection among academic styles, which were essentially fungible (Plate 3). Thus, throughout this book far more attention will be given to degree of ornamentation than to the particular style of those elements.[84]

Figure I.8. The modestly decorated tenement. *Left*, E. T. Deferest Tenement, 44 East First Street, New York (1877). George T. Johnston, architect. *Right*, John Knopf Tenement, 50 East First Street, New York (1872). Theodore Beu, architect. A style-focused approach would emphasize the difference between the Italianate ornament *(right)* and the Neo-Grec ornament *(left)*. These academic differences were less consequential to the speculative builder and their audience, for whom degree of ornamentation was a far more important factor: in that sense, these two buildings were nearly identical. Photograph by Sean Litchfield.

The decorated tenement embodied many of the most salient characteristics of this period: not only mass urbanization and its attendant economic dislocation, and mass immigration and its inherent cultural conflicts, but also mass industrialization that made a phantasmagoria of new, stylish goods—including architectural products—within reach of this newly urbanized population. The concomitant breakdown of old signifiers of wealth and power, as well as the breakdown of a shared sense of modesty and propriety, was deeply symbolic of the challenge to Anglo-American cultural and economic hegemony (Plate 4). Rejection of these decorated facades as part of wider anti-tenement, anti-immigrant, and anti-urban rhetoric was grounded in this sense of dislocation. Old symbols, old ways of life, old hierarchies, and old landscapes were rapidly passing away. What was taking their place seemed foreign, decadent (in both senses of the term), and morally suspect. Yet for the larger audience not so threatened by these changes, ornament, employing the language of historicism, sometimes with specific cultural or even sacred meanings, helped ground unfamiliar places and things in comfortable traditions. The tendency to use these forms to overelaborate new and perhaps slightly sinister objects—from steam engines to steam radiators—has been noted.[85] Ornament, then, was the fundamental visual vocabulary of nineteenth-century respectability and helped soften the edges of the process of immigration, industrialization, and urbanization.

The Decorated Tenement as Immigrant Enterprise

Writers have often portrayed the tenement, at least by implication, as the product of wealthy absentee landholders: Trinity Church in New York, for example, was repeatedly exposed in the nineteenth century as holding a large number of notorious west-side slum properties.[86] However, by the mid-nineteenth century American-born elites in both cities increasingly eschewed the construction of new working-class housing, extracting the remaining value from the property they did hold, or finding other, more passive forms of investment as remunerative with less hassle and social stigma.[87] The archetypical slumlords, these owners were often loath to perform basic maintenance on, let alone make improvements to, the aging converted housing they owned, and seldom invested in new tenements. Some, like Trinity, even preferred to leave lots vacant, awaiting the demand for a business block or another polite use, rather than to build new working-class housing there.[88]

As a result, construction of new tenements was left to the small, usually amateur builder and investor. By this period almost universally immigrants and highly leveraged, these builders often lived in the communities in which they worked.[89] Their entry into the field further hastened the elite's exit; this association heightened the disdain they already felt for multifamily housing. Further investment in it was considered unwholesome, even immoral, unless couched as a philanthropic endeavor.[90] Elgin Gould lamented that the close connection between tenement building and immigrant groups caused many supposedly more respectable investors to flee the market. "The tenement-house business . . . has been under the shadow of disrepute," Gould complained in 1900, "the saloon-keeper, the sweater, the padrone, the irresponsible speculator, have figured so largely in tenement building and ownership simply because the financier and the Christian man of business have not felt it entirely respectable to become tenement landlords."[91] In so clearly invoking the stereotypical and seemingly disreputable trades of many German, Jewish, and Italian immigrants, respectively, Gould sought to draw a bright line between the buildings these groups built and the inherently laudable work of the (Anglo-American Protestant) "Christian" businessman.

The decorated tenement was an important immigrant enterprise that allowed the working class to aspire to, and eventually demand, accommodations whose dignity and accommodations matched their taste and self-conceptions while settling in what had been notorious slum landscapes. The extent of immigrant involvement in tenement building has been noted, at least in passing, since the 1870s, when anti-tenement reformers first identified the small, amateur builder and landlord as an easy scapegoat for the era's housing problems.[92] Serious modern scholarship, particularly Jared Day's *Urban Castles,* has demonstrated the extent of immigrant involvement in this field and added important dimensions, situating it within the context of the period business community and the pressure groups building owners formed.[93] Yet, while the speculative tenement has largely been the purview of the social or business historian, it is also crucial to understand its built form as an artifact of immigrant working-class material culture.

The bulk of decorated tenement construction occurred within flourishing cross-class ethnic neighborhoods that were the center of communal life for the groups they housed. They were home not just to the impoverished and working class but also to a not insubstantial group of petty merchants, semiskilled workers, and even an immigrant elite with greater economic resources, all living in relatively close quarters and in generally similar types of buildings. The more established members of the community were important figures in the civic and commercial improvement that occurred in the cities in the last years of the nineteenth century. They were very often involved in tenement construction. They acted as a guiding force and often a source of capital for a large number of smaller and more precarious builders. An important market for improved tenements, they frequently demanded the introduction of innovations previously unknown in the neighborhood. Indeed, the best tenements served to attract this more economically stable group, although even the best buildings showed a remarkable mixing of occupations shortly after they were completed. A year after it was finished, for instance, Harris Fine's commodious Broome Street building was occupied largely by tailors and dress and cloak makers, joined by a range of others who worked in the garment and construction industries, all immigrants or their children.[94]

While many were tied to community institutions and often had business interests in these enclaves, the most economically stable residents of the downtown tenement neighborhoods were often the most geographically mobile, the first to decamp to pe-ripheral neighborhoods as transportation options expanded. As they moved to areas such as Yorkville and Harlem in New York, and Roxbury and Chelsea in Boston, they often brought the decorated tenement with them. Eventually, this movement of the immigrant elite away to these peripheral areas, largely complete by the time of World War I, resulted in the sharp decline, and eventual end, of large-scale construction of new tenements downtown, although it continued apace on the periphery. This move-ment severed the close neighborhood connections that had been the impetus of many builders and removed an important segment of the market for their new buildings. As a result, a fundamental tension arose in these neighborhoods between ideas of com-munal neighborhood improvement and the geographic mobility of their most promi-nent residents. More consistent with American myths and reformers' ideals, both of which posited the solution to the housing problem as the movement of the working class away from the center city, this trend has received more attention than the same groups' slightly earlier penchant to improve downtown neighborhoods.[95]

Given the makeup of immigration to American cities, it follows that the plu-rality of decorated tenement builders in both cities were Jewish immigrants from Germany and eastern Europe. (It is also noteworthy that nearly all of the remainder were Catholics: Italians, Irish, and some Germans, including the Herters.) The Lower East Side was said to contain fully 10 percent of the world's Jewish population at the turn of the twentieth century, and the North and particularly the West End of Boston hosted the largest concentrations of that group in New England.[96] Although it was not an exclusively Jewish phenomenon, the decorated tenement is profitably seen within the framework recently developed in studies of Jewish economic activity.[97] This field has undergone substantial reconsideration in the past two decades, overcoming a long-standing reticence, seeking to avoid the appearance of essentialism or worse, in highlighting the important role of Jewish immigrants in economic and cultural life, as well as their occasional conflicts with mainstream expectations.[98] The involvement of Jews within insular fields that relied on tight-knit networks, not only real estate and retail, but the rag and junk trade, the liquor business, among others, related in part to structures of discrimination they historically faced in the broader economy.[99] As architectural historian Andrew Dolkart has noted, "Jewish immigrants and their children seized on speculative building as a way to make a living." In this line of work, he noted, a Jewish builder was "not limited by discriminatory hiring practices and could generally rely on his compatriots for financial investment."[100] Crucially, as historian Paul Lerner and others have pointed out, Jews, often treated as outsiders, were less bound by mainstream taboo and custom than more established groups and therefore were less hesitant to enter fields that carried social stigma and more will-ing to participate in expansion and innovation within economic niches that, while vitally necessary and widely desirable, were shunned by others.[101] Both frameworks are extremely useful to understanding why these immigrants in particular so readily embraced the tenement and enthusiastically worked toward its innovation and improvement, while many in the hegemonic culture eschewed it or found their work to be distasteful, even vicious.[102]

Standing outside the economic mainstream, the figure of the ethnic working-class developer and landlord complicates the threadbare dichotomy between the virtuous, downtrodden producer and idle, parasitic owner. Indeed, as many new tenements were frequently owner occupied, the line between builder and tenant cannot be sharply drawn. These builders entered a market for working-class housing that had long been woefully underserved by an economic elite who had disdained it and evinced little interest in understanding its wants and needs. The tenement was embraced and elaborated, technologically and visually, by successive generations of immigrant builders, who adapted it to their tastes, purposes, and changing living standards. It is notable, then, that the use of decorated facades closely tracked the identity of the builder: immigrant builders used ornament consistently, while well-established builders mostly or entirely avoided it. Therefore, the decorated tenement facades were not simply crass merchandizing; their often highly symbolic ornament was not a cheap marketing ploy but a reflection of the wants and aspirations of newly arrived groups.

Among social and architectural historians there has long been a hesitation to talk explicitly about money, a concern seemingly either too workaday or indiscreet. Yet concerns about money, how it was made and how it was spent, were in the background of nearly all discussions of the tenement. Given that money is a proxy for social and cultural priorities, it is crucial to understand its role in the creation of this landscape. At the same time it is a fallacy of late capitalism to assume that something made for profit, as the tenement certainly was, should necessarily reflect a myopic concern for maximum return, to the exclusion of all other factors. Indeed, it would be wrong to cast most tenement builders, many drawn from communities with deeply rooted socialist, communist, and anarchist principles, in the mold of arch capitalists. These principles were common, as historian Kenyon Zimmer has noted, even among many business owners, including, perhaps paradoxically, its builders.[103] While the absentee landlord was always a hated figure, and while builders were sometimes making mass profits from the tenement, concerns about the conditions of the workers still abounded in this milieu. Bringing about the liberation of the working class necessarily started with taking its material needs seriously, and if we consider the decorated tenement as calibrated to meet these needs, the paradox of the socialist tenement builder might not seem so great after all.[104]

At a finer grain of analysis, if creating the decorated tenement was newly affordable thanks to industrial production, it was not exactly inexpensive, either. A heavily ornamented tenement facade of the type Peter Herter routinely designed could add up to 3 percent to the construction cost. Well-established builders and observers, who considered tenement residents a group without agency or a right to their own tastes and preferences, thought this money could be ill afforded. This view was reflected in their austere buildings, whether or not they were built as reform institutions

Figure I.9. James Loudon Tenement, 7 Phillips Street, Boston (circa 1895). Architect unknown. This tenement was built in a strict utilitarian mode by a private builder at the height of the decorated tenement phenomenon. Photograph by Sean Litchfield.

(Figure I.9). Yet as immigrant tenement builders, driven by pride of ownership or social concern, recognized an opportunity to fulfill long-held desires for more visually pleasing environments, prodigious spending on ornament soon became crucial to the profitability of their schemes. When the first decorated tenement builders, in New York mostly clients of the three Herter brothers, and in Boston of Charles Halstrom, began to put up elaborate buildings with technical improvements to match, tenants quickly learned they could demand such things. Other builders soon followed suit, lest their buildings be considered less desirable in the highly competitive housing market of the period, marked by frequent oversupply. In this case, as elsewhere, builders' concern for profit intersected with their social and cultural priorities. So while it may be taken as a given that money was an important aspect of this process, and its role should not be elided, higher-level social and cultural concerns will be the primary focus of my attention throughout this book.

Methodology

In many respects the reformers' penchant for encyclopedic documentation of the tenement landscape has seemed to serve historians well. It has provided a ready trove of published, period sources, chock full of statistics and graphical representations, as well as a pre-made narrative on architectural form. This has proved especially use-ful to scholars more interested in social and cultural history or whose focus was in later periods or social policy. However, the scholarly narrative based on these sources becomes increasingly predictable, almost rote. Furthermore, as we have seen, these sources had their prejudices and myopias, particularly when it came to the parts of the landscape that did not fit their preconceived notions of the slum. They framed working-class architecture through middle-class standards and viewed ethnic land-scapes through the lens of a dominant culture often disconcerted by the changes being witnessed. They were, therefore, particularly prone to exaggerating the abun-dance of the worst conditions and frequently portrayed ethnic and class-based pref-erences as problems in need of a solution. Yet these sources have often been the sole basis of our understanding of the tenement.

This book, on the other hand, uses the built tenements themselves as its most im-portant primary source of evidence. In doing so, it is based on the fundamental prem-ise of vernacular architecture studies: that common buildings and landscapes encode meanings for their builders and occupants often absent in written sources, which reflect a more elite view. Scholars of vernacular architecture have long put close ex-amination of architectural details, including ornament, at the center of their method, using these details in combination with analysis of construction methods, plans, and historical contexts to elicit implications from everyday buildings.[105] In that spirit, I began the research for this book with fieldwork, documenting all extant tenements in the North and West Ends of Boston and then in the Lower East Side of New York: over three thousand buildings.[106] For each of these, I analyzed the context of its construc-tion, builder and architect, cost, internal features, and the cultural significance of the architectural materials used in their construction.

This rigorous examination of the physical fabric of actual buildings, and related documents, allowed otherwise obscure meanings to emerge. Thanks in part to its digi-tal humanities approach, this process leveraged newly digitized collections of histori-cal building permit and housing inspection records in both cities, among other newly accessible sources, and took advantage of the democratization of data processing and analysis tools that allowed tens of thousands of disparate data points to be compared and analyzed.[107] This process allowed for a new understanding of these built forms that does not rely solely on reformers' narratives. So, while their literature was use-ful to give this story color and complexity, with more neutral sources now readily at hand, the reformer's literature can be read, in archaeologist Alan Mayne's words, "across the grain."[108] To supplement all this, I also delved into the rather robust field of immigrant fiction and memoir from the late nineteenth and early twentieth cen-turies. This was also an important source of narrative richness.[109]

I chose to look at both Boston and New York despite their vastly different scales of population and divergent growth trends. To examine either city in isolation would risk undue localism. Indeed, the exceptionalism with which the history of these two places has often been treated obscured much of what is common about the working-class material experience there. These neighborhoods have persistent and long-standing romantic associations that complicate much about their history. Historian Beth Wenger has noted that as early as the 1930s the Lower East Side gained "mythical" status, particularly for second-generation Jewish immigrants who had decamped to other neighborhoods.[110] The North End of Boston acquired similar status by the middle part of the twentieth century. And interest in the West End was particularly great after the demolition of large portions of the neighborhood during urban renewal in the 1950s, with the remaining part subsumed by the elite Beacon Hill.[111] The sense of nostalgia associated with these places, coupled with anti-tenement reformers' mystification of the tenement building process, has been an impediment to serious analysis of this landscape. On the other hand, because of the rigorousness of analysis of the buildings in these downtown neighborhoods, I chose to give the many thousands of decorated tenements that exist in the peripheral working-class neighborhoods of both cities only cursory attention.

In *The Decorated Tenement* I am concerned primarily with the design and production of space and its initial period of occupancy. Thus, I stake out a methodological position somewhat at variance with important strains of contemporary scholarship, which in the past two decades has prioritized the lived experience and the evolving meanings users impart on their spaces.[112] However, in the fraught and complicated landscape of the tenement, a strict focus on design and construction reveals meanings and significance that were largely obscured by later experiences. The tenement builders' transformation of a deeply contested landscape in which they were comparative newcomers was a profoundly consequential act. Beyond mere formal significance, the design choices they made in this process bore upon their ideals of home and community, respectability and progress. It is therefore worth pausing and examining them in that moment when they were new, before the passage of time and inevitable decay caused their buildings to fade into the background of everyday urban life, and indeed eventually come to resemble the slums they replaced. Yet in its long period of occupancy, successive generations of newcomers changed the meaning of this landscape again and again, for better and for worse. Beyond the sharply delineated focus of this book, the multivalent meanings of and experiences in the urban tenement over the course of the twentieth century are a topic of tremendous importance that would benefit considerably from additional research and analysis. While a brief outline of this field is sketched in the epilogue, in this book I will focus on the physical form of the tenement at its apogee.

The "Slum" and the "Tenement"

The word *tenement* was, and is, a hotly contested term. I use it prominently throughout this book advisedly, despite the long-standing negative connotations and the wide variety of building forms it encompasses. On one level, it is important to recover the more complicated history of the buildings to which this generally derisive moniker has been applied. But the term also has important historical meanings. Before the middle of the nineteenth century, the word *tenement* was generically applied to any sort of rental housing—independent of building class, type, or size—following the British tradition of tenement as lands occupied but not owned. The compound *tenement house* appeared by the middle of the nineteenth century to refer to a single building containing multiple dwellings, while the individual units within these buildings were frequently referred to as tenements.[113] In the 1860s, in the context of the first housing reform laws, legislatures in both Massachusetts and New York first defined a tenement as any building with separate living units for three or more families or having two separate units on any floor—regardless of the class of those tenants or the quality of the building—often to the chagrin of builders of high-class multifamily housing.[114] Indeed, some developers of early multifamily housing assiduously tried to avoid it.[115] Many preferred the term *flats.* While this was essentially the consensus term for multifamily housing, when applied to the buildings under discussion, it evades more than it clarifies, devolving to the level of euphemism. The New York building department, for instance, frequently permitted the tenements under examination with the pretentious (and comically inappropriate) designation "French Flats," which was more appropriately applied to a much higher class of multifamily housing that arose in parallel to the decorated tenement.

Yet to the figures who are the primary focus of my attention, like Peter Herter and Harry Fischel, whom we will meet in chapter 4, the definition of their buildings as tenements was crucial to the work they thought they were doing. They explicitly saw themselves as trying to improve a building type that others had viewed as shameful and that had poorly served its intended users. The word also speaks with clarity to where buildings like theirs stood in the range of multifamily housing of the moment. These buildings were certainly improved tenements, but many were subpar flats. The most honest builders did not attempt to obscure this fact. Further, *tenement* has often been synonymous with the word *slum,* although as I indicate in chapter 1, I will use the latter term strictly to refer to the ad-hoc landscape made up of primarily older buildings converted to multifamily housing from other uses. I use *tenement* here strictly to refer to purpose-built multifamily buildings for the working-class.

In the third quarter of the nineteenth century, *tenement* came to have its more specific and class-infused present meaning as a place of residence outside the confines of respectable domesticity.[116] By 1906, to a reformer like William Hazlet, a tenement was any building in which "the family bedding is aired upon the front fire-escape."[117] But of course such class distinctions had economic dimensions. Peter Herter was more precise, declaring in 1900, "we will call all buildings where apartments bring less than $20 a month 'tenement houses' and all buildings wherein the rent is higher 'apartment houses.'"[118] Throughout this book I will follow Herter's distinction between *tenement house* (or *tenement*) and *apartment house,* reserving the latter term for buildings of middle class or higher. However, I will occasionally use the word *apartment* in the modern sense (as Herter did at the beginning of the last quote) to describe a single living unit within a tenement. While this term historically was also reserved only for the higher class of housing, it is a necessary anachronism here to provide a synonym for *unit,* itself an anachronism, and a particularly soulless one, that came out of the technical housing literature of the twentieth century. While Herter and others often referred to tenement units with the collective *rooms,* that usage is too antiquated for general use here. I use *flat,* the other period alternative to *unit,* as a technical term to refer to a specific division of space within a tenement, described in chapter 2.

Herter added that tenements were generally built only on lots costing less than $20,000. This formed an important corollary in the definition of the tenement. He recognized that such lots could be found only in certain areas of the city, and therefore the tenement had specific geographical as well as physical, social, and economic dimensions. In the popular imagination the same building could be a respectable apartment building or a disreputable tenement depending on what neighborhood it was in. If it was in a neighborhood already perceived to be a slum, the building was a tenement, no matter its physical characteristics. If it was located in a neighborhood perceived as middle class or better, it was a flat, even if it was of poorer quality. Whatever its original biases, then, throughout this book I follow this class- and geography-based definition.

On Photography

Photography was a key weapon in anti-tenement activists' crusades. Jacob Riis's deployment of it has long been credited with galvanizing late nineteenth-century interest in these neighborhoods. It has been used consistently since then to reinforce the slum image, using the medium's putatively mimetic quality to reify long-standing tropes about urban working-class life. These images have regularly cast the neighborhood at its worst, by employing narrow framing, harsh force-flash, and other techniques that emphasize dirt and decay.[119]

Later photographers have generally followed this Riisian frame, particularly in the New Deal and post–World War II eras, when photography came to be used to support claims for the need for widespread slum clearance. Midcentury clearance advocates, for example, frequently employed images of narrow alleys and of the poor-looking backs of buildings. These austere spaces, often replete with garbage, hanging laundry, and other improprieties, were typically hidden from public view. Clearance advocates invaded and publicized these private spaces in a perhaps willful evasion of the often respectable and even pleasant appearance of buildings' street fronts.[120]

Yet even modern scholarly works will often select photographs that seem to portray the tenement in its worst light, again often from the rear or in a state of conspicuous abandonment or decay. Scholars frequently avail themselves of reformers' troves of images of trash-strewn yards, laundry-bedecked back walls, and peeling paint and plaster.[121] Sometimes these depictions suffer from a lack of close reading of the physical forms illustrated. Warehouses and commercial buildings (usually old and dilapidated) are frequently misidentified as tenements, and in one recent example the most conspicuous item in a photograph of a decrepit kitchen, captioned "cold-water apartment," was a hot water boiler.

The new photographs commissioned for this book, on the other hand, consciously eschew this usual framing. They employ the conventions of modern architectural photography to frame this landscape objectively, full of physical artifacts worthy of sustained attention. Further, by prioritizing new photography, where buildings are extant and reasonably intact, examples can be selected based on the needs of an intentionally constructed narrative considering the entirety of this landscape, not the accident of surviving historical views.

Likewise, the historical images chosen here do not rely on the hackneyed views that often illustrate discussions of these places, except in a few strategic instances. Indeed, many of the historical images here have never been reproduced before. Of particular note is a remarkable group of images now in the collection of the New-York Historical Society. Taken of properties to be expropriated for the Williamsburg Bridge approach in 1901, they were perhaps the first systematic photographic survey of these neighborhoods. Not reliant on the visual tropes of the slum, they revealed a landscape remarkable for its variety, with older converted building interspersed with large, new decorated tenements (Figure I.10; see also Figure 4.13).

Figure I.10. Streetscape of Delancey Street, New York, March 1901. Drawn from a group of images of properties to be expropriated for the Williamsburg Bridge approach, these are likely the first systematic representations of a neighborhood often portrayed with a narrow range of visual tropes. Instead, these images show normal urban streetscapes with a mix of tenements of various ages, including a large decorated tenement. Courtesy of New-York Historical Society, Lower East Side Photography Collection, PR 251, box 2, folder 9, image 95156d.

Chapter Structure

The Decorated Tenement explores this landscape through seven topical chapters, each covering the broad sweep of the period. Chapter 1 provides a brief background on the cultural landscape of the "slum" in both representation and material form, focusing on the ad hoc conversions of buildings built for other purposes and the deterioration these places suffered under the control of absentee landlords. While that chapter sets a scene well established by reformers, these outsiders will remain in the background for the next five chapters, which examine the tenement on its own terms.

The next two chapters deal extensively with the tenement as a built form. In chapter 2, I discuss the types of spaces and services found within a tenement, and the plans they took, in the context of rising working-class housing standards. Chapter 3 turns attention to the tenement facade, evaluating the various choices of tenement builders in terms of rising aesthetic standards, and provides a framework of meaning for builders' choice of ornamental forms.

The next three chapters help situate the decorated tenement within its social, cultural, and architectural context. In chapter 4, I describe the decorated tenement as an immigrant enterprise, introducing the cast of characters involved in the creation of these buildings and examining the networks of immigrant builders, architects, financiers, and finally prospective tenants. I build the profile of the type of person drawn to the design and construction of improved tenements, as well as their relationship to their communities. Chapter 5 takes a deep dive into the tenement design and construction process, elucidating the role of the architects and builders, as well as their methods and precedents, both at home and abroad. In chapter 6, I examine these buildings in terms of taste and material culture, situating them within the context of working-class taste, as well in relation to real estate prerogatives and other speculatively built buildings. In the main, then, chapters 1, 2, and 4 touch on topics typical to the discourse on the history of housing, while chapters 3, 5, and 6 address issues more common to discussion of architecture and material culture. These analytical frames are too often treated as separate, to the detriment of our understanding of residential building types. This book attempts to bring both to bear on the tenement.

Finally, we meet the reformers again at the end of the book. Chapter 7 examines the backlash against the decorated tenement, airing the anti-tenement activists' views that immigrant builders and architects could not be trusted to solve the housing problem, and that these buildings were cheap shams, for which the model tenement, and eventually the modest house in the suburbs, was the ultimate solution. As the epilogue shows, many second- and third-generation immigrants took up that solution, but the decorated tenement never completely went out of fashion, as demonstrated by the thousands still standing and occupied today, despite a tempestuous history in the twentieth century.

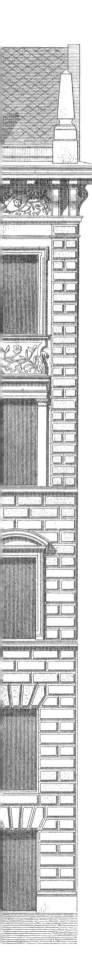

Chapter 1

Dens, Rookeries, and Hovels

The Slum Landscape and Stereotype

> Crazy old tenements, fit habitation for owls or bats, but scarcely for human beings
>
> **Samuel Adams Drake, 1894**

The shocking material disparity depicted in the frontispiece of Matthew Hale Smith's 1868 slum exposé *Sunshine and Shadow in New York* has been one of the most enduring pieces of Gilded Age American visual culture, framing its tale of two cities entirely through architectural imagery (Figure 1.1).[1] The top panel, with the word *sunshine* embowered in vines, is a perspective view of the department store magnate Alexander T. Stewart's mansion at Fifth Avenue and Thirty-Fourth Street. A five-story marble pile, designed by John Kellum, it was still under construction in 1868, four years after work on it had begun. From high basement to mansard attic, Stewart's house was elaborated with ornamental forms in the grand tradition that had long symbolized wealth and power. As period architecture critic Montgomery Schuyler noted, it "set the standard for rich men's houses of the gilded age."[2] Briefly considered the finest in the country, by the end of the century the marble house would appear staid compared to the more extravagant mansions that would come to surround it.

In contrast, the bottom panel depicted architectural squalor in the form of the storied "Old Brewery" on Cross Street in the Five Points neighborhood of the Lower East Side. In this image the word *shadows* literally casts a shadow on the wet roadway, littered with debris, with children playing as they dodge wagons filled with barrels. At the center is a Federal-era industrial building constructed on the site of the polluted Collect Pond, described as "a dirty, cream-colored, gable-ended building—a sort of cross between a jail and a dead-house."[3] The building, which had been hastily converted from a brewery to multifamily occupancy in the 1830s, contained eighty rooms, comprising dozens of small individual units. As part of its conversion, the building had sprouted a series of additions, including a large shed dormer with an irregular roofline, connecting it to a neighboring structure. The building was ill suited to its purpose and poorly maintained. Its owners were simply extracting the remaining value from the structure. Receding on both the Cross Street and Water Street sides of the brewery are equally dingy buildings, including a number of former single-family row houses, also with jerry-rigged additions.

The Old Brewery is the centerpiece of this image as it was central to the slum tropes of the era. Described in slum-exposé hyperbole as a "den of thieves" that was "the nightly scene of disgusting and obscene orgies," the building had existed in the

Figure 1.1. Frontispiece of Matthew Hale Smith, *Sunshine and Shadow in New York*, 1868. A frequently reproduced woodcut depicts the yet-to-be completed Fifth Avenue mansion of A. T. Stewart juxtaposed against the infamous but long-demolished Five Points tenement dubbed the Old Brewery, in an attempt to highlight the social distance between the slum landscape and more polite residence quarters.

imagination of concerned citizens for decades, appearing frequently in lurid news-paper accounts.[4] For Smith's illustrator, the image was something of a work of imagi-nation, however, as the building had been demolished fifteen years earlier, replaced with a building for the Five Points Mission of the Ladies' Home Missionary Society.[5] Nonetheless, its image, like most slum stereotypes, remained static, emblazoned in outsiders' minds as a symbol of everything the neighborhood represented. The dramatized contrast of a yet-to-be completed mansion juxtaposed against a long-demolished tenement helped construct the image of the slum as a place intracta-bly foreign and incomprehensible, suggesting that the social distance between Five Points and Fifth Avenue was far greater than the three miles that separated them.

The Slum Stereotype

While Smith's frontispiece used exaggerated iconography, the image of the Old Brewery itself was suggestive of the range of buildings that were common in the slum landscape. More likely a converted single-family house or structures shoehorned into a backyard or alley, these buildings were lightly built or quickly converted from other uses. Many of the worst—wood-frame shanties, two-story gabled structures, and large wooden blocks with stacked porches—also seemed the least urban. These buildings were frequently depicted as ramshackle, lacking in the most basic pro-visions for air, light, and comfort (Figure 1.2). The slum landscape was ephemeral, made up of hasty and cheap alterations to extract the last remaining value from old buildings, then largely still owned by the families who had abandoned them for more fashionable neighborhoods.[6] Low-rise and irregular, they were the product of a thou-sand historical accidents, adaptations of outmoded neighborhoods to new economic realities.

But presented with this unfamiliar landscape, period observers were apt to call these sorts of buildings rookeries, dens, and rude hovels, language evocative of the habitat of animals, not humans. As historian Steven Conn has noted, the neighbor-hoods themselves were often cast as a "wilderness" to be colonized and (re-)"settled" by a respectable population, in much the same way the putative wilderness of the West was to be redeemed by the onslaught of civilization.[7] Like the native popula-tion of the West, slum residents were cast as others, their homes as wild places that civilized society could do with as it pleased in the name of progress. They were a place apart from the polite landscape and something seemingly new on the American shores: "slums" like those depicted in Charles Dickens's novels, a fundamental prob-lem of old Europe, and places of increasing fascination for a middle class and elite now at an ever-greater social, cultural, and geographic distance.[8]

This caricature, what historical archaeologist Alan Mayne has dubbed the "slum stereotype," was developed to make these landscapes more understandable to bour-geois audiences. Encoding the fears and prejudices of the dominant culture, this

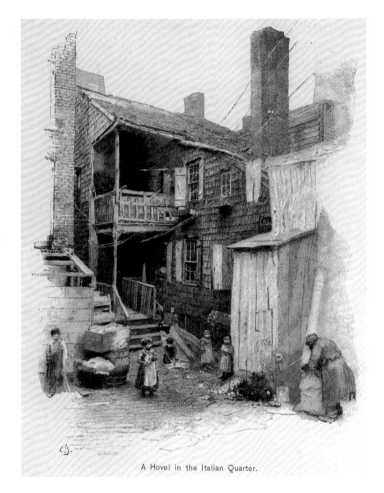

Figure 1.2. "A Hovel in the Italian Quarter," New York, 1892. The conditions of the rear lots of converted, wood-frame buildings were a popular theme for nineteenth-century illustrators portraying the slum stereotype. From Elsing, "Life in New York Tenements," 706.

A Hovel in the Italian Quarter.

stereotype, according to Mayne, "subsumed the innermost working-class districts of every city . . . into one all-embracing concept of outcast society."[9] It cast urban working-class neighborhoods and their residents as primitive, foreign, fraught with danger, and, most of all, ugly. Indeed, the unmitigated ugliness embodied by the slum stereotype was vital to the project of casting these places as incomprehensibly different than the polite landscape.

By portraying these neighborhoods in this manner, purveyors of the slum stereotype denied agency to its residents. In doing so, these neighborhoods came to appear more and more menacing. Part fiction, but grounded in the reality of poverty and decay, the slum stereotype helped convince outsiders that these areas needed to be controlled before they became a greater threat. These fears were further reinforced by demographic changes, as mass immigration began to swell the population of these areas in the 1840s. The concomitant political and social unrest heightened bourgeois fears that the slums represented a fundamental threat to their hegemony.

This type of sensationalized framing of horrors and infamies is crucial to our understanding of how these neighborhoods and the buildings in them were perceived. Never had the poor and working class in America been so strictly segregated or heavily concentrated. The shock of these new neighborhoods and the rising calls for their re-form put the sensationalized image of the slum squarely into the discourse on urban American culture.

I will use the words *slum* and *slum landscape* to denote the package of stereo-typed verbal and visual images that were employed by outside observers to describe the living conditions of the working class beginning in the mid-nineteenth century. While the slum myth has been exploded by careful scholarship, I use the word to draw an explicit contrast to the *tenement* landscape that emerged later in the nineteenth century.[10] As subsequent chapters will demonstrate, the slums were made over into the tenement landscape, something that was regular, purposeful, substantial, and more responsive to the needs and desires of their residents. Yet, that improvement remained largely absent from the public perception of these neighborhoods due in part to the persistence of the slum image. These places were portrayed as static and ahistorical; their conditions were viewed as intractable and destined to decline fur-ther without outside intervention. Therefore, many journalists, housing reformers, and "slumming" tourists uncritically embraced these clichés well into the twentieth century, by which point they were more of a chimera than they had ever been.[11] But to many, slum and tenement have been long synonymous. It is therefore crucial to understand, briefly, the physical context of the places called slums in order to under-stand the improvement that later buildings represented.

Reuse in the Slum Landscape

Situated in the oldest part of both cities, much of the building stock of the emergent slums was made up of remnants of the colonial and Federal-era built landscape. Some of the buildings there dated as far back as the seventeenth century, with a consider-able number from the middle of the eighteenth century common in the North End of Boston. In parts of these neighborhoods middling and genteel structures continued to be built as late as the 1840s.[12] As a result, the buildings in these neighborhoods in the antebellum period generally conform to the standard urban building types of that long period, with a mix of attached and detached buildings of wood frame and masonry.[13]

While these environments were complex, a key feature was a dense mixing of uses and people. In the social structure of the preindustrial city, many employees and ap-prentices boarded with their employers, often in the same building as their place of work.[14] Common to this landscape were mixed-use buildings containing street-level commercial space, workshop space often at the attic level, and living space in the second floor and basement (Figure 1.3). Such a building would contain space for all aspects of a proprietor's business and provided accommodations for his family, do-mestic help, as well as apprentices and employees.[15]

These relationships of dependence broke down with the decline of artisan pro-duction and the rise of wage labor. The emergent middle class purged their houses of commercial and workshop space and accommodations for anybody but the family and their domestic help. The result was a fundamental shift in how the new working class was housed, as workers were left to find accommodations on the market, which typically meant sharing an old house with others. The result was the newly forming slums in that old mixed landscape.[16] This separation meant greater freedom for many workers, no longer subject to their bosses' surveillance during off hours, and allowed for the flourishing of a distinctive working-class culture that rejected certain tenants of polite refinement.[17]

Among the most common building type in these neighborhoods was the side-hall row house, the basic urban house plan in the first decades of the nineteenth century (Figure 1.4A). Designed for narrow, regular lots of newly subdivided land, they were from two to five stories in height and generally less than twenty-five feet in width, though often twice or more deep. On the interior, these houses typically consisted of a rank of rooms—about two-thirds the width of the building—aligned against one party wall. Circulation space and a series of smaller rooms, called hall rooms, occupied the remaining width. These houses proved versatile and well suited for conversion into multifamily occupancy. The easiest transformation, requiring essentially no structural changes, was to rent each floor to individual families and would result in units of at least four rooms (Figure 1.4B). These comparatively generous units were

LITH. OF MAJOR & KNAPP, 449 BROADWAY, N.Y.   FOR D.T. VALENTINE'S MANUAL, 1864.

OLD SHANTIES COR. LUDLOW & DELANCEY ST.S 1864.

Figure 1.3. "Old Shanties Corner Ludlow & Delancey Streets 1864," New York. This image suggested the range of small mixed-use structures in wood and brick that were common in antebellum neighborhoods. Courtesy of The Miriam and Ira D. Wallach Division of Art, Prints and Photographs: Print Collection, The New York Public Library.

often divided again into two, two-room units per floor, each with one large room and one hall room. These smaller units could be further divided by walling off portions of the large front and rear rooms to create a series of small windowless bedrooms (Figure 1.4C).

The introduction of freestanding metal stoves, for both heat and cooking, beginning in the mid-nineteenth century, allowed for greater flexibility in the conversion process. These stoves eliminated the need for a fireplace in each room and meant

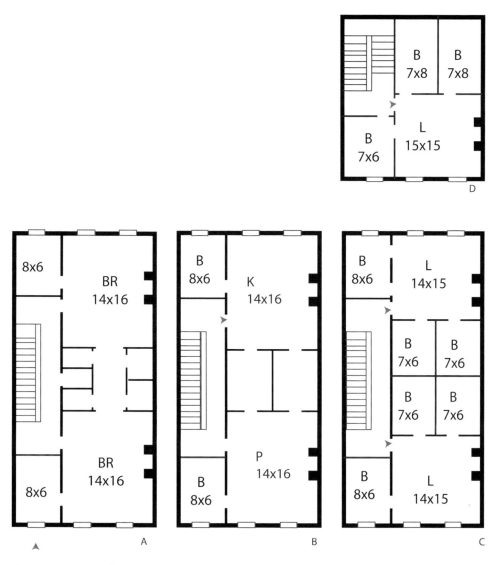

Figure 1.4. An upper floor plan representing the typical conversion of a twenty-five-foot-wide New York side-hall row house: A, original condition; B, converted to a one-unit-per-floor tenement; and C, converted to a two-unit-per-floor tenement, with two four-room units, each with two windowless bedrooms. It is further expanded by a rear tenement (D), built in the house's backyard; this building would usually be set close to the rear lot line. See Figure 1.11. Note that on all plans in this book, all scale is approximate, and an arrow indicates main entrance to unit (only one arrow is shown per unit, even if multiple doors exist). Drawing by author.

that multiple units of individual housekeeping could be provided without the construction of additional flues. All that was needed was access to a chimney, reasonably close to the stove, and connection by a sheet metal pipe. Like the middle-class hearth, the cast-iron stove became the symbolic center of many living spaces (Figure 1.5). The image of stovepipes haphazardly crossing spaces became a standard trope in reformers' literature: a totem for the overcrowded and jerry-rigged conditions that surrounded them.[18]

The flexibility of row house plans allowed for a variety of types of occupancy. Indeed, dense occupation of these buildings did not require even low-cost alterations. As architectural historian Jeffrey Klee has noted, on the North Slope of Beacon Hill some newly constructed, speculatively built side-hall row houses of the 1840s and 1850s housed multiple households even when they were new. Simple, two-story brick houses, many built on narrow alleys and courts such as Rollins Place, had small interior rooms with modest finish. Tenants seem to have used cookstoves in private rooms. Sold to investors, many of them wealthy and elite, shortly after they were built, these buildings were intensely occupied, with as many as seven households per building.[19]

While not the exclusive pattern in the conversion of these buildings, many single-family row houses were first converted for boardinghouse use. Indeed, although purpose-built lodging houses were occasionally constructed, particularly in the late nineteenth century, the majority of boarders in most cities occupied converted houses.[20] Not only did the boardinghouse fill an important role in sheltering individuals and small families from a wide range of classes, they were a critical step in the reuse cycle of urban residential architecture. They were also often indicative of a neighborhood's transition to a working-class area.[21] While some properties followed a stepwise cycle of conversion first to a boardinghouse, then a lodging house, then a

Figure 1.5. An African American tenant in a run-down New York City tenement with cast-iron stove, circa 1904. Note applied mantel and elaborate Eastlake-style headboard. Courtesy of Milstein Division of United States History, Local History, and Genealogy, New York Public Library, Astor, Lenox, and Tilden Foundations.

multifamily building, others skipped the first two steps and were converted directly to a multifamily residence.

An 1898 report describing conditions on Boston's numerous alleys and courts depicted a landscape that had been common to many slum neighborhoods for over a half century. The blocks contained a heterogeneous mix of barracks tenements, older mixed-use buildings, and small row houses, all converted for multifamily occupancy (Figure 1.6). In one example spanning two blocks of South Margin Street in the North End, inspectors found an equal mix of wood and brick buildings, between two and one-half and five stories high. These were arranged perpendicular to the street, with most of their windows facing narrow alleys. One such building was an old wooden house at 14 South Margin Street. Probably a colonial-era hall-parlor house, its multifamily iteration contained two, two-room living units on either side of a central hallway, with six units total in the building. Each housed between five and

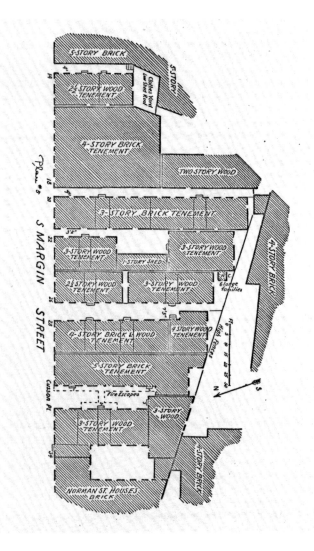

Figure 1.6. Plate from Harold Kelsey Estabrook, *Some Slums in Boston*, 1898. This sketch of a block in the North End, Boston, employed many visual conventions common to exposés on working-class housing stretching back to Friedrich Engels's *The Condition of the Working Class in England* (1844). From *Some Slums in Boston*, 15. Courtesy of Harvard College Library.

eight residents. One of the rooms in each of these units was very dark, with windows looking onto a narrow gap, just inches away from the four-story adjoining building.[22] The largest buildings on the court, a purpose-built five-story brick block, had no windows on one side. Its apartments also likely consisted of two-room units, with a dark bedroom. These conditions seem to have been typical of the neighborhood. Boston historian Traci Roloff, citing labor statistics, noted that as late as 1892, 259 North End families lived in one-room apartments, another 1,100 were in two-room units, the most common housing size in the neighborhood. These statistics strongly suggest the prevalence of converted houses and old barracks blocks.[23] The plans of these buildings left little option but the creation of small units with dark inner rooms, with insufficient space for light and ventilation, and only the most primitive sanitary and cooking facilities.

History in the Slums

Some houses converted for multifamily use were artifacts of the colonial-era elite and had a pedigree that was downright aristocratic, heightening observers' characterization of these as fallen places. Examples abound in period literature. For example, in Nathaniel Hawthorne's 1853 *The Blithedale Romance,* the character Fauntleroy flees his friends' failing utopian experiment in the countryside and settles in Boston on a "squalid street or court of the older portion of the city." There he takes up residence in part of a house that

> had been a stately habitation in its day. An old colonial governor had built it, and lived there, long ago, and held his levees in a great room where now slept twenty Irish bedfellows; and died in Fauntleroy's chamber, which his embroidered and white wigged ghost still haunted. Tattered hangings, a marble hearth, traversed with many cracks and fissures, a richly-carved oaken mantel piece, partly hacked away for kindling-stuff, a stuccoed ceiling, defaced with great, unsightly patches of naked laths—such was the chamber's aspect, as if, with its splinters and rags of dirty splendor, it were a kind of practical gibe at this poor, ruined shadow of a man.[24]

This setting was likely based on the 1690 Foster-Hutchinson house, former home of colonial governor Thomas Hutchinson. Once the finest in the city and an early manifestation of Renaissance classicism in the American colonies, the three-story house was demolished about a decade before Hawthorne's novel. It was replaced by a block of small side-hall row houses.[25] The "dirty splendor" of its richly ornamented interiors drew an explicit contrast to the poverty and squalor that surrounded it. Ornament in this case was simply the ghost of an elite past. Similarly, the setting in which protagonist Julian West was nearly burned alive in Edward Bellamy's 1888 utopian novel *Looking Backwards* was "a large, ancient wooden mansion, very elegant in an old-fashioned way within, but situated in a quarter that had long since become undesirable for residence from its invasion by tenement houses and manufactories."[26] Infused with a romantic irony, the image of the decaying early-American house in a disreputable neighborhood helped sell the slum image to the Victorian public.

Not simply the product of literary representations, important historical monuments had not escaped conversion to multifamily use. In Boston, the seventeenth-century North End house that had been occupied by Paul Revere during the Revolutionary period had been greatly expanded, subdivided, and intensely occupied as a tenement. Images of that building, covered in signs for Italian businesses and surrounded by tenements, excited the imagination of a public increasingly concerned by a changing culture (Figure 1.7). Likewise, in New York the Cherry Street houses in the neighborhood once occupied by George Washington had been converted to multifamily use.[27]

The historical associations of these buildings seemed incongruous with the poverty and putative depravity and danger of the surrounding neighborhoods, as well as with their foreign residents; the changing neighborhoods were to many a signal of

Figure 1.7. Late nineteenth-century color postcard view of the Paul Revere house, North Square, Boston, while it was used as a tenement. Note the large decorated tenement at left that had been recently constructed by an Italian immigrant. That building was later demolished as part of the restoration of the Revere house. Courtesy of Trustees of Boston Public Library.

cultural decline. Indeed, particularly in New England, the perceived threat to Yankee identity from mass immigration and rapid urbanization seemed to take threatening material form in these decayed colonial-era landmarks, increasingly the sites of historical veneration. In 1894, Boston historian and notorious immigration restrictionist Samuel Adams Drake noted the changes in the formerly elite North Square, where the Foster-Hutchinson house once stood and the Revere house remained. "What would probably surprise the stranger most of all, would be to tell him that the cheap tenement-houses, now swarming with occupants, could ever have held up their heads among the most aristocratic residents of the city or town." Drake was clear that he was most disconcerted by cultural, not architectural, changes. "The atmosphere," he sniffed, "is actually thick with the vile odors of garlic and onions—of macaroni and lazzaroni. The dirty tenements swarm with greasy, voluble Italians, and bear signs such as Banca Italiana. . . . One can scarce hear the sound of his own English mother tongue." Drake shuddered to think how his vaunted forebears would have perceived the scene.[28] Such sentiments would provide impetus for the early twentieth-century restoration of the architectural, and by extension cultural, purity of these spaces. Early restoration efforts at the Revere house and the Federal-period Harrison Gray Otis house in the West End consisted of stripping away layers of alterations made to convert these buildings for tenement or boardinghouse use.[29] The restoration of the Revere house eventually included the demolition of a large decorated tenement, built next door at the end of the nineteenth century by Italian immigrants, for the re-creation of garden space.

By the end of the nineteenth century, the forlorn row houses of the artisan and elite classes, then approaching a century old, became the subject of admiration not only for their history but their architecture as well. Observers were deeply troubled not just by the appearance of the slums but by this older landscape's replacement by large, new purpose-built tenements. The presence of rapidly disappearing but fine architecture in the slums provided ample opportunity to draw contrasts. Jacob Riis explicitly juxtaposed these "old Knickerbocker houses" with "their proud steps, sloping roofs and dormer windows" against the new landscape of "ugly barracks" (Figure 1.8). "Never," he declared, had these new buildings "had another design than to shelter, at as little outlay as possible, the great crowds out of which rent could be wrung. They are the bad after-thought of a heedless day."[30]

The carefully constructed, delicately ornamented row houses of the Federal period seemed to contrast sharply with the "heedless" new tenements, their foreign residents, and overloaded facades. The old houses would come to be admired for their simplicity and their restrained ornamentation. At the turn of the twentieth century, architecture critic Montgomery Schuyler admired the small New York row houses of the Federal period, largely associated with mechanics and other artisans, for their finely balanced ornament. In an 1899 article in *Architectural Record,* Schuyler lauded the superior taste of the artisans who made these buildings, illustrating two Federal-era row houses contrasting with new tenements closing in upon them. The most strik-

AT THE CRADLE OF THE TENEMENT.—DOORWAY OF AN OLD-FASHIONED DWELLING
ON CHERRY HILL.

Figure 1.8. "At the Cradle of the Tenement—Doorway of an Old-Fashioned Dwelling on Cherry Hill," New York, 1890. From Jacob Riis, *How the Other Half Lives*, 30.

ing of these was the image of a house on St. Mark's Place, its republican-era simplicity contrasting with the richly decorated tenement newly built next door. Three years later, the row house, too, would fall for a decorated tenement.[31]

The Elite Slumlord

Fine architecture and historical associations notwithstanding, even late into the nineteenth century, many slum buildings were still owned by well-established American families and institutions. The boardinghouse and multifamily conversion provided a convenient means by which old buildings could become a paying investment, which many continued to hold despite decreasing ties to the neighborhood. Some of these owners manifested a disinterest in, even a disdain for, the housing they owned. This was exacerbated as conditions worsened and public sentiment against the slum reached a crescendo. Owners frequently devised strategies to buffer themselves legally and morally from the conditions of their property. In both Boston and New York property owners often employed a sublease system, passing control of the building through a series of agents and lessors, effectively diffusing the blame for the conditions found there.[32] Indeed, in his testimony before a legislative committee in 1856, prominent New York real estate owner and coal dealer Samuel Weeks insisted that this subleasing system, employed by others, was the root of most of the trouble found in the tenement districts. Weeks insisted on controlling his own properties, instead of leasing them.[33]

Yet, for a number of decades after the appearance of the slum, well-established families continued to hold and actively manage properties in these neighborhoods. Among them were the heirs of Joshua Bennett, a successful Boston rum distiller and hops merchant in the early nineteenth century who came to own dozens of properties in the North End, the West End, and Beacon Hill, as well as in Lowell. His holdings in the larger city were made up almost entirely of buildings that were likely built by others and already old and declining when he purchased them. The estate held a mix of colonial-era buildings and later row houses converted for multiple occupancy, as well as wood-frame alley and back-lot structures. These represented all of the types of buildings common to the slum landscape. While their holdings were typical of elite Boston families in the middle of the nineteenth century, the Bennetts were unusual for holding many of these properties well into the twentieth century. These dilapidated alleys and courts were owned by the estate as late as World War I, long after most of the surrounding neighborhood had been rebuilt.[34]

These absentee owners, in general, were loath to make improvements, even basic maintenance, to their property, believing they were simply holding unproductive structures until they could be replaced with more remunerative uses. This was the single most important factor in the formation of the antebellum slum. Boston reformer Harold Kelsey Estabrook noted in 1898 that landlords of slum property "rarely improve them or tear them down voluntarily. Old tenements, without improvements, are the most profitable," largely because of their low tax valuation and water rates.[35]

In New York, Trinity Church, a major landowner since the colonial period, was particularly intransigent. The church controlled a large portfolio of old houses converted to multifamily occupancy and leased numerous others. Their buildings were said to have some of the highest death rates in the New York slums.[36] Yet they were disinclined to address the situation for both cultural and financial reasons. The church corporation refused to install running water and shared sinks in the halls of the tenements it controlled as late as the mid-1890s, even in defiance of orders of the Board of Health. (By this point private sinks and shared flush toilets were standard in all newly built tenement apartments, some of which even had private baths.) They dismissed such municipal directives as "an excessive exercise of power." Not only was the church vestry concerned about the costs of such improvements and the resulting increase in water rates, fundamentally they did not believe their poor tenants deserved nor could be trusted with these features. "The tenants of such houses are unusually dirty," a church trustee flatly told the Tenement House Commission in 1894; "if they had water in the halls the floors would always be wet." Trinity maintained that tenants and the Board of Health should be content with the well in the yard that had existed for generations.[37] Neglected by its owners, convinced of their tenants' inferiority, the ad hoc landscape of hastily converted structures soon grew inadequate to the needs of a rapidly expanding population.

Yet, many in the American elite, like the vestry members of Trinity Church, sought to divest from working-class housing altogether as quickly as they could, promoting industrial or commercial uses as a type of slum clearance. When old converted tenements could no longer be maintained or when leases on tenant-built buildings expired, the church demolished them and developed business buildings on the site, if there was demand for such a building. If there was no such demand, the church preferred to leave the lot vacant than construct a new tenement there. By the early twentieth century, the church even included deed restrictions on property it sold forbidding the site from tenement use in perpetuity. As one vestryman noted, "erection of the ordinary four or five story tenement on a single lot is contrary to the policy of the church."[38]

The Slum Tenement

Despite their disinclination toward investing in new working-class housing, a minority of elite landholders, sometimes the landowner, more commonly their lessors, chose to gradually replace their slum holdings with large, towering, new structures, often where previous buildings had been destroyed, or to fill in unused space in yards and courts (Figure 1.9). The Bennett estate in Boston, and the Weeks family in New York infilled and occasionally replaced the slums they held with new, large buildings built expressly for the purpose of housing multiple families (Figure 1.10). As with the alterations made to existing buildings, they were often built as quickly and cheaply as possible, with the barest standards of accommodation, sanitation, and even circulation.

Figure 1.9. A large, new tenement rises above run-down, wood-frame buildings in the Five Points neighborhood of New York, stereoview, circa 1875. The facade demonstrates a strict utilitarian austerity. Note the rear tenement visible in the background. Courtesy of the Miriam and Ira D. Wallach Division of Art, Prints and Photographs: Print Collection, The New York Public Library.

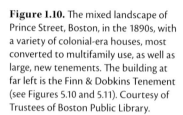

Figure 1.10. The mixed landscape of Prince Street, Boston, in the 1890s, with a variety of colonial-era houses, most converted to multifamily use, as well as large, new tenements. The building at far left is the Finn & Dobkins Tenement (see Figures 5.10 and 5.11). Courtesy of Trustees of Boston Public Library.

The most common of such new tenements occupied the area behind converted houses, in spaces formerly occupied by yards. In New York, where lots were generally regular, rear tenements had rectangular footprints, four- or five-story structures containing one three- or four-room unit on each floor. These were accessed only through the main house. Buildings such as these continued to be built into the mid-nineteenth century, even behind new front tenements (Figure 1.11). In Boston, where lots were often deeper and more irregular, land was frequently subdivided through a system of alleys and courts. The labyrinthine nature of these alleys and courts in the West End was a particular boon in the 1850s when the neighborhood was an important hub of the Underground Railroad, allowing for ample hiding places and carefully controllable sight lines.[39] Along these throughways were placed small and generally irregular buildings. Sometimes the expansion of older structures, these were generally long, narrow buildings with multiple entrances and often used stacked exterior porches as their primary means of circulation between units.[40]

These buildings were some of the earliest purpose-built multifamily housing, part of an increasing trend in the first half of the nineteenth century toward specialized building types. Yet these early tenements were uniform in the meager accommodations they provided. In general they contained two-room units consisting of a general-purpose living space and a sleeping space. This layout reflected the kinds of spaces that were familiar in the subdivided and converted buildings of the slums. Indeed, this was the most common arrangement for working-class housing in the early nineteenth century (Figure 1.12). In many European cities, for example, parallel rows of similar units were found in wide but comparatively shallow buildings, often arranged off double-loaded corridors. In the most extreme cases, such as in Berlin, parallel ranks of these buildings sometimes three or four deep were placed on a lot. In those situations, the best units were in the front building, with progressively less desirable spaces, sometimes mixed with industrial uses, placed farther back (see Figure 5.17).

Tenements of this type were particularly common in Boston, where they were built through the late 1880s. For example, in Luther Briggs's 1856 Broad Street building for Matthew Bartlett, two long, narrow buildings were placed perpendicular to the street. The two-room units of the buildings' upper floors were reached through open wooden porches, running the length of the rear of the buildings.[41] An important money- and space-saving feature, these appendages significantly darkened the already poorly fenestrated units. Long, narrow tenements with external circulation like this became popularly known as the barracks block (Figure 1.13).[42] Another such Boston building, known ironically as the "Crystal Palace," contained sixty small apartments on four floors and had entrance porches across the facade of the building, and stair towers capped by distinctive Mansard pavilions. It was considered among

Figure 1.11. A purpose-built four-story rear tenement behind an 1850s or 1860s Eldridge Street building, New York. A second, three-story rear tenement is at right, inches away. The front tenement for that building is now demolished. These have been made visible only by the demolition of neighboring buildings. Note the acanthus cornice on the four-story rear tenement. For a plan of a similar building, see Figure 2.2B. Photograph by Sean Litchfield.

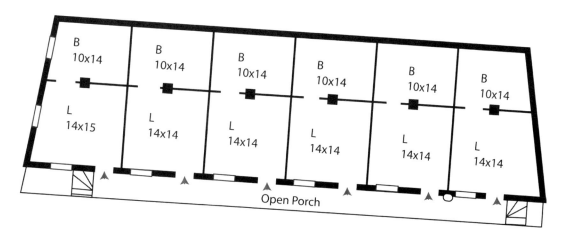

Figure 1.12. Plan, rear building, Matthew Bartlett Tenement, Broad Street, Boston, 1856 (demolished). Typical of two-room accommodations found in much early purpose-built, working-class housing. In this type (commonly referred to as a barracks block), circulation was entirely through wooden, exterior porches. Another building with a similar plan was placed between this and the street. Shared sinks were located on the porches, and sanitation was through privies in the yard. Drawing by author.

Figure 1.13. A Lower East Side barracks block in New York with external circulation. Located on a rear lot, the plan of this building almost certainly resembled Figure 1.12. From Jacob Riis, *How the Other Half Lives* (1890), 45.

AN OLD REAR-TENEMENT IN ROOSEVELT STREET.

the worst in the city, despite efforts at reform.[43] Likewise, the infamous Gotham Court in New York, built in 1850 initially as a philanthropic endeavor, had similar two-room plans. The heirs of Joshua Bennett built a more substantial purpose-built tenement in 1856 at 16 Phillips Street in the West End of Boston (Figure 1.14).[44] The brick and wood-frame building had a storefront along the first floor and at least twenty units, most likely of two rooms each, upstairs.

These earliest tenements would consistently be austere buildings with meager accommodations, reflecting an absentee landlord's view of these areas as slums. Indeed, a late nineteenth-century slumming tourist, exposing lurid stories of the neighborhood's opium dens in the *New York Times,* directed his ire to one of these large, purpose-built tenements in particular, unusual for both its age and size. To him, it was simply "a wart on top of a festering sore." Eschewing the usual animal-habitat imagery, this description of a seven-story Mott Street building built by the Weeks family in the 1820s recalled Thomas Jefferson's well-known formulation of the city itself as a "sore" and a "canker" on the body of pure government (see Figure 2.1, *center*). That same observer noted that Weeks's building had "a front that might lead you to take it for a mill or a factory, or an over-grown car-stable, or anything but a human habitation. The filth in it is so thick and deep that it is hanging out of the windows like icicles." The owner, the writer concluded, "ought to be ashamed of himself," declaring that "nobody who has ever looked upon the building will pity him" if his tenants committed acts of violent assault on the landlord while he collected his rent. [45]

While it did little to change Weeks (who returned to a Fifth Avenue mansion after collecting his rent from Mott Street), this sort of criticism, bordering on subtle threats of violence, may have hastened the departure of many elite landholders from the tenement-building and tenement-owning business. Their departure from the market for working-class housing created an opening for immigrant entrepreneurs, who were the leaders in an urban regeneration project that wiped away much of the slum landscape. A general rebuilding of these areas began in the post–Civil War building boom and continued in fits and starts into the early twentieth century. This new tenement building, carried out in waves of frenetic construction, witnessed much of the slum landscape being replaced with purpose-built tenements representing an increasing standard of interior accommodations. These technical conveniences were reflected

Figure 1.14. Joshua Bennett Heirs Tenement, 16 Phillips Street, Boston (1856; demolished). Architect unknown. Courtesy of Bostonian Society, collection number VW0050.

in visual improvements, most noticeably exteriors that no longer reflected the visual vocabulary of poverty that had long marked the slum landscape.

By the early twentieth century, after decades of changing ideas and rapid tenement construction in these neighborhoods, the slum landscape had been radically altered. Yet the layering of differing housing solutions, representing different aesthetic and living standards, remained clearly visible. In a plate in *The Leaven in a Great City* (1902), New York reformer Lillian Betts presented a scene of a New York street that she titled "Past, Present and Middle Period" (Figure 1.15).[46] While using the same sort of architectural juxtaposition, the image strongly contrasted to the more usual slum tropes like those employed in Matthew Hale Smith's frontispiece. Betts's image illustrated the range of housing conditions present in these neighborhoods in the early twentieth century and demonstrates clearly the rapid, if uneven and incom-

Figure 1.15. "The Past, Present and Middle Period," 1902. The elaborate Herter Brothers–designed tenement (since demolished) at left of this New York streetscape contrasted sharply to the old Federal-era house converted to a tenement at center, and the modestly ornamented tenements of the mid-nineteenth century at right. This image depicts the corner of Rivington and Cannon Streets. The three older buildings would be demolished for a large, modern tenement shortly after the image was made. This corner vanished for a public housing complex in the mid-twentieth century. From Lillian Betts, *The Leaven in a Great City* (1902), 44.

THE PAST, PRESENT AND MIDDLE PERIOD.

plete, improvement that had taken place there. Instead of comparing a downtown hovel and an uptown mansion, the contrast was between an old, converted slum and a new, modern tenement. The past, at the center of the frame, was represented by a converted Federal-era row house, quite dilapidated and a clear manifestation of the slum image that had been common for the past half century or longer. The middle period was depicted as a block of comparatively early purpose-built tenements, in the right foreground, austere but for their metal cornices. Finally, to the far left, the figure of the present was represented by a large, new tenement designed and built by Herter Brothers. This building was substantially taller than its neighbors, in warm buff brick, its roofline broken by galvanized iron pinnacles a story tall, and its windows surrounded by terra-cotta ornament in high relief: it was a decorated tenement, contrasting sharply with its environment, despite the laundry hanging from the fire escape. Evocative of the rising standards for working-class housing witnessed over the course of the nineteenth century, it was a sign of immigrant tenement builders' resistance to the static slum stereotype at just the moment when reformers were once again becoming intensely interested in this landscape. This new iconography of the improved, decorated tenement will be the focus of the remainder of this book.

Chapter 2

The Better Sort of Tenement

Competing Notions of Improvement and Living Standards

When they speak of . . . the evils of tenement houses, have they in mind the buildings that were erected twenty, fifteen, or ten years ago? Or are they speaking of the buildings that are permitted today? Clearly it is useless, except for sentimental purposes, to talk about structures of the bygone type.

Peter Herter, 1900

Jacob Weeks's startling architectural "wart," as the *New York Times* dubbed it in 1880, stood at 65 Mott Street, rising seven stories above the "festering sore" of the Lower East Side of New York (Figure 2.1). It sprang up, likely around 1824, rising above a street then lined with two-story row houses.[1] If the building continued to elicit strong reactions more than a half century later, it was certainly a novelty when it was new. Built specially to house multiple families living independently, in this case four per floor on a narrow lot, it was an early experiment in a new specialized building type, one of the many new forms emerging in this early stage of American industrial capitalism. Indeed, it may have been the first purpose-built tenement in New York, and perhaps anywhere in the country. Inside, the small, two-room units would have been familiar to many working-class New Yorkers (Figure 2.2). Weeks's building only increased the scale and density of housing in the neighborhood; it did not substantially improve conditions, having few amenities and cramped quarters.[2] According to historian Elizabeth Blackmar, new

Figure 2.1. Evolution of the Mott Street tenement, New York. *Center,* Jacob Weeks Tenement, 65 Mott Street (circa 1824). *Right,* Martin Ficken Tenement, 67 Mott Street (1875). William Graul, architect. *Left,* Barney Isaacs Tenements, 61 and 63 Mott Street (1887). Schneider & Herter, architect. *Far right,* Rebecca Ficken Tenement, 69–71 Mott Street (1907). Charles Straub, architect. Photograph by Sean Litchfield.

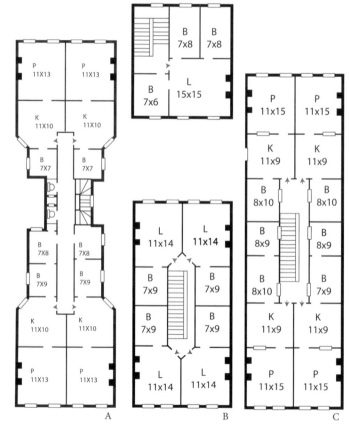

Figure 2.2. Evolution of the Mott Street tenement plan. *A,* Barney Isaacs Tenement, 63 Mott Street; *B,* Jacob Weeks Tenement, 65 Mott Street (note second tenement at rear lot); *C,* Martin Ficken Tenement, 67 Mott Street. The plan of the later Rebecca Ficken Tenement is not shown here but was similar to Figure 2.16*B.* Each plan was the most common tenement plan of its moment. Drawing by author.

buildings like this "legitimated" the poor housing standards of the early nineteenth-century slum.[3] But at least it was not a rookery carved out of a converted building, and therein lay its innovation.

The Weeks tenement set the basic spatial pattern for New York multifamily housing for much of the rest of the century. It was dubbed a "double-decker" tenement, a useful period term for a building in which two families shared the street frontage of a standard twenty-five-foot lot, usually with another two across the rear. Soon new tenements with better accommodations would grow up around it, and Weeks would increasingly come to play the role of absentee slumlord, making few improvements. While Weeks was born and raised in modest circumstances on Mott Street, his family, like many others like it, fled the changing neighborhood with a series of northward moves, first to an elegant townhouse near Gramercy Park, then to a large brownstone on Fifth Avenue, next to Cornelius Vanderbilt.[4] But the family held the Mott Street property into the early part of the twentieth century.

The Weeks building was rapidly seen as meager, even squalid, in an era of rising expectations. In 1875 Martin Ficken, a German immigrant grocer and liquor dealer and prominent Tammany Hall supporter, bought the old house at 67 Mott Street and demolished it for a new tenement.[5] Ficken's new building was markedly different than Weeks's, inside and out. Substantially deeper, the four-room units now contained an important new amenity: a parlor, a place of modest gentility separate from the workaday kitchen. There were now distinct places for living, for cooking and working, and for sleeping. Ficken also provided running water to a sink on each floor, reducing the hassle of lugging water from an outside well. The new amenities, along with the fancier facade, did not just help Ficken rent apartments but improved his own living conditions, as he moved into the new building and lived there, along with scores of other tenants, for years after its completion.

In 1887, as a new wave of immigration began to swell the already crowded neighborhood, Barney Isaacs, a Polish Jewish cigar maker who had lived on nearby Orchard Street, bought the two houses just south of the Weeks building and replaced them with a pair of elaborate six-story tenements designed by Schneider & Herter.[6] The buildings were far advanced over Ficken's tenement of just over a decade earlier. Not only did the inner rooms now have light thanks to air shafts, but each floor had two flush toilets, a great improvement over the unsanitary privies in the yard. These changes were newly required by code, but plenty of other improvements were not. The kitchen had its own sink with running water and sewer connection, a cooking range, and potentially a hot water boiler. A dumbwaiter served each floor. The wallpapered parlors were provided with folding blinds and faux marble mantels.

Within a decade, by the mid-1890s, nearby builders were going further, building tenements with five-room plans that included dining rooms, hot and cold water, bells and annunciators to the outside, private toilets, and even full private bathrooms. These innovations would be standard by 1907 when Martin Ficken's widow, Rebecca, then living in Yorkville, replaced the old houses at 69 and 71 Mott Street with a large, modern tenement whose conveniences and spatial amenities would represent nearly a century's worth of rapid improvement on Weeks's model.[7] Much of this betterment was carried out separate from, indeed often in spite of, the housing reform movement that was roiling around it.

Representing the most common New York tenement plan of their respective moments, the changes seen on this Mott Street block, along with a parallel evolution occurring in Boston, were material manifestations of the rising expectations among the working class about the spaces and services in their housing. This was enabled by rising wealth and the increased presence of builders with the interest and incentive to provide better housing. Each of these arrangements was calibrated to the tastes, desires, and economic circumstances of their residents within the harsh realities of the urban land market. Yet, such plans were routinely maligned by reformers as "heedless," designed with no other goal than to wring the maximum rent from tenants. Indeed, builders did have to keep an eye on what tenants would pay for, and had to prove that expensive innovations would be popular. Doing so, however, meant their designs responded to the rising expectations of immigrant tenants for spatial and technological accommodations and aesthetic improvements, reflecting changing standards, preferences, tastes, and cultural practices. During times of rapid tenement construction, tenants could demand better accommodations and frequently moved to achieve this goal.[8] A hypothetical tenant of 65 Mott Street in 1870 could have readily moved to 67 Mott Street in 1875, then to 63 Mott in 1888, and in the process their living conditions would have substantially altered over a fairly short period of time. In meeting these demands, builders reflected the interests of a group of consumers with agency, not a vulnerable and exploited class, as reformers, whose project relied in part on demonstrating the helplessness of these tenants, suggested.

The Misunderstood, Improving Tenement

Many of the characteristics of the tenement that reformers deplored most, indeed some of their seemingly most compelling evidence of its exploitative nature, were the direct result of builders' attempts to accommodate their tenants demands. In reflecting these preferences, the design of the tenement encoded not just tenants' economic position but important aspects of their culture as well. Yet the real design improvements that took place in these buildings were not readily perceived by middle-class outsiders, who sometimes even mistook accommodations to tenants' preferences as signs of heedless avarice on the part of builders. Indeed, there was a sharp disconnect between what tenement residents wanted and what housing reformers wanted for them.

In this vast cultural disconnect we can see the roots of the persistent charge that the tenement was "evil" and its builders "vicious." For example, reformers prioritized air, light, and family privacy: nostalgic notions tied to discomfort over the loss of the supremacy of the freestanding single-family house, as well as a distaste for high lot coverage and the industrial products that filled and decorated these new urban spaces. Yet builders knew tenants preferred to have an increasingly complex suite of rooms for varied purposes, including parlors and dining rooms, even if these rooms were smaller and more poorly lit and ventilated than they would be if undivided. Additionally, as life in many immigrant communities was lived largely on the street, as it had been in Europe, privacy was not yet an abiding concern.[9] To the contrary, residents wanted the closest possible connection to the street, ideally outside their formal parlor. The increasing demand for varied rooms and the need for a parlor close to the street required deeper footprints, pushing bedrooms and kitchens into darker and stuffier positions on the interior of the lot. Many tenants, builders like Ficken and Isaacs understood, made this trade-off readily. In addition, tenants increasingly demanded not only improved sanitary features but modern conveniences like dumb-waiters, hot water boilers, and coal grates. And since most took in boarders to help make rent, multiple entrances from the common hall were a great convenience, even if reformers viewed common areas as an inscrutable waste of space. Even the much-maligned insistence on building on single twenty-five-foot-wide lots even when more space was available, as in the case of Isaacs's twin buildings, was an important design decision. As chapter 4 demonstrates, it kept the tenement an accessible investment to small builders and owners.

Familiar with the cultural differences of their tenants, immigrant tenement builders in particular had both the understanding and inclination to meet these demands. The most successful builder, the *Real Estate Record and Builders' Guide* declared in 1899, "is likely to be the one who best meets the want of the consumer, who in tenements is just as eager to get the best for his money." Builders could not simply assent to reformers' demands without also accommodating their prospective tenants' tastes and desires. "An owner cannot provide any kind of house that will suit his own notions and order tenants into it," the *Record and Guide* continued, "He has to consult the wishes of his patrons."[10] Yet most reformers failed to acknowledge that much of what they found distasteful about the tenement resulted from builders' attempts to "consult" the wishes of their residents. Often tenement dwellers themselves, or formerly so, immigrant and working-class builders and architects were best positioned to "consult the wishes" of the tenement resident. Indeed, the conflicts over these spaces set those who believed the desires of the working class should be accommodated against those who thought it needed to be reformed.

The evolution of the Mott Street tenements was the result of vibrant experimentation and competition in tenement design that played out over the course of the nineteenth century. As the *Record and Guide* noted in 1899, "builders of tenements are continually wrestling with the problem of giving the best accommodation possible." A year later, in his public quarrel with reformer Ernest Flagg, Peter Herter declared, "our architects and builders . . . have had to deal with financial conditions, with the prices of lots, the value of money, the tastes of tenants, the desires and requirements of tenants, the several laws, the different municipal departments, and so forth." He declared, "there is not in the tenement house as we know it a single feature that is not the necessary product" of one of these factors. As a result he decried Flagg's temerity in assailing this work, suggesting that "the efforts of hundreds of architects and builders extending over a great many years, were all wrong, even vicious, and based upon erroneous principles. Mr. Flagg says in effect that all these men for all these years have been working . . . to see how unsanitary and uncomfortable tenement houses can be."[11]

While scholars of urban housing usually give tenement laws of the type promoted by Flagg an outsize importance in explaining the improved tenements, their actual effect on built form was limited. The thrust of the earliest reform laws centered on ameliorating the ill effects of high lot coverage and dense living conditions and sought to contain the hazards inherent in these environments.[12] While many of the provisions of the tenement laws were reasonable responses to the worst abuses, they also reflected reformers priorities of air, light, and family privacy. Yet often, especially in the case of the signal 1901 New York Tenement House Act, they codified improvements already offered by the best builders. Despite housing reformers' belief that these "culturally-inferior" groups were unable to improve their own environment and therefore positive changes could only be brought about by outside intervention, there was substantial improvement in both spatial and technological amenity beyond what was demanded by evolving building code. As Boston observer Lee Friedman noted, the immigrant tenement builders of the turn of the twentieth century were "in the van of something progressive, unconsciously creating standards for themselves and catering to demands which rejected the kind of houses which had served as living quarters for earlier generations."[13]

The improvements in the tenements of Boston and New York were part of evolving expectations for housing that took place nationwide in this period, in the context of an unprecedented rise in material standards. Recent scholarship has demonstrated that the working class was generally housed in small, often two-room living arrangements, like those in the Weeks tenement, well into the middle of the century.[14] Modest living quarters were the norm in both urban and rural areas, both in America and abroad. At this "pre-modern" stage, as architectural historian Thomas Hubka, has defined it, many had minimal spaces with undifferentiated rooms and primitive technologies for cooking, heating, and sanitation. Spaces evolved throughout the second half of the century, with rising notions of family privacy and increasing access to technology. The period after about 1870 witnessed greater separation between cooking and living spaces, as well as places for adult privacy, as Martin Ficken's tenement showed. Generally running water and stoves for cooking were introduced in this period. Beginning around the turn of the twentieth century, working-class residents came to expect an increased number of bedrooms with closets, the addition of a dining room as well as separate parlor or living room and kitchen, and modern technology such as gas cooking, electric lighting, and a full bathroom. Hubka has called this generally five-room arrangement the "Progressive Era plan."[15] These features began to appear in buildings like Isaacs's and were more clearly seen in slightly later examples, like Rebecca Ficken's. At each stage, newly built tenements in Boston and New York incorporated these changes slightly ahead of their adoption nationally, with the smaller city often quicker to embrace new amenities. On Mott Street, as elsewhere, older buildings built to previous standards existed alongside the up-to-date structures, providing important economic diversity but helping to perpetuate to the casual observer the notion that the tenements were universally bad housing.

The evolution of the spaces and services in the tenements of Boston and New York, unexceptional but for their smaller size and density, mirrored changes taking place within national housing culture. At each stage we find the tenement evolving alongside national norms. While the large, attached buildings containing perhaps dozens of units would be foreign to workers in most American cities, the types of spaces and services available would be generally familiar. Indeed, by the end of the nineteenth century the standards of the newly built Boston and New York tenement were quite advanced technologically compared to even middle-class rural housing, at a stage in which even indoor plumbing was uncommon. In rural areas most except the well-to-do would not see these improvements until well into the twentieth century. Their location in the metropolis gave many in the working class access to many more technological and spatial amenities, though certainly not more space, than their counterparts elsewhere. It was perhaps the anti-urbanism, indeed nostalgic agrarianism, of many reformers that led them to ignore the fact that most new tenements had substantial benefits over what the majority of rural residents, in America and abroad, experienced.[16] Indeed Jacob Riis, wed to the notion that all tenements were necessarily vicious, asserted this fact did not matter.[17]

Tenement Technology

Progress in urban working-class housing was measured most definitively around technological advances, which could be much more readily accommodated than spatial improvements, which required more fundamental shifts in the utilization of expensive land.[18] The most widespread and dramatic of these evolutions took place in the areas of cooking and sanitary facilities. The average tenement of the antebellum period had the barest of infrastructure, with well water and earthen privies in the yard and little else in terms of conveniences. By the end of the century a similar class of building would have running water and sewer connection to each unit, ranges, sinks, and hot water boilers in each kitchen or provided by a central facility, flush toilets on each floor (and potentially full bathrooms in each unit), a coal grate or perhaps steam heating, a dumbwaiter to each floor, gas lighting, even a bell and speaking tube to the outside door.

There were complex economic incentives for providing these features. They added substantially to the cost and complexity of construction and presented maintenance headaches for the life of the property. Rarely, except in the case of full baths or central heat, did these improvements yield a significant increase in rental income, which re-mained closely tied to the number of rooms in a unit. (At the turn of the century this averaged about $5 per room per month in the Lower East Side of New York.)[19] But as these improvements served to attract tenants to the building at times of rapid construction and assured a lower vacancy rate, builders provided them fairly consis-tently, even when they were not required by law. By providing more amenities than their neighbor and competing favorably with older tenements, the builders ensured that their buildings would be full upon sale or refinancing and that the long-term owner would have less trouble attracting tenants.

No room was more radically transformed than the kitchen. Once primitive spaces with little else than a fireplace or stove thimble, by the end of the century kitchens were the most technologically advanced spaces in the building. Throughout the last decades of the nineteenth century, tenants could expect an increasing number of ser-vices and amenities in their kitchen. By the 1880s, stoves were provided by the land-lord, as were private sinks, formerly located in the hallway, with at least cold running water. By the end of the decade, boilers to provide domestic hot water increasingly came to be seen as an indispensable feature. In 1889, for instance, New York builder Joel Hyams decided, during the course of construction of a Varrick Street tenement, to install hot water heaters in his Herter Brothers–designed building. The change cost an additional $900 on the twenty-three-unit, $40,000 building.[20]

Many of these new appliances dazzled and sometimes confused tenants, at least according to observers, eager to show the juxtaposition of old-world attitudes with modern technology. In her early twentieth-century account of Italian "peasants" liv-ing in a newly constructed tenement in New York, Lillian Betts described the confu-sion surrounding the hot water boilers, heated by a fire in the range, installed there:

> Few . . . can be taught that to get hot water in the boilers it is necessary to keep
> it there for some time. It is impossible to make the connection in their minds
> between the fire in the stove and the water that comes out of the faucet . . . it is
> accepted as one of those mysterious American puzzles, unsolvable but accepted.[21]

Betts was, of course, playing on long-standing racist and classist tropes that por-trayed tenement residents as naive and childlike, baffled by the conveniences of the modern city (Figure 2.3). More were probably like those Lower East Side tenants of Peter Herter, who by the 1890s were savvy enough to demand the latest amenities.[22]

Like the other services available to residents, the sanitary facilities of an average tenement underwent a significant evolution during the nineteenth century, matching an increasing concern for sanitary conditions witnessed in American culture at large. Over the course of the century, the tenement became connected to a public water and sewer infrastructure that grew up in large measure as a response to the health hazards of urban living in close quarters.[23] Built before the introduction of municipal sewers, the earliest tenements, like most of their neighbors, had backyard privies connected to earthen vaults that would contain waste. Unsanitary, particularly in dense neighborhoods, these privies were replaced in the middle of the nineteenth century with school sinks, connected to the sewer and water system. These school sinks contained up to a dozen private stalls, each connected to a single, large masonry vault. This vault could be flushed by a running-water connection into the sewer system. Considered a sanitary improvement over the older, more primitive privies, school sinks were quickly found to be inadequate due to the difficulty in fully flushing them. Interior, flushing toilets of the modern type were considered preferable and were required in new tenements built after 1879 in New York. School sinks were banned, even in existing buildings, in 1901. In the 1879–1901 period in New York, generally two interior water closets were provided on each floor, sometimes serving four families. After 1901, each unit was required to have its own private water closet.

In both cities private baths became a status marker in tenements in the last decade of the nineteenth century. While public baths were increasingly an option, prior to this point bathing more frequently took place in portable galvanized metal washtubs in the kitchen that were also used for laundry.[24] After experimenting with shared

Figure 2.3. An improved New York tenement kitchen with a parlor to the left, circa 1902. Note the presence of gas stove, hot water boiler, and shelves and table covered with cloth hangings. The parlor had grained woodwork, a mantel, and a frescoed ceiling. Photograph taken by the New York Tenement House Department. Courtesy of Milstein Division of United States History, Local History, and Genealogy, New York Public Library, Astor, Lenox, and Tilden Foundations.

bathrooms, Herter Brothers began providing full, private, three-fixture baths as early as 1889 in tenements they developed on Madison and Pearl Streets.[25] Harris Fine began providing them to some of his Broome Street tenements by 1895. These became standard in New York after 1901. The Tenement House Department noted in 1903 that 90 percent of tenements constructed after the new law over the previous year had full baths even though only a water closet was required.[26] Full, private bathrooms began to appear in Boston tenements by 1893 and quickly became standard. Indeed, the provision of a private bath became a status marker in many tenement apartments. Some Boston buildings, like Sarah Silverstein's 1900 Frederick Norcross–designed tenement at 40 Grove Street, provided a full bath for the commodious front-facing apartment, and a single-stall water closet for the smaller rear unit (see Figure 2.11*D*). By the early twentieth century in Boston, observer Lee M. Friedman noted, "it was impossible to find a tenement without a toilet, running water and a bathtub. Sometimes the bathtub was only an indication of social position, since its principal use was as a place for storing fuel . . . but it was absolutely necessary if good rents were to be obtained."[27]

The impulse of some tenants to use these space-consuming facilities for storage when they were not in use led many outsiders to suggest that naive tenement residents could not be trusted with private bathing facilities. Many reformers avoided them in their model tenements. In testimony leading up to the 1901 law, well-known pattern-book architect George Palliser declared to the New York State Tenement House Commission in 1900 that bathtubs should only be required in tenements if tenants "could be compelled to use them, too—not for duck ponds or coal bins, either." Many of these experts recommended showers instead of bathtubs, a feature that was rarely adopted.[28]

Heating was a particular problem in tenements. Throughout the nineteenth century virtually all tenements were heated with individual stoves or coal grates. The construction of the many flues necessary to serve these devices posed a challenge for builders. Most New York tenement units had at most two flues—one in the parlor, the other in the kitchen serving the range. This necessitated eight exterior chimneys, four per side, each with five or more flues. Even with this, inner rooms were cold in the winter. Large Boston tenements occasionally had an additional flue, but most bedrooms were still unheated.

Working in a colder climate, Boston developers adopted central steam heating earlier than New York builders, using it in tenements as early as 1898. While considerably more expensive and burdening the landlord with fuel costs instead of the tenant, steam heat allowed for more flexible layouts, particularly in smaller apartments, as living spaces no longer had to be tied to flues and encumbered by large stoves. This was particularly useful as tenement footprints became larger and more complex around the turn of the century. While a feature of better-quality New York apartments since the 1870s, steam heat was rare on the Lower East Side. In 1900 Peter Herter noted that this was an improvement he reserved for tenements in more desirable locations on the west side, providing them in tenements he built in the 1890s on

West Fourth and Charles Streets. For this improvement, he was able to charge about $1 a month additional rent per room, in buildings that were targeted to a more economically stable clientele.[29] Central heat did not commonly appear in Lower East Side tenements until after World War I, when it was retrofitted in many older buildings in an attempt to increase their desirability.[30]

A number of more minor features, some important conveniences, acted as inducements for prospective tenants. By the 1880s builders began providing a number of other conveniences, including piping for gas lighting, and door bells and annunciators providing communication from the street to the unit. More importantly, dumbwaiters were installed to alleviate the task of vertical lugging in buildings that could rise to seven stories in height. This was particularly useful in bringing coal from basement storage bins for use in the range and heating stoves. Only a handful of New York tenements, all built around the turn of the twentieth century, had elevators. These tended to be located in the most desirable parts of the neighborhood, such as near Rutgers Square or Second Avenue, and had other amenities, such as dining rooms, full private baths, and steam heat.

Tenement Space

In an era of rising standards, it became increasingly difficult to shoehorn new types of spaces and services onto narrow, and in Boston often irregular, urban lots. This made light and air, especially from the street, a valuable but scarce commodity. Not only did they more easily meet code requirements, units facing the street were generally more valuable than those facing the back as they received better light, and tenants were said to prefer the more interesting view afforded by the street over the comparative solitude of the yard with its fetid air.[31] Much of tenement life was lived in public, as it had been in the Old World; in European multifamily housing, often extending deep into a lot, a street-facing apartment was a major status symbol. On the small and narrow lots of Boston and New York, outlook onto the street seems to have been a guiding factor in tenement design, with builders insisting that units without an "outlook" could not be rented easily. In Boston builders often situated larger and more generously appointed units at the front of a tenement, while locating smaller units, sometimes with reduced plumbing facilities and fewer room types, at the rear. In New York front and rear units generally did not vary so greatly, although most builders continued to situate smaller units facing the yard.

The tenement was designed to accommodate a wide variety of cultural practices, many of which were antithetical to middle-class notions of domesticity. A builder had to anticipate heavy use by his future tenants, who would occupy the space in a variety of ways: some families lived independently; some rented space to boarders; others lived within partner or collective households wherein two or more families, often related but living independently, would share use of the kitchen and other facilities of a single apartment.[32] Space had to be available for the temporary lodging of relatives.[33] All told, a tenement apartment, few of which were much larger than five hundred square feet, needed to provide space to sleep, in extreme but not uncommon cases, upwards of a dozen people.[34] In addition to these quarters, significant other demands were put on the space. While middle-class homes were increasingly free from economically productive activities, tenement apartments maintained their status as workshops not only for the needs of the family but also for the cash economy.[35] The domestic requirements of a tenement household dictated the production of meals and laundry for a large number of people.[36] In addition, a key portion of many tenants' income was the home production of goods for market, whether these be garments made on the sweatshop system, laundry washed for pay, or the assembly of cigars, artificial flowers, or other consumer products.[37] Or perhaps the goods of a family's pushcart business had to be stored in the apartment, to the chagrin of reformers concerned about the hygiene of food.[38]

These strategies, necessary to cope with the economic realities of high rent and low wages, often demanded architectural solutions foreign to many elite designers, including, particularly, a flexibility in circulation and common facilities like rooftop space for laundry drying. Planning a satisfactory tenement, therefore, was a challenge of the first order, and the results were frequently less than ideal for all concerned. Yet most tenement residents could expect to find a fairly standardized range of spaces and amenities in the buildings.

Hallways and Common Areas

Common access to areas and services shared by other residents was part of the very definition of a tenement. The most visible of these was the public hall, serving anywhere from three to twenty-one apartments. The public hallways and other common spaces of a tenement were the most heavily used. Despite reformers' suggestion they should be minimized, speculative tenement builders persisted in devoting a fairly considerable amount of space to hallways. As private circulation within units was a rare luxury, the public hall often took on this role, with multiple doors, sometimes from nearly every room. In some Boston tenements the only way to move from one part of the unit to the other was to go through the public hall. Hallways provided communal services, like sinks with running water, before these were located in residents' kitchens. Later, water closets, dumbwaiters, and sometimes even features like public telephones were also located in the hall. Sometimes, particularly in Boston, water closets and sometimes full bathrooms were accessed off the public hall even if they were not shared by any other families.

Space was also provided for tenants in the cellars for storage of coal or other fuel, a crucial amenity for small apartments heated by stoves. To accommodate this, cellars were divided by thin wooden partitions into coal bins, one for each unit. The roofs of tenements provided important informal communal space for tenant use. Primarily, the roof provided space for laundry drying; wooden clothes-drying racks were fre-

Figure 2.4. General view of the North End of Boston, early twentieth century. Intersection of Battery and Hanover Streets at lower right, showing a number of important decorated tenements. Note the prevalence of laundry drying racks on tenement roofs. Courtesy of Trustees of Boston Public Library.

quently seen in period photographs of tenements (Figure 2.4). Peter Herter's buildings also provided individual water lines to the roof for the use of each tenant, referring to this part of the building as the "laundry roof."[39] The rooftop also provided a modicum of relief on hot evenings, in which sleeping became impossible in close and poorly ventilated interior spaces.

The Kitchen

The presence of a kitchen within each unit made the tenement distinct from the lodging house, boardinghouse, and hotel, where residents did not have their own space to cook.[40] Tenement kitchens were the workshop for the family, where they produced much of the food and other goods used by the household. Consequently many family members spent the majority of their waking hours at home there. In many tenement apartments, kitchens were also the largest room, averaging twelve by fifteen feet in New York and just slightly larger in Boston. In the typical plan in New York, the kitchen was the central space and served as the primary entryway to the apartment, separating the parlor from the bedrooms. In Boston, the kitchen was more commonly located in the rear of the apartment, following a long-standing convention of separating the kitchen from living spaces.[41]

The construction of most tenements came about in a transition period between the home production of items needed for household consumption and the introduction of industrially made products for this purpose. Tenement kitchens represent this hybridity. No longer the extensive workshops they used to be, the demands of the household still dictated these were large and well-equipped spaces.[42] Small "kitchenettes" would not appear until after World War I and were never popular with working-class residents, for whom the kitchen remained the center of the home.[43] In the smallest and barest tenement plans, those that omit the parlor, the kitchen was frequently designated the "living room," a general-purpose space meant to contain most of the household's activities, other than sleeping.

Given the level of activity taking place there, the kitchen was apt to be the social center of the apartment, even if the family also maintained a separate parlor.[44] Many tenants chose to use the kitchen as their primary living space. In her memoir of life in Boston tenements, Russian Jewish immigrant Mary Antin recalled using the kitchen as an all-purpose living space. Of her sister's apartment she noted, "Frieda had a beautiful parlor, with plush chairs and a velvet carpet and gilt picture frames; but we preferred the homely, homelike kitchen."[45]

The Parlor

While the Antin sisters, like many tenement residents, may have spent most of both their leisure and working hours in the kitchen, many still insisted on maintaining parlors (Figure 2.5). And tenement builders readily obliged. In part they were eager to do so because rental rates were based on the number of rooms in a unit, and thus adding a parlor meant being able to charge for an additional room. Builders began including parlors as early as the 1860s and consistently after about 1870 in New York. In Boston parlors appear as early as 1870 and were common by 1890, although often builders provided parlors only in front-facing units, leaving smaller, rear apartments with combined kitchen/living rooms well into the first decade of the twentieth century. In practical terms, providing a parlor in a typical New York tenement plan necessitated a building footprint that was twenty-five or thirty feet deeper than earlier two-room plans, increasing the difficulty in providing air and light to kitchens and bedrooms, now pushed deeper into the lot.

Yet for many tenants this trade-off in air and light, as well as the additional rent charge, was worth it for the benefits of the new room. Usually roughly the same size

Figure 2.5. Parlor, Louis Segel Tenement, "The Gothic," 47 Allen Street, Boston (1898; pictured in 1959, shortly before demolition). Charles A. Halstrom, architect. Note the applied mantel installed without a flue behind. The mantel was particularly redundant as this building was equipped with steam heat from the beginning, indicated by the ornate radiator at left. For exterior, see Figure 5.13; for plan, see Figure 2.15A. Library of Congress, Prints and Photographs Division, HABS MASS,13-BOST,63-3.

as the kitchen, the appearance of a parlor nearly doubled the living space available. More importantly, the separation, albeit by a thin stud wall often punctured by an interior window, of the work space of the kitchen from a space that could be devoted to domesticity was an important evolution. These spaces were often architecturally distinguished with better-quality moldings, eventually with features like folding blinds set into deep embrasures. At the center of most was a mantel, sometimes of fine material like marbleized slate, which became the physical and ceremonial centerpiece of the room. It meant, fundamentally, a place in which the rituals of nineteenth-century domesticity could be performed in whatever manner tenants' economic and cultural circumstances dictated. While the working-class parlor was not an uncomplicated embrace of middle-class standards, many residents aspired to these kinds of spaces for a host of reasons.[46]

Indeed, the parlor was central not only in Anglo-American culture of this moment but in Jewish domestic practice as well. As historian Andrew Heinze has noted, many Jewish immigrants were attracted to the parlor by the "old Sabbatical imperative to make the home a sanctuary from the world of work."[47] This notion closely mirrored Victorian, Anglo-American ideals of domesticity. For many in both groups, the parlor was a room in which the residents of a household would put on display their gentility and worldliness through the use of material goods.[48] The increasing importance of the parlor in the second quarter of the nineteenth century for the middle class has been called "one of the great democratic moments" of that century.[49] The appearance of such rooms in the homes of the working class a generation later continued this trend of democratization. By the end of the century, virtually everyone could live in an apartment with a parlor, an important sign of rising wealth and increasing standards of living.

Even if the kitchen was the center of the apartment, the parlor held a dear place in the heart of many tenement residents. Of course the ability to use the room for its intended purpose was highly contingent on tenants' circumstances. Indeed, for many, a domestic sanctuary was an unaffordable luxury, even if they lived in an apartment with a designated parlor. In her semiautobiographical 1925 novel *Bread Givers,* Anzia Yezierska portrays a conflict in one immigrant family when it became necessary to rent the parlor, which they referred to as the "front room," to boarders. The space had previously been held sacred by the family patriarch, a rabbi, who used it as his private study, while the family remained cramped in the remainder of the apartment. "As the kitchen was packed with furniture, so the front room was packed with Father's books. They were on the shelf, on the table, on the window sill, and in soapboxes lined up against the wall." The books were the only possessions the family had brought with them to America, dispensing with many other cherished goods. Distressed at the thought of losing his private space, the father exclaimed: "But where will I have quiet for my studies in this crowded kitchen? I have to be alone in a room to think with God." "Only millionaires," his wife replied, "can be alone in America."[50]

While the middle-class and elite parlor has often been interpreted as a place for the performance of female domesticity, in Yezierska's account the quiet tenement parlor was a place of privilege for the male head of a Jewish household. While the parlor generated additional housekeeping duties for all classes, in the small spaces of the urban working class this was a particular burden on women. The physical presence of the parlor also infringed on the comfort of the female space of the kitchen, often relegated to the dreary outlook of a narrow air shaft, if it was provided with an outside window at all. In Yezierska's tenement, as in most tenement households with parlors, air and light were sacrificed in the kitchen, space of most female domestic labor, in order to make the nominally male space of the parlor larger and more comfortable with its breezy and desirable outlook onto the street or rear yard.

Dining Room

If the parlor had been the marker of gentility in the years immediately after the Civil War, by the end of the nineteenth century prospective tenants of the best tenements would come to expect a designated dining room as well (Figure 2.6).[51] Indeed, the democratization of the dining room around the turn of the twentieth century played much the same role as the widespread adoption of the parlor had a generation or two earlier. In New York, these rooms often occupied a central position in the unit and were frequently poorly lit. Radiating off the dining room would be the kitchen, parlor, and at least one bedroom. In many units, the apartment door opened directly into the dining room. Given this position, these spaces may have often served as the primary living areas in the unit, with the designated parlor being used as an additional bedroom. The presence of a dining room, of course, did not mean that tenants would use the space for this purpose, whether it was in a tenement or a middle-class home. New York housing inspectors often identified these as a second living room. In many later tenements with dining rooms, the parlor became nearly indistinguishable from

Figure 2.6. Dining room in Louis Segel Tenement, "The Gothic," 47 Allen Street, Boston (1898; pictured in 1959, shortly before demolition). Charles A. Halstrom, architect. This space adjoined the parlor pictured in Figure 2.5 and provided access to a bedroom at right. It was illuminated only by a small light shaft but had quartered oak wainscoting. The building was demolished in the urban renewal of the West End. Graffiti on the doors read, "Good buy old home, happy days so long." For exterior, see Figure 5.13; for plan, see Figure 2.15A. Library of Congress, Prints and Photographs Division, HABS MASS,13-BOST,63-4.

a front-facing bedroom on the plans. As they did the parlor, economically precarious tenants likely expected that these spaces could be used for their intended purposes in good times and rented out for additional income in leaner ones. Nonetheless, the provision of more than one formal room, or at least potentially so, was an important improvement at the end of the nineteenth century. Some Boston builders even provided built-in china closets in their dining rooms, a feature that was nearly standard in middle-class housing.

Bedrooms

The bedrooms of tenement units were, in general, the smallest and most incommodious spaces.[52] Seemingly an afterthought on most plans, they averaged no more than eight feet wide and seven to nine feet deep in New York, just slightly larger in Boston. That represented just enough space for a single bed and dresser. They also had the poorest access to air and light, frequently located on the narrowest portion of the air shaft. Before windowless rooms became illegal, in New York in 1879 and Boston in 1892, many bedrooms had no access to air and light at all. Even after they were technically illegal, windowless bedrooms frequently appeared on Boston plans with disingenuous labels such as "alcove" or "closet." On hot summer nights these spaces frequently became unbearably hot and stuffy. On these nights fire escapes and roofs acted as important alternative sleeping spaces. Conversely, in the winter these rooms were unheated. Warmth was borrowed from the kitchen stove, although on the coldest days residents crowded in the warmer kitchen or parlor.[53]

The bedroom's position within a unit suggested their secondary importance. In the standard New York plan, the one or two bedrooms were grouped at the rear of the apartment. In two-bedroom plans, the room closest to the kitchen acted as a pass-through for the second bedroom, although this room sometimes had a door to the public hall. In Boston pass-through bedrooms were less common; in these apartments bedrooms usually adjoined the parlor or kitchen directly. Depending on family size, these rooms were likely shared by a large number of residents. However, as historian Elizabeth Cromley has noted, the notion of private, individualized bedrooms was a new idea even for the middle class.[54] In a tenement, they were likely even shared by distant relatives or boarders, potentially with different residents occupying the space at different times of the day.

Closets

Except in rare circumstances, New York builders did not provide full, studded closets, although built-in cabinets were often provided in parlors. Some larger flats did occasionally include a full-size storage room or pantry, but these appear only in the best tenements. In Boston, tenement builders began providing closets by the late 1890s. Sometimes builders in that city took the provisions of closets to an extreme.

For example, in his 1901 tenement at 112 Salem Street, builder Joseph Shoolman lined nearly the entire windowless party wall of the building with closets. He also provided a built-in china closet in each unit's dining room, a feature standard in most middle-class flats in that city but comparatively uncommon in tenements at that point.

Commercial Spaces

Small shops close at hand and selling all sorts of necessities of daily life were essential to a population whose work and family commitments meant that going out of the neighborhood for daily needs would have been difficult and undesirable.[55] The presence of commercial space was integral to the social and economic life of these neighborhoods. These stores frequently offered goods on credit to members of the close-knit and highly localized community. Such shops were an important means of economic stability for many immigrants. Many store owners also acted as petty wholesalers, providing goods that were later sold by the neighborhoods' many push-cart vendors, many of whom would come to occupy a physical storefront as their business expanded. Other spaces were occupied by community institutions such as the saloon, the dance hall, the movie theater, and meeting rooms, all of which acted as important extensions of cramped apartments.[56]

As a result, the tenement was rarely an exclusively residential property: only 20 percent of tenements in these neighborhoods had no stores whatsoever when they were built. This number was lower in New York, where only 9 percent of tenements did not originally include a store, and higher in Boston, where just over 30 percent were exclusively residential. These spaces were located either in the basement or on the first floor of the building, undesirable for residences because of dampness, noise, and dust. Commercial spaces were most common and valuable on the busiest streets, where storefronts were continuous along each block.[57] Buildings without storefronts were more common on quieter side streets and in peripheral neighborhoods, where buildings with stores often appeared only at the corners. In newly built tenement neighborhoods, builders often constructed whole blocks following this pattern. On the other hand, many downtown tenements were located on busy and desirable shopping streets.

Commercial spaces within tenements followed regular patterns. Particularly in New York, two levels of storefronts could be provided, up to four on a single twenty-five-foot-wide facade (Figure 2.7). Two would be located in the raised cellar, reached through an areaway, and two more on the first floor, usually reached through a cast-iron stoop. These commercial spaces often had dual entrances, one public, through a street-facing door and plate-glass storefront, the other typically off the internal public hall connecting to the living space above. This door may have allowed tenants access to the store without having to go outside. The commercial space was usually quite small, twelve feet by thirty feet on average, but frequently had a suite of ancillary rooms attached to it at the rear (Figure 2.8). These rooms included not only additional

Figure 2.7. In many tenements, storefronts were located in the half base-ment, as in this elaborate Schneider & Herter–designed building on East Broadway, New York. (Pictured in the 1930s; since demolished). The door to residential space is located a half story up (most of these stoops have been removed). Sometimes these first-floor apartments were also occupied by stores. In other cases, as in the Herter Brothers–designed building at right, the storefronts occupied the entire ground floor. Courtesy of Milstein Division of United States History, Local History, and Genealogy, The New York Public Library, Astor, Lenox, and Tilden Foundations.

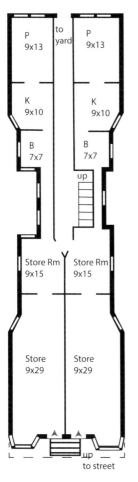

Figure 2.8. Ground-level plan, Morris Rosendorf Tenement, 78 Forsyth Street, New York, 1886. Blankenstein & Herter, architects. Note the suite of residential spaces adjoin-ing behind the stores. For exterior, with storefronts now altered, see Figure 3.10; the original appearance of the ground level was similar to Figure 2.7. Drawing by author.

storage or preparation space for the store but often a kitchen and living space to allow for live-in shopkeepers.

The income these commercial spaces generated was an important component of the profitability of many tenements. Their rent was higher—sometimes four to ten times the rents of the living units upstairs—and their tenancy was more stable.[58] And since many streets on the Lower East Side were well-established shopping districts, Peter Herter noted he could demand "almost Broadway rents" on a per-square-foot basis for storefronts there.[59]

Tenement Plans

Despite the varying demands, basic arrangement of tenement space had crystallized by the mid-nineteenth century in New York, and by the 1890s in Boston. While a limited number of variations occurred, these, too, tended to follow set patterns, reflecting modifications demanded by the building code, when rising standards called for new room types or amenities, or when small or awkward lots were developed. Preestablished modules were reproduced to the extent possible. The typical tenement occupied a single city lot ranging from twenty to thirty-five feet in width, with twenty-five feet being the standard in New York, and eighteen to twenty-two feet being typical in Boston. The spatial arrangements within these buildings can be grouped by their means of divvying up this desirable, and limited, street frontage. Common tenement plans in both cities before the 1890s were classed into two basic types: the double-decker and the flat.[60]

The Double-Decker Tenement

In a double-decker, two apartments were arranged side by side across the width of a building. In lower Manhattan these were usually also subdivided again laterally, creating four units per floor.[61] Double-deckers were easily identifiable by their four windows across the front, and if divided laterally, their fire escape connecting the two center windows. The double-decker tenement emerged as the earliest widespread multifamily house type in New York and was the basis for most later developments. In the earliest examples, such as 65 Mott Street, four two-room apartments connected off a hall on each floor. In that building each apartment, which contained just over 200 square feet, had two doors from the public hall, one into the ten-by-fifteen-foot combined kitchen/living room, and the other into the eight-by-eight-foot windowless bedroom. These apartments were similar to the small two-room units found in barracks blocks in the slum landscape; the key innovation in buildings like 65 Mott Street was arranging these units around a central hall and fitting four per floor on a twenty-five-foot lot.

The double-decker tenement underwent an evolution through the course of the nineteenth century. By the 1860s, the standard double-decker was built to a greater depth, allowing four apartments of either three or four rooms to be arranged around a central stair hall, instead of the two-room plans of the earliest iterations. Only the front room in these early units had outside light. The other interior rooms borrowed light from the parlor or from the skylit central hall, through interior windows and transoms (Figure 2.9). To remedy this lack of light, as early as 1870 builders began indenting the sidewalls, forming light shafts that provided modest light and air to interior rooms.[62] This was codified in New York in the 1879 tenement house act and strengthened in 1886, the latter amendment ushering in the era of the "dumbbell" shaped tenement. To accommodate these shafts, kitchen walls were narrowed, and already small bedrooms became tiny, averaging about eight feet in width. The narrowed public hall now had two water closets on each floor, and the staircase became narrow and winding instead of a straight run at the center of the building. On corner

Figure 2.9. Double-decker tenements with three or more units per floor. A, James Fitzsymons Tenement, 123 Elizabeth Street, New York, 1867. Richard Shapter, architect. A comparatively early, shallow double-decker plan, shown here with four two-room units per floor. A doorway between the units allowed for a flexible configuration; two four-room units, with a parlor in the front and kitchen at the rear, were also possible. That configuration was standard in Brooklyn for most of the nineteenth century. For exterior, see Figure 3.3. B, Sternkopf & Strohaecker Tenement, 165 Orchard Street, New York, 1892. Kurtzer & Rohl, architects. An asymmetrical three-units-per-floor double-decker. Rear unit had a slightly more generous plan, with windows on three sides, including a narrow side court. C, Herman Silberman Tenement, 111 Eldridge Street, New York, 1901. Michael Bernstein, architect. A common variation on the eve of the 1901 law, this three-units-per-floor double-decker showed a range of improvements, including dining rooms, private full baths, and private halls. D, Peter Herter Tenement, 101 Rivington Street, New York, 1891. Herter Brothers, architects. This plan shows a large corner building with seven three- or four-room units per floor with four shared water closets. For exterior, see Plate 10. Drawing by author.

lots the dumbbell shape was flattened on one side, as light could be provided to all rooms on one side of the building. This made for more spacious bedrooms, or it could result in the placement of a greater number of units per floor by eliminating the need for one airshaft, arranging rooms along the outside wall. The general shape and plan of the dumbbell remained for the inner portion.

In some of the best double-deckers, builders did not divide their tenements laterally. Instead they provided units, often of up to seven rooms, that extended the depth of the building, with a parlor in the front with the kitchen, and sometimes a dining room in the rear. While only a handful of such buildings were built on the Lower East Side, this arrangement was standard for tenements uptown, throughout Brooklyn, and in the handful of double-deckers in Boston (Figure 2.10). In other cases, only the front of the building was divided, providing two units with desirable street views, while the rear unit occupied the width of the building (Figure 2.9B). This meant both the kitchen and parlor of the otherwise less desirable back unit had outside light.

The Flat Plan and Variations

In a flat-plan tenement, often built on a slightly narrower lot, only one unit was arranged across the width of the building, with two front-facing rooms, usually a parlor and bedroom. Flats could be recognized by their three-bay fenestration, with

Figure 2.10. Two-units-per-floor double-deckers. *A*, Finn and Dobkins Tenement, 124 Prince Street, Boston, 1894. Charles A. Halstrom, architect. Two units per floor, with shared water closets. A comparatively unusual double-decker arrangement on a wide but shallow Boston lot. For exterior, see Figure 5.10. *B*, I. Goldberg Tenement, 171 East Broadway, New York, 1901. Frederick Ebeling, architect. Two seven-room units per floor with dining rooms and private baths. Drawing by author.

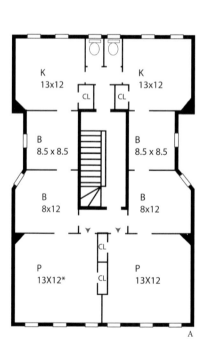

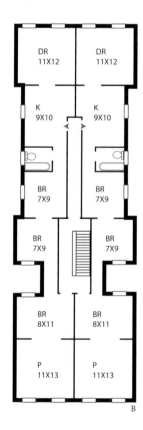

two windows in the parlor. While the double-decker dominated New York tenement construction before the mid-1890s, flat plans were the go-to for most Boston builders (Figure 2.10). An evolution from the side-hall row house, these plans were often indistinguishable from those in converted buildings. The flat was also a common feature of many New York neighborhoods, where it often appeared over storefronts on commercial streets, even in middle-class or elite neighborhoods. In the Lower East Side it could be found as the plan of rear tenements, some of the worst housing in the neighborhood, or above stores and at corners, particularly on the avenues above East Houston Street, where it represented some of the best. By the early twentieth century, the plan of these tenements, particularly in Boston, closely matched the contemporaneous five-room arrangement of much of the wood-frame, working-class architecture of that city's inner suburban neighborhoods, commonly arranged as two-families and triple-deckers.

An important feature of the flat plan was the front-facing bedroom. Dubbed "hall bedrooms," these rooms were particularly convenient for boarders.[63] The kitchen and

Figure 2.11. Common flat types, most above stores on prominent shopping streets. A, Joseph Shoolman Tenement, 112 Salem Street, Boston, 1901. Frederick Norcross, architect. One large seven-room unit with private bath on each floor. For exterior, see Figure 5.1. B, First-floor plan, Jenny Rollins Tenement, 17–19 Hanover Place, Boston, 1870. A pair of early three-unit flats in a basic row house form, located down a narrow alley. Second-floor plan (not available) would likely have included a small bedroom at each end of the hall. C, Edward Otterman Tenement, 236 Hanover Street, Boston, 1875. A typical, modest flat plan. Dining room is often a bedroom, and air shaft is frequently omitted. D, Frederick Pfluger Tenement, 101 Second Avenue, New York, 1880. Julius Boekell, architect. Typical corner flat with similar arrangement to C but with light in each room. Drawing by author.

another hall bedroom were usually aligned across the rear wall of the building. In deeper buildings, a series of bedrooms, larger than the hall bedroom but often windowless, separated the parlor from the kitchen. Units in a flat plan contained larger rooms aligned to one side, and smaller rooms on the other. When not located on corner lots, units often contained one or more windowless inner rooms. In Boston, where windowless rooms were outlawed in 1892, builders often dubbed these spaces "alcove" or "closet" on plans, provided small light shafts, or shifted the kitchen to a rear ell. When more than one unit per floor was provided, these were often divided laterally, with one unit in the front of the building, another in the rear. In divided flat buildings, the rear ell often sprouted a wing, making L- or C-shaped footprints (Figure 2.12). These configurations were most common in the West End, where uniform row houses had previously been quite common.

Figure 2.12. Two-units-per-floor flats. A, Thomas McCormick Tenement, 32–36 Fleet Street, Boston, 1886. A typical complex early Boston tenement on a shallow lot. Note the interior bedrooms but generous provision of built-in closets. B, Joseph Buttenweiser Tenement, 94 East Seventh Street, New York, 1896. George F. Pelham, architect. A large double flat with a dumbbell footprint. Includes private halls and water closets. C, A. Bilinsky Tenement, 135 Endicott Street, Boston, 1893. Charles A. Halstrom, architect. Note differentiation in quality between front and back units, showing one water closet per floor. D, Sarah Silberstein Tenement, 40 Grove Street, Boston, 1900. Frederick Norcross, architect. This plan shows more pronounced differentiation between front and back units with one full bath and one water closet, both shared between the two units. Dimensions marked with asterisk are inferred. Drawing by author.

In the more varied landscape of the North End, sharply contrasting to the regular block and lot pattern of New York, many oddly shaped lots, narrow alleys and courts, some extremely deep lots, and other irregularities prevented the implementation of regular types. Although builders clearly attempted to fit a standardized module to these circumstances, once accommodations were made for light and air, tenements were sometimes built with thirteen corners or nearly triangular shapes. Particularly common in the North End were shallow lots on which the standard narrow, deep tenement plan would not be feasible. In these areas buildings were frequently square or wider than they were deep. In either case, the building's main entry was centered on the facade, and the apartments were entered through a windowless stair hall in the center of the building. Each unit's rooms were arranged in a circuit around this hall. One or two apartments could be provided per floor in this type of building. If one apartment, circulation between rooms on either side of the hall was often difficult without going through the public hall.

The Improved Tenement in New York

While the double-decker remained fixed as the public image of the New York tenement, particularly as the reform agitation that would lead to the 1901 Tenement House Act ramped up, construction of tenements of this sort had dropped off considerably after 1895, when they were increasingly supplanted by more commodious plans, usually built on wider lots. Quite apart from reformers' claims, with the rising expectations of the 1890s the inadequacies of the old plans to meet tenants' new demands, particularly the desire for dining rooms and full baths, became increasingly apparent.[64] New tenement plans began to break away from the rigid linear arrangement of those older models.

The earliest plans of this type to become common were constructed on lots slightly wider than twenty-five feet. These lots allowed for a sort of double-decker/ flat hybrid plan. In this case, one unit was identical to a standard double-decker with only one front-facing room, while the second unit across the front would have a front-facing bedroom (Figure 2.13). With the addition of a dining room, this arrangement soon evolved into a cellular plan, which placed the new room at the center, with the kitchen, a bedroom, and parlor radiating off it, and sometimes an additional bedroom and often full bath off the kitchen. Depending on the width of the lot, one or both of the front units had two front-facing rooms; the kitchen, bath, and rear bedrooms were lit from the air shaft. One or two units, often of lesser quality, were placed at the rear. During this period, particularly on corner lots, builders experimented with a number of more complex arrangements, including ones that provided short private halls in some units.

Within these buildings, builders began incorporating features then virtually unknown in these neighborhoods. New York tenements such as Philip and Meyer Horowitz's 1900 Henry Court at Henry and Jefferson Streets (Figure 2.14) and Nathan

B 6x10	D 10x10		P 10x10	

Floor plan labels:

A (left plan):
DR 13x10 | K 11x10 | BR 7x11
Private Hall
K 12x10 | P 12x12
P 13x12 | BR 9x11
BR 9x9 | BR 9x9
P 13x12 | BR 8x11
Private Hall
BR 9x9 | BR 9x9
DR 13x10 | K 11x10 | BR 7x11
K 12x10 | P 12x12

B (center plan):
B 6x10 | D 10x10 | P 10x10
K 9X8 | H | B 7x8
B 7x8
B 7x8 | B 8x8
K 9X8 | K 9X8
DR 13x10 | DR 13x10
P 10X11 | B 6x11 | P 10X11

C (right plan):
P 10x12 | B 10x7 | B 10x7 | P 10x12
B 8x7 | D 10x12 | D 10x12 | B 8x7
K 12x9 | K 12x9
K 12x9 | K 12x9
B 8x7 | D 10x12 | D 10x12 | B 8x7
P 10x12 | B 10x7 | B 10x7 | P 10x12

A   B   C

Figure 2.13. A range of common, improved, old-law New York tenements. *A,* Harry Fischel Tenement, 164 Rivington Street, 1899. Samuel Sass, architect. A large corner building with four units per floor, with shared water closets but private halls, no pass-through rooms, and formal dining rooms. *B,* Harris Fine Tenement, 250 Broome Street, 1898. Hornberger & Straub, architect. A cellular plan on a twenty-six-foot lot, with dining rooms and full private baths. For exterior, see Figure 3.23, right. *C,* Harris Fine Tenement, 305 Broome Street, New York, 1899. Hornberger & Straub, architect. A variation on *B* on thirty-eight-foot lot. All four units have a front-facing bedroom. Note the amount of public hallway space to provide separate access to the front bedroom. For exterior, see Plate 1. Drawing by author.

Figure 2.14. Henry Court, an elaborate old-law tenement at 177 Henry Street, New York, designed by Michael Bernstein and developed by Philip and Meyer Horowitz in 1900. This photograph was taken as construction neared completion, probably in April 1901. Note the large sign advertising apartments "with bath, steam heat, water supply, electric lights, elevator, and telephone service." For plan, see Figure 2.15B. From Betts, *The Leaven in a Great City* (1902), 88.

Levy's 1901 The Columbia at Grand and Chrystie Streets had complex plans with multiple units per floor and were by far the best buildings ever built in the neighborhood.[65] These, along with Louis Segel's 1898 The Gothic in the West End of Boston, were notable for providing a high level of amenity, such as multiple formal rooms, private halls, generous closets, steam heat, electric lights, telephone service, and in the case of Horowitz and Levy's seven-story buildings, passenger elevators (Figure 2.15). Built for an economically stable clientele, they occupied desirable locations within the neighborhood.

Yet the improved tenements of the 1890s, even commodious buildings like the Columbia or Henry Court, did not meet the provisions of the Tenement House Act of 1901, which required more generous light courts, reflecting reformers' key preoccupations. Indeed, few builders were convinced that bigger courts were worth the sacrifice

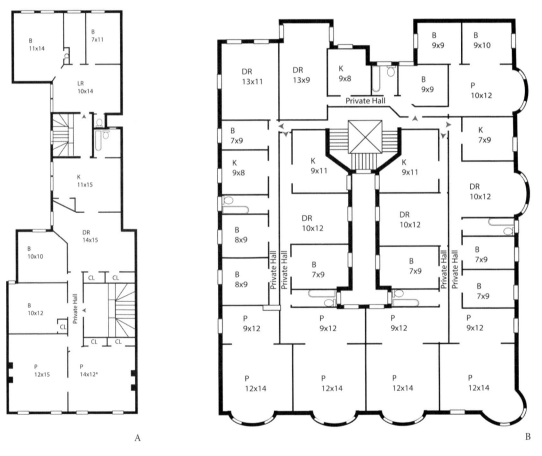

A   B

Figure 2.15. Plans for what were among the most commodious tenements in their respective cities. A, "The Gothic," 47 Allen Street, Boston, 1898. Charles A. Halstrom, architect. Front unit had two parlors facing the street, a dining room, and a full private bath; the rear unit had no parlor and only a private water closet. The building had steam heat. For exterior, see Figure 5.13. B, Henry Court, 177 Henry Street, New York, 1900. Michael Bernstein, architect. Units had long private halls, full bathrooms, double-parlors, and dining rooms. The building featured a passenger elevator and steam heat. Despite being freestanding on three sides, the building had a small, central light court, and its standards for light and air did not comply with the 1901 law. For exterior, see Figure 2.14. Drawing by author.

of accommodation. "It may be taken that the larger air shaft is an improvement," the *Record and Guide* noted in 1899, on the eve of the new law, "but not when its cost in living space and obstacles it presents to good planning are taken into account."[66]

Particularly problematic was that the post-1901 light court requirements made building desirable four-units-per-floor tenements on twenty-five-foot-wide lots difficult. An L-shaped plan was devised, dividing the building laterally, with one or two inner units in the narrowest part of the building having windows facing only the now-wider unenclosed light court (Figure 2.16*A*). These undesirable units had two or three rooms, while the better front unit had five, including a dining room and parlor. These buildings exhibited a greater diversity in quality of accommodations between units than had previously been common in New York (although this was typical in Boston). This arrangement did not prove popular. While over half of the tenements built before 1901 in New York were twenty-five feet wide, after that date only 10 percent were.[67] In general, buildings of this era were at least thirty-five feet in width, and fifty feet was increasingly common, and generally they followed the cellular plan introduced in the 1890s, often with slightly smaller and sometimes fewer rooms, to accommodate the larger courts (Figure 2.16*B*). Again these plans usually varied, having larger and more commodious units facing front, and smaller arrangements, sometimes reverting to two-room plans, with an undesirable outlook on the light court only in the middle and rear.

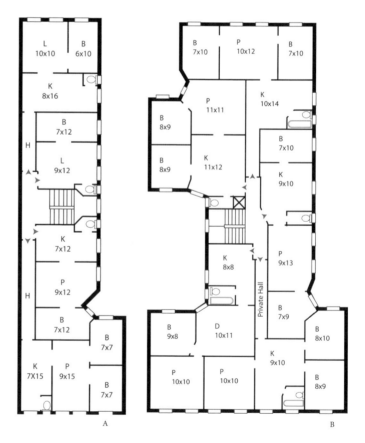

Figure 2.16. Two common variations designed to satisfy the 1901 New York tenement law, especially its requirement of wider courts. *A*, A hypothetical variation on four families per floor for a twenty-five-foot lot. Only one unit per floor looks out on the street, which was considered a serious disadvantage, so buildings of this type are comparatively rare. This plan shows only private water closets, the minimum required by law; full baths were more common. *B*, A more common wider plan with five units per floor. Note the similarities between the improved tenement of the slightly earlier period. Two of the parlors faced only the light shafts, and the design provides only one entrance per apartment. These were considered major drawbacks. Drawing by author.

A MODEL TENEMENT HOUSE
310 EAST HOUSTON STREET

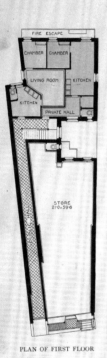

PLAN OF FIRST FLOOR

Built by   GEO. F. PELHAM
CHARLES I. WEINSTEIN   Architect
1905

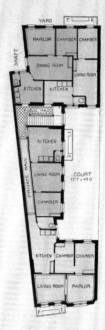

PLAN OF UPPER FLOORS

THIS building has a frontage of 22 feet 8 inches by 110 feet 2¼ inches by 36 feet 3 inches by 106 feet 6 inches. There are four apartments to a floor, in suites of three, four and five rooms. The kitchens have galvanized iron sinks and ranges with boilers, dish closets, shelves, etc. Chambers are painted and contain wardrobes, shelves, coat hooks, etc. The parlors are papered and have frescoed ceilings and mirrored mantels.

The entrance hall is laid out in patterns of ceramic tile with marble base and are burlapped. The ceilings are frescoed. The letter boxes are of bronze and the bells installed are adequately operative from every part of the house.

Rents from $17 to $28 per month.

Figure 2.17. A commercial, new-law decorated tenement dubbed a "model" tenement house. Built by developer Charles I. Weinstein from plans by prolific architect George F. Pelham, this example shows the adaptation to a narrow lot, in this case less than the standard twenty-five feet. Text of this advertising portfolio (titled *Apartment Houses of the Metropolis*) extolled the building's appearance and technical amenities, representing sharply divergent priorities from reformers' "model" tenements. Subsequent pages in this publication featured similar tenements by the same designer and builder standing on thirty-five- and fifty-foot lots, a more common strategy. Courtesy of Milstein Division of United States History, Local History, and Genealogy, The New York Public Library, Astor, Lenox, and Tilden Foundations.

Yet, the new law did little to slow down the building boom that had been taking place on the Lower East Side since about 1895. While the virtual prohibition of
the dumbbell plan was a disruption to some builders, the improved plans of the
1890s could be quite readily adapted to the new requirements, even if the need for
larger courts meant somewhat less commodious interior arrangements for tenants.
Construction continued apace, and the passage of the law may even have spurred new
investment by builders who had feared the uncertainty caused by reformers' agitation. "The whole lower east side is being rapidly rebuilt with new-law houses," the *New
York Times* noted in 1903, "there is almost no street in which there is not at least one
new-law house, and one generally finds five or six on each street."[68]

Some builders even took the imprimatur of the new law to recast their buildings
as radically different than what came before—reclaiming the reformer's term "model
tenement" and using it for speculative buildings. Yet the model tenements designed
by George Fred Pelham and Hornberger & Straub in this moment were far different
than those designed by Ernest Flagg and Grosvenor Atterbury. Indeed, these buildings more closely reflected tenants' desires than reformers' priorities. Three new-law
buildings appeared in the 1908 vanity publication *Apartment Houses of the Metropolis,*
all dubbed "model" tenements (Figure 2.17). Built over the course of the preceding
four years by prominent developer Charles I. Weinstein, to the designs of Pelham,
the buildings met all of the standards of the new law. Yet, in his advertising copy
Weinstein chose to highlight the improvements to amenities and appearance, not
light, air, or planning. Weinstein wooed potential tenants with galvanized sinks and
boilers in the kitchens, china cabinets in the dining room, the bronze mailboxes and
annunciator bells in the marble lobby, as well as the frescoed parlors with mirrored
mantels in each apartment. The hard-fought increases in light and air did not register
as a selling feature that Weinstein thought would particularly interest his tenants.
Those improvements were there for the reformers' sake.[69]

Weinstein's prioritizing of the aesthetic features of his buildings suggested a
strong engagement with the visual standards of contemporary architecture, signaling that improvement meant far more than better amenities and a greater variety of
rooms. The appearance of his buildings was important to Weinstein, as it was to his
tenants. This search for an appropriate visual standard for the tenement facade had
played out over the course of the nineteenth century in a way that mirrored many of
the interior improvements.

Chapter 3

Fantastic Shapes and Unfamiliar Profiles

Why the Tenement Facade Matters

> The builders of tenement houses . . . undergo throes of aesthetic parturition, and beat their zinc cornices into new and fantastic shapes and adopt moldings of unfamiliar profile. Mostly we wish they wouldn't.
> **anonymous writer for *Real Estate Record and Builders' Guide*, 1887**

The appearance of a building's exterior, even a common one, was not a matter to be taken lightly in the Gilded Age city. Indeed, the editors of the *Real Estate Record and Builders' Guide* had fretted over the question of "street architecture" regularly since the publication's founding in 1868. For years, its writers—who reflected a taste that, if not exactly highbrow, was at least mainstream among New York builders—had been condemning the rote appearance of lugubrious brownstone fronts with "bulging" cornices and "stereotyped" moldings.[1] However, with construction resuming apace in the mid-1880s, after a period of economic doldrums, the editors began to fear what they had wrought in demanding more expressive architecture. There was now more ornament, more broken fronts and rooflines, all taking on seemingly ever-wilder forms. The tenement builders of the Lower East Side particularly stood out as prone to flights of fancy, employing an even more "distressing" variety of fronts than seen on the "riotous" streetscapes of the new Upper West Side.[2] They "signalized the importance of the structure by more and bigger moldings," the journal complained, "and more projecting and umbrageous tin cornices."[3] The *Record and Guide* noticed there was something peculiar about these eclectic new buildings. Not only was the sheer volume of architectural ornament on working-class housing a new practice, but the particular forms chosen struck many viewers as mysterious, perhaps foreign. These "unfamiliar" moldings and "umbrageous" cornices were more than just a simple projection of economic status, these observers could sense; they were enlisted to perform specific cultural work in a contested visual landscape.

Prominent among the architects in the throes of "aesthetic parturition" in the 1880s were Peter Herter and his brothers; their 1889 tenement on Madison Street for Isaac Gellis would certainly have struck the *Record and Guide* as fantastical (Figure 3.1).[4] The terra-cotta and carved stone ornament was executed in an eclectic, Moorish Revival mode, unusual in and of itself, with fine arabesque panels, riveted moldings, and cushion capitals. The building's extensive sculptural program was evocative. Elongated bearded satyrs in heavy relief marked the keystones. A fully round griffin standing on an orb topped the portico. Shrine-like niches sheltered high-relief busts on each of the upper floors. Yet many of the forms would also have been familiar to the neighborhood's residents. The columns of the portico and niches, band moldings, panels, and even the recurring Star of David motif at the apex of each opening were nearly identical to those on the nearby Eldridge Street Synagogue, the signal landmark of the area's new Russian Jewish community, designed by Herter Brothers three years earlier, with this tenement's owner on the building committee (Figure 3.2).[5] Indeed, with the ornament on Gellis's new building, the Herters seemed to intend to provoke an emotional reaction in his viewers, elevating the workaday tenement landscape by invoking spiritual and fantastical themes.

The construction of the Gellis tenement seems to have attracted the attention of Jacob Riis, who noted in 1889 in *How the Other Half Lives*:

> Here, as we stroll along Madison Street, workmen are busy putting the finishing touches on the brown-stone front of a tall new tenement. This one will probably be called an apartment house. They are carving satyrs' heads in the stone, with a crowd of gaping youngsters looking on in admiring wonder. Next door are two other tenements, likewise with brown-stone fronts, fair to look at. . . . The owner was a wealthy builder who "stood high in the community." Is it only in our fancy that the sardonic leer on the stone faces seems to list that way? Or is it an introspective grin?[6]

The impish, anthropomorphized satyrs were thumbing their stone noses at outsiders like Riis, mocking their criticisms of a neighborhood whose appearance and culture they increasingly could not understand. More important than Riis's impression of the new tenement, however, were the wonder and awe it stirred in the neighborhood children, growing up amid famously squalid, although rapidly changing, conditions. It was to them and their parents' fancy that Gellis, indeed an important member of the community, had to appeal.

Figure 3.1. *Far left*, Isaac Gellis Tenement, 87 Madison Street, New York (1889; pictured in the early 1930s, demolished 1981). Herter Brothers, architects. The Gellis Tenement facade was lavish and comparatively unusual. The tenements at right, probably by Charles Rentz or an associate, were more typical of the decorated tenement at its apogee in the 1890s. This picture was taken by the New York Tenement House Department shortly before it vacated and demolished the two Rentz buildings. Courtesy of Milstein Division of United States History, Local History, and Genealogy, The New York Public Library, Astor, Lenox, and Tilden Foundations.

Figure 3.2. Detail showing portico detail, griffin, and niches on Gellis tenement.

These facades caused a stir of admiration and wonder as they were being built, and rightly so. In designing them, architects like Herter were then creating, for the first time, a finely textured and richly symbolic landscape that did not just indicate the community's rising wealth and increasing living standards but also encoded meaningful symbols of communal identity. Thus, the decorated tenement transcended pedestrian concerns about housing conditions and the real estate market (matters this chapter will also set aside) and served to nourish higher but long-neglected or even maligned concerns for beauty, meaning, even fantasy in the domestic environment of the urban working class.

The Importance of the Street Facade

Buildings like Gellis's were at once familiar to the critics writing for the *Record and Guide* as well as inscrutable. The widespread use of architectural ornament, in varying styles and degrees, had been standard practice among the city's builders for more than a generation. But in general it had been used in ways that reflected and reinforced the occupants' position within the social and economic hierarchy: buildings with more ornament were associated with the wealthy and powerful institutions, while those with less or none were associated with the poor and working class. Following this practice, the earliest tenements, predating the industrial production of architectural material, were uniformly austere (see Figures 1.9, 1.14, and 2.1, *center*). Many continued to believe this was the most rational approach to tenement design, reflecting the notion that industry and simplicity were chief virtues of the working class that should be manifest in their material culture (see Figures 6.8, 7.5, and 7.7). More commonly, by the mid-nineteenth century, builders provided a modest but respectable amount of ornament, consistent with their building's place in the range of speculative architecture. By the 1880s, others, like Herter, were not satisfied with this, and built tenements that in terms of sheer volume and flamboyance of applied ornament exceeded even middle-class standards. These buildings represented a democratizing tendency inherent in industrial capitalism. By providing visual markers previously inaccessible, they connected working-class residents to the practices of signaling fundamental to urban bourgeois culture. The class position of a building's residents could no longer simply be read by the extent of its exterior ornamentation. As one period observer noted, "a large number of tenement houses in the lower portion of New York are only a little below the common uptown flat. It is often difficult to tell where the flat leaves off and the tenement begins."[7] These buildings were an exercise in equality, breaking down, visually at least, the sharp class distinctions of the era.

The decorated tenement has been poorly understood in part because the system of architectural thought under which it was built was roundly discredited in the first half of the twentieth century. Since the rise of modernism's notions of architectural honesty, the "false-front" nature of nineteenth-century street architecture has been routinely maligned by historians and critics, who have long viewed it as a sign of the deceitfulness of the earlier age.[8] Cloaking the highly visible public fronts of build-

Plate 1. Harris Fine Tenement, 305 Broome Street, New York (1899). Hornberger & Straub, architects. For plan, see Figure 2.13C. Its ornate facade was typical of many immigrant-built tenements of this period. Compare to the austerity of the nearby reform tenement in Figure I.1. Photograph by Sean Litchfield.

Plate 2. Etta Lebowitch Tenement, 68 Prince Street, Boston (1895). Charles A. Halstrom, architect. Compare to the nearby reform tenement in Figure I.2. Photograph by Sean Litchfield.

Plate 3. A range of highly decorated tenements. *Center and left*, Albert Stake Tenements, 84 and 86 Madison Street, New York (1889). Alexandre I. Finkle, architect. *Right*, James Shea Tenement, 82 Madison Street (1906). Bernstein and Bernstein, architect. The same architect and developer built the two buildings on the left with different facades, a relatively uncommon strategy. The Shea tenement at right is a particularly late example. Photograph by Sean Litchfield.

WHAT HE WANTS TO SEE, BE GOSH!

Plate 4. The Gilded Age New York mansion as a tenement. In this cartoon from 1898, a comment on state income tax policy, the William K. Vanderbilt Mansion (Fifth Avenue and West Fifty-Second Street, 1878–82; Richard Morris Hunt, architect) is made over into a tenement, "The Vanderbilt Flats," populated by a diverse mix of ethnic and racial stereotypes at their trades. The decorated tenement reversed this paradigm in a similarly threatening way, using previously elite forms for the same groups, thought to be of low standing. Cover of *Puck Magazine*, October 16, 1898. Courtesy of Library of Congress, Prints and Photographs Division.

Plate 5. Albert Stake Tenement, 104 Forsyth Street, New York (1890). Alexandre I. Finkle, architect. An intricate and sophisticated facade by a Paris-trained architect. Note the use of encaustic tiles on the second floor. Photograph by Sean Litchfield.

Plate 6. Feinberg and Polstein Tenement, 91 Henry Street, New York (1898). Michael Bernstein, architect. This refined facade used pilasters to group multiple stories of windows, a level of cohesion absent in earlier examples. Photograph by Sean Litchfield.

Plate 7. Samuel Barkin Tenement, 100 Rivington Street, New York (1902). Alfred E. Badt, architect. The oriel windows of this wide tenement give it plastic form not seen in earlier buildings. The ornately framed oval windows signal the full interior bathrooms, an important feature of this ambitious new-law tenement. Photograph by Sean Litchfield.

Plate 8. Presentation drawing, Kahal Adath Jeshurun Synagogue, 16 Eldridge Street, New York (1886). Herter Brothers, architects. Likely drawn by Herter Brothers, this is the only known surviving drawing of this quality by that firm. Notice the implied grid and cornices on the hypothetical neighboring tenements. Herter Brothers would later design a tenement for the site just to the right. Courtesy of Museum of the City of New York, 29.100.2917.

Plate 9. Sender Jarmulowsky and Ascher Weinstein Tenement, 166 Henry Street, New York (1887). Herter Brothers, architects. This tenement, like others by Herter Brothers, bears formal resemblance to the Eldridge Street synagogue (Plate 8), of which Jarmulowsky was president. Globe-shaped finials are missing from the top of the central arch. Photograph by Sean Litchfield.

Plate 10. Peter Herter Tenement, 101 Rivington Street, New York (1892). Herter Brothers, architects. This building was one of a group of tenements published by *The Record and Guide* in 1892 illustrating a new visual, technological, and financial standard for the East Side tenement. For plan, see Figure 2.9D. For a sense of the original rooftop appendages, see Figure 1.15 *(left)*, depicting a similar building. Photograph by Sean Litchfield.

Plate 11. Jobst Hoffman Tenement, 228 East Sixth Street, New York (1890). Jobst Hoffman, architect. Hoffman was one of a number of tenement architects to develop a distinctive style, especially for buildings he developed. The cornice, originally similar to the Hoffman-designed building at right, has been truncated. Compare with Figure 3.12. Photograph by Sean Litchfield.

Plate 12. J. D. Karst Tenements, 34 and 36 East Fourth Street, New York (1888). Alexandre I. Finkle, architect. Two of three identical buildings designed by Finkle for Karst (the other is a block away). Note the exaggerated cornice and deep bas relief panels. Photograph by Sean Litchfield.

Plate 13. J. Emrich Tenement, 125 Madison Street, New York (1891). Alexandre I. Finkle, architect. Photograph by Sean Litchfield.

Plate 14. The New York decorated tenement, standardized and plagiarized. The four buildings at left, with nearly identical facades, were each designed by different architects. Rentz & Lang, who designed the 1889 building at 219 Madison Street (*far left*) seemed to first copy this form from A. I. Finkle but then used it extensively elsewhere. Next door, the design was copied by G. A. Schellenger in 1890 and M. V. B. Ferndon in 1891. This design was later used extensively by George H. Pelham. The large corner building was built in 1893 by Jacob Fischel to the more original designs (although repeated elsewhere) of Max Muller. Photograph by Sean Litchfield.

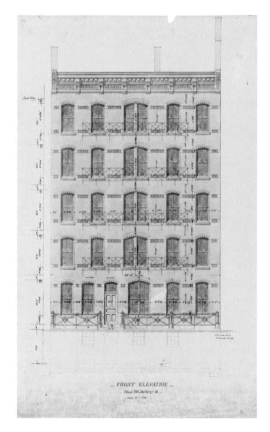

Plate 15. Elevation for tenement, 244–246 Mulberry Street, New York (1885; demolished). John B. Snook, architect. A finely inked drawing by a fairly prominent architect for a modest tenement. Courtesy of John B. Snook Architectural Record Collection PR64, folder 6, project 40; image 95387d, New-York Historical Society.

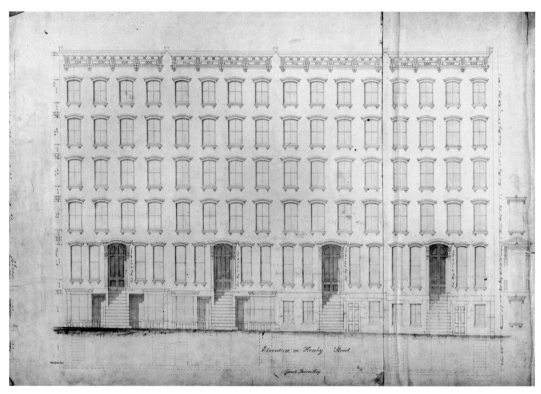

Plate 16. Elevation, Jacob Korn Tenements, 190–196 Henry Street, New York (1874; demolished). John B. Snook, architect. Snook's drawing for a row of common tenements. Courtesy of John B. Snook Architectural Record Collection PR64, folder 6, project 40; image 95387d, New-York Historical Society.

Plate 17. Detail, Albert Levering, "Flat Boomers of Gotham—The Rush for Apartments Is Getting Very Oklahoma," *Puck Magazine*, April 11, 1906. A horde of furniture-carrying prospective New York tenants is barely restrained by police and a building janitor in front of half-finished tenements being erected with astonishing speed. While referencing a slightly later period of booming multifamily construction of a slightly higher class, this cartoon suggests how quickly these buildings were built and occupied. Note sign for "J. Skinn, builder." Courtesy of Library of Congress, Prints and Photographs Division.

Plate 18. James Thomson Building, 206–208 East Ninth Street, New York (1885). George B. Post, architect. Designed by an elite architect, this facade represented a respectable level of ornamentation for a small rental building in a middling location. Unlike the decorated tenement, it appropriately reflected the class of the buildings' residents. Photograph by Sean Litchfield.

Plate 19. Charles A. Buddensiek/Samuel Simons Tenements, 99–105 Third Avenue, New York (1881). Henry J. Dudley, architect. Fine brownstone-fronted flats over stores, of unusual quality in this neighborhood. At the time this building was built, Dudley was Buddensiek's in-house architect; later he would be a city building inspector charged with taking bribes from Buddensiek to overlook shoddy construction on another project, which collapsed dramatically. While the permit for this Third Avenue building was issued in the name of a straw purchaser, Simons (a common tactic of this builder), it was explicitly discussed by witnesses in Buddensiek's 1886 manslaughter trial. Photograph by Sean Litchfield.

COLLAPSE OF ANOTHER BUDDENSIEK STRUCTURE.

JOHN ROACH.—"It's all Whitney's fault. If he hadn't knocked so hard, it would be standing now."

Plate 20. "Collapse of Another Buddensiek Structure." This cartoon referenced an incident of shoddy work at a shipyard by invoking the name of discredited builder Charles A. Buddensiek. Note the collapsed building with ornate window trim. *Puck Magazine*, July 29, 1885, rear. Library of Congress, Prints and Photographs Division.

Plate 21. Workingmen's Building Association Houses, Sunnyside Street, Boston (1891). Many housing reformers considered philanthropic developments of single-family workers' houses to be the ultimate goal. Here, picturesque ornamentation was welcomed and encouraged. Photograph by Sean Litchfield.

Plate 22. Harris Fine Block, Broome and Orchard Streets, New York (1898 and 1901). Hornberger & Straub, architects. Recently rehabilitated, these buildings contain stores catering to wealthier new residents. Construction of the massive Essex Crossing project, a multibuilding development on the site of an aborted urban renewal project, is visible at right. Photograph by Sean Litchfield.

ings of all types with ornate, historicist forms, while letting functional concerns dictate the form of the hidden sidewalls and rarely seen rear, seemed to many in the twentieth century a reflection of a corrupt bourgeois fantasy. The ornate street facade's use on multifamily housing heightened this disdain. When these fanciful forms covered what were assumed to be squalid living conditions, it came to be seen as a powerful metaphor for the masking of the true nature of urban society under industrial capitalism. Coupled with fears over the exploitative nature of the urban housing market, the overburdened facades of tenements and apartment buildings were thought to represent the worst impulses of nineteenth-century architecture. Indeed, they found early and vocal critics as prominent as Adolf Loos and Thorstein Veblen.[9]

Yet the ideas on which much of this critique was grounded were unknown to most builders and working architects in the nineteenth century, who understood street architecture in a fundamentally different way. Instead of masking reality, the elaborate facade honored the building and those within it, and mediated their relationship to the community. Throughout the streets of the city, ornament was used to stake claims for the respectability of people and institutions within a landscape of new urban forms. The new, complex, and perhaps threatening cosmopolitan world of strangers could most readily be understood and decoded visually.[10] The act of seeing and being seen was fundamental to bourgeois culture. But this visual orientation was not limited to clothing and mannerisms. The outward appearance of the publicly visible areas of a building not only situated an owner and his tenants within an economic hierarchy but placed them within a continuum of historical and cultural forces as well. Indeed, style mattered to many in the nineteenth-century city. A highly visible, outward projection of an individual and community's place within the sweep of cultural development was accomplished by a creative, sometimes eclectic engagement with familiar and meaningful styles drawn from the history of architecture. This practice of evoking meaning and emotion through engagement with the past was fundamental to the design process. For members of all classes, it clothed new and unfamiliar landscapes and ways of life with familiar and comforting forms, imbuing them with higher meaning.[11] As historian John Kasson has noted in his discussion of the ornamentation on new machinery, nineteenth-century urbanites "admired elegance, exoticism and imagination as the passion for picturesque eclecticism in architecture and decorative arts suggests. Instead of objects that made their appeal strictly in utilitarian terms, they valued works that brought the viewer the greatest associations, the most powerful emotional resonances."[12] Like many other new and seemingly utilitarian objects, the ornamented street facade of an everyday building was valued for the psychological responses its associations provoked.

Enabled by rising wealth and industrial production, these new visual standards for urban architecture at large were due in part to the ascendance of the middle class, who increasingly demanded a level of articulation and elaboration that had been long associated with the elite, even the nobility. These new expectations were aided by greater interest in historical styles, which were the subject of intense debate among architectural critics but were also frequently reflected upon even in public discourse.[13]

The practices of bourgeois visuality, an increased interest in the excavation and understanding of historical forms, as well as the infrastructure of industrial production provided the circumstances necessary for broad swaths of the urban population to delight in the use of material forms to transcend traditional class boundaries, rejecting the comparatively dull, republican simplicity of American urban architecture in the first part of the nineteenth century, in which simple, staid, but often repetitive forms had been perceived as an appropriate architectural response to the democratic impulses of the new nation.[14]

Cast-Iron New York

No American city had higher visual standards for architecture than New York, increasingly the center of national culture. By the mid-nineteenth century, builders of all types routinely took advantage of the city's commercial prosperity as well as a flourishing industry in production of architectural materials, particularly cast iron, to produce everyday buildings that would have been perceived as elegant elsewhere in America.[15] And not only did middle-class New Yorkers demand these forms, the working class increasingly did as well.[16] As early as the 1850s, tenements could be found with elaborate cast-iron cornices, sometimes with tall pediments, as well as molded window caps (Figure 3.3). These Italianate elements were a reflection not only of the commercial palazzos of the Broadway dry-goods concerns, many of which were designed by the same architects, but also of the long-standing association of the Italian Renaissance with urban modernity. These elements became the go-to for most immigrant and working-class builders in New York between the 1850s and 1880s, and later in peripheral districts. These were the first decorated tenements, and thousands of such buildings were built, particularly in the building boom that occurred between 1867 and 1872. They were constructed by the full range of investors working on tenements, at least two-thirds of whom were immigrants, largely German and Irish. Although modest compared to later developments, this first generation of decorated tenements was a radical departure from long-standing expectations. Tenements, like other supposedly utilitarian buildings, had long been expected to be plain, helping to reify class differences. These new tenements were the first to subvert that expected visual hierarchy.

On the streets of another city of this moment, even Boston, these decorated tenement palazzos would have passed for a fine commercial block. A Main Street merchant in any small town of the 1860s or 1870s would have been proud to afford such finery; many made do with far less. They far exceeded the usual standard of appearance for working-class housing in other cities. Indeed, in more conservative Boston, articulated tenements using intricate brick corbel work did not appear until the 1870s, and cast iron was almost never used on their exterior (Figure 3.4).[17] These tenements closely resembled contemporaneous industrial buildings. The Boston tenement did not commonly match even the modest standard of the palazzo tenement until the 1890s, when pressed sheet metal and cast stone came into wide use (Figure 3.5). Although this mode had passed out of fashion in New York in the 1880s, it remained the most

Figure 3.3. James Fitzsymons Tenements, 123–125 Elizabeth Street, New York (1867). Richard Shapter, architect. For plan, see Figure 2.9A. With iron cornices and window caps, these facades were typical for thousands of early decorated tenements. Photograph by Sean Litchfield.

Figure 3.4. Daniel McLaughlin Tenement, 175 Endicott Street, Boston (1875). Daniel McLaughlin, architect. An early decorated tenement in Boston, achieved strictly through brick corbel work. Photograph by Sean Litchfield.

Figure 3.5. Louis Goldstein Tenements, 14, 14 1/2, and 16 Hull Street, Boston (1906). Frederick Norcross, architect. Not until the late 1890s did Boston tenements typically reach the level of ornament seen in New York since the 1860s. Photograph by Sean Litchfield.

Figure 3.6. Patrick Skelly Tenement, 385 Broome Street, New York (1884). John B. Snook, architect. Builders of this modest tenement employed manufactured materials, such as the cast-iron cornice, that were essentially ornamented by default. Photograph by Sean Litchfield.

common type of decorated tenement built in Boston, appearing well into the first decade of the twentieth century.

In New York, these facades soon became a symbol of dull monotony in architecture, as their sharply limited range of industrially produced ornament quickly lost its ability to evoke a meaningful response.[18] Indeed, like many products of this era, cast-iron cornices and window lintels were decorated essentially by default. Thanks to the nature of cast-iron production, most ornamental forms could be rendered with little additional expense. Purchasing these items saved the masons substantial labor in constructing complicated parts. Therefore, elaborate cornices in particular came to be applied to buildings that otherwise evinced little interest in a decorative treatment (Figure 3.6). For a more austere treatment, a mason had to be called in for corbel work, a more expensive choice for a simpler result. With ornament becoming cheaper and more common, more elaborate treatments involving a greater number of parts were increasingly necessary if the decorated street facade was to retain its symbolic meaning.

A New, Imported Standard

For builders working to reshape the former slum districts, an expressive street facade was of utmost importance, a crucial marker that differentiated their new buildings from their often ramshackle surroundings (Figure 3.7). As noted in chapter 1, the stereotyped visual image of the slum had been one not just of squalor and dilapidation but of low, irregular, and insubstantial buildings, sometimes constructed of wood, many of which did not form a street wall. Towering and substantial facades with intricate and evocative detail stood out sharply in this environment and were readily embraced as soon as they became feasible. And for their builders, many from central and eastern Europe, the elaborate street facades that were commonplace on residential buildings in the cities of that region, unlike anything in American architecture, formed an important frame of reference for urban modernity.[19]

Indeed, the decorated tenement of Boston and New York was part of a tradition of elaborated residential street facades that developed on the European continent in the mid-nineteenth century. There, plaster and stucco ornament, often industrially produced, came to ornament the facades of multifamily buildings of all classes. These were the most common building type in many cities of the region. Formally an evolution of the urban palazzo common since the Renaissance, at first glance these tenements were typologically quite different than their American cousins. Most notably, as they did not have to accommodate the narrow lots typical of the American cities, platted with single-family houses in mind, they tended to be far wider, extending deeply into lots with a series of courtyards or back buildings. Yet their approach to the street facade was quite similar, sheathing, regardless of class, a comparatively

Figure 3.7. A decorated tenement's intricate facade *(third from left)* stands out prominently amid the tumult of the Hester Street market, then an icon of New York's immigrant enclaves. Rich in symbolism, facades like this represented a rejection of the squalor of the slum landscape, seen in the surrounding low buildings as well as in the dull monotony of an earlier generation of tenements farther down the street. The building's blank sidewalls and laundry roof illustrate the "false-front" character of many decorated tenements. This building was designed in 1887 by Schneider & Herter for Morris Goldberg and Nathan Schancupp, both Polish immigrants. Courtesy of Milstein Division of United States History, Local History, and Genealogy, The New York Public Library, Astor, Lenox, and Tilden Foundations.

standardized building form in rich, even overloaded ornament that was both varied yet harmonious with their neighbors, closely set along continuous street walls (see Figure 5.15). On those facades, discussed in more detail in chapter 5, architects used a complex array of belt courses and panels with playful and inventive classical forms, usually incorporating a great deal of human and mythological figuration. This building culture valued rich, imaginative forms, originality, and a projection of cultural and material progress throughout the use of historical forms.[20]

These buildings complicate the tendency to read architectural ornament and other material finery as a reflection of merely personal, individual identity. The latter interpretation privileges an Anglo-American worldview that placed the private single-family home at the material center of personal identity formation. Instead, in these streetscapes of palace-like multifamily buildings, identity was expressed through the outward appearance of the community's built landscape. While the discontinuity between the fine front and the crowded conditions within troubled many, the decorated tenement meant the decoupling of the facade from the identity of the individual resident. Instead it presented a group identity, sometimes with explicit references to national, historical, or religious discourses.

The elaborate street facade of the American decorated tenement was one of the great democratizing moments of the period. Just as the standards for interior accommodation were rising, so too were the expectations about the exterior appearance of the tenement. These rising demands were enabled by industrial production, were supported by the rising wealth it generated, and advocated by architects and builders for whom such material was an outward sign of progress, modernity, and an engagement with long-standing cultural forms. In an era during which much was communicated through visual symbols in the urban landscape, these facades were important sites of resistance to the outward projection of class and cultural hierarchies onto the immigrant working class, making their way in a new urban environment.

A Richly Symbolic Environment

Henry Herter, Peter's brother, may have been the most important originator of the elaborate New York tenement facade. Working in the office of German-born architect August H. Blankenstein soon after his 1881 arrival in New York, Herter first built American tenements of the common Italian palazzo type. Blankenstein & Herter's 1885 tenement for Solomon Jacobs at 131 Eldridge Street was virtually indistinguishable from the work of numerous other tenement architects, stretching back three decades (Figure 3.8).[21] Yet later the same year Herter, alone, designed for Jacobs a radically different-looking building at 94 East Broadway (Figure 3.9).[22] The far richer and more complex facade of Jacobs's East Broadway building demonstrated the techniques and motifs Herter would more fully articulate in later work, with terra-cotta panels and belt courses, and a sheet-metal cornice. Jacobs clearly favored the new mode and seems to have embraced Herter's aesthetic experimentation. In 1886 he hired Blankenstein & Herter to design a five-story tenement at 73 Eldridge Street.[23] The new building had a more coherent facade arrangement than East Broadway, fully divided by colossal pilasters supported on oversized grotesque masks and topped with terra-cotta capitals. Robustly rendered female figures graced the corbels flanking the door, and the building was capped by a tall, pedimented sheet-metal cornice. The more elaborate treatment cost one thousand dollars more than the smaller and simpler Eldridge Street building of the previous year. Shortly thereafter the firm designed a similar building for Morris Rosendorf, setting a pattern that was quickly emulated (Figure 3.10).[24] With the success of the new model, Herter would soon leave Blankenstein to join Ernst Schneider, forming Schneider & Herter.

When these tenements were new, in the mid-1880s, they were indeed extraordinary. This much more elaborate mode was soon widely emulated, particularly by the other German-born architects who dominated tenement design. William Graul, who

Figure 3.8. Solomon Jacobs Tenement, 131 Eldridge Street, New York (1885). Blankenstein & Herter, architects. An example of the palazzo-type tenements that had been built in New York since the mid-nineteenth century. Photograph by Sean Litchfield.

Figure 3.9. Solomon Jacobs Tenement, 94 East Broadway, New York (1885). Henry Herter, architect. Among the first American projects by one of the three Herter brothers, this building was also among the first in New York to employ elaborate terra-cotta belt courses, panels, and prominent sheet-metal pediment. The building at right, shorn of its cornice, was typical of Herter's later work. Photograph by Sean Litchfield.

had been designing modest palazzo tenements for a decade, soon adopted a facade quite similar to Schneider & Herter's; likewise Jobst Hoffman and Charles Rentz. The latter architect even cribbed the firm's Eldridge Street design for a series of 1887 buildings he built for himself on Delancey Street. By the early 1890s, ornamental facades were standard for tenements on the Lower East Side (see Plate 14). While the buildings erected between 1886 and 1893 were the most inventive, similar facades continued to be common through the first decade of the twentieth century, during the period of widespread tenement rebuilding.

At the apogee of the decorated tenement in the 1880s and 1890s, architects imposed an ornamental grid of pilasters and belt courses, a trick to break up the monotony of the street facade learned in the architecture schools of central Europe. This grid became the framework for a host of richly symbolic forms, executed in new or newly accessible materials, including terra-cotta, cast stone, and pressed sheet metal. During the economic doldrums of the late 1870s and early 1880s, builders had first begun experimenting with these techniques. Architect William Jose's 1876 Grand Street tenement for F. Mahnken was an early demonstration in the use of brick piers to divide a facade (Figure 3.11).[25] By the early 1880s, many builders began subtly dividing their facades by recessing the two central bays slightly to accommodate the newly

Figure 3.10. Morris Rosendorf Tenement, 78 Forsyth Street, New York (1886). Blankenstein & Herter, architects. This building was nearly identical to the building Blankenstein & Herter designed for Solomon Jacobs at 73 Eldridge Street (extant but altered), just months after designing the much more modest building pictured in Figure 3.8 and the transitional example at 94 East Broadway (Figure 3.9) for the same developer. Together they show Herter's transition to the decorated tenement and the maturation of his style, which would be widely emulated. Photograph by Sean Litchfield.

required iron fire escape. This is seen, for example, on Jobst Hoffman's buildings at 11 and 13 Eldridge Street designed in 1883 for Ernest Von Au (Figure 3.12).[26] Unlike the piers then common on industrial architecture, which served to reduce wall thickness and allow for more interior light, these projections were strictly decorative.[27]

Later these architects employed a broad range of highly elaborate techniques to divide the facade vertically. These often took the form of large brick pilasters forming colossal orders and topped by terra-cotta or sheet-metal capitals. This was a favorite technique of Paris-trained architect Alexandre I. Finkle, as seen on his dramatic Garfield and Lincoln tenements of 1889 and 1890 (Plates 3 and 5). A more common treatment placed a pair of engaged columnettes, often in polished granite, surrounding the central two bays on the top floor. In the most ambitious such installations, the pilasters were replaced by nearly fully round caryatids or atlantes, as in

Figure 3.11. F. Mahnken Tenement, 219 Grand Street, New York (1876). William Jose, architect. This building shows the articulated piers common in later decorated tenements. Photograph by Sean Litchfield.

Figure 3.12. Ernest Von Au Tenement, 13 Eldridge Street, New York (1883). Jobst Hoffman, architect. A transitional example built during a period of slow construction. Note the recessed central bays, designed to accommodate the original fire escape, which was narrower than its replacement. See Figures I.10, 3.1, and 4.1 for the original appearance of most tenement fire escapes, which usually had lighter iron railings and vertical ladders instead of stairs. Photograph by Sean Litchfield.

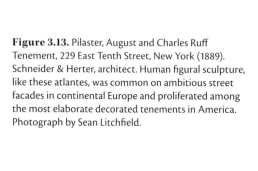

Figure 3.13. Pilaster, August and Charles Ruff Tenement, 229 East Tenth Street, New York (1889). Schneider & Herter, architect. Human figural sculpture, like these atlantes, was common on ambitious street facades in continental Europe and proliferated among the most elaborate decorated tenements in America. Photograph by Sean Litchfield.

Schneider & Herter's 1889 tenement at 229 East Tenth Street for August and Charles Ruff (Figure 3.13).[28] These centered columns gave the appearance of supporting an arched panel between the top floor and the cornice, usually a large terra-cotta panel incorporated into a pediment or arch.[29] These often featured large cartouches, griffins in profile, eagles, or other sculptural relief. Onto the upper levels of the sheet-metal cornice were often piled multiple layers of arches, pediments, or false domes, all topped with finials.

To divide a facade horizontally, builders could choose between a wide variety of styles of moldings and belt courses, usually also rendered in terra-cotta. The most elaborate buildings would include multiple belt courses in the piers between the windows, sometimes deeply projecting foliate bands, as well as larger and more thickly molded courses between each floor. This facade division left a rectangular space in the spandrel between the top of a window cap and the sill of the window above. This created the opportunity for a decorative panel. These panels featured a wide variety of motifs, including shells, cartouches, lamps, and heraldic devices, as well as heavy foliation. The *Record and Guide* complained in 1887 of these "unmeaning panels which are often freely used, more, it would seem, for the object of patronizing the makers and dealers than anything else."[30]

A Profusion of Forms

While the *Record and Guide* may have thought that these spandrel panels and other terra-cotta ornament were "unmeaning," the decorated tenement was noteworthy for the richness and complexity of symbolism found in its ornamentation program. None of these motifs was unique to the tenement, but few other common building types consistently used them in such variety, profusion, and fancy. This included, to a large extent, the houses of the wealthy, most of which were rather more staid not only in their density of ornamental forms but also in their iconography. Indeed, of the Fifth Avenue mansions of the Gilded Age elite, only the 1883 house of Bavarian-born beer magnate Jacob Ruppert came close to matching the decorated tenement in approach to ornament and iconography. And that house was roundly criticized, with the *Record and Guide* calling its facade, designed by German-born architect William Schickel, "course and ignorant."[31]

Perhaps the most noteworthy of the ornament commonly employed on the decorated tenement was the range of masks and grotesques, many of them quite bizarre (Figure 3.14). Such sculpture had appeared from the beginning of industrially

Figure 3.14. Detail of Peter Herter Tenement, 101 Rivington Street, New York (1891). Herter Brothers, architect. Note Moorish horseshoe arches and oversized grotesque masks. Photograph by Sean Litchfield.

produced ornament in America. James Bogardus's first iron facades of the late 1840s had prominent Medusa heads; the motif would become a trademark of that pioneer of cast-iron architecture.[32] Yet the decorated tenement was remarkable for the extent, profusion, and creativity of these figurative forms in its relief sculpture, some of which appear to have been manually carved in situ rather than cast off-site. A majority of the most elaborate decorated tenements of the 1880s employed these masks, particularly on keystones and at the base of pilasters, often with dozens of instances. Frequently, multiple figures appeared on a single facade, sometimes with a different variation at each window. Herter Brothers' 1889 building for Chaim Harris at 162 Henry Street, for example, was marked by at least twenty such figures (Figure 3.15). Unlike the simpler, conventionalized Medusa heads on Bogardus's buildings, a large portion of the tenement's sculpture program took the related form of satyrs, foliate masks, or the "green man," one of the oldest and most evocative forms of architectural relief sculptures. These figures frequently appeared with horns or snakes rising from their heads and had long beards and wavy hair, sometimes of acanthus or other vegetation. Many of them seemed to writhe in pain or were frozen in midst of a scream or a grimace.

The interpretation of the foliate mask was varying and contradictory, having meanings in classical mythology, where it was connected to both Medusa and the

Figure 3.15. Detail of Chaim Harris Tenement, 162 Henry Street, New York (1889). Herter Brothers, architect. This facade displays twenty different satyr heads and grotesque masks. Photograph by Sean Litchfield.

Bacchic cult. It appeared in the Roman-era temple of Hatra in Mesopotamia in the second century CE. Later it was connected with pagan May Day celebrations in northern Europe. In both these instances the icon was associated with death and rebirth.[33] It was later widely adopted in Christian church ornament of the Middle Ages.[34] In this context, particularly in the thirteenth century, these figures began to take on demonic forms.[35] Their presence on the decorated tenement seemed at once to suggest the domination and alienation of the residents within these buildings, or, conversely, their warding off the "evil eye," a meaning particularly supported by their placement over openings. Historians Margot and Carol Gayle have suggested this latter interpretation for the Medusa heads that appeared on Bogardus's buildings.[36]

The Oriel Tenement

One of the most important innovations in both appearance and accommodation was the introduction in the 1890s of the sheet metal–clad oriel window. These appendages became the defining feature of the decorated tenement in Boston, where more permissive building codes allowed such encumbrances above the sidewalk. The earliest of these buildings were almost entirely the product of architect Charles A. Halstrom, whose role in introducing improved appearance and accommodation to working-class housing in Boston mirrored that of Herter in New York (Figure 3.16). Unlike the fully decorated tenement of New York in the 1880s and 1890s, the oriel tenement in

Figure 3.16. Phillip and Israel Silverstein Tenement, 108 Myrtle Street, Boston (1896). Charles A. Halstrom, architect. This building is typical of Halstrom's pioneering work in Boston decorated tenements. Photograph by Sean Litchfield.

Boston was not universally adopted. Many builders, often working with the same architects, continued to build more modest, though still decorated, tenements that focused decorative attention at the cornice and window caps.

In these more ambitious tenements, decorative attention was focused not on masonry forms but on the sheet-metal cladding of the oriel windows, which code in Boston dictated be covered in fireproof material (Figure 3.17). Stamped sheet-metal panels had been enthusiastically embraced after their introduction in the 1880s. Facades fully clad in metal panels, which often accomplished very elaborate effects, were common on small-town commercial buildings, particularly in the American West. Architectural historian Pamela Simpson noted that these facades were advertised by western manufacturers as suitable "when cheap work to meet the competition is wanted."[37] Although full sheet-metal facades appeared on a number of Brooklyn tenements in the manner of the western commercial building, the material was most commonly used as cladding on oriel windows, in that city as well as Boston.[38] (Building codes did not allow this in Manhattan, politically separate from Brooklyn until 1898.) In the two decades after its introduction in the 1890s,

Figure 3.17. Louis Segel Tenement, 18 Cooper Street, Boston (1896). Charles A. Halstrom, architect. In addition to ornate sheet-metal panels on its oriel, this tenement by an important builder has loosely Moorish Revival–style window caps on the lower floors. Photograph by Sean Litchfield.

Figure 3.18. Bear Solomon (*far right*) and Henry Gustat Tenements (*center*), 32 and 36 Grove Street, Boston (1911). Silverman Engineering Company, architect. Sheet metal–covered oriels span the width of these buildings' facades. Photograph by Sean Litchfield.

some Boston builders took this material to its logical extremes, as in the full-front, metal-clad bay windows on the Grove Street tenements designed by the Silverman Engineering Company in 1911 (Figure 3.18).

These bay windows were a literal as well as symbolic outward projection of the tenement parlor, with all of its implications for respectable domesticity. Indeed, the appendage played an important role as a signal of the domestic practices of tenement dwellers. As architectural historian François Loyer has noted about bay windows on the apartment houses of Paris at the same moment, the bay window had dual and contradictory meanings. On the one hand, it was long associated in the English context with notions of domesticity, the paragon of which was the picturesquely massed Gothic cottage of which the bay window was a frequent feature. Similarly, in nineteenth-century American domestic discourse, the bay window was linked to the practice of home religion.[39] The provision of a bay window at one end of a parlor provided an apse-like area, linking the home to the sacred spaces of Protestant Christianity, imbuing the practices of the home with religious significance.[40] Additionally, in the urban context the oriel window was also an expression of modernity. Built in Paris on metal frames (those in Boston were constructed with heavy timber), they represented a technological evolution linked to many of the same advances that allowed for tall office buildings in Chicago. Whatever their meaning, not only did bay windows allow for a substantial increase in light and air within tenement spaces, they also injected plastic forms within the visually heavy masonry walls that had long marked the urban street facade.

"The Crude and Flamboyant Monstrosities of the Jewish Builder"

The next chapter will explore in depth who built the decorated tenement. Many of its most important early adopters were eastern European Jewish immigrants, for whom building a palatial structure that matched models of urbanity and modernity they had experienced in Europe was freighted with significance. This led Boston reformer Robert A. Woods, for instance, to bluntly identify the decorated tenement as simply "the crude and flamboyant monstrosities of the Jewish builder."[41]

In general the specific ornamental forms chosen by decorated tenement builders did not break down along ethnic lines, certainly not as cleanly as Woods suggested. One important exception was seen in the early work of Herter Brothers. They consistently chose the neo-Islamic (or Moorish Revival) style and employed forms closely associated with synagogue architecture for their Jewish clients on the Lower East Side. For example, in their 1886 Wolf Baum tenement, and a series of copies, the architects used moldings and other elements borrowed directly—indeed some seemingly cast in the same mold—from the Eldridge Street Synagogue they had designed earlier that year (Figure 3.19). Building with the same buff brick (since painted), they employed the same foliate belt courses, window tympana with allegorical figures, and bas relief spandrel panels, each with a prominent Star of David surrounded by twelve spheres. Baum's tenement was topped by a sheet-metal cornice with a broad, horseshoe-shaped arched pediment set on polished red granite columns, mirroring the broad arch on the front of the synagogue and closely matching in shape, proportion, moldings, and other decorations the elaborate walnut ark inside. Indeed, Herter Brothers' projection of a specifically Jewish identity for these buildings was quite overt. Among the finely scaled ornament on many of Peter Herter's buildings were numerous Stars of David, some quite prominent. He even employed this style of ornament on tenements he later built on his own account, in which, he noted, "Jewish tenants predominate."[42]

Herter Brothers' (or their client's) choice of this style, far from neutral, had complicated and contradictory implications within the nineteenth-century discourse on architectural form. As historian Saskia Coenen Snyder has noted, many German architects, mostly Christian, considered Moorish Revival architecture a "specifically Jewish style" in a period of increased, if not uncomplicated, economic emancipation.[43] The style had become the standard in Continental Europe for ambitious synagogues since midcentury. Having studied at the Berlin Bauakademie in the late 1860s,

Figure 3.19. Wolf Baum Tenement, 375 Broome Street, New York (1886). Herter Brothers, architects. This building was the first in a series of tenements with highly evocative forms related to the Eldridge Street synagogue. The buff brick has been painted. Photograph by Sean Litchfield.

Peter Herter surely would have been directly familiar with the new, prominent, and controversial 1866 Oranienburgerstrasse Synagogue in that city and may also have been familiar with the similar Dohany Street Synagogue in Budapest. New Yorkers would have recognized the style from the grand uptown Temple Emanu-El and the Central Synagogue, the latter designed by fellow Bauakademie graduate Henry Fernbach.[44] The style appeared into the late nineteenth and early twentieth centuries, most dramatically on Schneider & Herter's 1890 Zichren Ephriam, directed by prominent tenement builder Jonas Weil, as well as on their 1900 Congregation Shaare Zedek, an elaborate East Harlem synagogue of which Harris Fine was a member (see Figure 4.6).[45] As architectural historian Carol Krinsky and others have noted, many considered Moorish architecture an appropriate Jewish response to the largely nationalist search for a meaningful historical architectural style, one of the most important controversies in nineteenth-century design.[46]

Yet this style was considered by a number of Western architectural critics to be a weak and overly decorative mode, inferior to the classical and Gothic, with their connection to vaunted ideas of Western Civilization. Indeed, prominent German architectural theorist Carl Bötticher (almost certainly a teacher of Peter Herter at the Bauakademie) declared the style a "phantasmagoric art" that "destroyed its artform" by overlaying "their buildings with an opulent but meaningless coating."[47] To mainstream taste, it was, at least, exotic, magical, or frivolous and used as such. In a secular context it was most often found in places that called for folly and fancy, used for garden structures, pavilions, and summerhouses.[48] It was also often used for less-than-legitimate theaters, as in the case of the fantastical 1882 Casino Theater at Broadway and Thirty-Ninth Street in New York by Francis Kimball and Thomas Wisedell, and the 1892 Columbus Theater in Boston's South End tenement district.[49]

In this context it is noteworthy that, as in synagogue architecture, tenement architects almost never used Gothic styles for Jewish clients. Although quite fashionable, the style was alienating for its overt associations with medieval Christianity, which were increasingly tied to nostalgic notions of European national and cultural superiority.[50] Perhaps only a singular exception to this rule existed in each city: the 1885 David Brinkerhoff Loft and Tenement at 229 Grand Street in New York (Figure 3.20) by architect Elisha Sniffen, and Charles Halstrom's "The Gothic" in Boston for Louis Segel (see Figure 5.13). In the latter case the building was Gothic essentially in name only, with a single pointed arch and nominally Gothic moldings on the door surround. On the other hand, Herter Brothers was well versed in the use of Gothic forms in their nontenement work. For instance, they combined this style with Romanesque elements for their ambitious St. Elizabeth's Roman Catholic Church in Philadelphia in 1889, at the height of their New York tenement work, as well as the tenement-like rectory along with the interior decoration of the St. Nicholas Church on East Second Street in New York, where Frank Herter worshipped (Figure 3.21).[51] The rather conventional nature of these designs presented a telling contrast to their highly exotic work for Jewish clients.

Scholars have questioned the implications of this insistent use of Moorish architecture by mostly Christian architects (Fernbach was an exception) working for Jewish clients. According to Krinsky, it could be seen as having shades of anti-Semitism, as it "promoted a suspiciously foreign and Eastern image of Jews . . . who were accused of having their minds on earthly display and not on spiritual matters."[52] Beyond a mere transference from religious architecture, in this context, then, the use of the Moorish style on some of the earliest and most elaborate New York decorated tenements for prominent Jewish clients can be seen in a similarly problematic light. As Krinsky noted of synagogue architecture, "if a building has round arches, elaborate small-scale ornament, muted and warm color, and colored glass windows that admit dim light, many people still think the style is Jewish, even if it means equating murk and mystery with Judaism."[53] All of these same elements were characteristic of the decorated tenement, which employed exotic and small-scale decorative motifs on a building type well known for its internal murk.

These forms, intentionally or not, played into a dominant understanding of the

Figure 3.20. David Brinkerhoff Loft and Tenement, 229 Grand Street, New York (1885). Elisha Sniffen, architect. A rare Gothic Revival building purpose-built to house residential space and an industrial loft. Photograph by Sean Litchfield.

Figure 3.21. St. Nicholas Rectory, 125 East Second Street, New York (1903). Frank Herter, architect. The Herters worshiped in the Gothic Revival Catholic church (since demolished) that adjoined this building at right. Photograph by Sean Litchfield.

tenement and their builders as foreign and suspect, its ornament mere flights of fancy, its tenants having their mind only on display (Figure 3.22). This message was encoded not merely by the presence of the ornament—which was contested in the first instance—but also by the specific forms. In this way, the "fantastic shapes" and "unfamiliar profiles" chosen by the tenement builders and their architects perhaps deliberately heightened the otherness of these structures and their residents. Certainly these forms served to heighten the sense of fancy and mystery represented by these buildings.[54]

Yet despite these contradictions, neo-Islamic tenement architecture should not be read exclusively as an imposition of an orientalizing strategy by gentile architects on Jewish clients. They did not unilaterally force these othering forms onto builders and

Figure 3.22. Detail of Rachel Kurzman Tenement, 60 Bayard Street/1–3 Elizabeth Street, New York (1887). Herter Brothers, architect. This fine degree of ornamentation was typical of much of Herter Brothers' early tenement work. Note the small Star of David in the top roundel. Photograph by Sean Litchfield.

their working-class tenants. Indeed, the style was readily embraced by sophisticated clients, tenement builders, and building committees alike, who could have easily resisted inappropriate forms being foisted on them. Instead, they likely embraced its evocative forms as an assertive projection of a distinctive Jewish identity. The style was charged with meaning for many who used it. As Snyder has noted, not only did it appeal to a consumerist sense of exoticism of the East, but the "phenomena is directly related to Jews' soaring confidence and optimism about their socioeconomic and politic progress, which caused them to see no harm in publicly announcing their non-European origins."[55]

A Return to Simpler Forms

The use of neo-Islamic architecture with highly evocative forms diminished among tenement builders in the last decade of the nineteenth century (as it did in synagogue architecture). Many reverted to still quite elaborate forms of neo-Renaissance or neo-Baroque classicism. The increasing use of these more conventional forms reflected a broader trend in American architecture away from the eclectic styles that had been common in the previous decades. It is noteworthy that American tenement builders did not follow the lead of their European counterparts who adopted the sinuous forms of the *Jugendstil* and related movements that soon became standard on many Continental apartment buildings. Instead, like other American designers, they turned toward a more archaeologically correct, although still fundamentally creative, classicism.

While decorated tenements were constructed throughout the building boom of the second half of the 1890s and first half of the 1900s, builders pulled back on the evocative ornament of the previous decade. They continued to use ornamental forms in profusion, but the switch to a near-exclusive use of terra-cotta and sheet-metal ornament tended to produce a more standardized appearance. Recessed facade planes and broken cornice lines became increasingly less common, although belt courses, panels, and pilasters were still widespread. Foliate patterns frequently appeared, although there were fewer grotesques and less other figural relief. Cornices, still executed in sheet metal, reverted almost exclusively to unbroken rows of acanthus leaf consoles. The increased use of pilasters to group multiple stories of windows created in some buildings a level of order and cohesion that was absent in earlier facades. Architect Michael Bernstein's 1898 building for Polstein and Feinberg at 91 Henry Street was a particularly refined example of this new technique (Plate 6). Even more typical of the work done in the later 1890s was the block of buildings built in two phases between 1898 and 1901 for Harris Fine, designed by Hornberger & Straub (Figure 3.23).[56] Unlike Bernstein's more cohesive design, these buildings followed the earlier technique of piling up moldings, panels, and window surrounds, although the specific forms were more in line with the Beaux Arts classicism of the moment.

With the improved tenement plans of the 1890s as well as the 1901 tenement law encouraging the construction of wider buildings, these more expansive facades were augmented not only with pilasters and other applied elements but with oriel windows, corner bump-outs, and other appendages. These new plastic forms brought them in line with the commodious Boston tenements, although they were executed in masonry. The large building built by Samuel Barkin in 1901 at the corner of Rivington and Ludlow Streets to the designs of Alfred E. Badt (Plate 7) and John Pallimeri's Broome Street tenement of the next year by Sass & Smallheiser (Figure 3.24) were typical of ambitious tenements of the early twentieth century.[57] By this period buildings tended to have conventionalized elements drawn exclusively from classical and baroque motifs. As construction of improved tenements in these neighborhoods slowed after 1907, so too did the profusion of ornament on the new buildings. The few tenements built over the next decade demonstrated increasingly simplified forms.

Figure 3.23. *Left*, Harris Fine Tenements, 252 Broome Street, New York (1901). Hornberger & Straub, architect. The building at right was built by the same architect and developer in 1898. For plan, see Figure 2.12B. These two buildings show a return to conventionalized ornamental forms of the 1890s and early 1900s. Photograph by Sean Litchfield.

Figure 3.24. John Pallimeri Tenement, 382–386 Broome Street, New York (1902). Sass & Smallheiser, architect. A more typical early twentieth-century decorated tenement employing masonry oriels and modest neo-baroque ornament. Photograph by Sean Litchfield.

The decorated tenement at its apogee was a radical departure in American architecture not only in its use of ornament for buildings housing the working class but in
the evocative and contested forms it employed. These buildings, however common,
were not a mainstream approach to urban architecture or an inevitable response to
the real estate market but were the product of a particular set of cultural and economic forces. It is important, therefore, to understand the nature of the communities
that created them.

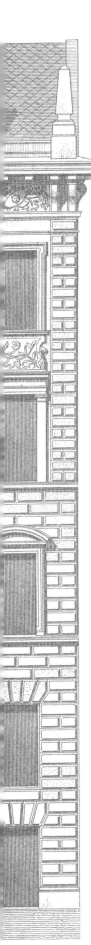

Chapter 4

Skin Builders and Plan Mills

The Tenement Business as Immigrant Enterprise

> The Tenement house is a knotty problem to anyone who has anything to do with it. The builder finds that it bristles with difficulties; the architect finds it one of the hardest propositions he has to deal with; the resident never seems to be quite satisfied and the investor finds that there lurks in his investment financial dangers of many kinds.
>
> **Peter Herter, 1900**

By the end of 1887, Peter Herter might have been excused for believing in the ideal of America as a place of reinvention; not only was he recasting the New York tenement, he was remaking himself in the process. The thirty-six-year-old architect, educated at the Bauakademie in Berlin, one of central Europe's most prestigious architecture schools, had seen his career as "one of the most prominent builders on the Rhine" shattered a decade earlier by politically motivated public corruption allegations, later proven spurious. He fled Germany penniless in 1884, settling in New York, where his older brother, Henry, had arrived three years earlier and established a fledgling architectural practice.[1] Their younger brother, Frank, also an architect, arrived in 1885. He and Peter soon began operating as the Herter Brothers, apparently unconcerned (or perhaps hoping) that they would be confused with the famous interior designers and cabinetmakers, unrelated, who operated under the same name. (Henry Herter had joined with Ernst Schneider, also a recent German immigrant, to form Schneider & Herter, a separate firm.)

The brothers soon became connected with a circle of Russian Jewish businessmen, the pioneers of a growing community on the Lower East Side, of which Sender Jarmulowsky was an important member.[2] In his role first as steamship agent, then as banker, notary, and lawyer, Jarmulowsky had enabled the passage to America for thousands of immigrants and attended to their needs once they arrived. He was also then president of Kahal Adath Jeshurun, one of the largest Orthodox Jewish congregations in the city, which in 1886 was planning a grand new building on Eldridge Street.[3] Although it was their first major commission in America, Herter Brothers was selected to design this significant project, a clear indication of the esteem with which the brothers' European training was held. The architects produced an ornate and loosely Moorish Revival–style building with extensive and highly symbolic terra-cotta ornamentation, which as we have seen, reflected the tradition of the grandest such buildings on the Continent, the products of an assertive projection of a Jewish identity in a period of increasing emancipation and economic freedom (Plate 8).[4] But in New York the Eldridge Street synagogue was clearly also part of a larger strategy of realignment of the landscape of the Lower East Side to the new physical, cultural, and spiritual needs of the rapidly growing immigrant population. The Herters, all three of whom initially settled on the heavily German lower Second Avenue, found the long-neglected buildings there "gloomy," "ill-smelling," and "unhealthy," completely unfit.[5] Their experience matched that of many new arrivals to the neighborhood. But their European background and architectural training, in which advanced forms of multifamily housing were fundamental and not considered vicious or foreign, put them in the position to reinscribe the meaning of the New York tenement to more closely align with the priorities of the new communities.

Members of the synagogue building committee played a pivotal role in this process. Using designs of the Herters, they helped introduce affordable visual and technological improvements previously unimaginable in working-class housing in New York. In December 1886, just two weeks after the ground breaking for the synagogue, Herter Brothers filed plans for a six-story tenement on Broome Street for Wolf Baum, and its appearance, based on the synagogue's architecture, and accommodations were radically new (see Figure 3.19). Over the next few months, as the walls of the synagogue were rising, the firm received a crush of commissions for new tenements like Baum's. On a single day in February 1887, they filed plans for ten new tenements, mostly for owners closely connected to Eldridge Street. Clients for these projects included Isaac Gellis, building committee member, who commissioned Herter Brothers to design a small tenement on Market Street, and later the extraordinary tenement at 89 Madison Street, discussed at the beginning of chapter 3. Jarmulowsky was also among the clients that day in 1887 for a tenement on Henry Street, joined by a young dry-goods merchant named Ascher Weinstein. They built a near copy of Baum's Broome Street building on Henry Street (Plate 9). Weinstein lived in that building for a short period after its completion, but he quickly grew to be one of the largest tenement builders working on the Lower East Side, building numerous similar tenements each year.[6] By 1890, Herter Brothers had designed one or more projects for each of the

Eldridge Street building committee members, including Nathan Hutkoff, the organization's treasurer, as well as David Cohen, who built an elaborate six-story tenement next door to the synagogue, employing the same moldings and buff brick (Figure 4.1).[7]

Indeed, scores of new tenements on the Herter Brothers' model had been built in the Lower East Side by the end of the decade, confirming Peter Herter's sense of the untapped potential for better housing in the neighborhood. By then all three brothers were not only designing these buildings but developing them as well (Plate 10).[8] "That the Eastsiders had a desire for better things is very conclusively shown," Peter bragged to the *Real Estate Record and Builders' Guide* a few years later, "by the success that has attended the erection of better tenement houses." Not only did these "noteworthy" new buildings have all the modern improvements, they looked considerably different than anything that had been built before.[9] These no longer fit the

Figure 4.1. A photograph of an early twentieth-century streetscape looking north on Eldridge Street, New York, with roadway under construction. The David Cohen Tenement (1890; Herter Brothers, architects) is the tall white-brick building with painted signs at right (since demolished). From this angle, its buff brick and belt courses blend nearly seamlessly into the Kahal Adath Jeshurun next door. The buildings at left show a progression of the most common type of decorated tenements between the 1860s and 1890s. Courtesy of NYC Municipal Archives.

stereotypical image of an east-side slum but were a new visual and economic model of a building that was much more responsive to the desires of its residents and highly profitable as well.

The Herters and their early clients on the Lower East Side were critical in establishing the decorated tenement as an important immigrant enterprise, a source for vastly improved housing for tenants, and the basis of considerable wealth for builders and financiers. As did many immigrant enterprises, this network arose because the existing market poorly served the needs and desires of new communities, misunderstood or disdained in hegemonic culture.[10] Here as elsewhere, the entrepreneurs who arose to meet this demand were both altruistic and opportunistic, guided by both communal concerns and business savvy. They recognized fellow members of their community not as foreign, helpless others who needed to be kindly instructed and provided for, but as consumers with choice and agency, whose culturally bound preferences and aspirations needed to be attended to. These businessmen recognized needs not being met elsewhere and stepped in to fill the gap. For instance, Isaac Gellis was most important (and best remembered) not as a tenement builder but for his primary trade: he was the first kosher meat dealer in New York. Kosher meat, like improved tenements, was a product that was being provided by no one else. These entrepreneurs, and many others, understood and provided for unique needs, even if this role occasionally caused conflict with their poor and working-class clientele. Gellis was famously excoriated at the synagogue in 1902 by a group of women upset about the premium pricing he commanded for his meat products.[11] Despite these conflicts, builders like him, living close at hand and sharing social, cultural, and religious ties, intimately understood the misery of the slum and recognized it could be ameliorated by new, modern buildings familiar to their idea of urban modernity.

The Aspirational Tenement

Buying or building an improved tenement appealed not just to immigrant elite like Sender Jarmulowsky and the officers of the Eldridge Street synagogue but to thousands of small investors, who built one or two buildings, which they often occupied. These were the most common builders of the decorated tenement. Indeed, the type flourished in the waning days of the amateur, working-class builder. The figure of the real estate developer, in the modern sense, historian Sara Stevens has recently noted, was a product of the professionalization of the real estate industry in the first half of the twentieth century. Developers, eager to cast themselves as experts on city building, joined with realtors (a newly coined and trademarked phrase) and related trade groups to naturalize their authority as agents of urban change.[12] For much of the nineteenth century, however, most urban housing was the product of working-class builders, often small-scale entrepreneurs with connections to the building trades.[13] As urban historian Jared Day has noted, building or owning a tenement particularly appealed to many immigrants "anxiously seeking a fast route out of urban squalor and up to a secure and independent living which was, for many, at the core of their 'American dream.'"[14]

Indeed, the great interest of these groups in owning or building their own housing was related to broader patterns of land tenure in the American city. Margaret Garb and a number of other scholars have demonstrated that homeownership became important to the immigrant working class in the nineteenth century even before it became a fundamental value of the middle class, who often preferred to invest excess capital elsewhere.[15] For the working class, on the other hand, homeownership acted as a safety net. It allowed a modicum of security and independence at times of uncertain employment, could be mortgaged to provide cash in hard times or to expand businesses, and acted as a type of old-age pension.[16] In addition to these often-discussed financial motivations, ownership also allowed the working class direct control over their living standards.

Much of the discourse on this phenomenon has been centered on the small single-family house, particularly common in the cities of the industrial Midwest and mid-Atlantic.[17] In the older and more intensely developed landscapes of Boston and New York, however, much higher land values and difficult transportation sharply limited access to space on which to build such houses, particularly in the center-city immigrant enclaves. These factors dictated that the tenement was the most rational choice for many working-class owners. While a tenement was much larger, considerably more expensive, and freighted with far different associations than a single-family house, for many the decision to buy, or especially build, one in Boston or New York operated on many of the same principles as buying a small cottage in Detroit, Chicago, or Milwaukee.[18] Frequently owner-occupied, the tenement provided an important opportunity to drastically improve living standards while also providing financial security. Additionally, the monetary returns possible with these buildings provided a powerful incentive for tenement owners to develop additional buildings in quick succession, a factor that led to the rapid transformation of these neighborhoods. For some with the inclination, luck, and wherewithal, a tenement even became the basis of more ambitious acts of city building, branching out into commercial lofts, grand theaters, and tall office buildings.

The simple fact of moving into a new building was a major improvement for many. A persistent lack of routine maintenance had long plagued multifamily housing. Absentee landlords' generally poor record of upkeep was the single biggest factor in the creation of slum conditions. The new decorated tenements were appealing not only because they had a stylish new appearance and all the latest conveniences, but because, for a while at least, they also had plaster that was not cracked, a roof that did not leak, and doors that closed properly. Living in a building where everything, presumably, worked as it should would have been a major step up for those used to slum conditions. This advantage, among other factors, led many in the working class to prefer building a new tenement instead of the safer act of buying an existing one.

Indeed, for many the act not just of owning but of building a new and seemingly palatial building in an American city was fraught with meaning. Many European immigrants had been routinely denied access to landownership in their home countries or had faced sumptuary or other laws that severely restricted what they could build there. These economic restrictions alone were enough to impel some migrants to America. Indeed, the concern for improving working-class housing, particularly notable among Jewish builders, was rooted in these and other cultural forces, in particular notions of communal improvement and faith in the emancipatory power of the American system. In reviewing Jewish involvement in housing construction for *The American Hebrew* in 1913, reporter Abraham Schepper encapsulated much of the spirit embodied in the tenement-building process, connecting it to the structural discrimination they had faced in Europe. "Having lived for many years under political conditions that practically prohibited landownership, the foreign Jew becomes intoxicated with the idea of being able to buy and build in safety, he considers the privilege of owning land without molestation as one of the great outward symbols of American freedom." This led these immigrants to "picture the future of undeveloped neighborhoods, and present to the mind's eye visions of beautiful homes." Schepper acknowledged that this process had a social as well as a financial dimension. Referring to wealthy developers who preferred to build modern tenements instead of making more prestigious and remunerative investments in luxurious hotels or exclusive apartment houses, he noted, "he has done something of a more beneficial nature and greater social value. By offering rooms with modern improvements at moderate rentals he has placed within the means of even poorer people to live decently and comfortably." This process, Schepper asserted, not only did "something pretty definite toward beautifying New York," but also "materially added to the well-being of humanity."[19] In a similar vein, observer Lee Friedman noted of Boston's tenement builders, "these Jewish artisans . . . labored long hours and finally produced, at surprisingly low costs, livable and good looking flats." Even writing from a distance of more than four decades, Friedman claimed that "the poor and middle classes of the community owe thanks to the Jewish builders for . . . much of the betterment in living conditions" that took place around the turn of the twentieth century.[20]

Not only the choice to build a home but also the particular design of the decorated tenement were far from a neutral or inevitable response to the real estate market. Instead, they were informed by builders', architects', and financiers' cultural frames of reference, personal pride, and communal commitments, as well as their sense of opportunity. Building, financing, or designing such a building, disdained by mainstream culture, appealed only to a certain sort of person. These actors operated in a tight-knit network and formed webs of association that were often insular in nature and frequently divorced from the larger community of more elite real estate investors, from whom they initially faced discrimination.[21] The insular nature of the decorated tenement business, in part, resulted in not only a commonality of ideas but what appears to be in-group pressure to strive toward innovation and improvement. Thus, it is important to understand the place of the builder, architect, and financier in both

American culture and the context of their community. For this reason, facts of the builder's and architect's biography are essential for our understanding of built form. These facts intersected with market forces that informed not only their choice to build but their design decisions as well.

The Decorated Tenement Builder

In many ways the story of New York builder Harry Fischel is emblematic of many of the factors driving the builders and designers of the decorated tenement. Indeed, his background filled out the profile of the type of person most likely to build such a building: he had deep personal, religious, and cultural ties to the community; he was intimately involved in its institutions; and he had a major stake in its improvement. Born in Mertz, Russia, to an Orthodox Jewish family, from a young age Fischel aspired to be an architect, informally studying in that field as a child and acting as a building foreman in Russia as a young adult. When economic and cultural forces impelled his immigration to New York in 1885 at age twenty, it was natural that he saw the move as the fulfillment of this long-standing dream. Working menial jobs during a period learning English in night school and taking architecture classes at Cooper Union, within two years he secured a well-paid position as a draftsman with Schneider & Herter, then flush with tenement commissions. "Never had he found work more congenial, more to his liking, having in it the possibilities for promotion and service, opening to him a new vista of long deferred hopes," his biographer later wrote of his time with the architects. In his first week Fischel conspired to make himself as useful as possible to his new employer in hopes they would grant him a reasonable accommodation: reduced pay in exchange for being excused from work on the Jewish Sabbath, then a standard workday (two-day weekends did not become common until the labor movements of the twentieth century). His request was roundly rejected, with one unidentified principal of the firm threatening him with termination if he did not report for work the following Saturday. After a crisis of conscience that day, he decided to prioritize his religious tradition by reserving the day for study and prayer, trusting he could prevail on the goodwill of his employer that Monday by suggesting a further reduction in pay. Schneider & Herter again refused, even withholding payment for the week he had already worked.[22]

Unable to gain a foothold in the New York architecture profession, where even immigrant firms like Schneider & Herter, who worked primarily for Jewish clients, were operated by unsympathetic gentiles, Fischel knew he had to strike out in business on his own. But instead of pursuing architecture any further, he turned to real estate. Like the Herters, Fischel was plainly aware of the need for improved tenements on the Lower East Side (he complained bitterly of the conditions he faced in his first years there) and put his knowledge of architecture to use to solve the problem. A few difficult years' work as a building foreman allowed him to attain connections, credit, and, most important, $2,000 in capital by the end of 1889. He knew he could improve on the design by which many new tenements were still being built. His first purchase was an irregular lot at 168 Clinton Street, which he was able to buy cheaply because most builders, with less training in architecture, were unable to envision how to profitably build there (Figure 4.2).[23] The building he constructed the next year on that site was a decorated tenement, though modest compared to the Schneider & Herter–designed buildings next door. Yet, the project proved a financial success. The building would be sold for a $5,000 profit, which was quickly turned around into numerous similar projects. In his biographer's exaggerated words, being "the first successful Jewish builder on the east side was fraught with much larger significance than the individual rewards," including opening numerous building trades to Jewish craftsman and insisting that his building operations shut down on Saturday.[24]

For Fischel, effecting major improvements to the squalid housing conditions he found when he first arrived in the neighborhood was a major motivation. "He was able to introduce," his biographer noted, "many novel features in his buildings of benefit to those who were to live in them. These conveniences procured their resale when completed."[25] Fischel would design his own tenements for at least four more years, although later he would rely on outside firms, particularly Hornberger & Straub, for

Figure 4.2. Harry Fischel Tenement, 168 Clinton Street, New York (1890, pictured in a 1940 tax photograph; since demolished). Fischel and F. A. Minuth, architect. This was Harry Fischel's first project as a New York developer. Note the contrast to the more elaborate tenements at right designed by Fischel's former employer, Schneider & Herter, who had fired him two years earlier for observing the Jewish Sabbath. Courtesy of NYC Municipal Archives.

the numerous elaborate buildings he built throughout the neighborhood in the 1890s and early 1900s. Like many who started as tenement builders, he soon expanded his interests to other building types in other areas. One of his last projects in the neighborhood would also be his most important, indeed one of the most substantial private buildings there: the Grand Theater at Grand and Chrystie Streets (Figure 4.3). The ornate brick and terra-cotta structure housed the first important Yiddish theater in the country.[26] Fischel would go on to be a major philanthropist, instrumental in the founding of Beth Israel Hospital, Yeshiva University, and pioneering settlements in Palestine, among dozens of other institutions and causes. His story demonstrates the close relationship between tenement builder and tenement architect; one can imagine such an interest in architecture driving other smaller-scale builders whose biographies have not been preserved.

Stories like Fischel's—of the "rise, in little more than thirteen years, from a condition of direst poverty to one of affluence"—were beguiling to many poor immigrants.[27] Indeed, while few rose to such heights, there were thousands of builders like Fischel working in the immigrant enclaves of Boston and New York. Nearly 90 percent of all tenements in these neighborhoods, and nearly 97 percent of the most elaborate

Figure 4.3. Grand Theatre, 255 Grand Street, New York, 1902 (pictured shortly after completion; demolished 1930). Harry Fischel, developer; Victor Kohler, architect. The seven-story tenement at right was the Columbia, built in 1901 to some of the highest standards in the neighborhood. The Columbia is extant but altered. Courtesy of Byron Company (New York, New York)/Museum of the City of New York, 29.100.811.

buildings, were built by immigrants or their children, mostly amateur builders. As pioneering urban planner and architect Clarence Stein derisively put it in a slightly later period, "most of New York's miles of apartments were erected by butchers, by bakers, by anyone who could borrow enough money to get the material and labor."[28] Abraham Cahan's 1917 novel *The Rise of David Levinsky,* about an immigrant who worked his way up to successful cloak maker, captured the "intoxicating" spirit of the booming years of immigrant tenement construction. "Small tradesmen of the slums, and even working-men, were investing their savings in houses and lots. Jewish carpenters, house-painters, bricklayers, or installment peddlers were becoming builders of tenements. . . . Deals were being closed, and poor men were making thousands of dollars in less time than it took them to drink the glass of tea . . . over which the transaction took place."[29] And these transactions were democratic, taking place at lively curb markets.[30]

The ethnicity of tenement builders closely matched the patterns of European immigration to America. In both cities, over the whole period from the Civil War to World War I, nearly half of tenement builders were eastern European Jews from areas identified by the census takers primarily as Russia, while another 17 percent were Germans. Despite their prevalence in parts of these neighborhoods and their prominence in the building trades, Italians represented only about 7 percent of the builders overall. Likewise, Irish made up only about 3 percent (Figure 4.4). While the builders' ethnic makeup was generally similar between the two cities, some differences can be noted. In more diverse New York, 38 percent of tenement builders were eastern European Jews, while 25 percent were German. Italians and Irish made up 4 and 3 percent, respectively, despite the prolific work of the firm of Fay & Stacom, composed of two Irish-immigrant partners, who frequently engaged German architects for elaborate buildings. Anglo-Americans built 12 percent. Various other groups made up the rest. In Boston, the tenement builders represented a simpler ethnic breakdown, reflecting the greater homogeneity of immigrant groups in that city: more than 70 percent of the builders were eastern European Jews, and 13 percent were Italians. Anglo-Americans represented 8 percent of the builders there, and the Irish built only 4 percent of the tenements, most before 1890.

As Cahan suggested, many involved in tenement development were in the construction trades. This was typical of many developers of working-class housing throughout the nineteenth century. Historian Donna Rilling has noted that early nineteenth-century Philadelphia builders, facing precarious economic conditions, often turned to developing housing on speculation as a way to remain busy during off times.[31] The returns from these projects, though risky, were an important means for many in the building trades to gain economic independence and long-term security. Historian James A. Jacobs has recently noted the same trend among contractors who became suburban home builders in the mid-twentieth century.[32] Many in the building trades frequently moved from positions as developer, contractor, or tradesman, depending on economic conditions.[33] Besides the construction trades, tenement build-ers were commonly drawn from the garment industry, a major economic activity in these neighborhoods, where they often faced similar risks and cyclical income.

In Cahan's depiction, "women, too, were ardently dabbling in real estate."[34] Indeed, women were frequently found to be the building owner on many tenement permits

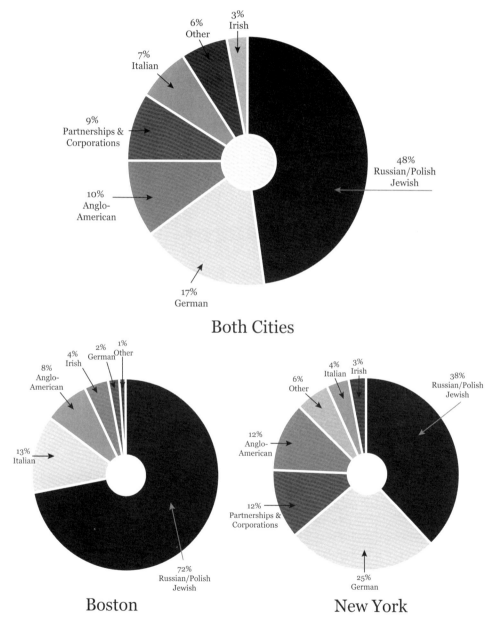

Figure 4.4. The ethnicity (first or second generation) of builders of tenements in Boston and New York. Drawing by author.

and deeds, although these women were almost always the wives of tenement build-ers. This ownership has been interpreted simply as a defensive tactic to protect the husband's assets against creditors in the expensive and risky building process.[35] In Peter Herter's case, much of his capital for his first tenements came from the family of his wife, Anna Maria Mayer. Her family wealth had supported Peter after his property had been confiscated by German officials in connection with his corruption convic-tion and would later be the basis for Peter's own real estate investments. During the panic of 1893 he transferred his property to her name to shield it from his substantial outstanding debt.[36] Yet the role of women tenement builders does not appear to have been entirely passive. As in many other immigrant enterprises, where the labor and prowess of all members of the family were necessary for economic survival, there is evidence that women played a more active role in tenement building than they did in the otherwise overwhelmingly male-dominated building and real estate trades. In Cahan's telling, for example, Mrs. Chaikin, the wife of protagonist Levinsky's former business partner and clothing designer, was active in real estate while her husband devoted attention to his primary trade.

The Mass Production of the Decorated Tenement

While small builders provided the bulk of the decorated tenements of both cities, a small number of partnerships began to build improved tenements on a large scale starting in the late 1880s. This trend increased dramatically after the turn of the twen-tieth century, as construction became more expensive, generally requiring larger lots. One of the earliest and most important of the large-scale tenement developers was the New York firm of Weil & Mayer, founded by German-born Jonas Weil and Bernhard Mayer. Once again, the innovations in the housing provided by this firm seem to have benefited greatly from their connections to the Herter brothers. The benefit was mu-tual. Indeed, the success of Schneider & Herter was due in large measure to their work with Weil & Mayer as the pair was quickly becoming one of the largest real estate operators in the city.

Jonas Weil, the senior partner, was born in Emmendingen, Germany, the son of an important religious leader; he immigrated to New York in 1861. First engaged in the livestock business and later as a real estate loan operator, he and Mayer be-came concerned by the slums on the Lower East Side in the 1880s. Like Fischel and Jarmulowsky, they set about doing something about them.[37] By the end of the next decade, they were developing more than fifty tenements annually, most designed by Schneider & Herter, a scale of production that encompassed at least eight hundred to upward of a thousand housing units per year (Figure 4.5). In these buildings the firm began using standardized plans, frequently repeating facade arrangements and ornamental trim, sometimes in long identical rows with only minor variation in the decorative forms. In this newly expanded field of production, the architect's comfort with the use of industrially produced architectural material, now mostly executed in terra-cotta and sheet metal, proved crucial to the success of the firm's ambitions.

Weil & Mayer were the only developers of working-class housing that the *Real Estate Record and Builders' Guide* included among its list of most important New York builders in 1898. They credited the firm with "destroying the rookeries" that had existed in the neighborhood of Cherry and Madison Streets and replacing them with "a substantial class of tenements and flats."[38] Like Fischel, Weil became a major philanthropist based on his real estate earnings. One of his most important projects was the dedication of a synagogue in honor of his father. The Zichren Ephriam Temple was also designed by Schneider & Herter (Figure 4.6). The formal connections between this building (in an uptown neighborhood that would have been unfamiliar to many of Weil's tenants) and the downtown tenements the architects designed for Weil & Mayer were not as explicit as they were with the Eldridge Street project and its members' buildings, but a similar instinct seems to have been at play.

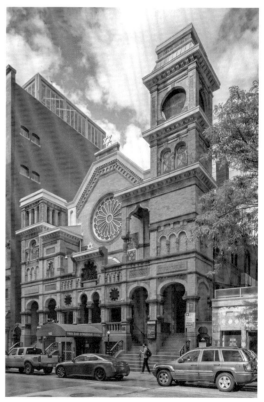

Figure 4.5. Weil & Mayer Tenement, 106 Madison Street, New York (1892). Schneider & Herter, architects. Upper part of cornice is missing. Weil & Mayer, one of the first firms to mass-produce the decorated tenement and New York's largest builder of working-class housing in the late nineteenth century, built hundreds of similar tenements. Photograph by Sean Litchfield.

Figure 4.6. Zichren Ephriam Temple, 163 East Sixty-Seventh Street, New York (1889). Schneider & Herter, architect. The construction of this elaborate uptown synagogue was sponsored by prominent tenement developer Jonas Weil, with designs by prolific tenement architects. Photograph by Sean Litchfield.

Housing the Tenement Builder

Clearly, the inclination of many immigrants to build tenements in their new neigh-borhoods resulted from an amalgam of forces. A vehicle for profits that could lead to financial security, a source of pride for groups long denied the right to control prop-erty, and a means of pulling the community out of the mire of the slums, a tenement could also result in a major rise in its owner's own living standards and that of their family members. While a prominent tenement builder like Jonas Weil could afford an elegant brownstone on the Upper East Side, the more numerous smaller build-ers looked to the tenement to change their own standard of living. As Lee Friedman noted, many tenement builders in Boston at the turn of the twentieth century "knew from their own experience what they wanted" when designing their buildings, as often the builder "planned to live in one of the flats himself and be landlord and jani-tor as well as tenant."[39] A more pronounced trend in the smaller city (although not uncommon in New York), the use value of the tenement for its builders, as opposed to the mere exchange value for a speculator, was an important but often overlooked aspect of the decorated tenement phenomenon.

Joseph Rudnick, along with his wife, Rose, and brother-in-law Louis Segel, dem-onstrated through a series of moves over the course of a decade the power of tene-ment building not only as a means of financial security but also as a vehicle to align the living standard they and their family aspired to with the realities of a new coun-try. The Rudnicks and Segels arrived in New York from their native Vilna, in present-day Lithuania, in 1890. But unlike so many, they did not remain there long. Instead they headed north to the dense but tiny dockside Jewish quarter of Portland, Maine, where Joseph's brother Simon lived (Figure 4.7). The Chatham Street neighborhood in which they settled was a motley collection of old wood-frame slums, where run-down early nineteenth-century buildings had been carved up into small one- and two-room units. It was here, according to family history recounted by historian Maura

Figure 4.7. Chatham Street, Portland, Maine, pictured in a 1924 tax photograph. This was the heart of the city's tiny dockside Jewish quarter, with crowded slum conditions. Joseph Rudnick lived on this street in the 1890s, in a building at the far left, where he determined to become a builder of improved housing in Boston. Courtesy collections of City of Portland—Planning and Development.

Fitzpatrick, that Rudnick, frustrated by his work as a tailor and demoralized by his squalid surroundings, resolved to pursue a long-held interest in becoming a builder.[40] Yet the region's slow growth and limited immigration made demand for anything like the elaborately decorated, palatial tenements that lined the streets of their native Vilna—or their port of call in New York—unlikely in the near future.[41] (A few decorated tenements were built here in the early twentieth century.)

Instead, Rudnick set his sights farther south on Boston and that city's growing North End, where the Jewish population had more than doubled in the past decade, but where, like Chatham Street, the new residents were crowded into ancient, run-down buildings.[42] In 1893 Joseph, Simon, and Rose Rudnick, along with Rebecca and Louis Segel, pooled their money to purchase a lot and old house at 20 Cooper Street in the center of the North End, securing a loan from the seller. The family hired architect Charles A. Halstrom, a second-generation Swedish immigrant raised in the tenements of the North End, who up until that point had mainly designed wood-frame buildings in the inner suburbs, including a complex of worker housing for brewer Julius Haffenreffer.[43] Like the Herter brothers in New York, Halstrom seemed positioned to break the conservative and ill-commodious mold with which most Boston tenements had been built for decades. His building for the family was perhaps his earliest experiment in the improved forms of working-class housing that Halstrom, Rudnick, and Segel would come to pioneer over the next decade. The brick facade was enlivened with terra-cotta panels, while the oriel window was covered in stamped sheet metal. It was one of the first to achieve the level of ornamentation that was then common in New York tenements, although Rudnick left the columns and arch of the door piece rough, awaiting future carvers that never came (Figure 4.8). Rudnick served as builder of the $8,500 building, begun in November 1893 and finished the following April. When the building was completed, the family moved into one of the four-room units at the front of the building, which had a parlor with a bay window facing the street, a modern kitchen with range and washtub, and two bedrooms. The two families on each floor shared a flush toilet in the hall, but the commodious front unit had a private bathtub, awkwardly placed in the front bedroom. Still, not only was the building a great improvement over the conditions they had found in Portland, but there was essentially nothing else like it in the immigrant quarters of Boston.

Within months of moving into Cooper Street, the family seems to have discovered that their risk in building a better tenement for their own benefit had paid off. They quickly cashed out, turning the profits into a number of other projects in the neighborhood. First, they commissioned a new, twelve-unit building nearby at 89 Prince Street (Figure 4.9). The Prince Street building, permits for which were filed under the name of Louis Segel's wife, Rebecca, cost $18,000, and it was more elaborate than Cooper Street. Four stories tall, it had a pair of storefronts on the lower level, with terra-cotta and sheet-metal ornament on the oriels above. On Broome Street in New York and on St. George Avenue in Vilna, this level of ornamentation would have seemed familiar, but on Prince Street in Boston, it stood shoulder to shoulder with some of the oldest buildings in the nation, long since given over to multifamily use. The fancy swags and filigrees of the sheet copper–clad bay windows contrasted sharply with the colonial-era Joseph Tileston house next door: its single-slope roof and clapboard siding were remnants of the past, and its sagging, haphazard additions and fire escapes overloaded with bedding were indicative of the poor housing conditions that existed inside (Figure 4.10). The Rudnicks and Segels would move into 89 Prince Street, its door surround still uncarved, after its completion. The ground-floor storefront served as the headquarters for the family's budding building and real estate business.

Yet even these conditions did not satisfy the Segels and the Rudnicks for long. After developing a number of other sites in the North End, in July 1897 Segel again hired Halstrom for a new tenement, this one in the slightly more prestigious West

Figure 4.8. Joseph Rudnick et al. Tenement, 20 Cooper Street, Boston (1893). Charles A. Halstrom, architect. Rudnick's family lived in this building shortly after their move from Portland to Boston. Notice the lack of carving on the granite door surround, likely intended to be finished in a manner similar to the building at left, built three years later by Rudnick's brother-in-law Louis Segel. Photograph by Sean Litchfield.

Figure 4.9. Rebecca Segel Tenement, 89 Prince Street, Boston (1894). Charles A. Halstrom, architect. The second tenement developed by the Segel and Rudnick family, shortly after their move to 20 Cooper Street. Photograph by Sean Litchfield.

Figure 4.10. The colonial-era Tileston house at Prince and Margaret Streets, Boston, contrasted with Rebecca Segel's elaborate new tenement at left when it was built in 1894. The Tileston house would be demolished shortly after this picture was taken in the late 1890s. Courtesy of Boston Public Library.

End, with wider streets and more regular lots. Their new, ten-unit building, The Gothic, cost $28,000 and had an elaborate cut-stone front and one of the most commodious interiors ever built in the neighborhood, setting an unmatched standard for working-class housing in Boston. Unlike the rough, undressed stone door surround of the family's first buildings on Cooper and Prince Streets, the limestone surround of The Gothic was finely carved, with a stained-glass transom announcing the building's name (Figure 4.11). Despite the project's high level of ambition, Segel still served as the building's builder and carpenter. The family moved in when it was finished in January 1898. Less than a decade after arriving from Vilna and only four years after those dark days in Portland, the family now lived in a modern seven-room, steam-heated apartment with two parlors stretching the twenty-seven-foot width of the building (Figure 2.5), a formal dining room wainscoted in quartered oak (Figure 2.6), a kitchen with hot water boiler, and a full bathroom with its tub in the proper place. These transactions propelled the family from the garment trade to the real estate industry, setting them up as among the foremost builders of working-class housing in Boston for the first three decades of the twentieth century.

Even if builders did not live in their own new tenements, they were rarely outsiders in their community. While some well-established German immigrant builders in New York lived in single-family town houses in the heavily German Upper East Side during their most active periods of tenement development, they were the exception among builders in that city. More commonly, prominent builders, particularly Russian Jewish immigrants, rarely lived in conditions much more luxurious than that of their tenants. In New York many of the most important builders' homes clustered around Rutgers Square in the Lower East Side (Figure 4.12). Not only Sender Jarmulowsky but also Isaac Gellis, Harry Fischel, Nathan Schancupp, and Harris Fine made their home there in the last decades of the nineteenth century. Instead of building large new tenements for themselves, they chose to convert Federal-era row houses into flats,

Figure 4.11. Detail of entrance, Louis Segel Tenement, "The Gothic," 47 Allen Street, Boston (1898; pictured in 1959 shortly before demolition). Attributed to Charles A. Halstrom, architect. Library of Congress, Prints and Photographs Division, HABS MASS,13-BOST,63-2.

Figure 4.12. 280 East Broadway, New York (pictured in a 1940 tax photograph; since demolished). This early nineteenth-century row house, built by merchant Eastman Smith, was remodeled and expanded into flats in 1891 by tenement builder Nathan Schancupp. Schneider & Herter added the fourth story, window caps, and cornice, all similar to motifs the architects designed for the builder's tenements (see Figure 3.7). Schnucapp lived in one unit in the building and rented out the others. Isaac Gellis, Harris Fine, and Harry Fischel all lived nearby in similar buildings, many also remodeled by the Herters. The large 1922 apartment building at right, designed by Seelig, Finkelstein & Wolfinger for Louis Cohen, was more typical of buildings built by many of the same developers in more peripheral neighborhoods after World War I. Courtesy of NYC Municipal Archives.

usually occupying a floor within each (for plans, see Figure 1.4). In the process they frequently hired the Herter Brothers or Schneider & Herter to give these buildings a stylish new facade, often with upper-floor additions and elaborate cornices. These renovations brought the appearance of the tenement builder's home in line with that of their other buildings. In this way the homes of working-class tenants and upwardly mobile builders, as well as the important civic, religious, and commercial structures of the neighborhood, were linked together through common visual characteristics.

The Operator and Investor

An aspiration of many, from a well-established merchant like Jonas Weil to a struggling tailor like Joseph Rudnick, the tenement as an investment was steep, though not unattainable, especially given the networks of financing available in many immigrant communities. These investments were available to a remarkable number of relatively poor people. As the *New York Times* mused in 1903, "The capitalist who erects business skyscrapers on Broadway or elevator apartment houses in Harlem will hardly believe that the east side is being rebuilt with comfortable dwelling places for working people by men whose capital is seldom more than $5,000; often no more than $2,000 or $3,000."[44] Lower land costs in Boston meant one could own a new tenement for an outlay of less than $1,000.[45] Given the low capital with which many builders began, tenement projects had to be heavily leveraged.

Indeed, tenement construction costs were high, averaging about $1.50 to $1.80 a square foot, just shy of a laborer's average daily wages. Investment in construction costs alone for the smallest project in Boston was about $2,500 on the low end, about equivalent to the cost of a middle-class single-family house, up to about $60,000 for the largest project in these neighborhoods. The median cost in Boston was $9,000 for a typical four-story tenement and store. In New York the investments were much greater. There, the cheapest buildings could be built for about $4,000, and investments ran as high as $130,000 for the largest tenements in the neighborhood, with elevators and steam heat. The median investment was about $20,000 to $23,000, which bought a typical sixteen- or twenty-two-unit, five- or six-story tenement in the 1880s or 1890s. A decade or two earlier, when tenements were built to a lower standard, this figure was closer to $14,000.[46]

People like Sender Jarmulowsky played an important role in this process. His bank, which grew out of his role as a steamship agent, and others like it were common features of immigrant communities throughout the country. In Boston's Italian community, Banco Stabile seems to have played a similar role.[47] These banks appear to have been the primary source of funding for most tenement projects. As historian Jared Day has noted, mainstream sources of capital were not available to most immigrant entrepreneurs, particularly those of Jewish origin, whom banks and credit rating agencies "routinely viewed . . . as fundamentally dishonest."[48]

The process worked generally the same in both Boston and New York.[49] The ground on which tenements were built was purchased from a dealer, known as a building operator, who specialized in holding properties in anticipation of tenement construction. These dealers often arranged financing for the construction that was to take place on the lots they sold, often for inflated prices that exceeded the cost of the buildings to be erected there. Sometimes as little as 5 percent down was all that was required to secure a loan and a lot. After construction was finished, the construction loan was replaced by a longer-term mortgage, which was in place while the building was filled and marketed.[50] Executing both loans required commissions and bonuses to be paid, greatly increasing the cost of the project, to the consternation of many reformers.[51] The final mortgage, sometimes held by more established banks, often reflected a valuation considerably higher than the initial outlay. The process gave builders the means and incentive to undertake tenement investments in quick succession, one of the primary drivers of change in these neighborhoods.[52]

These operators played an important role in promoting and perpetuating the decorated tenement, helping to standardize designs, which were then implemented by a large number of individual builders, limiting what might have otherwise been misguided schemes of amateurs, and grounding their work in a systematic understanding of the realities of the communities in which the builders and operators worked. Indeed, in the context of other types of speculative architecture, it has been well understood that financiers often had a hand, sometimes a significant one, in shaping the design of the buildings they financed.[53] The decorated tenement was no exception. Peter Herter called the tenement financier the builder's "partner" (occasionally both names appeared on the building permit application) and suggested that financiers would refuse to fund projects whose appearance or accommodation did not align with their expectations of proper tenement design. "You can't get a partner to join you," he noted, "unless your operation is distinctly of a sound business character. He won't invest in Utopias."[54] In this sense, then, figures like Jarmulowsky took on even greater importance in financing the initially risky venture to introduce better buildings. He and people like him were crucial in determining that improved and ornamented buildings were not just desirable but a worthy financial investment.

Another important role of the building operator, one Herter would know well, was connecting builders to architects and other professionals. Indeed, they often seem to have played the role of a clearinghouse for these sorts of references, connecting amateur builders with the wide variety of firms—architects, contractors, and material dealers, to name three—needed on the project. This function of the building operator was likely the source of the favored status certain architects enjoyed among tenement builders. Indeed, a tenement construction project was no simple endeavor, especially for an amateur builder. The process required specialized knowledge not only of the real estate market but of structural engineering, the building materials trade, the increasingly complex building code, and the needs, taste, and desires of prospective tenants. For this, builders had to turn to an architect, often a well-established member of their community, for guidance. The architects played an important, if poorly understood, role in the creation of the landscape of the decorated tenement.

The Tenement Architect, and Architect as Developer

Immigrant and working-class architects were best positioned to understand the importance of the tenement. While often better established and more likely to be American-born than their clients, most tenement architects hailed from working-class backgrounds, frequently with immigrant parents. While the training, methods, and precedents of the tenement architect will be largely the topic of the next chapter, it is important to understand them in the context of the decorated tenement network. These architects translated builders' and tenants' often European notions of modernity and gentility to American building forms and land patterns. In doing so, they played a crucial role as arbiters of fashion within the tenement districts. While nearly two hundred different architects designed the tenements of these two cities, for the most part prospective tenement builders generally turned to a relatively small group of firms who specialized in this sort of work.

The Herter Brothers' and Schneider & Herter's role in introducing the improved, decorated tenement to the Lower East Side has been noted, but their innovations attracted immediate attention and emulation. Within a year of the latter firm's founding, it was said to be "gaining quite a reputation" among the builders of the city. The *Jewish Messenger* advised its readers to "obtain the views of this enterprising firm."[55] Soon, however, they would have increased competition, almost entirely from German-born architects. Despite the competition, Schneider & Herter eventually designed just under 4 percent of the tenements in New York, thanks largely to their large-scale work with Weil & Mayer. They were eclipsed in volume by George Fred Pelham, who in the 1890s adapted many of the innovations into a standardized model, plans for which were cheaply sold to builders (and to which Weil & Mayer increasingly turned after the mid-1890s). Pelham's office ran on the model of the "plan mill," a usually spurious charge of reformers that will be explored in more depth in the next chapter. Yet his reputation was strong among speculative builders. In 1908 he was called one of the "foremost and best-known architects in New York City" and one of the few who specialized in multifamily housing.[56] Over a long career he ended up designing about 5 percent of the tenements in the city.

In a manner similar to the Herters, Charles A. Halstrom introduced an improved model to Boston tenement builders, including the Rudnicks and the Segels, in the early 1890s. While he sometimes had competition from William E. Clarke, few other Boston architects worked on tenement commissions. The two, however, were soon eclipsed by Frederick A. Norcross, who began architectural practice in Boston in 1896, after years of apprenticing with an engineer. Norcross (unrelated to the prominent Boston contractors the Norcross Brothers) not only attracted away many of

Halstrom's clients, he seems to have poached many of his design ideas, initially reproducing a decorated tenement form that was very similar to Halstrom's pioneering work. Norcross's commissions would quickly surpass the scale of the older architect, and he would for many years be the premier specialist in working-class housing (and other speculative building forms) in the city, operating much like Pelham did with his New York plan mill. But in the smaller city Norcross had an even greater impact; he would eventually design half of Boston's tenements of this era.

A number of tenement architects also transitioned into the role of developer as soon as it was practical. In 1889, after just three years in architectural practice in New York, Peter Herter started building tenements for himself. He would build half a dozen buildings over the next four years. Despite an 1893 bankruptcy, by 1900 he claimed to be one of the largest owners of tenement house property in the city.[57] Likewise, the firm Schneider & Herter started building tenements on its own account as early as 1892, with an elaborate tenement at 233–235 Delancey Street (Figure 4.13). After the turn of the century, these architects became heavily invested in uptown apartment houses, contributing four buildings that they both designed and developed to the illustrated *Apartment Houses of the Metropolis,* published in 1908 (Figure 4.14).[58] These buildings share formal similarities to their tenements of an earlier era, but their features were solidly middle class, with apartments containing maid's rooms, libraries, and private halls and a facade employing more-expensive limestone trim, instead of

Figure 4.13. Schneider & Herter Tenement, 233–235 Delancey Street, New York (1892; pictured in a 1901 survey photograph of properties to be expropriated for the Williamsburg Bridge approach; demolished 1901). Schneider & Herter, architect. This unusually paired tenement (two adjoining buildings treated as one) was one of the first both designed and developed by these prominent tenement architects. Courtesy of Lower East Side Photography Collection PR 251, box 2, folder 8, image 95155d, New-York Historical Society.

THE PENNINGTON

314-318 WEST 95th STREET

LOCATED on the south side of 95th Street, between West End Avenue and Riverside Drive. Two blocks from the Subway and three from the Broadway, Amsterdam and Sixth avenue surface cars.

BUILDING—Indiana limestone is used throughout the front, no terra cotta of any kind being employed.

Size, 75 feet front by 85 feet 6 inches deep.

Fireproof throughout.

Built by
SCHNEIDER & HERTER
1904

SCHNEIDER & HERTER
Architects

APARTMENTS—There are four apartments on a floor, in suites of four, five, seven and eight rooms and large foyer.

Entrance hall is wainscoted six feet high with marble. Trim in all rooms is of hardwood and rubbed to a high finish in parlors, libraries and dining rooms. All improvements, such as high class mantel pieces, with gas log grates, in parlors; tiled baths, porcelain lined washtubs and sinks and glass lined refrigerators in kitchen.

Rents from $50 to $100.

PLAN OF FIRST FLOOR

PLAN OF UPPER FLOORS

Figure 4.14. "The Pennington," a large elevator apartment building on West Ninety-Fifth Street, New York, designed and built by Schneider & Herter in 1904. It demonstrated the firm's evolution away from tenement design to the construction of elegant middle-class apartment buildings. Note the similarity between the plan of these apartments and those of the improved tenements of the 1890s. From *Apartment Houses of the Metropolis* (New York: G. C. Hesselgren Publishing, 1908), 201. Courtesy of Milstein Division of United States History, Local History, and Genealogy, The New York Public Library, Astor, Lenox, and Tilden Foundations.

terra-cotta, then too closely associated with tenements. Despite occasional financial troubles, the tenements were good to the three Herter brothers, as both architects and developers.

The Suppliers

The decorated tenement was only feasible because of the widespread industrial production of architectural ornamentation and other products.[59] These suppliers, many of whom were drawn from the same immigrant groups who dominated tenement construction, responded to the widening demand from all classes for elaborate forms. The competition among these firms, especially those specializing in sheet metal, seems to have been great; often a half dozen or more advertisers would appear in the *Record and Guide* offering cornices alone. This competition, along with increased mechanization, kept prices low and was a major factor in the democratization of elaborate forms. Ornament firms specialized in the manufacture of a range of other materials, including terra-cotta, artificial stone and cast concrete, tile, decorative brick, stained-glass, decorations made of composition or staff, and millwork and lumber.[60] Even traditional stone-cutting yards advertised their ability to rapidly reproduce carved forms in material such as Indiana limestone.[61] By the 1890s, there were nearly a half-dozen firms in New York that specialized in architectural terra-cotta alone. Some, such as the Excelsior Terra-Cotta works, also had offices in Boston.[62] The existence of these firms allowed architects and their clients to select from catalogs of stock designs that were fashionable and highly decorative.

Many of these firms maintained a high degree of pretense about the materials they sold. Their catalogs were elaborate, were heavily illustrated, and often contained ornate frontispieces and other graphic design elements.[63] In 1887 the Perth Amboy Terra Cotta Works of New Jersey, a well-known supplier, produced a catalog in much the same format and graphic style as the architectural sketchbooks that were popular at that moment. A woodcut "view of the works" suggested a preindustrial workshop-like setting.[64] Others, such as the New York Architectural Terra Cotta Company catalog of 1888, prefaced the listing of items for sale with a long essay not only extolling the particular virtues of the firm's product but connecting its use to the long tradition of Western architecture.[65]

One of the most important suppliers of material for the New York decorated tenement was the Empire Cornice Works, founded by Russian Jewish immigrants Leon Lanrowitz and Morris Fine. Their firm demonstrated the close interplay between tenement builders and ornament suppliers.[66] Both Lanrowitz and Fine immigrated in the 1880s and by the next decade were receiving numerous commissions for all sorts of work in pressed sheet metal.[67] They were a frequent supplier to Peter Herter.[68] Like many tenement architects, they were not content to simply provide materials for a booming market. Empire Cornice Works became a fairly significant player in tenement house development in East Harlem after the turn of the twentieth century. The corporation built a half-dozen six-story tenements there in 1905 alone, all designed by Bernstein & Bernstein. Despite the corporation's primary business, none of their buildings had particularly noteworthy cornices.

The Market

The primary concern for the tenement builders and their architects necessarily had to be pleasing the prospective tenants who would occupy their buildings. The intended population of the average new tenement ranged from petty merchants and skilled artisans to casual laborers, most of whom lived in family units, although many took in boarders. The precarious nature of their work and their low wages meant they needed to be as close as possible to the employment opportunities of the central city. Peter Herter made it clear that the intended market for his buildings was largely Jewish families, many of whom worked in the clothing trade, who were "willing to pay high rents because by reason of nearness of their homes to their places of work they save expenses in the matter of dinner and carfare."[69] This high rent translated to about five dollars a room at the turn of the twentieth century. These rents were almost 20 percent higher than in more peripheral neighborhoods but were fairly consistent with the neighborhood average.[70]

These rents would need to be drawn from precarious, and in some cases, declining wages; the decline in working-class wages in this period cast the betterment in living standards in greater relief. These improved apartments remained affordable for most in the working class. For instance, a male bricklayer, in New York in 1890 earned about $4 a day, down about 50 cents from his counterpart there immediately after the Civil War. In Boston a worker in the same trade could expect about $3.87 a day. A female dressmaker could expect about $1.67 a day in New York, and just over a $1 a day in Boston, down from about $2 for dressmakers in New York in 1870.[71] In either case the rent on these modern apartments would consume less than 30 percent of the full-time income of a single earner at these average wages.[72]

For a project to be successful, a builder had to have his building nearly fully rented within months of completion in order to successfully sell the building or obtain permanent financing before the construction loan came due, generally thirty to sixty days after the building was completed.[73] This period was the riskiest for builders. A delayed refinancing or sale could mean foreclosure and loss of the property. Excessive vacancies could result in a valuation for less than the outstanding loans, meaning financial ruin. This risk served as ample incentive to provide the best housing possible, as builders competed ferociously for tenants. To quickly fill their buildings, builders offered below-market rent, months of free rent, or other bonuses as an inducement to new tenants.

Even at market rates, newly constructed apartments were frequently offered for rent at little more than those in the tumble-down buildings they replaced. The primary rationale to build new buildings was that they were considerably larger than the buildings they replaced, generating much more revenue on expensive lots. Attractive and commodious new buildings also drew a more stable class of tenants. As the *New York Times* noted in 1899, "owners of old tenement houses have learned to their sorrow that the new tenement houses have constituted a drain on their tenants, the temptation being, not unnaturally, for tenants to seek better accommodations and conveniences." As a result, it was often more profitable to build improved tenements than accept lower rents or less desirable tenants in their smaller, old buildings.[74] But landlords knew even the best new building did not excite tenants for long; tenements were said to depreciate at about 3 percent a year.[75] That is why Peter Herter suggested in 1900 that a landlord should plan on making his money back in the first five years of ownership, before tenants could be attracted away by newer buildings, a perennial problem of rental housing.[76]

Because many small builders chose to build a tenement for the complex host of reasons discussed earlier in this chapter, and because they were not financed through traditional institutions, they often disregarded market conditions, leading to a frequent oversupply. If bad for owners, this oversupply gave tenants a fair amount of leverage. They frequently exercised some control over the buildings they chose to inhabit, and builders ignored their desires at their peril. Particularly when robust construction activity provided an abundant supply of new buildings, and of builders desperate for tenants, residents could exercise a good degree of choice. They often traded up for better apartments. Many tenants moved frequently in search of better deals and better spaces.[77]

The dynamics of this market, combined with the social and cultural inclinations of tenement builders and architects, were responsible for the dramatic rise in the quality of working-class housing experienced in these cities in the last half of the nineteenth century. But these buildings came about rapidly and affordably thanks to the deliberate and concerted efforts of designers who devoted considerable attention to the problems of tenement design and construction methods.

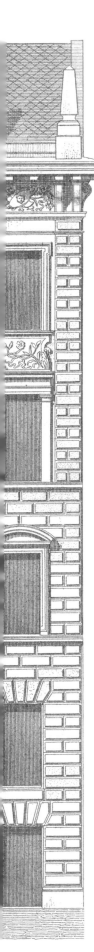

Chapter 5

Destroying the Rookeries

How the Tenement Was Designed and Built

The method of the new landlord in nearly every case is the same. He purchases an old building, tears out the plaster partitions, rearranging them so as to give a larger number of rooms, builds an ell so as to cover as much of the ground as possible, tears down the old front wall and erects a new one of showy yellow brick, which seems to be particularly attractive to tenants' eyes and almost universally makes the front cellar do duty as a basement store. The old material is used as far as possible. New material is of the cheapest grade.

Robert A. Woods, 1903

Joseph Shoolman may have bristled a bit at having to pay Frederick Norcross to draw up blueprints and specifications for the new tenement he was about to build at the corner of Salem Street and Carrol Place in the heart of the North End, Boston's burgeoning immigrant enclave (Figure 5.1). The perhaps one hundred dollars or so he paid for the documents in the spring of 1901 surely could have been better spent elsewhere, but the architect's help turned out to be a blessing in navigating the increasingly complex and mercurial bureaucracy of the city building department. Norcross had begun drawing plans before Shoolman had even purchased the lot, then occupied by a row of run-down wooden colonial-era buildings. He filed the plans the very afternoon the deed to the property was signed; the building department approved them and issued a permit thirteen days later. Absent meddling from city hall or reformers like Robert A. Woods, then casting a critical eye on the methods of new landlords in the neighborhood, Shoolman likely could have managed the project on his own. Boston tenement builders, like Daniel

McLaughlin, had made do without an architect a generation earlier, simply submitting a rough sketch for quick approval by the city. A carpenter by trade, Shoolman had arrived from his native Vilna via New York just ten years earlier, joined shortly by his teenage half-brother Max, who would go into business with him.[1] The older Shoolman planned to serve as the contractor for the Salem Street project, hiring day laborers to do the heavy lifting but overseeing most of the work himself. The $14,000 job was comparatively small, a store with three modern seven-room apartments above, each with a full bath and dining room with china closet (see Figure 2.11A). The specifications Norcross made were short and simple, a single handwritten page of just under 250 words that the architect filed in duplicate with the building department.[2] Absent were the calls for "workmanlike" construction or material "free of defects" usually found in building specifications. Instead the document was a mere accounting of the materials to be used on the project, specifying only general categories, like Indiana limestone trimmings, a galvanized iron cornice and skylights, and painted North Carolina pine trim on the interior, all of which were to be simply "merchantable," and for which Norcross employed shorthand, like "apply usual hardware." Such brevity, architectural historian Catherine Bishir has noted, suggested an environment in which most aspects of the design and construction process were well understood by the architect, owner, and builder, the latter two being the same in this case.[3] If he had little use for the specifications, Shoolman certainly did not pay much attention to Norcross's elevation drawing for the building's facade either (Figure 5.2). Norcross's design was basic, a rote Classical Revival structure with splayed lintels and molded keystones on the upper floors, and a modest console cornice. But Shoolman seemed to be calling the shots as far as the building's ornamentation was concerned, clearly interested in a building that would be attractive to him and his tenants' taste. Following the basic patterns set by Norcross, the builder chose window caps and a cornice that were heavier, more elaborate, and more idiosyncratic than the architect's design. These elements were stock items, likely selected by Shoolman from a catalog or showroom. From the time excavation began in April until the first tenant moved in that November, Norcross likely never visited the site.[4] The architect had at least eight other tenements on the drawing board at the same time.

As Shoolman's tenement was rising in Boston, Rosalie Hyams, the widow of Vilna-born Joel Hyams, was sitting in a Manhattan courtroom, facing architect Peter Herter and contractor Edward Conolly. Over a decade earlier, the pair had designed and built an elaborate tenement for Joel on Varrick Street, then surrounded by notorious slums owned by Trinity Church, along with a twin on Grove Street. It had been a hectic but businesslike operation that generated reams of paperwork, which now had to be dragged in to yet another hearing (Figure 5.3).[5] The volume of documentation suggested the process of building Hyams's building was quite different from Shoolman's. Hyams's twenty-three-unit Rosalie Flats, a $40,000, buff-brick tenement, had required extensive written specifications for the carpenters, masons, plumbers, and ironworkers, each containing dozens of typewritten pages.[6] The documents required,

Figure 5.1. Joseph Shoolman Tenement, 112 Salem Street, Boston (1901). Frederick Norcross, architect. For plan, see Figure 2.11A. Photograph by Sean Litchfield.

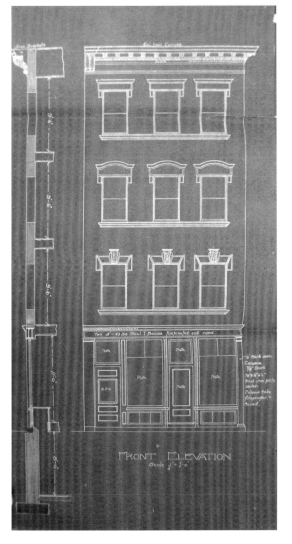

Figure 5.2. Elevation, Joseph Shoolman Tenement, 112 Salem Street, Boston, 1901. Frederick Norcross, architect. The architect called for a simpler design of the window caps and cornice than the builder ultimately chose. Courtesy of Trustees of Boston Public Library.

for example, that "all the materials used are to be of the best of their several kinds," and specified the make and model of everything from door latches to water closets. Herter provided numerous pages of drawings, elevations, sections, and framing diagrams. He submitted full-scale drawings of the cornice with its story-tall pinnacles and semicircular pediments in sheet metal, directing stonemasons on how to carve the cement and bluestone ornament ("which are to be strictly followed"), and even the elaborate interior trim for the parlor windows.[7] Little was left to chance, or choice, once construction had started. When Hyams later insisted on personally selecting the marbleized slate mantles and cast-iron summer screens for the parlors, in place of the models specified in the contract, accounting for even this slight variation would become a matter of contention.

As the contractually obligated six-month construction process began in the spring of 1888, employees of Herter's firm were constantly on-site supervising Conolly, his numerous subcontractors, and dozens of day laborers.[8] Herter attended the site every day, while Hyams, a feather dealer by trade, vacationed with his family at Long Branch, on the New Jersey shore. Once each of the eight phases of the project—from excavation, to superstructure, to plastering, to final decoration—was completed to his satisfaction, Herter would issue a certificate to Conolly, and Hyams would release

Figure 5.3. View of Baxter Street from Franklin Street, New York, pictured in 1913 with Herter Brothers–designed building at far left. The corner building was similar to Joel Hyams's 1888 Varrick Street building, the subject of a lawsuit between the contractor and builder's widow. (No surviving images of that building are known; its Grove Street twin is extant but altered.) Note particularly the story-tall cornice pinnacles with their polychrome paint scheme. On Hyams's building these were painted red with gold leaf. This Baxter Street block faced the group of buildings dubbed by Jacob Riis the "Dens of Death," pictured in Figure I.4. The buildings to the right of the Herter-designed tenement are visible in the background of that picture. Courtesy of George F. Arata/Museum of the City of New York, X2010.11.183.

payment for that portion of the contract. The process went smoothly through the first seven phases; the slipshod work became evident only as construction drew to a close. The massive cornice not only began to leak but was so insecurely attached that "every breath of wind" rattled it; it needed to be taken down and rebuilt. The drainage was not finished to code, and fines were due the health department. The gas for the lighting leaked. The real gold leaf that was to decorate the fire escapes and cornice was a dull imitation that tarnished quickly. Worse, fish oil was discovered to have been substituted for the interior paint. The deeply projecting stone sills were carelessly damaged. The fancy centerpiece was missing from the front vestibule. There were numerous other issues. Unsatisfied with the sloppy work, Hyams paid other contractors to fix the building's problems as he worked to quickly find tenants. Herter's inspectors agreed that the job was problematic, withholding the final certificate. As Conolly parted ways with a lien against the property rejected by the court, it seemed the matter was settled.

Then in 1899, fully a decade after the building was completed and occupied, Herter mysteriously and without his client's knowledge issued the final certificate to Conolly's son. It was an apparent act of fraud, and now the contractor was suing for payment. Perhaps trying to evade suspicion, in court Herter, a witness, would level the sensational accusation that the letters and invoices outlining Hyams's dissatisfaction with the building, and Herter's acknowledgement of it, were themselves forgeries, somehow pasted together and slipped into his letter book by a disgruntled former bookkeeper. Why, Herter claimed, the type on the letters did not match that of his secretary's old Remington typewriter, since given to his brother Frank. Other employees testified that the bookkeeper, then deceased, seemed to have been a bit too friendly with Hyams at his weekly visits to the firm's office on lower Broadway. Conflicting invoices were presented. The costs of mantels and summer screens were parsed and examined. The contents of Hyams's checkbook from the Germania Bank, showing transactions with dozens of suppliers and contractors, were dutifully entered into the court record. The case and its numerous appeals dragged on for years, with a court ultimately siding with Conolly, despite documents from both sides seemingly fishier than the building's paint. Hyams died during the proceedings, and his widow, Rosalie, whose name was stamped in sheet-metal letters covered in tarnished, fake gold leaf on the building's cornice, was forced to sell the property to pay the judgment. The complexity of the construction documents had not worked as intended. Instead of protecting the parties involved from disagreement, they only heightened the confusion and added opportunities for mischief.

The varying cases of Hyams's and Shoolman's tenements highlighted the contrast between two sharply divergent methods of design and construction and described two fundamentally different relationships between builder and architect and between the owner and the construction work. In the process of building Shoolman's Boston tenement, the architect's role was limited to bureaucratic matters, providing documents newly required by city agencies. Norcross operated what observers derisively called a "plan mill," providing stock, easily executable, and essentially fungible plans that were satisfactory to the building department but served little other functional or aesthetic purpose. He exerted little control over the building process itself, which continued along older, more informal lines, directed by an owner-builder who oversaw most aspects of the project. Crucially, in this relationship, the owner had a direct hand in shaping the building's appearance and directly oversaw the process of its construction. This has been widely understood to be the manner in which most tenements were designed; indeed, Norcross's name is found as the architect of almost half of Boston's tenements.

Hyams's tenement, on the other hand, was created through a formal and modern, if nonetheless problematic, process. Here the owner, whose business was in a trade other than building, kept his distance from the day-to-day construction work, perhaps to the detriment of the final product. Employees of Herter's comparatively large, hierarchically organized firm replete with typewriters and bookkeepers, secretaries and site supervisors, had a hand in each stage of the design process, overseeing the work of a professional contractor and numerous specialized tradesmen. The building owner's role was limited mostly to signing checks. Herter and Hyams's relationship was mediated by contracts, specifications, and drawings. Herter's firm, representative of the increased professionalization and specialization of American architectural practice in the late nineteenth century, operated along modern lines, apparent ethical violations notwithstanding.[9] Here, the owner exerted influence over the appearance of his structure only with difficulty, as demonstrated by the conflict over Hyams's purchase of mantels and summer screens. While the more expensive, ornate, and complex tenements of New York lent themselves to the development of these modern methods, both practices seem to have been at work in either city: architects George Pelham and Michael Bernstein were both accused by various sources as operating as plan mills.

Given the volume of construction, it is difficult to ascertain whether a firm operated in the manner of Norcross or Herter, that is, as a plan mill or a professional architectural firm, or somewhere on the spectrum between the two. Nonetheless, in either case the architects and builders had worked the design and construction process out to a science. In the process they effected a rapid transformation of slum neighborhoods, replacing them with large and modern buildings. Despite the complications and disputes inherent in such a process, construction proceeded at an unprecedented pace. Whole blocks, often filled with ancient buildings, were swept away seemingly overnight. But the breakneck pace of construction obscured a longer and more complex design and decision-making process that occurred before one brick was laid.

The Tenement Design Problem

Much of the tenement architect's design work centered around humanizing and enriching the working-class landscape. Streets lined with four-to-seven-story buildings, single-pitch roofed, with windows punched at regular intervals, were something heretofore unknown in the American city.[10] The lockstep repetition of elements within the landscape caused a sense of tedium and alienation that would have made these neighborhoods untenable, particularly in an era that increasingly valued individuality and complexity in architecture (Figure 5.4). It was largely the question of variety and individuality with which decorated tenement designers concerned themselves. It was left to the designer to invent solutions that could break this scale and overcome the tedium and repetition without fundamentally changing the building's program.

In this regard, tenement architects seem to have operated largely on precedent. Almost no published plans have been found for fully decorated tenements, and rarely do such buildings appear in American pattern books. A series of tenement plans and elevations were published in 1879 in the *Plumber and Sanitary Engineer* as part of a competition to improve the sanitary conditions of tenement interiors. Architect James E. Ware's winning competition entry, from which the dumbbell plan was derived, became the basic, improved New York tenement floor plan for a decade.[11] However, the generally austere facades suggested by competition architects were largely ignored by builders. Even the *Real Estate Record and Builders' Guide* rarely published tenement exteriors. Pattern books were also of little help when it came to designing the tenement facade, as they tended to focus on single-family houses or commercial architecture. Perhaps the most useful published source for tenement architects was William B. Tuthill's *The City Residence: Its Design and Construction.* Published in 1890 by William T. Comstock, Tuthill's nearly two-hundred-page guide offered extensive advice on formulating tenement plans, among other urban building types, as well as detailed specifications for their construction. Yet, despite this level of detail, he remained largely silent on the appearance of the tenement facade.[12]

The Home of a Thousand People.

Figure 5.4. "The Home of a Thousand People," New York, 1892. This drawing illustrates the monotony even of respectably ornamented tenements. Modest cornices and window caps did not break the tedium of this row of early buildings. From William T. Elsing, "Life in New York Tenement-Houses as Seen by a City Missionary," *Scribner's* 11 (1892): 697.

Despite the comparative lack of published plans, in both cities the pattern for tenement design was well understood, with innovations being quickly adopted by large numbers of builders and architects. Instead of relying on published plans, architects seem to have drawn on experience and the example offered by neighbors and colleagues within the comparatively small and close-knit tenement network.[13] Common tenement design was the result of the specialization of these firms that had enabled trial and error. This resulted in largely standardized solutions in terms of building shape, height, and floor plan. There was simply no reason to reinvent these elements for each new project.

Within the constrained program of the tenement, it was primarily through ornament that the tenement architect demonstrated knowledge of architectural fashion. Some architects developed, indeed, quite idiosyncratic styles. For instance, while German immigrant Jobst Hoffman's tenements of the early 1880s were relatively conventional, with pressed red-brick facades, with a limited use of encaustic tile, by the early 1890s Hoffman had developed a unique style that was shared by few other architects (compare Plate 11 and Figure 3.12). In the buildings of this decade, he employed buff-orange roman brick facades, elaborate figural panels, engaged columns that were heavily foliated in a naturalistic manner, and shallow cornices. While perhaps his style was the most unique, Hoffman was not alone in developing a recognizable style. These architects did not arbitrarily select conventionalized material that was readily available in trade catalogs but used stock architectural elements consciously and deliberately toward specific ends. Yet the architect still needed to mediate a relationship with a builder, who, as we will see, exerted influence over the building's final appearance.

Once an architect found a facade design that worked, even an elaborate or uncommon one, he frequently recycled it on other projects. Others were quick to plagiarize designs. For instance, Alexandre I. Finkle copied his own 1889 design for the facade of 84 Madison Street in New York (Plate 3, *center*), built by Albert Stake, in a building the next year for Stake at 104 Forsyth Street (Plate 5). He simply switched the name of the American president on the cornice: Lincoln for Madison Street, Garfield for Forsyth Street. This design was similar to an elaborate facade he employed a year earlier for J. D. Krast on three tenements in two separate locations a block apart (Plate 12). Yet, next door to the Lincoln building on Madison Street, Finkle employed an entirely different design for a second 1889 tenement for Stake. That more conventional design was repeated not only by Finkle for another client at 125 Madison Street (Plate 13) but also in 1890 by Charles Rentz at 43 Henry Street, and in 1892 by Severste & Cusack in a building at 73 Monroe Street. At least a dozen other similar versions were built, the work of various architects. Much of the early work of prolific architect George Pelham was also a variation on this facade, as it had been interpreted in the early 1890s by Charles Rentz (Plate 14). This facade was also used by developer Joseph Buttenweiser, on projects designed both by Pelham and by Louis F. Heinecke, a favorite architect of Italian tenement builders on Mott and Mulberry Streets. This formulation, perhaps developed by Finkle, represented the most common arrangement of ornamental forms during the widespread adoption of the decorated tenement in the 1890s.

Absent a common source, this level of cribbing makes it difficult to assign authorship and complicates any attempt for a meaningful connoisseurial approach to the tenement facade, even for the most elaborate designs. Indeed, as in the closely related garment trade, the open pirating of designs, sometimes with the aid of the designers themselves, was a common practice.[14] Sometimes repetition was even desired. In Boston, for example, the tenements at 28 and 32 Prince Street were nearly identical but for their varying brick colors (Figure 5.5). Each had unusual horseshoe-arch-shaped window caps on the third floor, and a parallel range of cast-stone decorations around the other windows. These adjoining buildings were built ten years apart by different architects and different builders.[15] A good tenement facade was not something to waste.

In both cities one of the most telling factors designers took into account when determining the extent of a building's ornamentation program was location. Paradoxically, the best facades were reserved for the worst locations, suggesting the use of architectural ornament in helping recast the downtown neighborhoods, long dismissed as slums, as once again respectable. At the same time, large tracts in more peripheral neighborhoods without such associations were also being developed with tenements. Here a lack of constraints allowed building operations to proceed on a much larger

Figure 5.5. *Left*, Vito Sessa Tenement, 28 Prince Street, Boston (1906). Frederick Norcross, architect. *Right*, Joseph Rudnick Tenement, 32 Prince Street, Boston (1896). William E. Clarke, architect. Two nearly identical tenement facades built a decade apart by different builders and architects. Photograph by Sean Litchfield.

scale, with many more long rows of identical buildings. While many of these buildings were still decorated tenements, they were as a rule considerably less ornamental. Compare Herter Brothers' early work, like the Wolf Baum Tenement at 375 Broome Street, to the block of a half-dozen store-and-tenement buildings they designed on the north side of Seventy-Eighth Street in Yorkville for German-born James Schnugg the same year (compare Figure 5.6 and Figure 3.19).[16] This location, although on blocks filled with newly erected tenements, was much more peripheral and at least nominally more respectable than Broome Street. In the Schnugg buildings, terra-cotta ornament was absent, replaced by brick pattern work, and the cornice, window caps, panels, and belt courses showed considerable restraint. No figural ornament of any kind appeared. The cornice was made of simple, widely spaced brackets with anemic roofline pediments. This simplification was standard on tenements in more marginal locations.[17]

These locations, being developed essentially ex novo, had few of the negative associations of the slum stereotypes that adhered to the older neighborhoods. These immigrant builders lavished the most ornament in neighborhoods considered slums,

Figure 5.6. James Schnugg Tenement, 447 East Seventy-Eighth Street, New York (1886). Herter Brothers, architect. A modest design for a long row of tenements at a peripheral location. Compare to the contemporary Wolf Baum Tenement at 375 Broome Street by the same architect (Figure 3.19). Photograph by Sean Litchfield.

while saving more austere designs for areas without such associations. Large concentrations of these modestly decorated tenements were to be found in Harlem; Williamsburg, Brooklyn; and Ridgewood, Queens, among other places.[18] A similar pattern existed in Boston, where tenements in peripheral East Boston, Roxbury, and Chelsea displayed modest ornamentation compared to those in the North and West Ends. Chelsea, which had absorbed a substantial outflow of immigrants from the North End, was extensively rebuilt with modest decorated tenements after a major fire in 1908 (Figure 5.7).

The Role of the Tenement Architect and Plans

The role of the architect in the design of the tenement was contested. At minimum they were employed by builders to furnish plans acceptable to city building inspectors.[19] Period sources indicate that architects were paid between $25 and $125 to prepare plans and submit them to the building department for approval.[20] This fee represented less than 1 percent of the construction cost of a typical tenement and was far less than the 4 to 6 percent that was then becoming common among elite architects.[21] Many thought even this did not buy much. "The rows of tenement houses run up by speculative builders," the *Real Estate Record and Builders' Guide* sniffed in 1884, "require no more than a draftsman who knows enough to reproduce forms given in the

Figure 5.7. Intersection of Park Street and Congress Avenue, Chelsea, Massachusetts. After a destructive fire in 1908, immigrant builders and architects, many with experience in the North and West Ends of Boston, employed modest versions of the decorated tenement in this dense port city's reconstruction. Compare the building at right (circa 1908) to the Etta Lebowitch Tenement, 68 Prince Street, Boston (Plate 2). Photograph by Sean Litchfield.

Stair Builder's Guide."[22] Tenement architects were frequently derided as "plan mills" that provided stock plans to builders without supervising the operations, potentially never visiting the site.

In this case, the builder or one of his employees would supervise the work of constructing the building. During his time working as an assistant to a tenement developer, future architect Lafayette Goldstone noted that his boss, likely Charles I. Weinstein, purchased plans from George Pelham for just $25 per set. "Standardized plans were used whenever the standard 25-foot lot was available," Goldstone said, noting, "The plans were well studied and ingeniously contrived considering the requirements: a maximum number of rooms of minimum dimensions legally allowed."[23] It was Goldstone's responsibility to check the measurements on-site, make corrections, and supervise the building process. While reformers complained constantly of this practice, its extent is difficult to document. Pelham was the most prolific architect in New York, designing at least 5 percent of the tenements there. Given this volume, surely the largest-scale tenement architects functioned in this manner.

But testimony in the *Connolly v. Hyams* lawsuit and numerous other period sources illuminated a different method, in which the architect or his employees provided close, daily supervision and administered the site.[24] Many architects, it seems, played a role beyond selling standardized plans to developers. Architects sometimes served as foremen and agents on tenement projects. During tenement builder Charles Buddensiek's 1885 manslaughter trial, some workmen described the role of his architect George Spitzer as that of bookkeeper, others as site foreman. Materials dealers recognized him as the builder's agent and took orders from him. A building department official even called the architect the despised builder's "alter ego."[25] Buddensiek himself testified that Spitzer was an employee who was hired as "a bookkeeper, and an architect to make plans and specifications for the building department." Yet, he claimed, he never saw the architect draw any of those plans and could not articulate what in his professional background qualified Spitzer to perform these duties. The architect himself was absent from the court proceedings in defiance of a subpoena.[26]

Other architects treated tenement design like any other commercial commission, preparing elaborate presentation drawings, detailed specifications, and other professional trappings and directing the supervision of the site with a large office staff.[27] For example, John Butler Snook was a prominent and prolific New York architect who worked mostly on commercial commissions, designing numerous cast-iron loft structures. In the post–Civil War period Snook oversaw a large and professional practice, with an office staff numbering nearly three dozen and with hierarchically arranged teams of draftsmen and tracers, as well as numerous support staff.[28] Among his firm's work was a number of tenements for a variety of clients, including the estates of well-established New York families, as well as for German immigrant builders. Most notably among these were Jacob and David Korn, Prussian-born clothing dealers who built a substantial number of modern tenements in the 1870s.[29] Snook's office, while prominent, was typical of tenement designers of this period. However, a remarkable group of his renderings, preserved in the collection of the New-York Historical Society, clearly illustrate that even when employing a standardized solution, architects generally treated a tenement commission with much the same level of care as other jobs, producing full sets of architectural drawings, specifications, and other documents, all carefully rendered. These documents confounded the notion that tenement designers universally operated as plan mills. Snook's drawings evince a high level of care and deliberation in planning and presenting a tenement facade, even an austere scheme. Finely rendered, full-color, ink-washed drawings exist for both the front and rear elevations for dozens of tenements (Plate 15). Colored drawings were provided even for the most austere type of utilitarian tenement, such as the 1891 building Snook designed for the G. L. Lordes estate at 130–138 Attorney Street (Figure 5.8).[30]

Figure 5.8. Elevation, Lordes Tenement, 138 Attorney Street, New York, 1891 (demolished). John B. Snook, architect. A colored pen-and-ink drawing for a modest speculative tenement. Courtesy of John B. Snook Architectural Record Collection (PR64), box 9, project 76; image 95523d, New-York Historical Society.

These drawings also suggest that both tenement architects and their clients engaged with architectural fashion, within the constraints of the industrially produced material available to them.[31] In his 1874 drawings for a block of Henry Street tenements for Jacob Korn, Snook provided carefully rendered and elaborate inked drawings of the front elevation (Plate 16). He also presented his client two options for the cast-iron window and door surrounds. Korn could choose segmental arch door and window surrounds with foliate patterns, an Italianate design common since the 1860s, or pediment caps with more angular motifs, an increasingly common choice more closely related to the Neo-Grec motifs then popular in French and German architecture schools (Figure 5.9). These new designs could also be produced even more cheaply than the more delicate foliate patterns. Interestingly, Snook did not sketch the matching angular, incised brackets that were usually selected by builders who used newer motifs (see Figure I.8, *left*). Plenty of builders mixed the two, including Korn's brother, David, in a tenement he built to Snook's designs at 169 East Broadway, choosing angular brackets and foliate window caps. While Jacob Korn eventually chose the Neo-Grec caps for the Henry Street tenements, the sketch suggested the role of the client in guid-

Figure 5.9. Detail of elevation, Jacob Korn Tenements, 190–196 Henry Street, New York, 1874 (demolished). John B. Snook, architect. Note the architect's suggestion of a choice between Italianate and Neo-Grec window surrounds, both common at this moment. For entire drawing in color, see Plate 16. Courtesy of John B. Snook Architectural Record Collection PR64, folder 6, project 40; image95387d, New-York Historical Society.

ing the final style of the building.[32] It also demonstrated the interchangeability with which builders and architects viewed ornamental items. The style was of little or no consequence, and the decorative effect, affordability, and function mattered most.

In many cases tenement builders simply could not make the reality of their finished buildings match the ideals represented in their architect's renderings. While few Boston tenement architects seem to have employed the elaborate inked drawings that Snook created, elevation drawings were frequently part of the set of documents filed with the building department to obtain a permit, even though elevations were not yet required by the city. As in the case of Joseph Shoolman's Salem Street tenement, these documents often illustrated a striking difference between the ornamental schemes that appear on the architects' blueprints and what actually was built. This was particularly the case with the work of Frederick Norcross, who often drew rather modest facades, with placeholders for items to be selected as the buildings went up. Similar trends were also noticeable in the elevations filed by Charles A. Halstrom. His 1894 elevation drawing for Finn and Dobkin's 124 Prince Street tenement, among the earliest decorated tenements in that city, depicted a unified composition with colossal brick piers, molded belt courses, fifth-floor roundels, and a heavily elaborated door surround (Figure 5.10). While the finished product followed the basic outlines of Halstrom's design, it was more simply and crudely rendered (Figure 5.11). The pilasters were reduced in width, and the terra-cotta corbels supporting them were omitted, along with the belt course and roundels. The substitutions made on the door frame most clearly showed the limitations builders faced in producing a decorated tenement, particularly at this early juncture in Boston, before the wide availability of architectural materials. The surround Halstrom drew was to be elaborate but well proportioned. But Finn and Dobkin's substitution of anemically proportioned pilasters, a more crudely carved frieze with cartoonishly rendered lion heads, and a glass fanlight instead of the laurel-encrusted tympanum the architect proposed, gave a result that was both simpler and more idiosyncratic than Halstrom's design. Sometimes the opposite case was true, and substitutions resulted in a better-quality treatment. This result was most clearly seen in Halstrom's 1898 design for The Gothic for Louis Segel in the West End (Figure 5.12). In this case, Segel seems to have insisted on a more ambitious treatment than Halstrom's simple brick facade with modest door surround. So in its place a facade of cut stone, a more richly carved door piece, and a sheet-metal cornice in a "gothick" pattern were provided (Figure 5.13).

These variations suggest that the owner/builder played a critical role in shaping the aesthetics of their building. They also highlight the flexibility of ornamental forms enabled by the industrial production of elements. It may in fact be the case that architects, some of whom had training primarily as engineers, simply vetted the builder's plans, providing the drawings required by the city. Yet the variety and enthusiasm with which industrially made ornament was adopted suggest designers engaged in contemporary architectural discourse even if they did not have full control over the final appearance of the facade.

Figure 5.10. Elevation, Finn and Dobkins Tenement, 124 Prince Street, Boston, 1894. Charles A. Halstrom, architect. Courtesy of Trustees of Boston Public Library.

Figure 5.11. Finn and Dobkins Tenement, 124 Prince Street, Boston (1894). Charles A. Halstrom, architect. For plan, see Figure 2.10A. For elevation, see Figure 5.10. Note the much cruder rendering of the door surround, pilaster corbels, and fourth-floor belt course. Photograph by Sean Litchfield.

Figure 5.12. Elevation drawing, Louis Segel Tenement, "The Gothic," 47 Allen Street, Boston, 1898 (demolished). Attributed to Charles A. Halstrom, architect. Courtesy of Trustees of Boston Public Library.

Figure 5.13. Louis Segel Tenement, "The Gothic," 47 Allen Street, Boston (1898; pictured in 1959 shortly before demolition). Attributed to Charles A. Halstrom, architect. For plan, see Figure 2.15A. For interiors, see Figures 2.5 and 2.6. For architect's elevation, see Figure 5.12. Note that the builder completely altered Halstrom's original scheme, choosing a finer cut stone facade and elaborate door surround. Library of Congress, Prints and Photographs Division, HABS MASS,13-BOST,63-1.

Training the Tenement Architect

The bulk of nineteenth-century tenement architects lacked formal training but learned their craft through apprenticeship, often finding early employment with engineers, building contractors, or other working architects.[33] This type of training was not unusual for many architects in this period. Frederick Norcross, designer of half of Boston's tenements, received only an elementary education in Boston public schools. The son of a railroad foreman, he left school at age fourteen and soon thereafter he went to work as a draftsman in the office of Frank E. Kidder, a structural engineer and architectural consultant best known for the popular guidebook *The Architect's and Builder's Pocket-Book.* Norcross remained in Kidder's office until 1896, when he began his own practice.[34] The slightly older Boston architect Charles A. Halstrom, from whom Norcross seems to have cribbed many of his ideas, also was from a working-class background. Son of Swedish immigrants—his father worked as a laborer and stevedore—Halstrom had grown up in a crowded tenement on Foster Court in the North End. He was educated in Boston public schools and does not seem to have had formal architecture training. English-born John Butler Snook, the New York architect, was also largely self-taught, having apprenticed with his father, a carpenter, before working as a building contractor.[35]

On the whole, by the twentieth century, tenement architects tended to be better educated than their nineteenth-century counterparts, paralleling trends in the field at large. They were also more likely to be second-generation immigrants. In Boston Nathan Silverman studied naval engineering at the Lawrence Scientific School at Harvard University, from which he received a degree in 1904. The son of Russian Jewish immigrants, he soon went into business with his brothers Peter and David, a draftsman and engineer, respectively.[36] Together they formed the Silverman Engineering Company, which became a major tenement design firm in the North and West Ends. They worked in a modest Classical Revival style that owed much to the work of earlier tenement architects, often indistinguishable from that of the older Norcross, whose office was in the same Cornhill building (Figure 5.14).

In New York, Lafayette Goldstone, son of Polish immigrants, was personally tutored by the architect William Cusack, who, among other things, sent the boy to the 1893 World's Fair to report on his observations. Later Goldstone apprenticed in the office of Cleverdon & Putzel, who were Weil & Mayer's go-to architects for loft buildings, where he experienced anti-Semitic harassment from the construction workers he supervised daily. After a period working as an assistant to a tenement developer, a job he found difficult and distasteful, he opened his own practice in the first years of the twentieth century. Many of his first commissions were for tenements, which he designed in a quite ornamental Classical Revival style similar to the contemporary work of Michael Bernstein. But he considered the tenement work to be of low standing and was worried about the social stigma that came with it. His biographer noted, "At that time any architect designing tenement houses or 'flats' was looked down upon by his fashionable confreres many of whom affected canes, flowing ties, spats, and ribbons attached to their eyeglasses."[37] He used his early tenement commissions as a stepping-stone to more prestigious work. He quickly became a prominent designer of fine elevator apartment houses, department stores, and even the 1912 Grand Street skyscraper for Sender Jarmulowsky's bank. This apparent shame at the stigma of tenement work seems to have impelled many to work in other fields as soon as it was viable.

In the earlier period a smaller group of tenement architects had a comparatively prestigious European training, at least in schools of building if not fine arts.[38] If their educational achievement and backgrounds did not impel them to the most elite American architectural circles, they were better educated than most builders and architects of working-class housing. They seem to have played an important role in promoting the ideas that would lead to the widespread adoption of the decorated tenement, designing some of the most sophisticated buildings of the type. These architects were the tastemakers for the decorated tenement, developing forms imitated by other builders. One of the most interesting of this group was Alexandre I. Finkle, a native of New Orleans and the son of Polish immigrants. From New Orleans he went to France, where he graduated from the National and Imperial Academy of Fine Arts. In Paris he studied painting under Henry Moore, and architecture in the atelier of

Figure 5.14. Israel Flink Tenement, 35 Myrtle Street, Boston (1910). Silverman Engineering Company, architect. Designed by a pair of fledgling, Harvard-trained architect brothers in a style that had been used by the older architect Frederick Norcross for more than a decade. Photograph by Sean Litchfield.

prominent architects Charles-Auguste Questel and Jean-Louis Pascal. This education perhaps more than prepared him for the design of a series of richly sculptural tenements with evocative iconography, such as his 1888 buildings for J. D. Karst on East Fourth Street (see Plate 12). An architect of speculative residential buildings, Finkle was said to have designed "a vast number of fashionable private dwellings."[39]

However, given the patterns of immigration to America in the nineteenth century, German institutions were the most common background for many immigrant designers of working-class housing. Peter Herter was among the most prominent German-trained tenement architects. Born in 1851, his education at the well-known Bauakademie in Berlin was interrupted in 1870 when he was called to fight in the Franco-Prussian War. After the war, he was engaged in a large business of both public and private commissions in his native Bonn, as well as in Berlin and other cities.[40] While it may be assumed that his brothers, Frank and Henry, had similar training, evidence for this has not yet come to light. Likewise, a number of other German-immigrant tenement architects in New York in the same period, including William Kurtzer, Frederick Ebeling, and Jobst Hoffman, among others, came to New York as adults and began working shortly after their arrival, although the nature and extent of their training abroad are also unclear. All were important designers of decorated tenements. A generation older than Herter, Henry Fernbach was also a graduate of the Bauakademie, which he attended before arriving in New York in 1855. A prolific commercial architect, Fernbach was well known for his designs of cast-iron lofts, although no tenement commissions of his have come to light.[41]

The Decorated Tenement and German Architectural Theory

The Bauakademie of the 1860s and 1870s, in which Herter was educated, emphasized functional expediency in matters of construction, material, and decoration. A polytechnic school for the practical education of prospective state building officials, the school's pedagogy was heavily influenced by Karl Friedrich Schinkel, one of the most prominent architects and theorists of the nineteenth century. Schinkel advocated an understanding and expression of the relationship between structure and ornament in classical architecture. His 1832 design for the institution's brick and terra-cotta building in Berlin, with its trabeated facade and high-relief spandrel panels, was a study in his late architectural theory, and its influence can be seen in the work of many academy students, including Herter.[42]

While it was by no means a pure representation of any high-level theory, two strains of nineteenth-century German architectural thought were important for their relationship to the decorated tenement. In the post-Schinkel era, the Bauakademie retained the neoclassical outlook of earlier periods but with a heightened interest in ornamentation and structural rationalism, based on classical Greek architecture. During Herter's attendance, the institute's primary theorist was Carl Bötticher, author of *Techtonik de Hellene,* a landmark study of Greek structure and ornament, which was a major part of the school's curriculum. Bötticher emphasized the differentiation of architectural construction and decoration. There was an interest in exploiting new structural methods and decorative techniques, particularly the use of iron and terra-cotta. He also advocated an "intellectual eclecticism" that encouraged the intermixing of loosely classical forms. There was also a greatly renewed interest in architectural ornament that contrasted with the monumental austerity of the earlier work of Schinkel. Students of Bötticher were noted for the richness of their ornament, their free combinations of historical forms, their interest in classical and figurative elements, and what architectural historian József Sisa has called the "almost playful" and inventive manner of their ornament, often incorporating human figuration. This ornament was restrained within the grid-like framework of articulated piers and spandrels developed by Schinkel. Bötticher was particularly noteworthy for his interest in trabeated facades in which brick piers and terra-cotta spandrel panels created a grid on the wall plane onto which freely interpreted classical motifs, executed in new materials, were placed. These elements, which were virtually unknown on New York tenements before Herter's arrival, were to become a trademark of the brothers' work. It is significant to note that Ödön Lechner was a classmate of Herter at the Bauakademie. One of the most important Hungarian architects of the late nineteenth century, a founder of the Hungarian Secession movement, Lechner's early works consisted mostly of elaborate street facades for Budapest apartment buildings. These buildings, in the architect's own estimation, demonstrated a clear Bauakademie influence.[43]

In a number of ways the German architectural theory in which Herter was steeped contrasted with important aspects of Anglo-American architectural thought. It was especially noteworthy for its rationalist embrace of new architectural materials and comfort with the apparent dichotomy between facade, structure, and interior. It displayed a lack of concern for truth to materials and little distrust of industrial production, especially in regards to ornament (although there were certainly critiques of this, particularly later in the century). Indeed, the mechanical reproduction of historical forms was held to be emblematic of the progress of the age. As architectural historian Mitchell Schwarzer has noted of German and Austrian architectural thought at this moment, "Because capitalism was not rejected, contemporary artistic existence was represented in a chain of historical developments culminating in the pragmatic arising of machine industry. For both traditionalists and utilitarians in Germany and Austria, the past represented an immanent force in industrial modernity."[44]

These architectural ideas contrasted with one of the most persistent criticisms of the decorated tenement and buildings like them, which centered on their use of industrial, machine-worked materials to reproduce historical forms of ornament.[45] The critique of this practice was grounded in the work of British theorists like Augustus Welby Northmore Pugin, John Ruskin, and William Morris, all widely read in the United States.[46] These critics generally held romantic ideas of the place of the artist in an increasingly mechanized system of production, which intersected with long-standing Anglo-American suspicion of display.[47] The commodification of architectural materials aping historical and often religious forms was seen by critics such as Pugin as a sign of decadence and moral degeneracy. It was in this matter that we see the most significant contrast between the cultural frame of reference of the Anglo-American mainstream and the decorated tenement architects and builders, who for the most part shared a German and central European cultural tradition in which technological progress, expressed through the wide embrace of ornamental forms, was widely considered a social and even moral good. There was little contradiction in expressing historical forms in new modern materials, as both were considered signs of cultural superiority and modernity. These competing views of the place of ornament in an industrialized society played out on the facade of the decorated tenement. They help to explain immigrant architects' and builders' enthusiastic embrace of these facades in spite of the scorn of Anglo-American critics.

The Decorated Tenement in European Architectural Practice

When Herter's classmate Ödön Lechner moved back to his native Budapest after graduating the Bauakademie and began designing elaborate street facades for tene-

Figure 5.15. Elaborate street facades of multifamily buildings of all classes were a common tradition on the European continent, particularly for central and eastern European cities in the cultural orbit of Berlin and Vienna. These 1887 Vienna tenements were typical of the facade designs, with plaster and cast-stone ornament, published in the prominent builders' magazine *Allgemeine Bauzeitung mit Abbildungen* throughout the second half of the nineteenth century. This tradition served as a direct precedent for the American decorated tenement. Courtesy of Science, Industry, and Business Library, The New York Public Library, Astor, Lenox, and Tilden Foundations.

ments and apartment buildings there, he was taking part in a much wider tradition. Elaborate facades increasingly adorned the front of new buildings of all classes, including tenements, over the course of the nineteenth century (Figure 5.15). Significantly, these buildings made up a large portion of the landscape of the industrialization of the eastern European cities from which many American tenement builders originated. Such decorated tenements could be found in great numbers not only in regional capitals like Saint Petersburg and Kiev but also in smaller cities like Posen, Lviv, Vilna, Chernivtsi, and Lodz.[48] The latter city, an important industrial center, was particularly noteworthy for its extensive landscape of dense and robustly ornamented four- and five-story tenements and apartment houses, largely the product of German and Jewish entrepreneurs.[49]

The city of Lodz, in modern Poland, was one of the most remarkable centers in eastern Europe, a nineteenth-century industrial boomtown that defined its new modernity and cosmopolitanism through the use of architectural ornament on buildings of all types (Figure 5.16). Although the blocks of company housing built for Izrael Poznanski's massive cotton factory, for example, were comparatively austere and

Figure 5.16. Piotrkowska Street looking north, Lodz, Poland, 1914, during World War I. Streetscapes like this represented many tenement builders' and architects' frame of reference of urban modernity. This scene shows a principal street of an important central European industrial center. The robustly ornamented tenements lining it were typical of those found throughout this city and many others in the region, including Vilna, from which many Boston and New York builders originated. With elaborate but conventionalized plaster or stucco ornament, the tenement at far left is particularly typical. Note the similarities between that building's overscaled baroque window surrounds and those found on many early twentieth-century New York tenements, such as in Figure 2.14 and Plate 7. Courtesy of Library of Congress, George Grantham Bain Collection, LC-B2- 3483–11.

matched the mill in their articulation, following the model of British and American manufacturing towns like Manchester and Lowell, many of the privately built tenements in the city that surrounded it had elaborate facades. Lodz's architecture was vividly described at the height of its building boom by novelist Władysław Reymont in his 1899 *The Promised Land.* Reymont was in awe of the "large beautiful houses that looked like museums but served only as warehouses; houses overburdened with ornamentation in every possible style, with Renaissance caryatids on the bottom story supporting stone balconies, bay windows, while the second story in Louis Quinze, floated upward in sinuous lines of the window frames, and the finishing touch was added by bulging ornaments reminiscent of full spools of cotton." The streetscape, according to Reymont, was a "veritable rubbish heap of every possible style, overloaded with stone balconies, caryatids, ostentatious facades, roof balustrades," but the tenements had "awful courtyards, reminiscent of mine shafts; full of shops, offices, warehouses, dirty little junk shops."[50]

For much of its inspiration, industrializing Lodz looked both to Vienna and to nearby Berlin; Reymont described the style of the tenements of Lodz as "Berlin Baroque." Indeed, the decorated tenement has been most commonly associated with

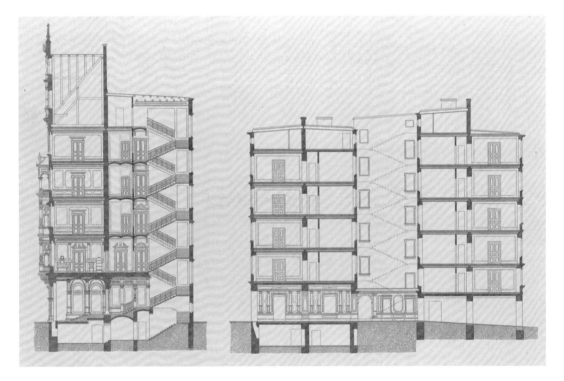

Figure 5.17. The ornate street facade of many European decorated tenements frequently obscured an economic zoning that situated palatial living spaces on the lower floors facing the street, with units of decreasing finish and accommodation above and behind. In this 1895 mixed-use building in Vienna, the best units, solidly middle class, were placed above stores in the elaborate front building, while two-room units occupied parallel ranks of barracks blocks at the rear. The class position of each unit could be easily read by the trim depicted in this cross-section drawing. *Allgemeine Bauzeitung mit Abbildungen,* 1895, Plate 40. Courtesy of Science, Industry, and Business Library, The New York Public Library, Astor, Lenox, and Tilden Foundations.

Berlin, a city whose population rivaled that of New York by the early twentieth century. The metropolis was said to be the largest tenement city in the world.[51] Berlin's speculatively built *Mietskaserne,* or rental barracks, were long, narrow buildings of two-room flats, which like those in Lodz were frequently economically zoned front to back and bottom to top, with residents of all classes sharing the same elaborate entrances (Figure 5.17). In part following the dictates of public officials who set rules for private construction, their facades were richly decorated with stucco, plaster, or cast-stone ornament.[52] According to architectural historian Eve Blau, who has discussed the similar buildings common in Vienna, these facades marginalized their residents by subsuming their working-class identity behind a bourgeois facade.[53] Indeed, buildings like this were famously criticized by anti-ornamentalist architect Adolf Loos. In his seminal essay "Ornament and Crime," Loos called the landscape of these buildings a "Potemkin village," streetscapes of false fronts attempting to mask the social and economic conditions that existed behind them.[54]

These buildings were an important precedent for American tenement builders and architects. In using them, they employed familiar modes of gentility, urbane decorum, and responsibility toward the streetscape, even if these were out of sync with the mainstream Anglo-American building culture, which viewed the tenement as a shameful object to be minimized, not elaborated. Given, for instance, Peter Herter's training at the Bauakademie and deep connection to the building culture of Berlin, as well as the origin of many tenement builders in Vilna and Lodz and the surrounding region, it is clear the decorated tenement embodied lessons learned in continental Europe adapted to the American streetscape.[55]

With a constant flow of people and ideas, Berlin clearly influenced the everyday streetscapes of New York and Boston more than any other European city, even Paris. Indeed, while historians have frequently suggested that Americans looked to Paris in the nineteenth century as the paragon of cosmopolitan urbanism, this is a rather elitist view, informed by the presence of the intellectually important École des Beaux-Arts and the influence of a number of important American architects trained there, including Richard Morris Hunt, Henry Hobson Richardson, and Charles McKim.[56] Paris's celebrated Haussmann apartment buildings, to which so many American designers of elite apartment houses referred, although part of this larger tradition, represented a particular elaboration of a much more common building type throughout the European continent. Yet these elite, Paris-trained architects failed to devise a mode of apartment house construction adapted to the American city that was as widely adopted as the decorated tenement.

Tearing Down and Building Up

The first step in turning an architect's design into an actual tenement in Boston and New York was finding and selecting a lot. This process was typically done by the building operators, who made the initial speculation that a lot would be suitable for tenement reconstruction. "He is constantly on the lookout for lots covered by little two or three-story dwelling houses, once homes of fashion or the prosperous middle class," the *New York Times* wrote of these speculators in 1903. "As fast as they come to market, through the death of owners, settlement of estates or desire to get rid of unproductive property, the speculator snaps them up" (Figure 5.18).[57] The speculator held the old buildings, sometimes using rental income to offset the carrying costs, awaiting sale to a tenement builder.

In these neighborhoods the quality of the surrounding buildings mattered less than the demand for accommodations there. If demand was growing, the tenement was deemed a safe investment. Unlike better classes of residential property, in which residents deigned to live near commerce or industry, only the nearby presence of the most odious types of businesses, like gas plants or abattoirs, would decrease the attractiveness of a lot for tenement development. On the contrary, nearby industrial

Figure 5.18. "No Longer Profitable," 1902. A pair of early nineteenth-century two-story row houses in New York are prepared for demolition to make way for a large new tenement, much like the highly decorated (and probably Herter-designed) building at right. Frontispiece from Lillian Betts, *The Leaven in a Great City* (1902).

NO LONGER PROFITABLE.

employers could provide a ready stock of potential tenants. Building in less fully developed or slower-growing neighborhoods, like those on the metropolitan fringe, while requiring less of an outlay of capital, were also riskier, since especially before robust public transportation options, the builder could be less sure that units would be filled quickly. Real estate experts considered any building that cost more than ten times the value of the lot it stood on to be misplaced or "top heavy," ahead of demand and thus a waste of capital.[58] In many areas the tenement operated as the default form of development.

Construction in these long-settled neighborhoods always needed to begin with demolition, which set builders in conflict with existing residents of the old buildings that occupied the site. These buildings needed to be vacated, and tenants frequently fought their removal. But in an era before rent regulations afforded tenants a modicum of protection against these sorts of evictions, landlords got their way eventually. The construction of Joel Hyams's Herter Brothers–designed tenement, for instance, was delayed for months by an intractable tenant who refused to surrender possession. Peter Herter was sued, unsuccessfully, in 1901 for $50,000 by the widow of a former tenant who claimed her husband's untimely death was caused by an illness exacerbated when Herter began demolition on the house they continued to occupy while the couple fought their eviction. The architect-turned-developer intended to replace their house with a large tenement.[59]

With tenants out of the way, the old buildings on the site had to come down. Occasionally these were sites of historical interest. When Louis Goldstein demolished an ancient wood-frame building on Boston's Hull Street, just above the storied Old North Church, he aroused attention by exposing the long-hidden facade of a neighboring early eighteenth-century house reputed to have served as the headquarters of a general during the Revolutionary War Battle of Bunker Hill (Figure 5.19). "It would behoove those who would see how their grandparents were housed in Boston to take a look very shortly," the *Boston Globe* advised its readers in 1906, "as the opportunity will doubtless be brief."[60] The *Globe* was right, as Goldstein would demolish the old house for another tenement later that year (see Figure 3.5). The demolition led the sexton of the Old North Church to scornfully lament, "The old buildings here . . . are going so rapidly. . . . The Hebrews are especially averse to living in old houses. Hence they tear down these old wooden mansions, each with an interesting story."[61]

More often the old buildings were hardly missed. But, usually less than half a century old, they contained valuable material that could be salvaged. Demolition contractors frequently took secondhand material as partial payment.[62] In other cases builders retained some or all of this material for reuse, or they purchased similar materials back from demolition contractors. The typical tenement of this era was made up of a substantial amount of salvaged material, particularly interior structural masonry. The specifications for Joel Hyams's tenement explicitly instructed the masons that "all the old materials such as stone, bricks, etc., which may be found on the premises shall be used for the new work, if in good and sound condition" after they were cleaned and washed.[63]

The extent of brick reuse was the subject of another early twentieth-century lawsuit. Prominent builders Philip and Meyer Horowitz, developers of Henry Court, attempted to withhold final payment on their 1901 Michael Bernstein–designed tenement at 54 Eldridge Street in New York, alleging contractor Edward Poerschke employed a far greater portion of used brick than the contract allowed, among other problems. The original agreement had anticipated Poerschke would demolish the old buildings on the site and use the brick in the new tenement. Construction was delayed when the building department rejected Bernstein's plans on suspicion, raised by reformer Lawrence Veiller, that the prolific architect improperly reused documents intended for other projects. When permits were finally secured, the developers sold the demolition rights to house-wrecker Morris Levison in a rush to have the new building under way before the new tenement law took effect. At this point, Poerschke claimed, the developers instructed him to use as much secondhand brick as necessary to compensate for the value. The value of the material in the two three-story buildings that had stood on the site amounted to about $700 of the $16,000 contract for the new building. At that point secondhand brick was particularly inexpensive; demolition for the Williamsburg Bridge had caused a glut. The 172,000 used bricks in the finished building, about 30 percent of the total, cost $300 less than if the building had been constructed of all new material. Two-thirds old brick was the maximum allowed by the building department, although Poerschke testified he had seen some buildings built entirely out of recycled brick.[64]

Sometimes the old buildings on the site did not even need to be fully demolished to achieve the same outcome. This was particularly true when the site was occupied

Figure 5.19. The historic Galloupe House, 16 Hull Street, Boston, built circa 1724 (pictured circa 1898). The house was used as a headquarters during the Battle of Bunker Hill. The demolition of this and the neighboring house in 1906 for three tenements built by Louis Goldstein (see Figure 3.5) caused an outcry among the Boston elite. Courtesy of Trustees of Boston Public Library.

by a row house or other building with party walls. A new tenement could be achieved by stripping off the front, constructing a new facade, extending the structure rearward and upward, and reconfiguring the interior layout. In the quote that opens this chapter, Boston reformer Robert Woods noted the prevalence of this technique among North End landlords at the turn of the twentieth century. A photograph in the collection of the Bostonian Society shows a Stillman Street row house undergoing this conversion to a tenement around the turn of the century, front wall and roof stripped off, leaving only the floor structure of the second, third, and fourth stories, as well as the party walls, wallpaper still attached (Figure 5.20). This process resulted in substantially new construction.[65]

In an era before widespread ecological concerns, this level of salvage and reuse was not regarded as a laudable practice. Quite to the contrary, the recycling of old material for new buildings was one routinely criticized by reformers. To them, it signaled a lack of integrity on the part of a miserly builder and his cobbled-together structure. Reuse, particularly of materials that were then hidden by fancy new facades, was to many observers simply a dishonest trick, a way to attract new tenants and provide

Figure 5.20. Early twentieth-century photograph of Stillman and South Margin Streets, looking toward Salem Street, Boston, showing the process of converting a former row house (*center right*) into a tenement. The old front wall had been stripped off, exposing the interior walls with wallpaper still attached. The building's front would be replaced with a facade of yellow pressed brick. Courtesy of the Bostonian Society, Collection WV001.

more usable space as cheaply and quickly as possible. More sympathetic observers, like Lee Friedman, called this "resourcefulness." Reusing material, combined with the long hours many builders worked, he claimed, contributed to the high mortgage or resale valuations that allowed tenement builders intent on improving the neighborhood to work in rapid succession.[66] Indeed, the judicious reuse and recasting of materials were fundamental not only to success in building but also in a number of other immigrant-dominated enterprises, particularly in the garment industry, where the practice aided in the expansion of access to a wide range of formerly inaccessible goods to the working class.[67]

The reused building material usually proved just as useful and durable as the new. This was something of a matter of contention in the Poerschke lawsuit. Architect Michael Bernstein, testifying for the Horowitzes, his clients, claimed that the presence of used brick diminished the life span of a building by five years.[68] Contractor Poerschke disagreed, asserting he had frequently used one-third old brick in his over twenty years as a builder and had never thought it made a difference in the life span of a building. (Indeed, the Horowitz building is still extant.) So long as it was properly cleaned, he claimed, it was "just as good" as new brick.[69] This testimony was corroborated by building material dealer Thomas Haywood, who sold Poerschke the brick, which he had bought from buildings demolished for the bridge and thoroughly cleaned.[70]

Whether old or new, the materials used in construction of tenements were consistently derided as inferior by outside observers. As architect and reformer William Hazlet wrote, tenement builders considered that "anything that will pass the inspection of an inspector—by hook or by crook—is good enough." Hazlet then went on to catalog what he saw as the deficiencies in these materials, including their use of "soft brick, second-hand brick, damaged cement or none, loam in place of sand, concrete that will not hang together, half dried wood, the thinnest of doors and sash, anything that can be concealed or covered with cheap paint and varnish."[71] Sometimes the failure to use proper materials, such as the accidental or intentional substitution of mud for mortar, jeopardized the structural stability of these buildings.[72] This was proved to be at fault in the infamous 1885 collapse of Charles A. Buddensiek's westside tenements, discussed in chapter 7. Such incidents led Jacob Riis to conclude that the decorated tenement was "shaky, but fair to look at."[73] But if the core structure of the tenement was often made up of potentially inferior, salvaged material, builders seldom reused one key element: the exterior trim.

Putting the Pieces Together

Speed was a crucial aspect in the success of a tenement project, and this put considerable strain on all involved. Lafayette Goldstone, later to become an architect on his own, worked for a period in the first years of the twentieth century as the assistant to a tenement builder, whom Goldstone does not name, although he may have been

Charles I. Weinstein. Goldstone found the work exhausting. His biographer noted that the job "required that he be at this builder's home week in week out, at six in the morning. In the front basement dining room the day's business started in bedlam: the builder's numerous children falling all over each other while their father ate his breakfast, the telephone constantly ringing, contracts being drawn—a turmoil lasting until about eight o'clock."[74] At this point Goldstone would then begin his rounds at the builder's dozens of construction sites. At the end of eight hours on job sites, he would spend the evening, some times past ten o'clock at night, revising plans provided by George F. Pelham and preparing reports. A similar pace of work was found in the practice of developer Ascher Weinstein, unrelated. His 1893 obituary in the *Record and Guide* described the level of commitment required to conduct such a business. "He was an untiring worker. . . . He would spend the day until 5, 5:30, or 6 o'clock visiting different brokers' and lawyers' offices, and afterward devote two, three or four hours answering and writing letters with the aid of an amanuensis. The latter, although fond of his employer, could not stand such hard work and resigned."[75]

Despite the complexity of these various phases, tenements were put up with lightning speed relative to their size to ensure they were completed before the initial construction loan came due. Although Veiller claimed that building an ordinary tenement could take six to eight months, building permit records in both cities indicate that the majority were finished in closer to four or five.[76] Goldstone insisted that buildings had to be ready for occupancy five months after the lot was purchased. "Under such a schedule," Goldstone noted, "it was often difficult to make the wall paper or paint stick to the wet plaster" (Plate 17).[77] Construction activity, particularly in New York, seems to have been carried on regardless of the weather, though buildings in both cities were finished in similar time frames. The primary duty of the builder during this period was to ensure that the contractors he had retained maintained this schedule.

Within half a year the new tenement was done and ready for occupancy. With the paint barely dry, it was time to find tenants and perhaps a buyer for the entire building. Now came the ornament's role in making the building attractive to potential residents and owners. In this regard the elaborate forms could even arouse suspicions that played into long-held beliefs about the tenement and those who built it.

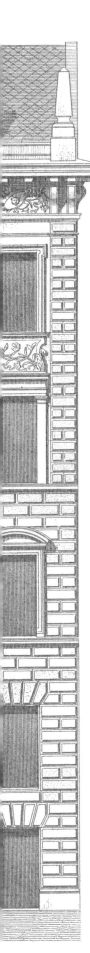

Chapter 6

A New Style of Poverty

*Understanding Working-Class Taste
and Material Culture*

... an ugly, pretentious brick building overloaded with hideous
terra-cotta, which we suppose its architect would call ornament. What
heartless irony the erection of a pretentious monstrosity such as this
for the occupation of poor people, who doubtless have increased
rent wrung from them to pay the interest on the cost of the ugly and
elaborate detail! Could there be a more striking example of the want of
taste, the absence of any sense of fitness, the craving for mere display,
the heartless vulgarity which is characteristic of certain elements in the
community?

The Brickbuilder, **July 1892**

The Brickbuilder, a Boston-based publication for the masonry trades,
refused to even reproduce the woodcut that had appeared in the July
1892 issue of *Scribner's Monthly*; it was simply too offensive (Figure 6.1).
Indeed, the anonymous *Brickbuilder* author even apologized to readers
for introducing the topic of "social issues" in a trade publication, but the
image just could not pass without comment.[1] An article titled "Life in
New York Tenement-Houses" by reformer William T. Elsing had included
the offending picture, which was simply titled "A New Tenement of the
Better Sort." The pair of buildings it depicted had been built in 1890 at
the corner of Broome and Goerick Streets, at the far eastern edge of the
Lower East Side, just a block from the East River, where they adjoined
docks and lumberyards. Designed by German-born architect William C.
Frohne, later a prominent designer of tall office buildings, they were
built by Bernhard Rosenstock.[2] Indeed, the buildings were of the elaborate type that were being built by immigrant developers and architects

throughout the neighborhood.[3] Each floor was marked by exaggerated terra-cotta bas-relief panels (a trademark of Frohne), with figural corbels, massive cartouches, an intricate filigree pattern on the fire escape, and overscale urns at the cornice. The building's appearance shocked the *Brickbuilder*'s sensibilities so much that it warranted an impassioned screed of nearly five hundred words that encapsulated many of the cultural conflicts embodied by the decorated tenement.

The building was a "better sort" of tenement in the eyes of Frohne, Rosenstock, and his tenants, yet the facade greatly offended the tastes of the *Brickbuilder* and its readers. To them, this level of ornamentation represented an untoward pretense, inappropriate for the working class. The "incongruity" of elaborate details on a tenement, the editors opined, was not just "ridiculous" but sadly becoming more common under the influence of "certain elements in the community." This was, of course, a thinly veiled reference to immigrant builders and architects, who were frequently portrayed as

Figure 6.1. "A New Tenement of the Better Sort—One of Many Recently Erected by Private Enterprise," 1892. Depiction of the Bernhard Rosenstock Tenements, 35 and 37 Broome Street, New York (1890; demolished). William C. Frohne, architect. This sketch prompted the leading masonry trade magazine to publish an impassioned screed against the "heartless vulgarity" of such ornament on a tenement. From William T. Elsing, "Life in New York Tenement-Houses as Seen by a City Missionary," *Scribner's* 11 (1892): 701.

LIFE IN NEW YORK TENEMENT-HOUSES. 701

A New Tenement of the Better Sort—One of Many Recently Erected by Private Enterprise.

both "heartless" and "vulgar." The author found the flamboyant facade, delighting in the democratization of previously elite forms, to be simply ugly, displaying a wanton lack of taste on a building considered to be of such low status. The issue of cost, addressed here with a feigned air of social concern, was a red herring. Certainly the editors of *The Brickbuilder* knew how cheaply terra-cotta ornament could be procured. The matter, simply, was one of taste and propriety. The author called on their trade to demonstrate an interest in "public character" to avoid such outcomes. He described the only type of tenement that could be considered appropriate: "A decently plain, strictly utilitarian building, whose affect should depend on pleasing proportion and mass, and relation of voids to solids, and whose details should be of the very simplest, all in plain brick."[4] That, he contended, was the only way a building for the poor and working class could be considered fit for its purpose, no matter what the residents wanted. This view was widely shared not only by housing reformers but also in the community of mainstream and elite architects and builders, as well as among real estate agents and investors. Yet these were not primarily the audience for decorated tenement builders like Rosenstock.

Tenement Taste

Instead, tenement builders were responding to a working-class taste that, as historian Lizabeth Cohen has noted, relished complex, elaborate forms and long-standing symbols of power and status, and to a market for architectural materials that catered to that demand. Before the middle of the nineteenth century, elaborate forms were an easily understood signifier of wealth. Expensive to produce, they were a sign of ample means and social status. Drawn, in architecture, from erudite study of historical motifs, ornament signaled social capital and was a primary marker of distinction.[5] Industrial production upset this order in myriad ways. The social and economic order was threatened by the rise not only of a middling industrial class not beholden to old regimes of power but also through the appearance of a large and assertive working class, whose cultural forms began to demand attention in the wider culture.[6] Factory production allowed for the creation of a wide array of goods in forms previously available only to the wealthy, destabilizing the link between elaboration and power. To an observer like sociologist Thorstein Veblen, these facades were simply "suggestions of expensive discomfort." He claimed in 1912 that ornament on the "better sort" of tenements was a sign of "conspicuous waste" and the substitution of "pecuniary beauty for aesthetic beauty," suggesting that the projection of economic and social status was the sole justification.[7]

Yet deeper cultural forces were also at work. Indeed, the decorated tenement was not simply a debased version of a middle-class or elite apartment building, its architecture not a pale imitation of high-style forms. Here elite taste was not passively accepted and emulated through the use of cheap, imitative materials, as critics suggested. Instead, these forms were selectively embraced, modified, emphasized, and embellished. These were deliberate choices responding to distinctive strains of working-class and immigrant taste. Builders often took fashionable forms and expressed them in exaggerated, flamboyant ways. Beyond what was simply fashionable, in some cases the forms chosen by architects and builders were part of a fraught negotiation of material forms that were thought to represent the identity of the communities of which they were part. Set within an urban landscape in which elaborate forms competed for meaning, the decorated tenement also occupied a contested position relative to a range of other structures, including the commercial loft buildings that were often their neighbors and the more elite apartment houses where builders sought to highlight the social distance between themselves and the tenements.

The choices made by builders of decorated tenements fit into a larger context of material culture where there was democratization of stylish and elegant goods in an era of rising mass consumption. Within the decorated tenements there were finely trimmed interiors, colored pictures, and elaborate furnishings, and residents, to the extent they could afford, clothing themselves in the latest fashions, worshipping in substantial new buildings, and celebrating elaborate rituals. These material choices formed a continuum that challenged the image of the slum as a place of unmitigated squalor.

These buildings, then, are profitably seen within the framework of working-class taste that has been developed by Lizabeth Cohen and extended by Andrew Heinze, Nan Enstad, Elizabeth Ewen, and Kathy Peiss. These scholars have granted immigrants and workers a considerable degree of agency in their choices to consume stylish goods and to engage in elaborate celebrations and amusements.[8] While of course not all members of a class or ethnic group shared the same taste, historians have identified these patterns as being generally associated with urban working-class culture.[9] Both Enstad and Ewen, for instance, have demonstrated that late nineteenth-century immigrant working women's clothing choices frequently exaggerated popular trends, exceeding middle-class standards. These choices showed a preference for forms that in immigrant women's countries of origin often signaled nobility. As Enstad noted, "when both Jewish and Italian immigrants embraced American fashions, they imbued them with meanings rooted in a collective memory of oppression."[10] Displaying many of the same traits, the decorated tenement was therefore the most enduring manifestation of this otherwise ephemeral material culture. Thus, the common charge that tenement ornament was not fashionable because it was industrially produced and available from a builder's yard is akin to dismissing as not interested in fashion the worker who bought ready-made clothes and wore them in a more or less flamboyant manner. For some, certainly, dressing with the times and to suit the purpose was a practical necessity. But for others, it was evidence of a rich cultural practice.

This democratization of stylish goods, resulting from industrialization and urbanization, must have been jarring for outsiders, who had long associated the poor and working class with rough and austere material forms. Returning to New York after decades in Europe in the early twentieth century, Henry James famously made note of the new appearance of the working class of the Lower East Side in his collection of essays *The American Scene*. He described the new scene as a "phantasmagoria," rich and complex in comparison to the slums he had witnessed in Europe and the antebellum New York of his youth. While elsewhere he described the neighborhood's residents in starkly anti-Semitic terms, James was fond of the new appearance of the area. Calling Rutgers Square a "New Jerusalem," he found the tenements there "evolved," praising particularly the white marble staircase he ascended to observe the scene from a rooftop of a new tenement. He thought that in this glittering new district "the wants, the gratifications, the aspirations of 'the poor,' as expressed in the shops (which are the shops of the 'poor'), denoted a new style of poverty."[11]

What James saw in Rutgers Square that evening was the result of the increasing availability of fashionable goods that began shortly after the Civil War. In this new style of poverty, the formerly stable association of stylish and elaborate material goods with the wealthy and elite was destabilized. For a brief moment, at the height of the Gilded Age, the material betterment of industrial capitalism helped reduce the sharp visual differences on the streets of the city. At the very least the ability to publicly negotiate style was becoming more democratized through the expansion of the market for numerous goods that were formerly status markers. An anonymous, though clearly comfortable writer commenting in the *New York Tribune* in 1898 saw little problem with this phenomenon:

> If my lady wears a velvet gown, put together for her in an East Side sweatshop, may not the girl whose fingers fashioned it rejoice her soul by astonishing Grand Street with a copy of it next Sunday? My lady's in velvet and the East Side girl's in the cheapest, but it's the style that counts. In this land of equality, shall not one wear what the other wears? Shall not Fifth Avenue and Grand Street walk hand in hand?[12]

So while the other half down on Grand Street may not have lived at all like those on Fifth Avenue, in aesthetic terms the two places looked a lot more similar than they ever had (compare Figure 1.1). While the discerning eyes of Fifth Avenue could easily spot the cheap knockoffs, to many in the tenement neighborhoods, it was the style, as a projection of their ambition and aspiration, that counted. Indeed, the nexus between the emergent ready-made clothing industry and the tenement districts meant that residents there were keyed into the vagaries of cosmopolitan fashion, which they felt increasingly free to express. Even in the notorious Five Points slum, archaeologists found material goods notable for their quantity and fashionability dating from as early as the 1850s.[13] In analyzing the ceramics found at that site, for example, archaeologist Steven Brighton discovered that tenement residents there had access to wares that were of a value "equal to that of the middle class in rural areas which were removed from the marketplace."[14] This finding suggested a more conscious accessibility of and engagement with fashionable goods in areas long considered sites of unmitigated squalor.

Period observers sometimes tried to draw explicit connections between the ethnicity of tenement builders and their design choices, sometimes with a sense of essentialism that tried to connect putative ethnic traits with material forms. In a 1905 chapter on East Boston, a neighborhood then filling up with decorated tenements, reformers Albert Kennedy and Robert Woods noted the difference between the ways in which Jews, Italians, Irish, and Anglo-American builders handled the exterior of their tenements:

> Most Italian buildings . . . show distinctive Italian touches. One notices inlaid mosaic pavements, colored glass in the windows, a more elaborate cornice, a bit of carved stone about the doorways or windows, a touch of color to the curtains. Though the massed effect of rows of tenements is dull, the individual houses do not show that dullness of pure discouragement which characterizes certain Irish communities, nor the riotous crudeness which is typical of Jewish neighborhoods.[15]

While Kennedy and Woods's remarks were laced with the ethnic stereotypes that typify much early twentieth-century sociological writing, these comments highlight that it was clear to period observers that recent immigrants employed a different taste and outlook toward architectural ornament than shown in working-class housing built by Anglo-Americans or the Irish. Interestingly, Kennedy and Woods also suggested that there were distinct sensibilities toward ornament between Irish, Jewish, and Italian tenement builders. Such assertions cannot be sustained by close analysis of built form. Except in the limited case of Herter Brothers' Moorish Revival tenements in New York, Italian- and Jewish-built buildings, for example, were nearly indistinguishable. Yet Kennedy and Woods's remarks were also clear evidence that observers sensed the differing approaches in these new tenements, perhaps projecting their own images of tenement residents' culture onto their buildings. Immigrant tenement builders were indeed quite consistent in their preference for flamboyant forms, often to the consternation of tastemakers.

The Decorated Tenement Interior

The fittings and furnishings of the interior of the decorated tenement were an important manifestation of the shared standards of the decorated tenement builders and their tenants, who utilized the space and achieved decorative effects as assertively and flamboyantly as possible within both a constrained site and budget. Inside these buildings not only the architects and builders but the residents themselves used mass-produced and elaborate material goods to furnish and decorate their homes. Builders and their architects needed to provide a suitable interior space for this display. Like their exteriors, the interiors of many decorated tenements were marked by stylish, industrially produced millwork and plaster moldings, sometimes including quite elaborate forms of wainscoting, stair newels and balusters, casings, and mantels, creating a rich effect within the constraints of harsh economic realities.[16]

The most consistently and conspicuously ornamented spaces inside a tenement were the public areas of the first floor, presenting the building's best face to the public (Figure 6.2). These spaces usually had encaustic or mosaic tile floors, often with intricate patterns of variously colored tiles (Figure 6.3). The casing of door openings in these spaces often contained a flamboyant head casing. Wainscoting executed in wood, tile, marble, or metal covered the lower portions of the walls in these areas. Whatever the material, this wainscoting served both a practical and decorative purpose, as it protected the lower portions of the wall from the daily abuses of these heavily used spaces. The upper walls were also frequently covered in durable but decorative materials, often leather and burlap, articulated with panels of riveted sheet metal. Upper-floor hallways were frequently covered with Lincrusta. Harris Fine's

Figure 6.2. Stair hall of a 1901 Schneider & Herter–designed tenement at 19–23 Catherine Street, New York. The floor is marble mosaic, and the walls are paneled with marble wainscot. Note the elaborate cast-iron newel post and balusters. The ceiling also shows remnants of decorative plaster work. Plaster has been removed from the upper portion of the walls of this otherwise well-preserved space. The vestibule of this building contained a modillion cornice, a more intricate mosaic pattern on the floor, and a heavily molded door surround. Photograph by Sean Litchfield.

1901 building at 250 Broome Street in New York had elaborate, carpet-like mosaic tile floors and pressed-metal wainscoting, also a typical treatment. Ceilings in these spaces were usually articulated by plaster moldings, some of which even contained runs of acanthus modillions. Walls were often even frescoed. Joel Hyams described in court proceedings the care he took in decorating the halls of his Herter Brothers–designed tenement: "I decorated the walls of this flat house, just the halls; I had a little border of stencil and fresco put in the hall . . . there is a little border done in water color through stencil work." Doing so, he claimed, was "absolutely necessary."[17]

The newel post for the main staircase to the upper floor was frequently the center-piece of these spaces. Another stock item, common wooden newels were either heav-ily turned posts, paneled boxes, or octagonal in shape, the latter having the highest status of the three options. Hyams's building had called for an octagonal newel post like this. When contractors substituted a square box newel instead, Herter Brothers' site supervisor Charles Braun testified that it was unacceptable. "It is not the same thing; quite a difference; more workmanship. The octagon one takes more time to put together."[18] Supporting the staircase banisters were often heavily turned balusters. While wood staircases were technically outlawed in New York after the 1879 tene-ment house act, and in Boston after 1892, building officials in the larger city routinely permitted hardwood construction, claiming, comically and to the consternation of

Figure 6.3. Encaustic tile floors in the vesti-bule of an abandoned Jersey City, New Jersey, tenement, pictured in the 1970s. Such tile lobbies were common in New York tenements before the introduction of marble mosaic tile in the 1890s. Library of Congress, Prints and Photographs Division, HABS NJ-868–3.

reformers, that such material was fireproof because it was slow burning.[19] After 1901 New York began to insist on truly fireproof staircases in new tenements. This requirement provided the opportunity for builders to use cast-iron stair parts, originally used for commercial buildings, often in quite fantastical shapes, provided by a range of iron manufacturers.[20] Marble was frequently used for stair treads, even though slate or iron treads were acceptable and affordable alternatives. Fine's Broome Street buildings employed metal newels and fanciful balustrades, as well as marble treads, in their staircases. The marble staircase in Rutgers Square that caught Henry James's attention was an outcome of this reform.

While the hallway set the tone for the building, the parlor was the ornamental center of the home. A place to display the residents' most cherished goods, it was also the space to which the builders devoted the most architectural attention. Boston reformer Robert Woods described one family's parlor, noting "the marble mantel which surrounds an imitation fireplace contrasts oddly enough with the small cookstove beneath it."[21] Many of these spaces had plaster cornices and center medallions. Woods noted, for example, the elaborate "centerpieces" in the same room. All of these features were basic to the finishing of a refined interior space.

The key to the parlor design was the fireplace mantel. A vestigial reference to the hearth, as tenement apartments were usually heated with stoves or coal grates, most parlors had applied mantels (see Figure 2.5). Stock items, industrially produced, these could be quite ornate and were often executed in slate painted and grained to look like marble, usually with a cast-iron summer screen covering the fireplace grate (Figure 6.4). As we have seen, Hyams also took special care in selecting the mantels for his 1888 tenement, later a matter of contention. In recalling a conversation with the building's contractor, Hyams noted, "I spoke about the design of the mantels and I said I like a very nice mantel there." The $18 per mantel budget called for in the project's specifications was not sufficient for Hyams, who, after visiting multiple suppliers, personally selected slate models that cost nearly 50 percent more, adding nearly $500 to the $40,000 project budget.[22] Hyams likewise took care to provide fancy woodwork for the parlor windows, surrounding them with molded and beaded pilasters five inches in width, with turned corner blocks, and a crown molding with bracketed corners. Molding was continued to the floor, heightening the appearance of the room, and panels were placed under the window. Folding blinds in deep embrasures were also provided for the parlor windows. Herter Brothers supplied the builder with half-scale drawings of these details to assure they were executed properly.[23] Finally, a plaster cornice and center medallions were provided for the room. Even in tenements less ambitiously finished than Hyams's, windows and doors could be cased with stock wood molding profiles.

Residents augmented these architectural finishes with furnishings that were often equally fanciful (Figure 6.5). Case pieces with heavy carving and items with plush fabrics seem to have been in particular demand.[24] Tenants frequently used lambrequin and other hangings, framed prints, and small objects artistically displayed

Figure 6.4. Slate mantel in an abandoned Jersey City, New Jersey, tenement, pictured in the 1970s. Mantels like this are typical of the high-end finish often seen in New York tenements. Similar mantels are extant in Peter Herter's building for Wolf Baum at 375 Broom Street (Figure 3.19) and were central to the dispute in the case of tenement builder Joel Hyams against his contractor, discussed in chapter 5. A slate mantel such as this would likely have been marbleized. Heavily painted over by the time this photograph was taken, this mantel had incised decoration that may have originally been gilded. Library of Congress, Prints and Photographs Division, HABS NJ-868–2.

A CORNER IN A WORKINGMAN'S HOME.

Figure 6.5. A tenement apartment furnished to high standards, showing the tenants' preference for plush furniture, carved dark wood, hangings, and patterned wallpapers. Photograph circa 1901. From Lillian Betts, *The Leaven in a Great City* (1902), 95.

to create rich, colorful spaces.[25] In Boston Robert Woods noted the movement of immigrants into "the new flats of the West End, where they have figured plush furniture, flowered carpets, and even pianos."[26] While these rooms did not meet metropolitan standards for parlors of the middle class and elite, they represented the same interest in elaboration and fashionability that was evidenced on the exterior of the decorated tenement (Figure 6.6).

Another important site of conflict over taste and propriety occurred on the ground level of many tenements, where saloons often filled the storefronts. While reformers often promoted the home, particularly the parlor, as an alternative to saloon culture, these remained important sites of working-class sociability and solidarity. Like the tenement, the saloon was often an economically precarious, immigrant-run enterprise with heavy competition among proprietors, who needed to be closely attuned to the needs and desires of their patrons. Important and often club-like cultural institutions, as historian Madelon Powers has noted, rather than mere purveyors of drink, these establishments were often elaborately outfitted and offered a refuge from daily

Figure 6.6. Elaborate parlor of a Mulberry Street tenement, pictured circa 1905. Notice the plaster cornices, frescoed ceiling, and heavy overmantel with fabric hangings at right. Bay windows were rare in New York tenements before 1900, though they had been common in Boston for at least a decade. The exterior of this 1901 building designed by Michael Bernstein, extant at the corner of Broome and Mulberry Streets, was just as ornate as this interior. From Lewis E. Palmer, "The Day's Work of a 'New Law' Tenement Inspector," *Charities and the Commons* 17 (October 6, 1906): 85. Courtesy of Harvard College Library.

life.[27] These institutions frequently provided entertainment, meeting rooms for social groups, and sometimes free meals with drink purchases, representing a significant savings to patrons, who were likely to spend a portion of their meager income on this sort of entertainment anyway.[28] The institution of the saloon came under intense scrutiny from reformers, perhaps more so than the tenement itself, who before the outright prohibition of alcohol nationwide in 1919, pushed for increasingly strict regulations on sites of public entertainment and alcohol consumption.[29] Many of these campaigns relied on the portrayal of the saloon keeper and liquor dealer, both frequently immigrants, as a diabolical other. Anti-drink reformers employed much of the same highly fraught spiritual language against the saloon keeper that anti-tenement reformers deployed against the tenement builder, routinely calling both "evil," implying they were the chief source of urban vice.

In this context, then, it is important to note that the interiors of most saloons were carefully calibrated to appeal to working-class tastes and therefore employed many of the same forms and techniques as the decorated tenement. Like the facades of the buildings they were in, the interiors of many saloons were elaborately ornamented (Figure 6.7).[30] The 1892 *King's Handbook of New York* described the interior of the aver-

Figure 6.7. An elaborate tenement-district saloon, pictured in the 1890s. This space featured mosaic floors, ornate woodwork, and fresco ceilings. Courtesy Art and Picture Collection, The New York Public Library, Astor, Lenox, and Tilden Foundations.

age saloon as containing "heavy plate and cut glass, richly carved wood, fine frescos and other elegant decorations, and valuable pictures." This description came immediately after a long discussion of the city's efforts to regulate such establishments.[31] As one reformer lamented, "in many a tenement block the saloon is the one bright, cheerful place to be found."[32] Indeed, the saloon was one of the few public spaces that assertively and often flamboyantly reflected the working-class taste and ambitions represented elsewhere in the decorated tenement.

Selling the Decorated Tenement

Like the parlor furnishing and piano, the clothes on residents' bodies, and the conviviality of the saloon, the decorated tenement was fundamentally a commercial product. While many tenements were owned and sometimes occupied by their initial builder for many years after their construction, all were beholden to the demands of the speculative housing market. Architectural ornament consumed a not-insubstantial portion of the builders' budget, even if that expenditure did not result in commensurate rent increases for tenants. Yet the elaborate facades of the decorated tenement cannot be explained away as simply a product of the builder's hope of boosting the resale value of their buildings enough for quick sale to a dazzled buyer. They certainly may have helped them inflate the valuations of their building for mortgage, resale, and insurance purposes, a practice many reformers said was widespread, and perhaps fill the apartments more quickly and with a more stable class of tenant.[33] Yet the builders of the most elaborate tenements violated well-established principles of the commercial real estate business that had little to do with the moralism of reformers or the snobbishness of tastemakers.

While industrially produced ornament may have been cheaper to buy than handworked alternatives, the decorated tenement was far from cheap to produce. Although the amount builders chose to spend varied quite widely, the ornamentation schemes of the most elaborate tenements frequently added 4 percent to the builder's budget. Builders would routinely spend upwards of $1,600 buying ornament for buildings whose cost averaged $20,000 to $30,000.[34] For just under $1,000 in materials, a twenty-five-foot-wide, six-story New York tenement could be adorned with a variety of styles of molded window caps and full-arched windows with grotesques on the keystones. It could have a fine portico with polished marble columns, multiple belt courses on each floor, including deeply carved floral reliefs between the arched windows, and the whole thing could be topped with a tall sheet-metal cornice with a complex parapet.[35] This level of spending was typical of, for example, most of the clients of Schneider & Herter. Alternatively, for just under $200 for a twenty-five-foot-wide, five-story building, a builder would have to be satisfied with simpler window lintels and no arched windows with keystones or elaborate door surrounds. This price would accommodate a couple deeply modeled spandrel panels and sheet-metal pilaster caps to top brick pilasters, and an elaborate sheet-metal cornice but with a more staid parapet.[36] By way of comparison, $200 could have provided the fixtures for at least five three-piece bathrooms, while the $1,000 would have been enough to buy the equipment for central steam heat or to buy and install equipment for domestic hot water.

This spending baffled many in the mainstream real estate profession. For instance, although skeptical of reform, the editors of the influential *Real Estate Record and Builders' Guide* could not understand the way most tenements were designed. Complaining even of the comparatively modest tenements that were common by the early 1880s, the editors deplored the "pretentious specimen of the florid tenement house," with tin cornices, pinnacles, and sanded paint. These buildings, the editors declared, were "the most vulgar type of building in the civilized world, and for that matter more vulgar than any type of building in the uncivilized world."[37] That view was not uncommon, even for other observers who did not write from a reform perspective. In an early twentieth-century training manual for real estate agents, Ransom E. Wilcox, of the prominent New York firm of Wilcox and Shelton, warned agents to be sure that buyers of tenement property were not so awed by a building's appearance as to ignore its fundamental flaws. "A buyer's eyes are so dazzled with the mahogany and marble of the vestibule and the embossed plush with which the walls are hung, that he cannot see the floors of the house are out of level, that the doors do not fit, and that scanty and poor labor and materials are everywhere in evidence. There is such a fine polish on the parlor mantle that he does not see that the balance of the woodwork has not received a particle of sandpapering since it left the mill."[38] Wilcox's view represented a common understanding of the material structure of a decorated tenement—a "very poor thing" in Wilcox' words—"that for a time looks as if it were good." This view that the decorated tenement was a dishonest trick, simply staged for quick sale to an unsuspecting buyer, reflected long-held and often racially based stereotypes about the fundamental dishonesty of working-class and immigrant tenement builders, their architects, contractors, and workers.

Likewise, representing the interests of the commercial real estate investing community of New York, Cecil C. Evers, vice president of the Lawyer's Mortgage Company, was in a special position to offer highly practical advice to potential investors in all manner of buildings.[39] His 1912 book *The Commercial Problem in Building* offered extensive and dispassionate guidance to investors in all stages of the development process. In general, Evers considered ornament, both internal and external, an important if tertiary factor in determining the commercial value of a building. So long as it was restrained, appropriate to the circumstances, and not provided at the expense of utility of plan, location, or structure, ornament could be safely considered a profitable investment. "Two buildings," he noted, "the planning and construction of which are equally satisfactory, that which the external appearance is pleasing and the internal decoration in good taste, will commercially be more valuable and thereby justify the expenditure, than in another building equally useful, but less pleasing to the eye."[40]

Evers recognized that the public's appreciation of fine buildings was continually increasing, and buildings judged to be ugly were bound to depreciate more rapidly.

Despite this approval for ornament in speculative buildings generally, Evers argued against its use on tenements for the working class. Indeed, he saw no commercial rationale for building better-than-average buildings in tenement neighborhoods. In these areas, he claimed, "the rents of the building would be fixed by the competition of its neighbors; and there is but little variation in the rent which the tenants in such a section can afford to pay," meaning that any additional expense in these places would not pay back its cost.[41] Evers also "regretted that . . . [multiple family dwellings] are mostly supplied by speculative builders, who . . . are apt to pay more attention to outward appearance than to those portions of the structure in which poor quality is not apparent at first sight," echoing the typical indictment of the decorated tenement as a cheap sham.[42] To this end, Evers followed the consensus articled for decades in publications like the *Record and Guide.* "Structurally [tenements] should be devoid of all unnecessary cheap ornamentation and of any material which will not stand rough usage. Good brick and terra-cotta properly used are more substantial and attractive than cheap stonework; galvanized iron cornices are objectionable, though their cheapness makes them attractive to builders."[43]

Perhaps the most revelatory example of the elite real estate investment community's consensus about the most rational approach to the design of buildings for the low-income housing market was a block of tenements built in 1885 in New York for the estate of A. B. Schermerhorn, a member of one of the oldest and wealthiest families in the city. Their project at 302–304 East Third Street was developed through the estate's agent, William C. Cruickshank. Cruickshank was a well-connected real estate agent, dealer, and developer, as well as a founder of the Real Estate Exchange.[44] He was executor to the large estate of William Astor, as well as others of the "best elements" of the real estate business, managing the estates and rental properties of some of the wealthiest families in America.[45] His firm was well known for its conservatism and the resulting high performance of these investments. If anybody represented the views and interests of the mainstream American real estate community, it was Cruickshank. So, the pair of buildings he oversaw for the Schermerhorn estate were quite telling. Twenty-five-feet-wide each, the buildings had only tiny light wells; a year later buildings with this little light and ventilation would be outlawed. They were planned to the minimal standards of the worst speculator-built tenements. Unlike most tenements, however, this block was designed by one of the most elite architects in the country, George B. Post, a favorite of the city's wealthy.[46] Post's facade was among the most austere of any tenement built in either city, with flat limestone lintels and modest brick corbel work at the cornice (Figure 6.8). The building looked little different than the austere first generation of tenements built before the Civil War. At the same time he was designing the austere Schermerhorn tenement, Post was engaged to design the Fifth Avenue house of Cornelius Vanderbilt II, perhaps the fundamental manifestation of elite architecture of the Gilded Age.[47]

The utilitarian austerity of the Schermerhorn tenement was particularly startling in contrast to an actual utilitarian building designed by Post, also in 1885, for
Schermerhorn heir Ellen S. Auchmuty (Figure 6.9).[48] Standing at a scrappy dockside
location amid other Schermerhorn holdings, the Auchmuty loft was elaborated by
terra-cotta window trim and a shell-shaped cornice, while moldings and keystones
featured aquatic motifs. This iconography signaled the uses within the building,
which was occupied by seafood dealers and stood next to the city's main fish market.[49]
The ornament of the Auchmuty loft, as a business building, signaled the respectability of its commercial tenants with durable, stylish terra-cotta forms.[50] No such
messages were required on the East Third Street tenement, Post and Cruickshank believed. Its working-class residents could be properly housed only in an austere, utilitarian building, fit for its purpose of making money and providing minimal shelter
but little else. It was an elite client's and an elite architect's view of an appropriate
tenement facade, encoding explicit class and cultural prejudices. Built by arbiters

Figure 6.8. A. B. Schermerhorn Estate Tenement, 302–304 East Third Street, New York (1885). George B. Post, architect. This tenement was more austere than the fish warehouse designed by Post for Schermerhorn family members later that year (Figure 6.9). Photograph by Sean Litchfield.

Figure 6.9. Ellen S. Auchmuty Loft, 142 Beekman Street, New York (1885). George B. Post, architect. A fish ware-house more elaborate than a contemporary tenement by the same architect. The four-story building at right was also designed by Post. Notice the similarities between that simpler building and the Schermerhorn Estate Tenement. Photograph by Sean Litchfield.

of taste who considered the neighborhood a slum, the Post-designed Schermerhorn tenement encoded this view on a facade more austere than even a fish warehouse.

Building for tenants with little ability to pay, for a market that found their choices questionable, builders of the most flamboyant facades failed to make the most economically rational choice in the construction of their new buildings. Yet the isolation of most decorated tenement builders from the broader real estate investing community meant that these buildings were built on scale. While ornamental forms clearly helped builders gain favor with working-class tenants, whose taste these facades reflected, they alienated a larger market of potential investors who were taught to be suspicious of such buildings, and seemed to have added little to their long-term value.

The Decorated Loft

The building type most closely related to the decorated tenement was the commercial loft building. These served, among other things, the needs of the garment industry, which was the economic backbone of these neighborhoods and became increasingly crucial as the scale of production led to tenement home work, long decried by reformers, becoming increasingly less viable. Concentrating an intense and largely formulaic building program on a narrow city lot, these buildings also often had elaborate street facades. Significantly, they were frequently the work of the same builders and architects. They became a favored investment of many successful tenement developers, most notably Weil & Mayer in New York, and the Silverstein brothers in Boston. Responding to many of the same economic and cultural imperatives, these buildings help situate the decorated tenement in a landscape in which ornament was becoming increasingly profuse on everyday buildings of all types. Yet the taste exhibited by decorated tenement builders remained unique. Despite their ornamentation, loft design revealed important contrasts in the scale, type, and placement of ornament on the facade. The two building types could seldom be confused upon diligent inspection. This was in part due to the wider fenestrations required of commercial buildings, although not all differences could be explained by the varying program.

The sudden appearance of these structures was met with some degree of consternation, largely due to the hordes of workers, particularly working-class women, they attracted each day. The reaction against commercial loft construction in elite New York residential neighborhoods has been well documented.[51] However, the loft did not carry the problematic stereotypes that the tenement did. As a result, ornament on these structures seldom met with the same level of criticism that met the decorated tenement. Indeed, ornament was often considered quite proper on a commercial structure. As we have seen in the case of the Auchmuty loft, these buildings were often designed by elite architects and employed a variety of ornamentations strategies. Likewise the Weeks family, responsible for the early, austere tenement at 65 Mott Street, developed a number of elaborate cast-iron loft structures on Broome Street, just west of the tenement district, in the 1850s and 1860s, designed by architect Elisha

Sniffen.[52] In general the ornament on these buildings was a reflection of their builders' high regard for their commercial tenants within.

While builders more closely associated with the tenements often used ornament on both structures, the ornamental forms of the decorated tenement were clearly perceived by their architects and developers as something appropriate to residential structures only. The commercial nature of their loft buildings was signaled by wider fenestrations, coarser forms, and less figural ornament. The loft building at 226 Endicott Street in Boston built in 1900 by prolific developers Isaac and Phillip Silverstein to the designs of Frederick Norcross was a good example (Figure 6.10). Just outside the core of the North End tenement district and with these associations, one might expect it to look like a decorated tenement. It did not. Instead, Norcross and the Silversteins chose a comparatively austere treatment with the windows on the upper floors grouped under two broad arches, a very common facade treatment for commercial structures.[53] In many ways this structure was quite a bit more conventional than the decorated tenement. The contrast between this building, and the de-

Figure 6.10. Phillip Silverstein Loft, 226 Endicott Street, Boston (1900). Frederick Norcross, architect. This industrial building was designed and built by a prominent decorated tenement architect and builder and bears little resemblance to this architect's tenement work. Compare with Figure 6.11. Photograph by Sean Litchfield.

Figure 6.11. Phillip and Israel Silverstein Tenement, 64 Revere Street, Boston (1898). Frederick Norcross, architect. Compare to the contemporaneous loft building of this client and architect in Figure 6.10. Photograph by Sean Litchfield.

velopers' building at 68 Revere Street of exactly the same moment and architect is noteworthy (Figure 6.11). These aesthetic differences cannot be fully accounted for by the differing programs. Similar contrasts could be seen in a series of loft buildings designed by the Herter Brothers in the early 1890s, which used less ornament and more prominent trabeation than in their contemporaneous tenement designs. These buildings were free of the delicate belt courses and filigrees, elaborate cornices, and highly symbolic figural ornament that appeared on the brothers' nearby tenements. Instead the building had broad first-floor arches and assertive corbeling on the upper levels and a simpler silhouette.[54]

The Elite Apartment Building and the Specter of the Tenement

As we have seen, the streets of the Gilded Age city were a chaotic, visually confusing place in which long-standing social markers were breaking down and in which class position was becoming increasingly difficult to read. Conflicts, therefore, over visual distinction became increasingly sharp. Perhaps one of the most dramatic of these conflicts, and one in which the decorated tenement was directly implicated, was over the middle-class and elite apartment building. Architectural historian Andrew Sandoval-Strauz has noted there was a long tradition of elites occupying hotels on a permanent or semipermanent basis, forming a major trajectory in the design of earliest apartment hotels. Buildings such as the 1856 Hotel Pelham in Boston, perhaps the first purpose-built elite apartment building in the United States, were large structures, typically not relying on a mere street facade (Figure 6.12). They were designed in a grand tradition that, according to Sandoval-Strauz, signaled hospitality as much as domesticity.[55]

Still, the tenement was a specter that haunted the prospects of respectability of multifamily living as it moved to the middle classes. Architectural historian Elizabeth Collins Cromley has documented the social and architectural lengths to which builders of middle-class and elite apartment houses went to burnish their buildings' reputations as respectable, proper, and genteel. To do so, they experimented with architectural forms, and as historian Matthew Lasner has noted, sometimes varying ownership structures as well, to distance themselves physically, socially, architecturally, and economically from the tenements, which had already become a major part of the landscape.[56] This goal meant solidifying the class stratification of the city by building structures imposing in both scale and ornament in only the most respectable neighborhoods.

Yet even the most elite apartment house found itself subject to some degree of the scrutiny and scorn that was directed at the tenements. This scrutiny included compliance with the increasingly tough regulations advocated by housing reformers, who were generally suspicious of all multifamily housing. As reformer Lawrence Veiller said of this fact, "no possible distinction in law can be made between the so-called tenement, flat, and apartment house . . . they are absolutely and irrevocably one

Figure 6.12. Hotel Pelham, Boylston and Tremont Streets, Boston (1855; pictured in an 1890s stereoview). Like many early elite apartment houses, buildings such as this were an evolution from the hotel and therefore clearly distinguished from the tenement by their large size and monumental treatment. Builders of smaller elite apartment houses had a harder time projecting this distinction. Author's collection.

and the same thing."[57] Indeed, some supporters of strict tenement inspection regimes were often gleeful in pointing out that it applied to all classes of buildings, often to the chagrin of upper-class residents. One 1906 article, for example, noted the amusement of a bellboy in the lobby of a luxurious Upper West Side apartment hotel at having to handle documents left by inspectors from the newly consolidated Tenement House Department. "Across the envelope in black letters was printed 'Tenement House Department.' The boy looked at the inscription, glanced over his shoulder at two silk-gowned women entering the elevator and whispered, 'Gee, wat would de loidies think if dey only knew.'"[58] Certainly the ladies knew they were not living in a tenement, no matter what the law or the building inspector said. The distinction was both architectural and geographical.

Builders of the much more common small rental apartment building, more clearly an evolution from the tenement instead of the hotel, had a bigger challenge disassociating themselves from working-class housing. This was particularly true with regard to buildings constrained to a twenty-five-foot-wide lot, marking a clear contrast to the often block-length apartment hotels that allowed for a more monumental treatment. Indeed, in New York, where small apartment buildings were particularly common, apartments were often arranged on the double-decker plan of most tenements. These buildings usually contained two deep units per floor as opposed to the laterally divided four units of a typical tenement. While they had more spacious apartments, with rooms often separated by private halls, many of the secondary rooms in these buildings rarely had much more air and light then those in a dumbbell tenement. As one period observer noted, the best status this sort of apartment building could hope for was that of "genteel tenement."[59]

Still, good taste and decorum typically dictated a certain modesty of treatment on these buildings, even for those who could afford more (and even if some builders insisted on using more). A representative example of this modest decorum was the 1885 apartment building designed by George B. Post for James Thomson, occupying two lots on East Ninth Street near Third Avenue, a location at the edge between a respectable residential district to the north and west and the tenement districts developing to the south and east (Plate 18). The building was especially remarkable in contrast to the austere tenement Post designed the same year for the Schermerhorn estate, four blocks south and three east on East Third Street, and matched Post's approach to other middling buildings, like the contemporaneous Auchmuty loft. The Thomson building represented a mainstream approach to ornamentation for the middle-class. Appropriately simplified, its historicizing forms were abstracted and conventionalized, mostly consisting of terra-cotta window tympana and door surrounds and a simple shell cornice. The ornament here was all executed in terra-cotta, a relatively new material, in which Post was considered an expert.[60] This approach, overall, represented a respectable level of ornamentation for a rental building in a middling location, appropriately reflecting, unlike the decorated tenement, the class of the building's residents.

Yet many observers were increasingly disconcerted with these buildings as the nineteenth century wore on. They projected their discomfort with the multifamily forms, and indeed urban modernity, onto the even comparatively modest amount of ornamentation on apartment buildings like Thomson's. Journalist Julius Henri Browne claimed in 1892 that the expense and discomfort of many of New York's apartment buildings were "measurably attributable to excess of ornamentation for the sake of show and effect" that builders provided in order to overcome "the prejudice against them by association with the common tenement."[61] Browne was echoed by Hubert, Pirsson and Hoddick, elite apartment house designers and early experimenters with the cooperative model of apartment ownership (Figure 6.13). Ernest Flagg apprenticed with principal Philip Hubert in this period.

The group sought to shed light on the situation through a series of articles in the *Architectural Record*.[62] They did so by reporting on an experiment, living one year in a flat in Paris, the next in New York. Their New York flat was in a common double-decker-type building, not of their design. Its facade was "prettily trimmed and decorated," and the interior was filled with "the delightful smell of new varnish." Yet they found their time unpleasant. The building was noisy and uncomfortable, and the

Figure 6.13. Hubert, Pirsson and Hoddick, Navarro Flats (Central Park Apartments), West Fifty-Ninth Street, New York (1883–85, pictured in 1903). High-class apartment buildings like this were growing up in tandem with the decorated tenement. The architects thought tenants of such buildings were "too exacting in their demands" for "ornamentation and conveniences." This complex of buildings was built on a pioneering, although ultimately unsuccessful, cooperative ownership plan, in part sponsored by Philip Hubert. Courtesy of Wallach Division Picture Collection, The New York Public Library, Astor, Lenox, and Tilden Foundations.

elaborate decorations in the hall quickly became threadbare. Their Parisian flat, on the other hand, was in an eighteenth-century building on an unfashionable street in a structure they described as "strong" and "very plain looking." (And therefore quite unlike the new apartment buildings that were then being built in Paris.) Yet the full-floor, seven-room apartment was well ventilated, private, and quiet.[63] The problem, the architects concluded, was that most American tenants (like Europeans of the nineteenth, not eighteenth, century) had misplaced priorities, considering better housing to be that which incorporated stylish new features and technological improvements, instead of the architects' nostalgic notions of privacy, propriety, and proprietorship:

> Are we not too exacting in our demands for modern conveniences and ornamenta-
> tion? If economy be an absolute necessity, had we not better do with less plumb-
> ing work, less steam heat, less electric bells, annunciators, regulators, etc, etc,
> and with less ornamentation in the way of terra cotta, stone carving, porticoes,
> colonnades, projecting cornices, sham turrets, sham mosaic, sham fancy glass,
> cheap carpets, frescos, and other embellishments and have a little more air, light
> and privacy? The old French house we have tried to describe is as plain as a storage
> warehouse; its devoid of almost all our cherished modern conveniences, but it has
> stood and will stand, if not disturbed, for centuries, and the apartments within its
> rugged walls are separate, individual homes.[64]

These architects were clearly bemoaning the loss through industrialization and urbanization of the vaunted characteristics of the freestanding, single-family home: air, light, privacy, and private ownership, and suggesting tenants should be content with uglier and less commodious spaces to get it. They were preaching an early version of the gospel of simplicity for middle-class and elite residents, a sentimental call for simpler forms and more modest accommodations, and certainly by implication a simpler way of life. To them, material improvements, even advances in plumbing, heating, and other technology, did not compensate for the philosophical stigma of rented multi-family housing; like Riis, they (by implication) found the shanty preferable.

And to their mainstream taste, the ornament, which like plumbing and steam heat was increasingly associated with industrial modernity, began to heighten their suspicion of these buildings. While "plain as a storage warehouse" would not yet fly for elite apartment buildings, there was a decreasing emphasis on ornament among the comfortable classes by this point. And, while Hubert, Pirsson and Hoddick did not acknowledge as much in their report, by 1892 it was clear that "terra cotta, stone carving, porticoes, colonnades, projecting cornices, sham turrets, sham mosaic" were becoming too closely associated with downtown tenements to remain in demand uptown for much longer. Indeed, the changing attitudes toward architectural ornament, as well as the suspicion these forms were a mere distraction from deeper problems, opened the decorated tenement up to a withering line of critique that called into question the motivations, even the morality, of its builders.

Chapter 7

A Heartless Irony

Cultural Conflict and the Tenement Reform Movement

> The practical question is what to do with the tenement. I watched a
> Mott Street landlord, the owner of a row of barracks that had made
> no end of trouble for the health authorities for twenty years, solve that
> question for himself the other day. His way was to give the wretched
> pile a coat of paint, and put a gorgeous tin cornice on with the year
> 1890 in letters a yard long.... That was the landlord's way, and will
> not get us out of the mire.
>
> **Jacob Riis, 1889**

William Buhler Jr., the son of a Prussian-born furniture dealer, was
among a group of prominent builders that included Weil & Mayer and
Ascher Weinstein, who in 1888 had set their sights on destroying the
old rookeries in the run-down New York blocks of Mulberry, Mott, and
Elizabeth Streets, just below Bleecker. Buhler bought perhaps the worst
building in the area, a row of six old tenements at 306–318 Mott Street,
dubbed the Barracks, that had been a favorite of reformers' exposés as
early as 1865. Located just across the street from the Board of Health
offices and the attached police headquarters, the buildings were right
under the nose of the laziest health inspector.[1] Built in the 1850s by
Martin Walsh, an Irish-born stonemason who lived on the block, the
three-room flats inside the Mott Street buildings were arranged two per
floor, but a back building set close behind made the rear rooms dark,
and sanitary arrangements were in the cellar of one of the buildings.[2]
In the third of a century since the tenement was built, the standards
for working-class housing had risen dramatically; by 1888 these accommodations were far below the standards of new tenements in the

neighborhood. The new owners set out to change things; the *Record and Guide* noted that Buhler and the others intended to "materially improve the appearance" of a long-neglected area.[3] Using plans by Walgrove & Israels, Buhler conducted a superficial renovation of the Mott Street Barracks, knowing that the buildings would soon need to be replaced. On the exterior, the changes were largely aesthetic.[4] The new owner knew that to signal respectability and propriety among the buildings' working-class tenants, he had to update their appearance, as many other new landlords were doing with old, austere tenements. Atop the original cast-iron cornice he added a fanciful sheet-metal parapet, nearly a story tall, with a lacelike cresting and pediments recording the date. With a polychrome paint scheme, the cornice's copious text may even have been gilded. The improvements caught the eye, and ire, of Jacob Riis, who spent long hours in the neighboring municipal complex searching for stories of neighborhood color. While both remained unnamed, Riis was eager to cast Buhler and Frederick Dassori, the Italian immigrant banker to whom he leased it, in the role of the villainous landlord, and their renovations as an inadequate sort of reform.

Yet Riis seldom used the picture he made of the improved front of the Mott Street Barracks from an upper-floor window at the Board of Health building (Figure 7.1). It was unlike most of his other images with their Dickensian scenes of poverty and despair that served to highlight the social distance between the viewer and the subject. His story of the Barracks was just better without this photograph; his much more commonly reproduced view of the narrow rear yard was better.[5] Try as he might, he could not make the building look particularly like a slum from the front. Instead, his picture depicted a seemingly everyday urban landscape. The "wretched pile," with its flats over storefronts, was not unlike thousands of others lining streets throughout the city, sheltering countless residents of even the middle class. His audience may have just as easily visualized themselves here, instead of the dirty crowds Riis was attempting to portray. Indeed, the signs of modest domesticity on Mott Street extended beyond Buhler's interventions on the building's facade. As literary historian Elizabeth Klimasmith has noted, Riis elided clear signs of the tenants' domestic practice at the Barracks: lace curtains and planter boxes, some with prodigious quantities of flowers, hanging from many of the parlor windows. These signs of home were ignored in an attempt to paint a picture of decay.[6]

Riis's observation of Buhler's renovations reflects the fear inherent in many of the portrayals of the decorated tenement: that fancy sheet-metal cornices, tenants' window boxes and lace curtains, and other such improvements were but a cynical attempt by tenement owners and residents to distract attention from the problematic living conditions found within their buildings. In this case the cornice literally obscured the children camped on the roof behind it. Riis's description presented the verbal, if not visual, contradiction inherent in tenement ornamentation; the "gorgeous" cornice contrasted with the dirt and "mire" just behind it.

Yet the Mott Street building did not last long after its improvements. In 1897 the Board of Health, using newly acquired powers, condemned and demolished the rear buildings. Courts later ruled the action was improper and that the building's condition did not warrant its demolition. Yet Dassori, whose own house had also been condemned a few years earlier for the construction of Mulberry Bend Park, was only awarded $110 in compensation from the city, the supposed value of the material removed, despite a drop in the taxable value of the property of more than ten times that amount.[7] The landlord even attempted to sue Riis and police commissioner Theodore Roosevelt, who had also pressed for the demolition, personally for compensation—one of the few documented cases of immigrants fighting back against powerful reformers—but nothing came of the claim. Riis and Roosevelt declared victory.[8] Dassori later sold the Mott Street property to Weil & Mayer, who demolished the remaining section, as they had scores of other buildings they deemed rookeries. In 1901 they hired Schneider & Herter to design its replacement: a row of seven-story

Figure 7.1. Jacob Riis, "'The Barracks'—Mott Street between Bleecker and Houston." Depicting the Martin Walsh Tenements, 306–318 Mott Street, New York (circa 1850; pictured about 1890). Notice the elaborate cornice added in 1890, as well as tenants' window boxes. This building would be demolished by Weil & Mayer in 1901 after the rear buildings were removed by the Board of Health. Courtesy of Jacob A. (Jacob August) Riis (1849–1914)/Museum of the City of New York, 90.13.4.119.

tenements with an elaborate Classical Revival facade of yellow brick and terra-cotta and an even more umbrageous cornice, and with all the modern improvements inside and dozens more units than the old Barracks.[9] That, as we have seen, was much more commonly the landlord's way and got many more tenants out of the mire.

Yet to anti-tenement activists like Riis, improvements made to these neighborhoods by immigrants like Buhler and Weil & Mayer were inherently suspicious. Surely, they thought, these distastefully elaborate new tenements were cheap shams that simply tempted tenants away from true reform, not just of housing but of taste, lifestyle, and morals as well. To Riis, the deceit of the tenement facade was most troubling because of the disconnect between the seemingly respectable exterior and the real or imagined affronts to middle-class propriety inside. "In spite of the brownstone trimmings, plate-glass and mosaic vestibule floors," he wrote of another new tenement, "the water does not rise in the summer to the second floor, while the beer flows unchecked to the all-night picnics on the roof."[10] More important than its sanitary problems the tenement in question seemed to violate standards of domesticity and sobriety, traits seemingly signaled by the formal facade and fine materials. These buildings were simply shams, "painted and varnished sepulchers," in the words of another reformer, for failed notions of shared American living standards.[11] Reformers were firm in their belief that immigrant builders and landlords could not be trusted to improve the housing conditions of these neighborhoods, which they still considered slums even after they were extensively rebuilt with modern buildings. Part of a growing cadre of experts who sought to reshape numerous aspects of working-class culture, reformers cast themselves as having superior knowledge and sought to provide housing they thought more suited to American standards of taste and domesticity. While Riis begrudgingly admitted, for instance, that the death rate was substantially lower in these new tenements than in the slums they replaced, anti-tenement activists were on the whole convinced that the best way to help urban tenants was through the paternalistic institution of the model tenement and, eventually, a move to the privately owned house in the suburbs, where the political, moral, physical, and aesthetic threat of the tenement could be neutralized.[12]

The Image of the Tenement Builder and Architect

Jonas Weil and his partners were among the most prolific of the thousands of immigrant builders, financiers, laborers, and architects who were responsible for creating the tenement landscape of the late nineteenth century. As in all fields, of course, certain figures, through greed, ignorance, or a combination of the two, caused real problems. Yet anti-tenement activists, convinced of the inherent immorality of multifamily housing as well as the cultural inferiority of recent immigrants, were quick to ascribe the worst motives to all tenement builders based on limited examples. To reformers, these builders were the chief villain at the root of a major urban problem. They were frequently portrayed as incompetent, cunning, and fundamentally dishonest, yet childlike and ignorant.[13] They were, at best, a "less intelligent class" of businessman, in the words of reformer Alfred T. White.[14] At worst they were criminally greedy, profiting while taking a sadistic joy in the discomfort of their tenants, knowingly and ruthlessly building shoddy, uncomfortable, and ugly buildings, and creating physically and morally dangerous spaces in the name of profits.[15]

These claims were frequently couched in ethnic stereotypes, often with open or thinly veiled anti-Semitism. "For the old absentee landlord, who did not know what mischief was afoot," Riis said of the changing identities of tenement builders and owners in his 1902 *The Battle with the Slum,* "we have got the speculative builder, who does know, but does not care, so long as he gets his pound of flesh."[16] Earlier Riis had called the Jewish tenement builders of the Lower East Side "intruders," nefarious outsiders impervious to criticism and insults. "He pockets them [criticisms] quietly with the rent and bides his time," Riis said in 1889 of the builders of modern tenements. "He knows from experience, both sweet and bitter, that all things come to those who wait, including the houses and lands of their persecutors."[17] Indeed, the mostly Protestant anti-tenement crusaders often portrayed their work as a religious battle against evil, invading forces. Riis was particularly blunt about the spiritual dimensions of his war against the tenement and its creators. "It is the devil's job," he declared of tenement building "and you will have to pay his dues in the end, depend on it."[18] These characterizations served to bolster the reformers' claims of superior knowledge and moral standing, reinforcing their claims to greater control over the working-class landscape.

Perhaps the source of the worst public perception of the tenement builder—the signal example of their supposed greed and stupidity—was a dramatic and highly publicized incident in New York in 1885. In April of that year a faulty mortar mixture caused a five-story tenement being built on West Sixty-First Street to suddenly collapse, triggering seven others under construction to fall in domino-like fashion.[19] The incident killed a worker and injured several others, and the builder himself narrowly escaped the basement of the failing structure. He was Charles A. Buddensiek, German immigrant and a butcher by trade, who lived in a Yorkville tenement of his own construction.[20] A prolific developer, Buddensiek was thought to have built many hundreds of tenements—one paper put the number at fifteen hundred—concentrated in Yorkville and Hell's Kitchen. Buildings were said to "spring up like mushrooms under his magic touch." The *New York Times* noted of his decorated tenements that "all must have showy brownstone fronts and pretentious interior decorations. But the woodwork in all is wretched and cheap beyond description."[21] Among Buddensiek's tenements were a number in the Lower East Side, including his row of fine brownstone-fronted flats on Third Avenue and Thirteenth Street (Plate 19).[22] The latter buildings were designed by Buddensiek's in-house architect Henry J. Dudley, who would later serve as a city building inspector charged with supervising many of his former employer's projects, including the collapsed buildings.

Buddensiek's manslaughter trial for the Hell's Kitchen collapse caused a media sensation, resulting in near-daily coverage in the *New York Tribune* and elsewhere, and seemingly opening to public scrutiny the entire process by which housing was built in New York. Blatant ethnic and class prejudices permeated much of the coverage. The *Tribune,* for instance, noted Buddensiek wore "cheap, ill-fitting clothes" and spoke in an "unintelligible" German accent. Yet, ample evidence of endemic corruption was also presented. Dudley and other city officials were charged with taking bribes to overlook shoddy workmanship. Key witnesses, including the failed building's architect, George Spitzer, were nowhere to be found, and others accused Buddensiek's associates of attempting to pay them to leave town. The suitability of various materials was questioned, with competing testimony. While only the finest brownstone was used on the front, stonemasons testified, brick dealers claimed that the interior structural brick used was soft, cheap, and perhaps inadequate. In his defense Buddensiek testified that he was not culpable for the worker's death because, as an amateur for whom building was a sideline, he knew little about construction methods, relying instead on his architect, foreman, and the building department to assure his projects were properly executed.[23] Eventually, Buddensiek was convicted of manslaughter in the worker's death and sentenced to ten years in prison; he spent six years at Sing Sing before being pardoned.[24]

While deadly construction accidents were common in all classes of construction in this era before workplace safety regulations, a special sort of moral indignation and outrage followed incidents on tenement building sites. A touchstone for public distaste toward multifamily housing, these accidents helped bolster the ethnic and class prejudices promoted by reformers. Indeed, they cast the structure of the tenement itself as a dangerous weapon in the hands of murderous builders who took pleasure in endangering their tenants, latent killers requiring the intervention of government and private charity to protect the public. Although workers, not tenants, were injured in this incident and in most others, Riis later claimed of Buddensiek's buildings "that they killed their tenants was no concern of the builder."[25]

The Buddensiek incident cast a long shadow over the whole field. As one architect wrote a decade later, "the name of Buddensiek will never be forgotten among the builders of New York."[26] The word became synonymous with "greed and tottering walls."[27] For decades, builders whose methods were impugned were said to be "of the class" or "of the breed of Buddensiek," and shoddily constructed buildings were called "Buddensieks" (Plate 20).[28] Some went so far as to say that it was not only Buddensiek's "business but his pleasure . . . to put up buildings that directly endangered the lives of those who inhabited them."[29] Buddensiek, according to press reports, was simply a "skin builder," that is, "one who borrows money to build tenement houses of material that is just strong enough to hold together till he can find a purchaser."[30]

The image of the "skin" builder with his good looking but flimsy "Buddensiek" building played a central role in the extension of the slum stereotype to the new landscape of the improved, decorated tenements. Indeed, subsequent incidents on tenement building sites seemed to reinforce the idea that the new buildings were "shaky," despite reformers' best efforts. For example, during a heavy rainstorm in 1903, a nearly completed tenement at the northeast corner of Madison and Rutgers Streets in New York collapsed, injuring eight workers, two critically (Figure 7.2). The building department found nothing improper with the mortar specifications or mixture, ruling that the incident was completely accidental, as the storm washed out a footing. However, owner Benjamin Rubenstein, along with his foreman and an injured Italian laborer (whom detectives hauled from his hospital bed), were arrested after a bricklayer testified that he had recently quit his job at the site because he did not believe the work was safe (workers had also quit for the same reason before the Buddensiek collapse). It is unclear if Rubenstein, who claimed he used only "the richest of materials" on the new-law tenement, or his associates were eventually charged with a crime; the collapsed building was repaired and is extant.[31] Tragically, five years later in Chelsea, just outside Boston, a large store and tenement under construction at 177 Winnisimmet Street by builders Morris Gordon and Morris Seegel collapsed, killing eight workers and injuring thirteen. That incident was blamed on the reuse and improper modifications of a brick party wall that had been damaged in a major conflagration that had leveled the city earlier that year. In covering Gordon's

Figure 7.2. Benjamin Rubenstein tenement in state of partial collapse, New York, 1903. Alfred E. Badt, architect. This collapse of this new-law tenement under construction at the corner of Madison and Rutgers Streets had echoes of the Buddensiek affair two decades earlier, although the builder was held blameless. Although the collapse seriously injured a number of workers, the nearly complete building was repaired and is extant. Courtesy of Milstein Division of United States History, Local History, and Genealogy, New York Public Library, Astor, Lenox, and Tilden Foundations.

manslaughter arrest, the *Boston Globe* was quick to note that "four men of his race" paid the Russian Jewish immigrant builder's bail.[32] In this and nearly all of the other cases, the inexperience of the contractor and his workmen was at the root of the problem. Incidents like these, however, helped to further the reformers' claims to control over these landscapes and the people within them.

Less dramatically, tenement architects were likewise the subject of intense scrutiny. The speed at which they worked particularly prompted suspicion. In the early months of 1901, just before the new law took effect, architect Michael Bernstein, a prominent decorated tenement architect, filed plans with the building department for seventy-six tenements to get ahead of the new requirements.[33] His volume of filings was somewhat greater than any other architect's in the major construction boom related to those laws but was not unusual for Bernstein. For example, a year earlier on a single day, December 22, 1899, he filed for fifty-nine permits to build tenements across the city.[34] The prior year's experience notwithstanding, the permits filed in 1901 raised the suspicion of reformer Lawrence Veiller, who had been the chief architect of the new law. He accused Bernstein of systematically evading the law by filing dummy plans, based on a building at 273 East Eighty-First Street, then amending them to conform to site conditions.[35] Some plans were found to contain the address of other buildings, and in other cases the dimensions did not exactly match the size of the lot for which the building was intended. Four-fifths of the permits were revoked by the department after Veiller's investigation. Bernstein issued a blanket denial, claiming he acted in good faith, and blaming his surveyors for the inconsistent measurements.[36] He declared, "No architect living has ever filed a perfect plan. There are always little improvements made here and there."[37] Indeed, the evidence of the eventually completed buildings cut against Veiller's claim; they hardly appeared to have been cast from the same mold, and few resembled the East Eighty-First Street building.[38] Yet Veiller maintained the violations were willful and that Bernstein was aided by corrupt inspectors in the department.[39]

While Bernstein asserted that he did not understand why the department "should have selected me out of the thousands of architects who do the same thing," the suspicion with which he, as one of the city's first successful Russian Jewish architects, was treated may have been a result of the undercurrent of anti-Semitism that plagued the leadership of the new Tenement House Department.[40] While Veiller, then deputy commissioner, filled the upper echelons of the department with former associates from the Charity Organization Society, in apparent violation of civil service rules, he was accused of showing extra scrutiny of Jewish applicants and subjecting those he did hire to harassment. The matter came to a head in 1903 when he fired inspector Louis Rosenbaum for refusing to work during the High Holy Days. Commissioner Robert DeForest, a prominent corporate lawyer and millionaire who had been appointed by mayor Seth Low to head the department, subsequently sent a notice to employees that all requests for time off during the upcoming holidays would be declined, and absence would result in dismissal, citing the large number of Jewish employees in the lower ranks of the department.[41] Some department employees disagreed that animus was at the root of the incident.[42] *The American Hebrew,* a newspaper targeted to assimilated German Jews sympathetic to reform, defended DeForest, suggesting the incident was blown out of proportion for political gain by Tammany operatives.[43] Yet, as we have seen, reformers frequently framed their critique of the tenement in anti-Semitic terms. It is clear, at the very least, that in a broader sense the concern over the changes wrought by mass immigration and immigrants themselves, with unfamiliar culture and mores, was an animating spirit of much of the reform movement. The Bernstein affair and related incidents reinforced a stereotype that reformers like DeForest, Veiller, and Riis had been promoting for years: that nobody associated with tenement construction, whether builders, architects, or even low-level building inspectors, particularly those of Jewish origin, could be trusted without intense oversight.

A Lesson in Stone

Early in 1906, architect Grosvenor Atterbury was struggling with how to handle a new commission, for which his training at Yale and Columbia had ill prepared him. Hired by wealthy steel magnate Henry Phipps to design the prototype for a series of model tenements, Atterbury knew that the buildings needed to be a "lesson in stone" for their tenants, instilling in them notions of frugality and cleanliness. "What is to be said to the tenement population is to be said plainly," Atterbury declared to the magazine *Charities and the Commons* later that year. "Flourishes are not wanted any more than they can be afforded."[44] Given this, Atterbury criticized his own design for the Phipps Houses, published by the magazine, as too elaborate (Figure 7.3). Indeed, he provided an unusually high level of architectural articulation for a model tenement, including a rusticated ground level, two broad-arched entrances, corner quoins, and a faux-hipped roof covered in metal tile. Yet few of these elements could be classified as applied ornament. In an architectural theory that anticipated the early modernism of many European social housing experiments, Atterbury declared that the ideal solution in the "matter of construction and decoration" was far from reached:

> While . . . these two elements [construction and decoration] should doubtless be synonymous and result in a building that will produce a decorative effect through ornamental construction, without constructed ornament, the model tenements erected so far have almost universally failed to express the "home" idea which seems such a vital element in any proper definition of a model tenement.[45]

In providing such decorative elements, he sought to avoid the institutional and "hopelessly dreary" aspects of most model tenements. Although Atterbury's buildings were more attractive than most model tenements, they ended up looking much like the institution they were.

"PHIPP'S HOUSES" MODEL TENEMENT NUMBER·1·SHOWING STREET FRONT *and* SPACIOUS INTERIOR COURT GROSVENOR ATTERBURY ARCHITECT NEW YORK CITY

Figure 7.3. Study for the Phipps Houses, 321–337 East Thirty-First Street, New York, 1906 (demolished). Grosvenor Atterbury, architect. Atterbury himself thought his use of ornament on this attractive model tenement was less than ideal but contrasted with the "hopelessly dreary" model treatments that were more common. From *The Craftsman*, April 1906. Courtesy of Art and Picture Collection, The New York Public Library, Astor, Lenox, and Tilden Foundations.

Ornament, redolent with associations with the speculator's decorated tenement, sent the wrong message to residents, whose tastes needed to be disciplined to reflect their station. Indeed, the architect perceived his role as a didactic one, that he should be composing in stone a lesson on thrift, honesty, and integrity. To this end, he regretted that some of the "flourishes" he provided were not strictly necessary or honest in their expression of the structure behind them. In particular, he found fault with the roofline. There, in order to avoid the "bald, poverty-stricken" appearance, he employed "the despised galvanized iron cornice and metal tile 'tin-eyebrows' for an otherwise substantially and honestly constructed building."

When it came to applied or "constructed" ornament, Atterbury and his colleagues usually settled in the same place. It was to be circumscribed or banished entirely, and buildings should be modest and efficient, like the workers who lived inside them. To Atterbury, the lesson was political; he hoped to use his designs to impose a traditional and monolithic view of national culture. In the design of his model tenements, to be occupied largely by immigrant tenants, he sought "the cultivation of national sentiment—of the American idea as exemplified in our great patriots." Through appropriate architectural forms, he asserted, the social and political dangers of the tenement district could be ameliorated. A well-designed project could "combat . . . the corner saloon and the district boss—the translators of 'freedom of conscience' of our forefathers into the 'free graft' of today."

Indeed, these model tenements encoded in built form much of the spirit of the housing reform movement: its good intentions and high-handed moralism, its public spirit but seemingly greater concern for spiritual than material well-being, its insistence on purity and simplicity, its mistrust or misunderstanding of urban working-class culture. Many of these ideals traced their roots to the earliest strains of puritan culture in America, which placed a premium on modesty, functionalism, frugality, and action that appropriately reflected one's standing in society. Yet, this policing of class boundaries was increasingly seen as backwards in an expansive age of industrial capitalism. Model tenements were designed by prestigious architects and financed by wealthy backers, many from a genteel New England background, who often based their designs on schemes pioneered in London, among other precedents.[46] The buildings' appearance was calculated to reflect and reinforce tenants' low standing in the social and economic hierarchy. As another reformer put it, model tenements that were "too high-toned" were to be "steadfastly avoided."[47] While these reformers sought a limited profit from their projects, usually 6 to 8 percent, they charged market rent, ideally investing excess profits into expansion. And backers used their position as landlord to police their tenements for the moral decay they thought was rife within commercial housing.

These austere, utilitarian tenements were elite designers' and backers' logical solution to new construction in the stereotyped slum, a place outsiders viewed with contempt and disgust, in which excess or display was held to signal not material progress but the profligacy and decadence of their residents. Thus, the reformers' buildings reproduced many of what tenants found distasteful about the slums. The lack of parlors, the austere, poverty-stricken appearance, and the lack of views onto the street signaled a refusal to engage with tenants' tastes and self-conceptions. The reformers' lack of accommodations for economic coping strategies such as home production, taking in boarders, and storage of material for trade, as well as the dearth of small stores and appealing diversions like saloons and dance halls within these complexes signaled a lack of understanding of their economic circumstances and cultural preferences.

Still, these buildings were constructed as the result of earnest crusades by reformers throughout the nineteenth century. In Boston, the first model tenement was constructed in 1852, well before purpose-built private tenements were common in that city. The institution was built by a group of clergy and businessmen calling themselves the Model Lodging House Association.[48] Prominent among this group was Harvard professor and influential cultural critic Charles Eliot Norton. Employing English model tenements as a precedent, the group built two buildings under slightly different designs by architects Benjamin F. Dwight and Charles Kirby. Now known only through a woodcut, plans, and descriptions in the *Atlantic Monthly*, the narrow five-story buildings had four small apartments on each floor, arranged around a central winding staircase. Tellingly, the exterior was strictly utilitarian, resembling contemporaneous mill construction. Norton, who at that time was a leading commentator on American architecture, not surprisingly took interest in the appearance of the buildings, which he described as "substantial and not unornamental."[49] Architectural historian Cynthia Zaitzevsky has called this double negative statement "high praise" from Norton. But that someone of his stature, closely connected to the American aesthetic discourse at midcentury, found this building appearance pleasing was telling.[50] It is a clear statement that the utilitarian tenement represented the Anglo-American ideal for appropriate architecture for the poor and working class. The Osborn Place buildings set the pattern for Boston model housing into the twentieth century. In the 1870s, Kirby designed a series of similar tenements on East Canton Street in the South End for the Model Lodging House Association (Figure 7.4). Funded by a bequest from textile magnate Amos Lawrence, they were nearly identical to the Osborn Place buildings but for the addition of a mansard roof.[51]

This mode was remarkably persistent in Boston: for sixty years (between 1852 and at least 1914) every model tenement in that city was built with a facade as plain as a storage warehouse. No other building type went through such little stylistic evolution through this very dynamic period in American architecture. The Boston Cooperative Building Association, the best known and most influential model housing association in the city, began using this austere mode as early as 1870 and as late as the 1910s for its Endicott and Thatcher Street buildings in the North End, as well as developments in the South End. The association employed well-known and respected architects, including Alexander W. Longfellow and the firm of Cabot & Chandler (Figure 7.5; see also Figure I.2). Historian Amy Johnson noted that the backers of the company "felt visual clarity and simplicity best established a pleasing appearance." Eschewing ornament, to them, was an attempt to avoid "stylistic fads" and connected to deeply conservative strains of Boston architecture. In doing so, Johnson argued, company architects "emphasized connections to the local vernacular."[52] Johnson, following architectural historian Margaret Henderson Floyd, suggested that Longfellow's designs were reminiscent of the modest Federal-era row houses of the architect's native Portland, Maine.[53] By attempting to design buildings that would not be subject to the vagaries of fashion, the association built tenements that were deeply and intentionally unstylish. These architects refused to engage in the high styles in which they were so well versed because they did not feel such styles, and the ornament associated with them, were appropriate for the tenants of these buildings.

The landscape of reform tenements was more varied in New York, where backers allowed residents a somewhat higher standard of appearance. While the earliest reform tenements in New York, such as the 1850 Gotham Court and the 1855 Workingman's Home, exhibited many of the same characteristics as the Boston reform tenements, later philanthropic tenements, such as Alfred White's Riverside Buildings in Brooklyn, evinced modest attempts at ornamentation (Figure 7.6).[54]

Figure 7.4. Lawrence Model Lodging House, 79 East Canton Street, Boston (1874). Charles Kirby, architect. On a block of similar buildings built over the span of twenty years, the Lawrence Model Lodging House was typical of the utilitarian treatment of most model tenements in Boston. Photograph by Sean Litchfield.

Figure 7.5. Boston Cooperative Building Association Tenement, 159 Endicott Street, Boston (1914). Alexander W. Longfellow, architect. Designed by an École des Beaux-Arts–trained architect, this model tenement was deeply and intentionally unfashionable. The tenement at right, nearly identical, was built in 1870 by the same organization. Photograph by Sean Litchfield.

Borrowing explicitly from models in London, the Riverside Buildings were articulated mostly through brick corbeling, a picturesque roofline, and ornamental ironwork on the open staircase balconies. Reformers considered the open circulation in these buildings a great innovation, reducing or eliminating the interior common spaces they thought were prone to mischief. Still, the appearance of the Riverside Buildings is more closely related to industrial rather than domestic architecture.

Around the turn of the twentieth century, housing as a social issue elicited considerable attention from elite architects in New York. This movement was spearheaded by Ernest Flagg, the École des Beaux-Arts–trained architect who was called the "father of the modern model tenement."[55] Writing voluminously on housing, he was a consummate scientific planner who decried the twenty-five-foot-wide lot as wasteful.[56] Instead he advocated for what he called the open-court plan with wide, square buildings, often partially freestanding, that provided generous courtyard space. Flagg's open-court plan, first constructed in 1896 in a project for the philanthropic City and Suburban Homes Company, became the basis for open space and courtyard dimensions after the passage of the 1901 Tenement House Act. While Flagg's designs for the large Mills Houses, model lodging houses, were generally institutional in both scale and articulation, his model tenements, such as those for the City and Suburban Homes Company, were consistently six-story buildings of sanitary glazed white brick, sometimes enlivened by a terra-cotta door surround (Figure 7.7).[57]

These buildings represented many of the compromises elite reformers were will-

Figure 7.6. Riverside Buildings, Joralemon Street, Brooklyn (1890). William Field, architect. Photograph by Sean Litchfield.

ing to make on behalf of their tenants, with whom they shared little cultural knowledge (Figure 7.8). While better lit, units were significantly smaller than the four-room units available in the standard tenement. More important, they lacked parlors or dining rooms, cherished symbols of domesticity for many residents, substituting the combined living-cooking space then favored by Progressive reformers. Peter Herter particularly objected to these rooms, often only nine feet wide, many of which faced onto light courts, and some of which had only narrow windows (Figure 7.9). "What a magnificent prospect for the 'reformed' tenants on a sultry summer day," he declared. "This [arrangement] may be hygienic, but the woman who doesn't know the meaning of the word but has to spend the greater portion of her day in that living room is not likely to appreciate it to the point of paying for it." Recognizing that these buildings replaced the cherished status symbols of the working class with at best nominal improvements in sanitation and privacy, Herter described Flagg's model tenements as "buildings which, like medicine, may be 'good' but are nasty to take. A public that demands its living rooms in the front of the house won't change its taste in such matters just because you tell it is better to be content with an outlook on an inside court."[58]

Figure 7.7. Alfred Corning Clark buildings of the City and Suburban Homes Company, West Sixty-Eighth Street, New York (1896; demolished). Ernest Flagg, architect. The company was one of the largest operators of model tenements in New York. As its name suggests, it also built developments of freestanding worker houses in suburban neighborhoods, notably Homewood in Brooklyn. A similar iron balcony originally appeared on the sixth floor of the Bishop Tenement (see Figure I.1). From Riis, *The Battle with the Slum*, 131.

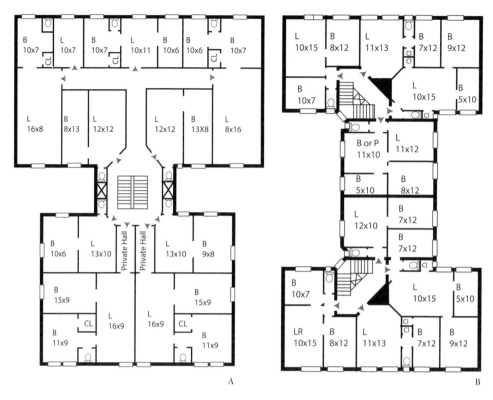

| B 10x7 | L 10x7 | B 10x7 | L 10x11 | B 10x6 | B 10x6 | B 10x7 |
| L 16x8 | B 8x13 | L 12x12 | | L 12x12 | B 13X8 | L 8x16 |

B 10x6	L 13x10	Private Hall	Private Hall	L 13x10	B 9x8
B 15x9					B 15x9
B 11x9	CL	L 16x9	L 16x9	CL	B 11x9

L 10x15	B 8x12	L 11x13	B 7x12	B 9x12
B 10x7		L 10x15		B 5x10
B or P 11x10	L 11x12
B 5x10	B 8x12
L 12x10	B 7x12
	B 7x12
B 10x7	L 10x15	B 5x10
LR 10x15	B 8x12	L 11x13	B 7x12	B 9x12

A   B

Figure 7.8. A, Ernest Flagg, winning floor plan from the Charity Organization Society competition for model tenements, 1896. Notice the similarities between the footprint of this open-court plan and the improved tenements of the 1890s. Unlike those buildings, however, this model tenement lacked parlors, dining rooms, and full baths. Based on Riis, *The Battle with the Slum*, 150. B, Plan, Florence Van Cortlandt Bishop Tenement, 58 Hester Street, New York (1901). Ernest Flagg, architect. For exterior, see Figure I.1. Drawing by author.

Figure 7.9. Narrow combined kitchen–living room of the Riverside Buildings, Brooklyn, pictured circa 1890. While tenants preferred separate kitchens and parlors (along with dining rooms), these larger combined live-work spaces were commonly advocated by reformers to discourage boarders and home work. Note the lack of wallpaper, mantel, and casings then typical of tenement parlors. For exterior, see Figure 7.6. Courtesy of Jacob A. (Jacob August) Riis (1849–1914)/Museum of the City of New York, 90.13.2.297.

Taste, Conflict, and the Model Flat

At the same time Grosvenor Atterbury was musing over the correct design for his buildings for the Phipps estate, Mabel Kittredge was fighting an uphill battle on the Lower East Side. Having rented a tenement apartment, under the auspices of the Henry Street Settlement, to use as a model flat, the nation's foremost expert on domestic propriety and scientific housekeeping was preaching the Gospel of Simplicity in the waning days of the Gilded Age.[59] Her very precise notions of how a tenement apartment should look, put on display in her 1906 model flat, stood in sharp contrast to the way many immigrants aspired to decorate their spaces (Figure 7.10). The walls were painted in a light color, perhaps yellow; wallpaper was out of the question— too unsanitary. The elaborate woodwork surrounding the windows was painted brilliant white and deemphasized; surely she wished it had not been there to begin with. There were no fancy lambrequins on the mantel in the front room, another object she

LIVING ROOM OF THE MODEL FLAT

Figure 7.10. Mabel Kittredge's ascetic vision of a model New York tenement living room, circa 1905. This image shows a tenement parlor transformed by the Gospel of Simplicity, which banished plush, heavily ornamented furniture and wallpaper. Compare to Figures 6.5 and 6.6. From Bertha H. Smith, "The Gospel of Simplicity as Applied to Tenement Homes," *The Craftsman* 9 (1905): 81. Courtesy of General Research Division, The New York Public Library, Astor, Lenox, and Tilden Foundations.

probably would have banished if she could. Floors were stained in antique oak, except in the kitchen, where wood was left bare. No carpets or rugs were permitted, except one small braided mat by the bed to accommodate evening prayers in a kneeling position. Open shelves were provided for the dining room in place of the sideboard, an aspirational object of many tenement residents that she felt was "very ugly." Blue and white stoneware dishes took the place of gilt china. All the furniture, custom ordered in the new "mission style," was bought new and finished with an alcohol-based stain. Plain muslin curtains took the place of fancy lace. To enliven the otherwise dull environment, "a few good pictures" were pasted to the wall.[60]

Just as her middle-class friends were purging their parlors of the plush furniture, elaborate fabric hangings, and carefully arranged bric-a-brac that had formerly defined a respectable home, tenement residents were enthralled in their new ability to purchase these same items.[61] Her call to tenement residents to turn their back on these things demonstrated progressive priorities that intersected with the long-standing Anglo-American discourse on the need for restraint in material goods for the working class. Kittredge and the other settlement-house workers made it plain that immigrants' taste and attitudes toward consumption were as much in need of reform as their housing situation. But doing so would come at a price: immigrants would have to abandon their newfound ability to use symbols of luxury. Visitors to the model flat seem to have been skeptical, if not downright insulted. For instance, Kittredge noted that many visitors recoiled at the bare floors, which they contended were "a sign of poverty." But Kittredge was unconcerned with such symbolic values, insisting that the improvement in cleanliness was far more important. Likewise the mission-style furniture did not seem like a good value for tenants who

> want all they can get for their money. They think more machine scroll work, gorgon heads and claws, and the more big brass handles, the more stuffing, the more colors in the plush, the better. What the furniture man shows, the immigrant house-wife buys, thinking, and quite truly be it confessed, she is becoming Americanized. Simplicity is not yet the creed of the many.[62]

Indeed, while the immigrant working class may have been revolted by it, reformers were quite enamored with the simplicity of mission-style furniture and the aesthetic purity it seemed to embody. Reformer Lawrence Veiller, for instance, reportedly even received a William Morris–style chair as a kickback from a furniture dealer to whom he awarded a large no-bid contract for a prodigious quantity of filing cabinets for the New York Tenement House Department, one of the agency's early scandals.[63]

To become respectable in the eyes of Kittredge and her ilk, the working class had to forgo the elaborate ornamental forms and showy dress that were newly available to them, selecting instead goods that were more appropriate to people of their station. This was the same gospel being preached in middle-class homes. But it held a much different implication for those of a more precarious social and economic position. The comfortable middle class no longer needed elaborate "things" to express their identity and could choose a more sophisticated and modern discourse of objects in which simplicity, restraint, and quality of materials and workmanship replaced the tradition of symbolic communication through ornamentation. Yet many urban immigrants were not yet in a position to accept a message so challenging to their preferences and the tastes of their neighbors. To them, Kittredge's model flat was an affront to their self-image, perhaps with sinister overtones of the sumptuary laws some had historically experienced in Europe. To be encouraged to revert to simplicity in an age still enthralled with gilt and complexity would not have seemed like becoming more "Americanized." It would have seemed like nothing more than an overt admission of their poverty and insecurity in an unfamiliar culture.

Ornament and the Suburban Workingman's Home

Many reformers felt that constructing urban tenements, even a flat in a model tenement furnished to the precepts of the Gospel of Simplicity, was still fundamentally problematic. William B. Patterson, the Methodist Episcopal faith leader who believed the tenement was an "impediment to God's plan for the home," implored his fellow reformers "to put less emphasis upon the matter of building 'model' tenements, and more emphasis upon the necessity of single houses for single families, in order that the home may be preserved."[64] This reflected a widespread sentiment among reformers.[65] Writer and reform advocate Marcus T. Reynolds agreed, noting in 1895 that model tenements "do not lift [the tenant] out of the tenement. At best they provide him with better rooms and better air, but they are tenement rooms and tenement air for all that. A cottage in the suburbs is certainly more attractive, and . . . far better results are reached than by any other means."[66]

Reformers saw the ultimate solution to the housing problem in small cottages for the working class, constructed in the suburbs. These projects would lessen the threatening density of the tenement districts, solve many of the planning problems of small urban lots, and most importantly allow workers to become invested in the system of private property through ownership of their homes. They considered "proprietorship" a moral good, and renting an evil having what they perceived as deleterious effects on social stability (even though many in the middle class also rented their homes). Some even cast the ownership of private single-family homes as a means of achieving racial purity, arguing that the private residence and the nuclear family it promoted were essential to the preservation of the social order, in which backers were deeply invested.[67] Responding in 1903 to the complaint that proposed new tenement laws would discourage the construction of the improved tenements that were then being built en masse, Boston reformer Robert Treat Paine told a newspaper, "So far as impulse is given to scatter the population into healthier suburbs, and into small, detached suburban homes . . . students of social welfare . . . must certainly rejoice."[68] Forcing the working population into the suburbs, ultimately, was the primary goal of housing reform in the nineteenth century.

In single-family house developments, workers—in practicality only the best-paid, skilled workers who already occupied the best tenements—would be sold modest single-family houses on suburban lots and provided with easy mortgage terms, usually arranged through the organization sponsoring them or through the sale of shares in a development company. The contours of such programs have been studied in detail elsewhere.[69] But in contrast to the model tenement, most of these houses made liberal use of architectural ornamentation. For example, in one of the most ambitious single-family home development projects of the period, the nearly one hundred houses developed by Paine at Sunnyside in the Boston suburb of Roxbury in 1891, facades were substantially more ornamental than those of even the average lower-middle-class single-family house in the neighborhood (Plate 21).[70] Fully engaged in the romantic picturesque iconography that had been part of the Anglo-American response to urbanism since midcentury, these houses featured complex rooflines, fish-scale shingles, elaborate bargeboards, spindle-work porches, and colored-glass windows. These buildings were a stark contrast to Paine's downtown model tenements, which were executed on strictly utilitarian lines. Later experiments in suburban worker housing, including Atterbury's Forest Hills Gardens in Queens, Percy Griffin's Homewood in Brooklyn, and Kilham & Hopkins's Woodbourne near Boston, would consistently employ picturesque landscape conventions, often with an emphasis on "homelike" appearance.[71] The aversion to ornament on buildings for the working class clearly applied only to center-city premises that were rented. Once the residents became owners and were located away from the corruption of the city, ornament became appropriate. Since these buildings would be occupied by homeowners, who were seen as having a higher status as they were engaging in bourgeois strategies of identity formation despite their working-class status, they were afforded greater access to elaborated forms.[72] Yet, like the reform tenement itself, these single-family projects did not directly answer the needs of the bulk of the downtown tenement population, largely because of the high cost and lengthy travel times of public transportation, as well as the social and cultural isolation of these areas.

But if reformers were not successful in moving the bulk of the working class into suburban single-family houses, tenement builders would soon look to the urban periphery as the next site for improved multifamily housing. In these outer districts the tenement and the suburban ideal would come into direct conflict, while also meaning an end for the decorated tenement downtown.

Epilogue

The Afterlife of the Decorated Tenement

Look at the moldings, look at the cornice. That's terra-cotta! . . . It's got style, it's got dignity! . . . This one's still here, it can be saved, it can be restored.

Mason Baylor, *Batteries Not Included*, 1987

When the Jarmulowsky bank, so crucial to the introduction of improved tenements in the immigrant enclaves of New York in the late nineteenth century, failed dramatically in 1914, battered by unrest in Europe, angry mobs of disaffected depositors descended on Sender Jarmulowsky's son Meyer, who had taken over the business of his late father.[1] But the dramatic scene did not play out at the converted Federal-era row house near Rutgers Square where Sender had lived after immigrating in 1873. Nor did the crowds remain at the bank's new high-rise office building nearby at Canal and Grand Streets, designed by Lafayette Goldstone. Instead, the mob coalesced in front of Meyer's home at Belle Court, a modern, six-story, brick and terra-cotta apartment house with steam heat, elevators, and a large marble lobby, designed by George Fred Pelham, the so-called plan mill architect.[2] Standing on a breezy site overlooking the Hudson River in Washington Heights, it was a long subway ride away from the Lower East Side. The family bank, with a syndicate of developers, had promoted its construction five years earlier, along with blocks upon blocks of buildings like it, built for members of growing and largely immigrant middle and upper working classes (Figure E.1).

Like many of the early promoters of the decorated tenement, the Jarmulowsky family's interests had expanded outward from the dense downtown neighborhoods where they had first settled in America, moving to new peripheral areas, like Yorkville, East Harlem, and Washington Heights, where they would come to carry on building operations that far exceeded their downtown developments in the nineteenth century. The loss of connection to these older neighborhoods resulted in a decreased interest in improvement there. In Boston, Louis Segel departed his 1898 The Gothic in the West End, the result of years of improving housing standards for himself and his family, around 1907 for a large William E. Clarke–designed brick apartment house built by himself and a partner just off Blue Hill Avenue in formerly suburban Roxbury.[3] The enclaves of tenement builders that had grown up in the West End and Lower East

Side rapidly disintegrated in the first decade of the twentieth century. Harry Fischel moved to Yorkville in 1904, Harris Fine to East Harlem by 1910, Peter and Henry Herter to a building Peter developed on Park Avenue and Fifty-Eighth Street around 1903, and Frank Herter and Ernst Schneider to the Bronx. As these figures increasingly disengaged from their former communities, their interests shifted away.

With the departure of the immigrant elite and the most economically stable residents to these new neighborhoods, the interest in building improved tenements downtown vanished. Indeed, many things were just better in these peripheral neighborhoods. With rising wages in the first decades of the century came further rising housing standards, which even the new tenements built in the turn-of-the-century building boom could not fully meet. The larger lots available in the outer neighborhoods were more affordable and represented far less of a planning challenge than the narrow, previously occupied downtown spaces, which housing reformers had long sought to discourage as tenement sites. Unconstrained by lot sizes intended for single-family row houses, these areas saw the construction of apartment buildings that looked much more like the wide, substantial European tenements that had initially acted as a precedent for the earlier decorated tenement phenomenon. Crucially,

Figure E.1. Broadway looking south from West 180th Street, New York, circa 1910. This was a block north and east of Meyer Jarmoswky's apartment at Belle Court, which was similar to these buildings but lacked the ground-level storefronts. This Washington Heights scene was representative of an assertively urban landscape of large and commodious new apartment buildings rising on the city's periphery, many sponsored by architects and builders who had previously lived and worked in the tenement neighborhoods. Courtesy of Thaddeus Wilkerson/Museum of the City of New York, X2011.34.1440.

with better, cheaper mass transit options, these locations were finally accessible to a wider swath of the working and ascendant middle class. Many of the same sorts of builders and architects who a decade or two earlier would have been found working on Broome Street in the Lower East Side or Blossom Street in the West End could by the 1910s be found working in Brownsville, Brooklyn, and Blue Hill Avenue in Roxbury. As Lee Friedman observed of Boston builders, by the time of World War I, "apartment houses, rather than tenements, became the goal" of many who had formerly been active builders in the North and West Ends.[4]

But the move to the periphery did not (yet) mean the suburbanization of the working class. Indeed, in many ways the development of these areas between 1905 and 1930 represented not an end but an expansion and elaboration of the decorated tenement phenomenon of the previous generation. Carried on by many of the same architects and builders, or their children and successors, it represented much of the same assertively urban outlook, insistence on decorative forms, and interest in improving housing standards that the earlier tenements had. Many housing reformers had hoped that the movement of the working class away from the center city would reestablish the supremacy of the freestanding single-family home. Although plenty of such housing was built, in many of these outer neighborhoods, particularly those that incurred a substantial outflow of residents from the tenement districts, a version of the dense urban forms perfected downtown was reproduced on the periphery. These areas were filled with attached, indeed often quite ambitious, three- to six-story masonry buildings. These were often built in developments that included a range of commercial and eventually civic and religious structures as well. These buildings showed a continued interest in the eclectic use of industrially made architectural ornament, although to lesser degrees with rising prices and changing tastes of the interwar period.

This preference for urban forms was particularly noteworthy as these builders reached beyond peripheral city neighborhoods to places that had been suburban in the nineteenth century. Instead of wholeheartedly embracing the suburban ideal of freestanding single-family houses on garden lots, as had been the tradition in these areas, these builders continued to prefer dense, multifamily forms, grander and more commodious but otherwise little altered from their tenement forebears. In the suburbs these builders battled not the slum stereotype but open discrimination by groups eager to maintain these areas as homogenous oases of single-family dwellings.[5] Regardless, former tenement builders filled previously suburban tracts in parts of outer Roxbury, the Bronx and Brookline, Allston and Flatbush with large apartment blocks. In the case of Eastern Parkway in Brooklyn, the Grand Concourse in the Bronx, Commonwealth Avenue in Allston, and Beacon Street in Brookline, they lined grand landscaped boulevards with large apartment buildings whose City Beautiful pretensions and spacious quarters belied their roots in the tenements. Frederick Norcross's 1913 apartment building on Commonwealth Avenue in Allston for Benjamin Levine was typical of decorated tenement practices and associations

Figure E.2. Benjamin Levine Building, 1300 Commonwealth Avenue, Allston, Massachusetts (1913). Frederick Norcross, architect. This large apartment building on a landscaped boulevard was typical of decorated tenement practices and associations appearing in a formerly suburban area on the outskirts of Boston. Photograph by Sean Litchfield.

transmuted onto a formerly suburban boulevard (Figure E.2). Construction of such buildings continued through the 1930s. The tradition of the decorated tenement reached the end of the line in these suburbs by the time of World War II, supplanted by changing tastes, changing meanings of decorative forms, and new demographics.

The New, Old Slums

Back downtown, the decorated tenement phenomenon came to an end quickly in the first decade of the twentieth century (Figure E.3). After half a decade of comparatively anemic construction, Marans Court, the 1913 building at the corner of Hester and Ludlow Streets, was among the last major decorated tenements built by European immigrants in the Lower East Side.[6] While Chinese developers in the post–World War I era would construct a number of purpose-built tenements, particularly around lower Mott Street, that group's contribution to this landscape would be largely in alterations to buildings built by previous groups within an expanding Chinatown.[7] Likewise, a few tenements by Italian American builders appeared in the persistent enclave of the North End during the interwar period, but these developments were the exception, paling in comparison to the quantity and quality of housing being developed elsewhere.

With the removal of many of the groups who had supported improved tenement construction, the trajectory of the downtown neighborhoods after World War I in many ways mirrored their history in the antebellum period, when the movement of the Anglo-American elite away had caused their initial decline. Importantly, the curtailment of European immigration, first by World War I, then by the tough nativist immigration policies of the 1920s, stemmed the flow of new residents, who had supported the construction of new tenements over the previous six decades. Inner-city working-class areas began an inexorable population decline that was particularly acute in the 1920s and 1930s. The old tenements were rapidly emptying out as they lost their appeal in an era of rising living standards with fewer new immigrant residents willing to accept what was increasingly perceived as lower-quality housing. This lack of demand, combined with the economic pressures caused by new rent regulation, meant the nineteenth-century tenements lost much of their value.[8] Stricter new building codes, now applied retroactively to existing buildings, put increasing pressure on landlords, many of whom (particularly in New York) chose to close their buildings for residential purposes rather than comply with the new laws and spend money they knew they would never get back.[9] Conditions worsened in these rapidly aging buildings, which by the New Deal era had taken on many of the aspects of the antebellum slum.

The slum stereotype of the nineteenth century gained new currency in this era of expansive reform, with the process of reconstruction and improvement that these neighborhoods underwent in the Gilded Age increasingly lost to memory, buried under an outpouring of reform narratives and a rehashing of old stereotypes. Yet, in this period particularly, tenants began to organize around their own interests, taking on increasingly assertive tactics, like rent strikes, which eventually led to effective

Figure E.3. Orchard Street looking north from Rivington Street, in an iconic early twentieth-century view. The modestly ornamented tenements at left were developed in the 1890s by Sender Jarmulowsky and designed by his son Meyer, who later became a professional architect. Courtesy of Milstein Division of United States History, Local History, and Genealogy, New York Public Library, Astor, Lenox, and Tilden Foundations.

political organization. These activists were concerned not just with problems like poor maintenance and inadequate heating but with the issue of high rent (and low wages), the fundamental cause of the housing problem, which most reformers of an earlier era had been loath to address. The nature of the housing problem as an artifact of social and economic inequality, not merely of faulty architectural design, was increasingly recognized.[10]

Tenement Demolition

Critics of the tenement landscape were convinced these buildings were not long for the world. As Earnest Flagg declared in 1894, "The [tenements] already constructed are of such a flimsy character that they cannot last forever."[11] Reformers and public authorities over the next seven decades would do everything they could to make that prediction a reality. Clearance efforts began in earnest in New York with the construction of Mulberry Bend (later Christopher Columbus) Park on the site of one of the city's most infamous slums in 1897, before the tenement building era had even ended (Figure E.4).[12] The subsequent decades in both cities would see an accelerating rate of tenement loss due to public works projects, including the widening of

Figure E.4. Mulberry Bend Park, New York, circa 1905. Jacob Riis's "Dens of Death," seen in Figure I.4, once stood on the left side of this site. Courtesy of Library of Congress, Prints and Photographs Division.

numerous Lower East Side streets and the creation of the Paul Revere Mall in the North End.[13] After the 1920s, many landlords welcomed the condemnation of their tenements as a way to rid themselves of increasingly unproductive property. Indeed, few saw the demolitions as anything other than a social good. There were, however, occasional pangs of recognition of what was being lost. Watching the demolition of an early twentieth-century tenement in the 1930s, Helen Hall, director of the Henry Street Settlement, recalled what an improvement these buildings represented when they were new. She mused that the tenement "must have been called elegant when it was built 35 years ago. . . . The passerby saw fancy pediments over the front windows, a decorative cornice across the top. But the impressiveness of this new law tenement was more than skin deep. It had fireproof hallways, inside toilets, and an air court."[14]

The demolition efforts would eventually lead to the clearance of large swaths of the Lower East Side and nearly the entirety of the West End of Boston, supported in part by the Federal Housing Act of 1949, which provided generous aid to demolition and redevelopment projects (Figure E.5). The campaigns supporting these clearance efforts relied heavily on slum stereotypes, many of which cast the housing conditions in these neighborhoods as little improved over what had existed there when Jacob Riis toured the neighborhoods more than a half century earlier. And like the earlier slum stereotype, these portrayals served to reinforce the claims of the urban planner—

Figure E.5. The demolition of Boston's West End in 1959, with Frederick Norcross–designed tenements in the background. Italian and Jewish developers had extensively rebuilt this neighborhood with decorated tenements in the early twentieth century. Its demolition exemplified the rehashed slum stereotype deployed by mid-twentieth-century urban planners to cast the working-class housing there as obsolete, substandard, and in need of radical intervention. Note the paneled wainscoting visible in the stair halls of demolished buildings. Photograph by Nick DeWolf.

who had largely overtaken the role of the housing reformer—for the need of drastic intervention.[15] With the federal government increasingly defining uniform national standards for housing design and construction, the urban working-class housing of the nineteenth century came to be systematically cast as substandard, and the dense neighborhoods in which it stood branded as obsolete, marked for disinvestment and eventually demolition.[16]

Many tenements would be replaced by tower-block housing projects for both the working and middle classes.[17] Combining the small-scale block and lot patterns of these neighborhoods into large superblocks, these projects contrasted greatly to the surrounding fine-grained landscape. These buildings were also the apogee of anti-ornamental architecture.[18] Representing a confluence of European modernist aesthetics, bureaucratic efficiency, and older American puritan notions about the propriety of decoration in multifamily housing, these buildings were among the most aggressively austere structures ever built in either city. While in the era of modern architecture this design choice did not carry the same symbolic weight as it had in the nineteenth century, many found the appearance of these new projects as deeply off-putting as the model tenement had been.

However, for many members of the middle-income working class in the postwar period, even (or perhaps especially) the assimilated children and grandchildren of the tenement residents, the modest house in the suburbs was now the goal. The postwar dichotomy between the regimented urban tower blocks and the modest but articulated freestanding house in the suburbs represented a continuation of the nineteenth-century paradigm of the austere model tenement and the ornamented workman's cottage. Many in the working class now decidedly preferred the latter, thanks in part to pervasive cultural messaging on the importance of the single-family house, a redoubling of individualism in an age of Communist hysteria, the rise of automobile travel, as well as generous government support for the suburban building boom.[19] To many, the tenement became a shameful episode of the American past. Despite continued investment in public housing and the persistent construction of new middle-class apartment buildings, particularly in New York, urban multifamily housing for the working class came to be seen as an anathema. Such housing being considered at best a temporary arrangement, permanent residence in such a building came to be seen as reserved for only those who by nature of race, income, or family structure were systematically excluded from the freestanding, suburban, single-family house that seemed to represent the apogee of material progress and the core of American life and social policy.

In some cases the urban renewal projects that replaced these old neighborhoods had deep resonances in the tenement building culture of the earlier period, a fact scarcely highlighted by their sponsors. For instance, architect Lafayette Goldstone, who as a young man worked as a tenement designer and builders' assistant, was proud later in life to design high-rise cooperative apartment buildings, which replaced blocks of Lower East Side tenements he designed and helped build in his youth.[20] In Boston, redevelopment authorities chose a development team headed by Theodore Shoolman to build Charles River Park, a complex of middle-class tower blocks built on part of the site of the cleared West End.[21] Shoolman was the nephew of Joseph Shoolman, who we met at the beginning of chapter 5 building a Salem Street tenement at the turn of the twentieth century. Both Joseph and his half-brother Max, Theodore's father, had been among the builders of the wrecked tenements.[22]

New Meanings of the Decorated Tenement

The regimented austerity of these tower-block projects, as well as the social conformity of suburbia, may have contributed to the downfall of the modernist urban project. By the 1960s critics such as Herbert Gans and Jane Jacobs advocated for the return to dense, diverse, and more human-scaled urbanism. Gans famously lived as a participant-observer in the West End in the years immediately before its demolition, noting that while the buildings had faults, most residents there were satisfied with the conditions, which allowed for low rents and a vibrant community.[23] Jacobs wrote extensively of the advantages of fine-grained urbanism and its capacity for self-regeneration over the deleterious influence of "cataclysmic" large-scale planning projects.[24] Together, their work was largely responsible for discrediting the century-old slum stereotype as a living entity relevant to contemporary life. This, combined with the withdrawal of funding for large-scale public works projects, the growing resentment over the use of eminent domain, increased interest in historic preservation, and the continued deindustrialization of these cities, meant an end by the early 1970s to wholesale tenement demolition by public authorities.[25] The tenement districts slowly came to be valued. For example, although it consisted mostly of early twentieth-century tenements, the surviving portion of the West End, rechristened the North Slope of Beacon Hill, would be subsumed in 1963 into the existing historic district that covered the older and much tonier South Slope, in part to buffer that elite neighborhood from further modernist interventions.

The following period of urban disinvestment, felt particularly acutely in New York in the 1970s and 1980s, once again changed the popular perception of the decorated tenement, as parts of the Lower East Side would be one of the areas hardest hit by the urban crisis.[26] (The generally newer and better tenements of the Bronx would be hit even worse.) In the shadow of blight caused by abandonment and arson, in neighborhoods overrun by crime, tarnished and battered architectural ornament became implicated in the popular-culture iconography of the urban landscape.[27] Grimy and abandoned tenements, usually with their iconic details prominently visible, were common tropes in the visual culture of this period. Perhaps the most famous work of this genre, the 1975 album cover of Led Zeppelin's *Physical Graffiti,* prominently featured a pair of 1890 Schneider & Herter–designed tenements on Saint Mark's Place, shorn of their cornice. They were thought by the album cover's designer Peter Corriston to have "interesting details."[28] Randall Wolff thought these details were interesting as well. Then a teenager, he, among others, spent late nights and early mornings surreptitiously salvaging ornament from the scores of abandoned tenements then awaiting demolition. His collection, parts of which were later donated to the Brooklyn Museum, would eventually number in the thousands of items, filling multiple loft spaces. Wolff would later spend a career reproducing these forms as an architectural sculptor.[29]

The decorated tenement even played a bit role in a major Hollywood film. Steven Spielberg's 1987 *Batteries Not Included* was set in a deteriorating East Village tenement, the appearance of which was based on a widely disseminated photograph of the ruins of East Fifth Street. In one scene in the film, residents appeal in vain to city historic preservation authorities in their efforts against an unscrupulous landlord, a thinly veiled Donald Trump character, trying to evict them to make way for a new high-rise. One resident, an archetypical bohemian enthralled with the romance of the place, implores a disdainful city preservationist to "look at the moldings, look at the cornice, that's terra-cotta . . . it's got style, it's got dignity . . . Oh? You don't like ornament." Unconvinced of the tenement's merits until it is restored to pristine condition through supernatural forces, the preservationist's fawning judgment of the building's facade as "fantastic, unbelievable, especially the moldings, corbeling, reliefs. It's perfect!" is among the film's concluding lines, signaling the residents' improbable victory.[30] Absent the intervention of Spielberg's benevolent extraterrestrials, however, such stories rarely had a happy ending. Even the fantastic facade of Isaac Gellis's Herter Brothers–designed tenement at 87 Madison Street (see Figure 3.1) did not protect its residents from a campaign of landlord harassment, including withdrawal of maintenance and building services, aggressive buyout offers, and a series of fires (all tactics depicted in Spielberg's movie), which ended in the building's 1981 demolition for a high-rise development that never materialized.[31]

But abandonment and disinvestment provided the opportunity for another important evolution in the meaning of the decorated tenement. From the 1970s to the 1990s, thousands of formerly abandoned or distressed tenements were rehabilitated through New York's *in rem* and urban homesteading programs that resulted from the urban crisis.[32] One of the most famous manifestations of the latter program, the Solar Tenement, an important 1970s experiment in solar and wind energy, would even take place in a Herter Brothers–designed and Ascher Weinstein–developed building on East Eleventh Street.[33] With these and scores of other creative and community-centered rehabilitation efforts, buildings that had been condemned, literally and figuratively, by housing reformers and urban planners for over a century now became the basis for the city's affordable housing program, stabilizing these neighborhoods and again providing decent homes for a large population. Many of the newly rehabilitated tenements, particularly on the periphery, were populated by waves of new immigrants, whose numbers by the early twenty-first century reached levels not seen since the nineteenth.[34]

At the same time, many of the infill projects that took the place of the demolished tenements resisted the imposition of austere modernist forms. Much like the austerity of nineteenth-century reform tenements, these forms were still frequently reviled as overt visual signals of poverty. Often sponsored by nonprofit community development corporations, sometimes in partnership with city agencies, these buildings began to use forms and articulation borrowed from the decorated tenements that surrounded them.[35] Project architects often wrapped otherwise conventional slab apartment buildings in a historicist garb of rusticated brick, splayed lintels, corner quoins, and sometimes even acanthus cornices. Like those of their tenement forebears, these elements were often executed in modern, substitute materials, such as cast concrete and fiberglass. And like the decorated tenement, these ornamental forms were used to signal respect, in this case respect not only of the social and cultural position of the residents but also of the historical and architectural context of the neighborhoods.

However, the shifting meaning of the decorated tenement in the late twentieth century did not end there, with the restoration of what was essentially the original significance of these buildings. In the 1990s, the establishing shots of the popular sitcom *Friends* featured another Schneider & Herter–designed tenement, marking an important evolution. No longer a symbol of decay, working-class immigrant culture, or even bohemianism, works such as this portrayed the tenement as a symbol of a revitalized urban middle-class lifestyle, an emblem of a turn back to the city and a popular rejection of suburban living. The yuppies of this back-to-the-city movement cherished, even fetishized, many workaday elements of the former industrial city, not just the tenement but particularly the industrial loft, which came to be a chic emblem of urban sophistication.

Amid a bonanza of real estate development over the next three decades in both Boston and New York, these neighborhoods have experienced widespread gentrification. While the cultural and economic landscape of these areas has changed rapidly and dramatically, their architectural fabric has not, and the decorated tenement has taken on a new role as the backdrop for increasingly wealthy neighborhoods. Yet again in a period of high rent and depressed wages, what many have dubbed a new Gilded Age, these neighborhoods have become increasingly inaccessible to those for whom they were built. Indeed, with an influx of new, comparatively wealthy residents, the tenement has been made to comport to a certain kind of high-end living standard.[36]

Perhaps emblematic of the new wealth in the neighborhood is the recent history of 47 East Third Street. A six-story, fifteen-unit, 1901 tenement designed by Michael Bernstein, built just ahead of the new-law reforms, its original building permit had been rejected by reformer Lawrence Veiller as improper. Over a century later, with the eviction of dozens of longtime, rent-regulated tenants, the building has been made over into a private, single-family, sixty-room mansion for a wealthy family after a multi-million-dollar renovation. The tenement's heavily ornamented facade, recently landmarked, was immaculately restored in the process, although in an echo of past debates the replacement cornice, a fiberglass reproduction of a long-missing element, was derided by neighbors as a cheap knockoff of the stamped sheet-metal original.[37]

But while many of the decorated tenements themselves have been rehabilitated, not so the image of those who built and designed them, a fact that has significant consequences for the crisis of housing affordability that again plagues these cities. The image of the builder and designer of low-cost housing as greedy and incompetent, so promoted by the reformers of the late nineteenth and early twentieth century, has remained remarkably persistent. And these biases against multifamily housing remain encoded in zoning, housing maintenance, tax, and building codes they promoted, and in the discourse they encouraged.[38] These largely unexamined biases may have the effect, as they did in the past, of stigmatizing and stymieing those most actively involved in housing creation that most closely matches the needs and taste of the communities in which they are built. Even today the debate about low-cost housing and its lack centers on public interventions, particularly the policy of encouraging large-scale, corporate development of affordable housing through zoning and other incentives, often in high-rise towers catering to, and mostly occupied by, wealthier residents. These mixed-class developments, like the apartment buildings of nineteenth-century Europe, tend to subsume the identity of the working class behind a bourgeois front (that is, if the affordable housing residents are not relegated to using inferior entrances, the so-called poor doors, recently prohibited). As in the past, those most deeply concerned with housing as a social issue tend to miss the cultural and economic significance of the new generation of generally small-scale, often immigrant builder and architect and their varying architectural forms. Or, if recognized, they tend to mistake them for the source, not solution, to the housing crisis.

Indeed, the current discourse tends to ignore or denigrate the everyday production of low-cost (if not, in the technical sense, affordable) housing that occurs throughout New York (far less so in Boston), much of it small-scale, infill housing. Indeed, much new construction, often of buildings quite denser than their surroundings, like the decorated tenements were when they were new, still occurs in many growing immigrant and insular communities, although this building is now concentrated in the outer boroughs. Widespread new construction has taken place, for example, in the Chinese and Taiwanese communities in Flushing, Queens, and the Hasidic Jewish neighborhoods of Borough Park and South Williamsburg Brooklyn. This housing is quite different in accommodation and appearance than that which is constructed, for instance, in the many older working-class neighborhoods now experiencing gentrification, a process that has deepened the affordability crisis even as it has rehabilitated many older buildings. And its construction, as in the past, often elicits strong public reaction, a reflection of discomfort over the social and demographic changes it represents. In this way, the built form of housing remains a touchstone for racial, class, and ethnic tensions, as in the recent heated controversy over the rezoning of the Broadway Triangle section in the South Williamsburg. There, longtime black and Latino residents were vocal in their concern that housing built on a vacant former industrial site would be designed with floor plans and other features designed to cater to the growing Hasidic population, of which the developer was a member.[39] Indeed, as in the past, many of the developers and architects of these new outer-borough developments are still drawn from within these communities. And their buildings, usually absent from the public discourse on affordable housing, often have a complicated relationship with mainstream architectural taste. Some, as do many of the new apartment buildings in Borough Park, even demonstrate a persistent use of applied, mass-produced architectural ornament in classical motifs on conventional forms, resulting in buildings quite different than the stark modernism of current elite taste (and which bear more than a passing resemblance to the decorated tenement). And in many ways their invisibility in this discourse on affordable housing matches that of their forebears in the tenements of Manhattan and Boston in the late nineteenth century.

Today, a steady stream of tourists can be found every day on the corner of Orchard and Broome Streets in New York. Drawn by the Lower East Side Tenement Museum, a half block up Orchard, inevitably they point their cameras upward toward Harris Fine's block of buildings.[40] That block, with its unrelenting fire escapes and layers of terra-cotta ornament, has become something of a symbol of the New York tenement (Plate 22). Photographs of it appear high in Google Images' search rankings for those terms.[41] Yet these tourists, unlike their predecessors on this spot a century ago, are not really slumming. Fine's white brick walls gleam again after a recent cleaning. Storefronts on the block, catering to wealthy new residents and visitors, ape fashionable and generically turn-of-the-century styles with exposed "Edison" lightbulbs, glossy black paint, and gilt-lettered signs. Just perhaps, ornament is part of this newfound interest in these areas, both on the part of the tourists and the new residents. Like their forebears, they may find something essentially humanizing about ornamented buildings in an anonymous urban environment. For them, too, keystone satyrs, zinc cornices, and terra-cotta egg-and-dart molding may help fulfill their search for beauty, variety, and delight.

Acknowledgments

A project such as this, nearly a decade and a half in the making, is impossible without the support, feedback, encouragement, and love of a robust network of people. The genesis of this research was a seminar paper in Jessica Sewell's Material Culture seminar at Boston University in fall 2005. That paper turned my curiosity about a group of North End buildings I did not understand into a sustained line of academic inquiry. My digging into the meaning of those curious tenements was nurtured by Keith Morgan, who encouraged me to interrogate their significance, "hiding in plain sight." He has steadfastly supported the project through its completion. William D. Moore, Patricia Hills, and Marilyn Halter all contributed critical insights at important stages of this work. My greatest intellectual debt is owed to Claire Dempsey, who has been enormously generous with her criticism and insight. Over the decade she has shaped the questions and methodology, read countless drafts, from my earliest musings through the penultimate manuscript for the book, and saved me from countless errors of fact and logic. (The many that certainly remain are my own.)

One could not ask for a better, more supportive academic "home" than the Vernacular Architecture Forum, whose members were liberal with their feedback and advice through the years, including during three different paper presentations relating to this work at the organization's annual conference. Their spirit has been foundational for my scholarship of the built environment. Certain key moments stand out. I particularly regret not having had a longer conversation with Pamela Simpson, whose work on industrially made architectural ornament had been critical at the early stages of this project, and who shared important insights and good humor after my first presentation on the topic as a scared graduated student at my first VAF conference in 2006. It took only a passing comment the same day from Andrew Dolkart on the differences between Boston and New York tenements to spark an interest in expanding the geographic focus of this project, which had up until that point been limited to the smaller city. I particularly thank Richard Longstreth for his willingness to join my dissertation committee, his steadfast support of the process of turning the dissertation into the book it is today, and his practical advice on how to make that happen.

Any project requiring extensive archival research, even one attempting to leverage digital resources to the extent possible, relies on the assistance and goodwill of librarians, archivists, and support staff at a number of institutions. Librarians in the Fine Arts Room at the Boston Public Library were of particular help and endured sustained requests over a period of years for (among other things) the hundred-plus-volume collection of large, bulky—and dirty—Boston Building Inspection Reports.

Similar assistance was provided by the fine staff of the New York Municipal Archives. The staff of the Print Room of the New-York Historical Society helped me discover and access the fragile and rarely seen drawings of the John B. Snook Collection. I appreciate Nancy Johnson of the Museum at Eldridge Street, who shared that institution's files on the Herter Brothers and helped me see more clearly the significance of that early work by the firm. Robert Delap at the New-York Historical Society, Kenneth Cobb at the New York Municipal Archives, Elizabeth Roscio of the Bostonian Society, and the staffs of the permissions departments of the New York Public Library, Boston Public Library, and Museum of the City of New York were helpful in responding to my numerous requests for images. The book's illustration program—more beautiful than I could have imagined—was made possible by the Society of Architectural Historians' Mellon Author Award. Research for this book was also supported at the dissertation stage by the Henry R. Luce/American Council of Learned Societies Dissertation Fellowship in American Art.

Pieter Martin at the University of Minnesota Press shepherded this project from naive first-time book proposal to finished manuscript with consummate patience and good humor. I very much appreciate his advocacy of this project. Thanks to two anonymous reviewers for the Press, I finally understand the standard cliché of academic acknowledgments that this book is "immeasurably better" because of their work. Indeed, I could never have expected that one reviewer would be so generous as to give a cumulative thirty-two (single-spaced) pages of insightful and ultimately encouraging feedback on three different iterations of this manuscript. I believe "immeasurable" is inadequate to describe how much richer, deeper, and indeed better a book this is thanks to the attention they afforded it. I hope the finished product lives up to their clearly high expectations.

None of this would have been possible, of course, without my parents, Richard and Linda, who, if they never exactly understood why I was fascinated by old buildings, were nothing if not indulgent and supportive in the extreme. Before I knew it could be a career or an academic practice, my first experience of "fieldwork" was as a child, leaning on my mom to drive me to every town in Maine within day-trip radius of Augusta, equipped with my dad's 1970s 35mm Minolta and a dog-eared copy of McAlester's *Field Guide* (bought, in the fourth grade, with my allowance), to try to hunt down every example of nineteenth-century architecture I could find. It was something I have never wanted to stop doing. Earle G. Shettleworth of the Maine Historic Preservation Commission encouraged the shaping of that avocation into a practice and career.

Finally, if all Sean Litchfield, my love, had contributed to this project was putting up with my neurotic behavior through the long and crazy-making process of writing an academic book, he would have done more than could reasonably be expected. But his beautiful photographs that grace the cover and these pages are an enormous gift not just to me but to all the readers of this book, who can see this landscape in a new way thanks to his talented eye and skilled hand. I cannot begin to thank him enough.

Notes

Introduction

1. The claim that the Lower East Side was the most populated place on earth has been frequently repeated but smacks of Victorian-era hyperbole. The statement may first have been made by Jacob Riis, *How the Other Half Lives: Studies among the Tenements of New York* (New York: Charles Scribner's Sons, 1890), 10. It was, without a doubt, the densest place in the country. For a discussion of these figures, see Max Page, *The Creative Destruction of Manhattan, 1900–1940* (Chicago: University of Chicago Press, 2000), 31–32.

2. I use the term *Gilded Age* throughout to refer to the period between the Civil War and World War I. While political historians generally locate the end of the Gilded Age with the mid-1890s rise of Progressive reform movements, those movements' effect on tenement architecture was not felt until after the turn of the twentieth century, at the earliest, and buildings in the type that arose during the Gilded Age were built as late as World War I. For an outline of issues related to this period, see H. Wayne Morgan, ed., *The Gilded Age: A Reappraisal* (Syracuse, N.Y.: Syracuse University Press, 1963).

3. The 1900 census lists Harris Fine as a builder living at 309 Henry Street in a rented apartment in a three-unit building—a converted row house—near Rutgers Square in the heart of the tenement district, where he lived with his wife, nine children, and a Russian-born servant. Before this, he had lived in a much smaller tenement unit, at 28 Jefferson Street.

4. This gold leaf detail on Fine's building was recently restored. There is evidence that cornice text on New York tenements were commonly gilded. See New York State Court of Appeals, *Henry A. Conolly against Rosalie Hyams: Case and Exceptions on Appeal,* no. 483 (New York: Evening Post Job Printing, 1903), 67, describing painting specifications calling for real gold leaf on the cornice and fire escapes.

5. The Tribune Monthly, *American Millionaires: The Tribune's List of All Persons in the United States Reputed to Be Worth One Million Dollars or More* (New York: Tribune Association, 1892), 59.

6. "What One Woman Is Doing," *New York Times,* July 1, 1894, 21.

7. The building permit for 56 Hester lists the owner's address simply as "Lenox, Massachusetts." New York New Building Permit (NB) 241–01.

8. Ernest Flagg, "The New York Tenement-House Evil and Its Cure," *Scribner's Magazine,* 1894, 108–17. See also Ernest Flagg, "The Best Method of Tenement Construction," *Charities and the Commons* 17 (1906): 77–80; Ernest Flagg, "A Profitable Tenement House: Plans, Suggestions and Criticisms," *Real Estate Record and Builders' Guide (RERBG)* 65 (1900): 865–67; Mardges Bacon, *Ernest Flagg: Beaux Arts Architect and Urban Reformer* (New York: Architectural History Foundation, 1986), 234–67.

9. Jacob Riis noted of a similar Flagg-designed model tenement that rents were $1 a week per room higher than in the surrounding buildings. While Riis calls this additional rent "trifling," it would represent a 20 percent increase on Lower East Side rents of the period. Model tenements were not intended as "affordable" housing. Jacob Riis, *The Battle with the Slum* (New York: Macmillan Company, 1902), 136.

10. [Peter Herter], "The Critic Criticized: Are Mr. Flagg's Plans Practicable?," *RERBG* 65 (May 26, 1900): 915.

11. [Peter Herter], "Mr. Herter-Mr. Flagg," *RERBG* 65 (June 9, 1900): 1004.

12. Amy Johnson, "Model Housing for the Poor—Turn of the Century Tenement Reform and the Boston Cooperative Building Company" (PhD diss., University of Delaware, 2004).

13. Economic historian Deirdre McCloskey uses the term *betterment* to refer to the material improvement that has resulted from the adoption of traditional liberal values of egalitarianism and dignity since the eighteenth century. Deirdre Nansen McCloskey, *Bourgeois Equality: How Ideas, Not Capital or Institutions, Enriched the World* (Chicago: University of Chicago Press, 2016).

14. Jared Day, *Urban Castles: Tenement Housing and Landlord Activism in New York City, 1890–1943* (New York: Columbia University Press, 1999); Donna Gabaccia, "Little Italy's Decline: Immigrant Renters and Investors in a Changing City," in *Landscape of Modernity: Essays on New York City, 1900–1940,* ed. David Ward and Oliver Zunz (New York: Russell Sage Foundation, 1997), 235–51; Donna Gabaccia, *From Sicily to Elizabeth Street: Housing and Social Change among Italian Immigrants, 1880–1930* (New York: Columbia University Press, 1990), especially chap. 2. For others talking about the role of immigrant developers, see Elizabeth Blackmar, *Manhattan for Rent, 1785–1850* (Ithaca, N.Y.: Cornell University Press, 1989), 245; Robert Ernst, *Immigrant Life in New York City, 1825–1863* (New York: Columbia University Press, 1949), 248, n150.

15. On the formation of the American working class, see Herbert Gutman and Ira Berlin, "Class Composition and the Development of the American Working Class, 1840–1890," in *Power and Culture: Essays on the American Working Class,* ed. Ira Berlin (New York: Pantheon Books, 1987), 380–95.

16. Blackmar, *Manhattan for Rent,* 197–211. For an economic background, see Sam Bass Warner, "The Engine of Enterprise," in *The Urban Wilderness: A History of the American City* (Berkeley: University of California Press, 1972), 55–85.

17. For a background on the importance of New York in this period, see David M. Scoby, *Empire City: The Making and Meaning of the New York City Landscape* (Philadelphia: Temple University Press, 2002); Stuart Blumin, "Explaining the Metropolis: Perception, Depiction, and Analysis in Mid-Nineteenth Century New York," *Journal of Urban History* 11 (November 1984): 9–38; Gunther Paul Barth, *City People: The Rise of Modern City Culture in Nineteenth-Century America* (Oxford: Oxford University Press, 1982); Howard Mumford Jones, *The Age of Energy: Varieties of American Experience, 1865–1915* (New York: Viking Press, 1971), chap. 3. For Boston, see Walter Muir Whitehill and Lawrence W. Kennedy, *Boston: A Topographical History,* 3rd ed. (Cambridge, Mass.: Harvard University Press, 2000).

18. David Ward, *Cities and Immigrants* (New York: Oxford University Press, 1971), 51–83; U.S. Census Bureau, "Nativity of the Population for the 50 Largest Urban Places: 1870 to 1990," https://www.census.gov/population/www/documentation/twps0029/tab19.html, accessed 15 March 2017.

19. Richard Plunz, *History of Housing in New York* (New York: Columbia University Press, 1990), 4.

20. James Ford, *Slums and Housing with Special Reference to New York City, History, Conditions, Policy* (Cambridge, Mass.: Harvard University Press, 1936), 143.

21. Ford, *Slums and Housing,* 272. In Boston, a substantial portion of these "tenements" in Ford's account were wood-frame three-deckers in the city's inner suburbs. Ford was following Robert DeForest and Lawrence Veiller, *The Tenement House Problem: Including the Report of the New York State Tenement House Commission of 1900,* vol. 1 (New York: MacMillian, 1903), 136. New England three-deckers have received a considerable amount of attention. See Kingston Heath, *The Patina of Place: The Cultural Weathering of a New England Industrial Landscape* (Knoxville: University of Tennessee Press, 2001); Kingston Heath, "Housing the Worker: The Anatomy of the New Bedford, Massachusetts, Three-Decker," in *Building Environments: Perspectives in Vernacular Architecture X,* ed. Kenneth A. Briesch and Alison K. Hoagland (Knoxville: University of Tennessee Press, 2005), 47–63; Diane Jacobsohn, "Boston's 'Three-Decker Menace': The Buildings, the Builders and the Dwellers, 1870s–1930" (PhD diss., Boston University, 2004).

22. While the American distaste for multifamily housing has a more nuanced history than is usually presented, it was an animating spirit for anti-tenement activists. See A. K. Sandoval-Strauz, "Homes for a World of Strangers: Hospitality and the Origins of Multiple Dwellings in Urban America," *Journal of Urban History* 33, no. 6 (September 2007): 933–64.

23. Julius Henri Browne, "The Problem of Living in New York," *Harpers Monthly Magazine* 65, no. 300 (November 1892): 918.

24. Henry Nash Smith, *Virgin Land: The American West as Symbol and Myth* (Cambridge, Mass.: Harvard University Press, 1950), 123–250.

25. The classic works on American anti-urbanism are Thomas Bender, *Toward an Urban Vision: Ideas and Institutions in Nineteenth-Century America* (Baltimore: Johns Hopkins University Press, 1975), 1–53; Morton White, *The Intellectual versus the City, from Thomas Jefferson to Frank Lloyd Wright* (Cambridge, Mass.: Harvard University Press, 1962); Leo Marx, "The Puzzle of Anti-urbanism in Classic American Literature," in *Literature and the Urban Experience,* ed. M. C. Jaye and A. C. Watts (New Brunswick, N.J.: Rutgers University Press, 1981), 63–80. For a more recent interpretation, see Steven Conn, *Americans against the City: Anti-urbanism in the Twentieth Century* (Oxford: Oxford University Press, 2014), 1–56.

26. Ward, *Cities and Immigrants,* 125–45; for an analysis of the literature of the geography of city neighborhoods in this period, with a particular focus on Boston, see William J. Lloyd, "Understanding Late Nineteenth-Century American Cities," *Geographical Review* 71, no. 4 (October 1981), 460–71.

27. The literature on this topic is extensive. See, for instance, Sam Bass Warner Jr., *Streetcar Suburbs: The Process of Growth in Boston, 1870–1900* (Cambridge, Mass.: Harvard University Press, 1962), 1–46; Kenneth T. Jackson, *The Crabgrass Frontier: The Suburbanization of the United States* (Oxford: Oxford University Press, 1985), chap. 2; David P. Handlin, *The American Home: Architecture and Society, 1815–1915* (Boston: Little Brown and Company, 1979), 167–232; Gwendolyn Wright, *Building the Dream: A Social History of Housing in America* (Cambridge, Mass.: MIT Press, 1981), 73–91.

28. See, for instance, Leo Marx, *The Machine in the Garden: Technology and the Pastoral Ideal in America* (New York: Oxford University Press, 1964), especially 145–226; Peter J. Schmitt, *Back to Nature: The Arcadian Myth in Urban America* (New York: Oxford University Press, 1969).

29. Roy Rosenzweig and Elizabeth Blackmar, *The Park and the People: A History of Central Park* (Ithaca, N.Y.: Cornell University Press, 1992), 22–30, 130–49. For a discussion of class-based conflicts over the use of the park, see 228–59.

30. For a background on the power dynamics of New York politics, see David C. Hammack, *Power and Society: Greater New York at the Turn of the Century* (New York: Russell Sage Foundation, 1982). See also Sean Wilentz, *Chants Democratic: New York City and the Rise of the American Working Class, 1788–1850* (Oxford: Oxford University Press, 1984); For its manifestation in one New York neighborhood, see Luc Sante, *Low Life: Lures and Snares of Old New York* (New York: Farrar Straus Giroux, 1991); Tyler Anbinder, *Five Points: The 19th-Century Neighborhood That Invented Tap Dance, Stole Elections, and Became the World's Most Notorious Slum* (New York: Free Press, 2001), chaps. 5 and 8.

31. Blackmar has suggested that working-class landlords and builders "formed the core" of the New York Democratic Party in this period. While further research is still needed on this question, there is every indication of a close connection between tenement builders and New York's Tammany establishment. Herter, for instance, was well connected to Tammany insiders even by marriage. Blackmar, *Manhattan for Rent,* 245.

32. Lawrence Veiller, "Reminiscences of Lawrence Veiller," transcript of oral history conducted by Allan Nevins and Dean Albertson, Columbia University, 1949, 21.

33. Marcus T. Reynolds, *The Housing of the Poor in America's Cities: The Prize Essay of the America Economic Association for 1892* (Baltimore: American Economic Association, 1893), 30.

34. Jane Eva Baxter, "The Paradox of a Capitalist Utopia," *International Journal of Historical Archeology* 16, no. 4 (December 2012): 651–65. For a discussion of radical thought among New York Jews, see Ronald Sanders, *The Downtown Jews: Portraits of an Immigrant Generation* (New York: Harper and Row, 1969), chap. 4. For a discussion of responses, see Paul S. Boyer, *Urban Masses and Moral Order in America: 1820–1920* (Cambridge, Mass.: Harvard University Press), 123–32.

35. Plunz notes the Draft Riots were the immediate impetus for the formation of the Citizen's Association for New York, which successfully lobbied for the passage of that city's first tenement house law in 1867. Plunz, *History of Housing*, 21. For a period account, see Charles Loring Brace, *The Dangerous Classes of New York and Twenty Years Working among Them* (New York: Wynkoop and Hallenbeck, 1872), 51–63. For a recent study of Jewish anarchists on the Lower East Side, see Kenyon Zimmer, *Immigrants against the State: Yiddish and Italian Anarchism in America* (Urbana: University of Illinois Press, 2015), 15–48.

36. For a discussion of Victorian Londoners' fear of revolts from the tenement districts, see Jerry White, *Rothschild Buildings: Life in an East Side Tenement Block, 1887–1920* (London: Routledge and Kegan, 1980), 7. On sexual mores, see George Chauncey, *Gay New York: Gender, Urban Culture, and the Making of the Gay Male World, 1890–1940* (New York: Basic Books, 1994), especially chaps. 1, 3, and 4.

37. Boyer, *Urban Masses and Moral Order*, 191–287; Rosenzweig and Blackmar, *The Park and the People*, chaps. 10–12; Michael B. Katz, "Social Class in North American Urban History," *Journal of Interdisciplinary History* 11, no. 4 (Spring 1981): 579–605; Daniel Bluestone, "The Pushcart Evil," in *The Landscape of Modernity: Essays on New York City, 1900–1940*, ed. David Ward and Oliver Zunz (New York: Russell Sage Foundation, 1992), 287–314; Val Marie Johnson, "Defining 'Social Evil': Moral Citizenship and Governance in New York City, 1890–1920" (PhD diss., New School University, 2002), 127–211.

38. Mae M. Ngai, *Impossible Subjects: Illegal Aliens and the Making of Modern America* (Princeton, N.J.: Princeton University Press, 2004), chap. 1; Roger Daniels, *Guarding the Golden Door: American Immigration Policy and Immigrants since 1882* (New York: Hill and Wang, 2004), 3–59.

39. These two methods correspond to the coercive and environmentalist approaches that Paul Boyer has identified as the two distinct but complementary faces of the urban moral reform movement of the late nineteenth century. Boyer, *Urban Masses and Moral Order*, 175–87.

40. The most important sources on housing reform are Plunz, *History of Housing*, 1–23; Nicholas Dagen Bloom and Matthew Gordon Lasner, eds., *Affordable Housing in New York* (Princeton, N.J.: Princeton University Press, 2016): 1–70; Roy Lubove, *Progressives and the Slums: Tenement House Reform in New York City* (Pittsburgh: University of Pittsburgh Press, 1962); Richard Foglesong, *Planning the Capitalist City: The Colonial Era to the 1920s* (Princeton, N.J.: Princeton University Press, 1986), 56–88; Ford, *Slums and Housing*; Edith Elmer Wood, *The Housing of the Unskilled Wage Earner: America's Next Problem* (New York: MacMillan, 1919), 29–442; David M. Culver, "Tenement House Reform in Boston 1846–1898" (PhD diss., Boston University, 1972); Eugenie Birch and Deborah Gardner, "The Seven-Percent Solution: A Review of Philanthropic Housing, 1870–1910," *Journal of Urban History* 7 (August 1981): 403–39; Robert J. Bremmer, "The Big Flat: History of a New York Tenement House," *American Historical Review* 64, no. 1 (October 1958): 54–62. For the model housing movement, see Johnson, "Model Housing for the Poor"; Cynthia Zaitzevsky, "Housing Boston's Poor: The First Philanthropic Experiments," *Journal of the Society of Architectural Historians (JSAH)* 42, no. 2 (May 1983): 157–67; Handlin, *The American Home*, 252–63.

41. For colonial-period attitudes, see Lawrence J. Vale, *From the Puritans to the Projects: Public Housing and Public Neighbors* (Cambridge, Mass.: Harvard University Press, 2000), 19–50. For the early reform movement, see Lubove, *The Progressives and the Slums*, 4–20; Vale, *From the Puritans to the Projects*, 57–62.

42. F. Duncan Case, "Hidden Social Agendas and Housing Standards: The New York Tenement House Code of 1901," *Housing and Society* 8, no. 1 (1981): 3–17.

43. They were joined, however, sometimes uncomfortably, by a number of wealthy and assimilated German Jews.

44. T. J. Jackson Lears, *No Place of Grace: Antimodernism and the Transformation of American Culture, 1880–1920* (Chicago: University of Chicago Press, 1981), xvi; Alex Jonathan Feerst, "Bowery Beautiful: Progressive Slumming and Ghetto Aesthetics, 1880–1930" (PhD diss., Duke University, 2005).

45. Foglesong, *Planning the Capitalist City,* 57.

46. Boyer, *Urban Masses and Moral Order,* 199–200; David Ward, *Poverty, Ethnicity, and the American City, 1840–1925: Changing Conceptions of the Slum and the Ghetto* (Cambridge: Cambridge University Press, 1989), 79–86.

47. Boyer, *Urban Masses and Moral Order,* 220–32.

48. For a discussion of Jacob Riis's deflection of blame onto inanimate objects, see Joel Schwartz, "The Moral Environment of the Poor," *Public Interest* (1991): 21–37.

49. On the settlement house, see Allen Davis, *Spearheads for Reform: The Social Settlements and the Progressive Movement, 1890–1914* (New York: Oxford University Press, 1967); Judith Ann Trolander, *Professionalism and Social Change: From the Settlement House Movement to Neighborhood Centers* (New York: Columbia University Press, 1987). On the role of women in social reform movements, most notably the municipal housekeeping movement, as well as the architectural manifestations of those movements, see Daphne Spain, *How Women Saved the City* (Minneapolis: University of Minnesota Press, 2001).

50. For aesthetic and cultural background, see Lears, *No Place of Grace*; Andrew Chamberlin Rieser, *The Chautauqua Moment: Protestants, Progressives, and the Culture of Modern Liberalism, 1874–1920* (New York: Columbia University Press, 2003); David Shi, *The Simple Life: Plain Living and High Thinking in American Culture* (New York: Oxford University Press, 1985); James B. Lane, "Jacob A. Riis and Scientific Philanthropy during the Progressive Era," *Social Science Review* 47, no. 1 (March 1973): 32–48.

51. Daniel Horowitz, *The Morality of Spending: Attitudes toward the Consumer Society in America, 1875–1940* (Baltimore: Johns Hopkins University Press, 1985): 13–67. For a sociologist's take on similar issues in a contemporary context, see Matthew Desmond, *Evicted: Poverty and Profit in the American City* (New York: Crown Publishers, 2016), 215–27.

52. "Changes on the Lower East Side," *New York Times,* July 9, 1899, 14.

53. "Changes on the Lower East Side," 14.

54. For expansion of the commercial districts, see Mona Domosh, "Shaping the Commercial City: Retail Districts in Nineteenth-Century New York and Boston," *Annals of the Association of American Geographers* 80, no. 2 (1990): 268–84.

55. For the literary representations of this change, see Carrie Tirado Bramen, "The Urban Picturesque and the Spectacle of Americanization," *American Quarterly* 52, no. 3 (September 2000): 444–77.

56. Plunz, *History of Housing,* fig. 2.20, 2.21, 46.

57. Lubove, *Progressives and the Slums,* 130–33.

58. Richard Hofstadter famously, and controversially, discusses fanaticism and anti-Semitism among Progressive Era reformers in *The Age of Reform: From Bryant to JFK* (New York: Vintage Books, 1955).

59. William B. Patterson, "The Religious Value of Proper Housing," *Annals of the American Academy of Political and Social Science* 51 (January 1914): 43.

60. Jacob Riis, *A Ten Years' War: An Account of the Battle with the Slum in New York* (New York: Houghton, Mifflin and Company, 1900), 36. The more rational-minded observers at the Council of Hygiene railed against uptown shanties with the same vigor as against downtown tenements. Plunz, *History of Housing,* 54. For background on New York's squatter settlements, see Lisa Goff, *Shantytown, USA: Forgotten Landscapes of the Working Poor* (Cambridge, Mass.: Harvard University Press, 2016), 54–84; Robert Neuwirth, *Shadow Cities: A Billion Squatters, a New Urban World* (New York: Routledge, 2005), 205–37.

61. Colleen McDannell, *The Christian Home in Victorian America, 1840–1900* (Bloomington: Indiana University Press, 1986), 45–50. This notion has been studied intensively, especially around the New Deal mortgage programs; see, for example, Jackson, *Crabgrass Frontier,* 190–95; Wright, *Building the Dream,* 240–47.

62. John Archer, *Architecture and Suburbia: From the English Villa to the American Dream Home, 1690–2000* (Minneapolis: University of Minnesota Press, 2004), 4.

63. For a study of the increasing importance of the single-family home among both the working class and housing reformers of this period, see Margaret Garb, *City of American Dreams: A History of Home Ownership and Housing Reform in Chicago, 1871–1919* (Chicago: University of Chicago Press, 2005).

64. Louis Wirth, "Urbanism as a Way of Life," *American Journal of Sociology* 44, no. 1 (1938): 1–24. On the resistance of many Jewish immigrants to notions of rugged individualism, see Hadassa Kosak, *Cultures of Opposition: Jewish Immigrant Workers, New York City, 1881–1905* (Albany: State University of New York Press, 2004), 7.

65. As historian Donna Gabaccia has noted, while many Sicilian immigrants preferred the systems of property ownership they had experienced in their home country, they were not inherently uncomfortable with multifamily living. Gabaccia, *Sicily to Elizabeth Street,* 52. For these attitudes in a later period in Boston, see Herbert Gans, *The Urban Villagers: Group and Class in the Life of Italian-Americans* (New York: Free Press, 1962), 19–22.

66. E. R. L. Gould, "The Economics of Improved Housing," *Yale Review* 5 (May 1896): 17.

67. Riis, *How the Other Half Lives,* 274.

68. Herbert Gutman, "Work, Culture, and Society in Industrializing America, 1815–1919," *American Historical Review* 78, no. 3 (June 1973): 531–88. For just one study of the conflict between immigrant and managerial efficiency, see Stephen Meyer, "Adapting the Immigrant to the Line: Americanization in the Ford Factory, 1914–1921," *Journal of Social History* 14, no. 1 (Autumn 1980): 67–82.

69. Gould, "Economics of Improved Housing," 13.

70. Andrew Heinze, *Adapting to Abundance: Jewish Immigrants, Mass Consumption, and the Search for American Identity* (New York: Columbia University Press, 1990); Ken Koltun-Fomm, *Material Culture and Jewish Thought in America* (Bloomington: Indiana University Press 2010). Consumption as a source of identity formation in immigrant culture has been a popular topic in American studies and material cultural studies for a number of years. See, for example, John A. Kouwenoven, "American Studies: Words or Things?," in *Material Culture Studies in America,* ed. Thomas J. Schlereth (Nashville, Tenn.: American Association of State and Local History, 1982), 79–93; Kathy Peiss, *Cheap Amusements: Working Women and Leisure in Turn-of-the-Century New York* (Philadelphia: Temple University Press, 1986); Donna R. Gabaccia, *We Are What We Eat: Ethnic Food and the Making of Americans* (Cambridge, Mass.: Harvard University Press, 1998); Marilyn Halter, *Shopping for Identity: The Marketing of Identity* (New York: Schocken, 2002).

71. Plunz, *History of Housing,* 1–123; Bloom and Lasner, *Affordable Housing in New York,* 1–107; Vale, *From the Puritans to the Projects,* 55–158; Anthony T. Jackson, *A Place Called Home: A History of Low-Cost Housing in Manhattan* (Cambridge, Mass.: MIT Press, 1976), chaps. 1, 2 and 3. Urban historian Robert Barrows argues that the tenement has been overemphasized in the literature on the history of housing. Robert Barrows, "Beyond the Tenement: Patterns of American Urban Housing, 1870–1930," *Journal of Urban History 9 (August 1983): 395–420.*

72. Wright, *Building the Dream,* chap. 7; Elizabeth Collins Cromley, *Alone Together: A History of New York's Early Apartment* (Ithaca, N.Y.: Cornell University Press), 52–61; Robert A. M. Stern, *New York 1880: Architecture and Urbanism in the Gilded Age* (New York: Monacelli Press, 1999), 495–515; Christine Hunter, *Ranches, Rowhouses and Railroad Flats, American Homes and How They Shape Our Landscapes and Neighborhoods* (New York: W. W. Norton, 1999), chap. 6, especially 225–32; Alan Mallach, *A Decent Home: Planning, Building, and Preserving Affordable Housing* (Chicago: American Planning Association Planners Press, 2009), chap. 1. For an excellent study of a related building type, see Paul Groth, *Living Downtown: The History of Residential Hotels in America* (Berkeley: University of California Press, 1994).

73. Of the limited published works on the speculative tenement, the most notable is on the

single building that now houses the Lower East Side Tenement Museum. See Andrew Dolkart, *Biography of a Tenement House in New York City: An Architectural History.* (Santa Fe, N.Mex.: The Center for American Places, 2006).

74. Even the free-market fundamentalists at the Cato Institute reproduce reformers' narratives of the failure of the market for working-class housing in nineteenth-century New York, which they also condemned for stymieing private homeownership. See Randal O'Toole, *American Nightmare: How Government Undermines the Dreams of Homeownership* (Washington, D.C.: Cato Institute, 2012), 45–50.

75. Alan Mayne, *The Imagined Slum: Newspaper Representation in Three Cities, 1870–1914* (Leicester: Leicester University Press, 1994); Alan Mayne and Tim Murray, eds. *The Archaeology of Urban Landscapes: Explorations in Slumland* (Cambridge: Cambridge University Press, 2001); Alan Mayne, "On the Edge of History," *Journal of Urban History* 26, no. 2 (January 2000): 249–58; Alan Mayne "Tall Tales but True? New York's 'Five Points' Slum," *Journal of Urban History* 33, no. 2 (January 2007): 320–31.

76. Joseph C. Bigott, *From Cottage to Bungalow: Houses and the Working Class in Metropolitan Chicago, 1869–1929* (Chicago: University of Chicago Press, 2001); Oliver Zunz, *The Changing Face of Inequality: Urbanization, Industrial Development, and Immigrants in Detroit, 1880–1920* (Chicago: University of Chicago Press, 1982); Garb, *City of American Dreams;* Michael Doucet and John Weaver, *Housing the North American City* (Montreal: McGill-Queen's University Press, 1991), especially chaps. 4, 5, and 9.

77. Thomas C. Hubka and Judith T. Kenney, "The Polish Workers' Cottage in Milwaukee's Polish Community: Housing and the Process of Americanization, 1870–1920," *Perspectives in Vernacular Architecture* 8 (2000): 33–52; Thomas Hubka and Judith T. Kenney, "Examining the American Dream: Housing Standards and the Emergence of a National Housing Culture, 1900–1930," *Perspectives in Vernacular Architecture* 13 (2006): 49–69; Thomas Hubka, *Houses without Names: Architectural Nomenclature and the Classification of America's Common Houses* (Knoxville: University of Tennessee Press, 2013); Lizabeth Cohen, "Embellishing a Life of Labor: An Interpretation of Material Culture of American Working-Class Homes, 1885–1915," in *Common Places: Readings in American Vernacular Architecture,* ed. Dell Upton and John Michael Vlach (Athens: University of Georgia Press, 1986), 261–80. See also Heinze, *Adapting to Abundance,* parts 2 and 3. Rebecca Yamin, ed., *Tales of Five Points: Working-Class Life in Nineteenth-Century New York,* 7 vols. (Washington, D.C.: General Services Administration, 2002); Lee Rainwater, "Fear and the House-as-Haven in the Lower Class," *Journal of the American Institute of Planners* 32, no. 1 (1966): 23–31; Elizabeth Collins Cromley, "Modernizing: or 'You'll Never See a Screen Door on Affluent Homes,'" *Journal of American Culture* 5, no. 2 (Summer 1982): 71–80.

78. Peter Herter, "How to Invest in Tenement Property," *RERBG* 65 (May 5, 1900): 765.

79. Although the specific context they are referring to is quite different than the buildings under discussion, the decorated tenement follows Robert Venturi and Denise Scott-Brown's concept of the "decorated shed," which they define as a building in which "systems of space and structure are directly at the service of program, and ornament is applied independently to them." Robert Venturi and Denise Scott-Brown, *Learning from Las Vegas,* rev. ed. (Cambridge, Mass.: MIT Press, 1977), 87.

80. Wright refers to the "ornamental facades" of commercially built tenements in *Building the Dream,* 124; Hunter, to interior and exterior ornament in *Ranches, Rowhouses, and Railroad Flats,*128; Dolkart, to stock material in *Biography of a Tenement,* 27. Some reproduce period critics' view that the ornament was a sham to distract from problematic conditions. Historian Luc Sante dismisses the "fiction" of ornamented tenement facades in *Low Life,* 23–26. Guidebook author Gerard Wolf calls the "Jewish stars in terra cotta" on one Herter Brothers–designed tenement, "a ruse by builders to attract religious but naive tenants." Gerard Wolf, *New York: A Guide to the Metropolis, Walking Tours of Architecture and History* (New York: New York University Press, 1975), 115.

In perhaps the longest treatment of the topic, a recent essay considering the architecture of the Lower East Side, neighborhood activist and historian Rob Hollander considers the "mystery" of ornamenting tenements. He suggests "tenement facades were elaborately adorned to attract renters who could afford a bit more . . . each tenement competed for a piece of family respectability." Rob Hollander "Architecture of the Jewish Ghetto," in *Jews: A People's History of the Lower East Side*, vol. 2, ed. Clayton Peterson et al. (New York: Clayton Books, 2012), 83–89.

81. The false-facade quality of the decorated tenements is commonly noted in the study of European housing. For a discussion of it in the context of nineteenth-century Vienna, see Eve Blau, *The Architecture of Red Vienna: 1919–1934* (Cambridge, Mass.: MIT Press, 1999), chap. 2. See also Douglas Mark Klahr, "Luxury Apartments with a Tenement Heart: The Kurfürstendam and the Berliner Zimmer," *JSAH* 70, no. 3 (September 2011): 290–307.

82. Cohen, "Embellishing a Life of Labor."

83. "Naïve" and "unsophisticated" are infelicitous labels by modern scholars. See National Register of Historic Places Registration Form: Lower East Side Historic District (June 2000), section 7, page 5; section 8, page 1. "Crude" and "vulgar" are from period sources. See Albert J. Kennedy and Robert A. Woods, *The Zone of Emergence: Observations of the Lower Middle and Upper Working Class Communities of Boston, 1905–1914* (Cambridge, Mass.: MIT Press, 1962), 63; "Municipal Architecture," *RERBG*, 33, no. 835 (March 15, 1884): 261.

84. For a critique of the misuse of architectural style, see Richard Longstreth, "The Problem with Style," *Bulletin of the Committee on Preservation, Society of Architectural Historians* 6 (December 1984): 1–4.

85. John F. Kasson, *Civilizing the Machine: Technology and Republican Values in America, 1776–1900* (New York: Penguin Books, 1976), 140–70.

86. "Trinity's Old Buildings," *New York Times,* December 9, 1894, 1; "Trinity Gives Reasons," *New York Times,* December 8, 1894, 3; Blackmar, *Manhattan for Rent,* 251.

87. On the departure of the elite from working-class real estate, see Blackmar, *Manhattan for Rent,* 251; Oscar Handlin, *Boston's Immigrants, 1790–1880,* rev. ed. (Cambridge, Mass.: Harvard University Press, 1969), 101–2.

88. Lawrence Veiller, *Condensed Report: Trinity's Tenements* (New York: Charity Organization Society, 1909), 17.

89. Largely due to the nature of the population in these neighborhoods, in this period ethnicity, rather than race, was the most operative factor in tenement construction. No African American tenement builders or architects have been identified here. Before large-scale migration from the American South in the twentieth century, these groups often occupied the worst housing, usually handed down from earlier European immigrants, and were subject to the worst abuses. Uptown, however, a number of black-run real estate firms focused on providing improved housing for these groups in much the same way as their downtown counterparts. These are worthy of additional research. See Seth M. Scheiner, "The New York City Negro and the Tenement, 1880–1910," *New York History* 45, no. 4 (October 1964): 304–15. Indeed, in racial terms, the rise of the tenement landscape downtown can be seen as having negative effects. For instance, the arrival of many southern and eastern European immigrants to the North Slope of Beacon Hill displaced the significant African American community that had long inhabited that neighborhood, a locus of abolitionist sentiment in the antebellum period. In that period a number of African American boardinghouse keepers have been noted. For a background on this community, see James Oliver Horton and Lois E. Horton, *Black Bostonians: Daily Life and Community Struggle in the Antebellum North,* rev. ed. (New York: Holmes and Meir, 1999).

90. Birch and Gardner, "The Seven Percent Solution."

91. Gould, "The Housing Problem in Great Cities," 393.

92. Lubove, *Progressives and the Slums,* 39.

93. Day, *Urban Castles,* 31.

94. 1900 U.S. Manuscript Census, Manhattan Enumeration District 177, 4–5.

95. John E. Bodnar, *The Transplanted: A History of Immigrants in Urban America* (Bloomington: Indiana University Press, 1985), 169–80; Deborah Dash Moore, *At Home in America: Second Generation New York Jews* (New York: Columbia University Press, 1981), chap. 2; Matthew Edel, Elliott D. Sclar, and Daniel Luria, *Shaky Palaces: Homeownership and Social Mobility in Boston's Suburbanization* (New York: Columbia University Press, 1984); Jeffrey S. Gurock, *When Harlem Was Jewish, 1870–1930* (New York: Columbia University Press, 1979); Gerald M. Gamm, "In Search of Suburbs: Boston's Jewish Districts, 1843–1994," in *The Jews of Boston: Essays on the Occasion of the Centenary of the Combined Jewish Philanthropies of Greater Boston,* ed. Jonathan Sarna and Ellen Smith (Boston: Combined Jewish Philanthropies of Greater Boston, 1995).

96. See Ira Katznelson, "Between Separation and Disappearance: Jews on the Margins of American Liberalism," in *Paths of Emancipation: Jews, States, and Capitalism,* ed. Pierre Birnbaum and Ira Katznelson (Princeton, N.J.: Princeton University Press, 1995), 174–203.

97. For a background on this field, see Rebecca Kobrin, "The Chosen People in the Chosen Land: The Jewish Encounter with American Capitalism," introduction to *Chosen Capital: The Jewish Encounter with American Capitalism,* ed. Rebecca Kobrin (New York: Rutgers University Press, 2012), 1–12. For the role of Jewish entrepreneurs as clients, see Frederic Bedoire, *The Jewish Contribution to Modern Architecture, 1830–1930,* trans. Robert Tanner (Jersey City, N.J.: KATV publishing, 2004). Deborah Dash Moore thoroughly analyzes the role of second-generation Jewish immigrants in the outer boroughs of New York in the 1920s and 1930s; Moore, *At Home in America,* 39–54. For a discussion of identity issues related to Jewish landlords in Toronto, see Richard Dennis, "Property and Propriety: Jewish Landlords in Early Twentieth-Century Toronto," *Transactions of the Institute of British Geographers,* New Series 22, no. 3 (1997): 377–97.

98. David Hollinger, "Rich, Powerful, and Smart: Jewish Overrepresentation Should Be Explained rather than Mystified or Avoided," *Jewish Quarterly Review* (Fall 2004): 596–602.

99. See, for instance, Adam Mendelsohn, *The Rag Race: How Jews Sewed Their Way to Success in America and the British Empire* (New York: New York University Press, 2015); Paul Lerner, *The Consuming Temple: Jews, Department Stores, and the Consumer Revolution in Germany, 1880–1940* (Ithaca, N.Y.: Cornell University Press, 2015); Marni Davis, *Jews and Booze: Becoming American in the Age of Prohibition* (New York: New York University Press, 2012); Neal Gabler, *An Empire of Their Own: How the Jews Invented Hollywood* (New York: Crown Publishers, 1988).

100. Andrew Dolkart, "From the Rag Trade to Riches: Abraham E. Lefcourt and the Development of New York's Garment District," chap. 3 in *Chosen Capital,* ed. Kobrin, 67.

101. Lerner, *Consuming Temple,* 67. See also Mendelsohn, *The Rag Race,* 7.

102. The important Jewish contribution to housing reform, first among well-established German Jews in the nineteenth century, and more broadly and deeply in the twentieth, should also not be overlooked.

103. Zimmer, *Immigrants against the State,* 22.

104. In this we can also see the roots of the important union cooperative housing movements of the early twentieth century that at last put real reform of housing conditions within residents' control, often fully grounded in socialist principles, but using urban building types similar to those found in the speculative landscape. See Matthew Gordon Lasner, *High Life: Condo Living in the Suburban Century* (New Haven, Conn.: Yale University Press, 2012), 97–103; and Plunz, *A History of Housing,* 151–62.

105. For an introduction to these methods, see Thomas Carter and Elizabeth Collins Cromley, *Invitation to Vernacular Architecture: A Guide to the Study of Ordinary Buildings and Landscapes* (Knoxville: University of Tennessee Press, 2005); Edward A. Chapppell, "Fieldwork," in *The Chesapeake House: Architectural Investigation by Colonial Williamsburg,* ed. Cary Carson and Carl Lounsbury (Chapel Hill: University of North Carolina Press, 2013), 29–47.

106. It should be noted that fieldwork examination was limited to the exterior of most of these

buildings. Understanding of interior arrangement was achieved by examining the systematic period housing inspections records that exist in both cities.

107. For technical details on this process, see Zachary J. Violette, "The Decorated Tenement: Working-Class Housing in Boston and New York, 1860–1910" (PhD diss., Boston University, 2014), 461–544.

108. Mayne, *The Imagined Slum,* 4. See also Mayne and Murray, eds., *The Archaeology of Urban Landscapes,* chap. 1.

109. The literature of the tenement has been considered in much more detail elsewhere. See David M. Fine, *The City, the Immigrant, and American Fiction, 1880–1920* (Metuchen, N.J.: Scarecrow Press, 1977); David M. Fine, "Immigrant Ghetto Fiction, 1885–1918: An Annotated Bibliography," *American Literary Realism, 1870–1910* 6, no. 3 (Summer 1973): 169–95; David W. Fleming, "Restricted Spaces: The Urban Tenement and the American Literary Imagination" (PhD diss., Indiana University, 1994).

110. Beth S. Wenger, "Memory as Identity: The Invention of the Lower East Side," *American Jewish History* 85, no. 1 (1997): 3–27; Kathleen Neils Conzen, "Immigrants, Immigrant Neighborhoods, and Ethnic Identity: Historical Issues," *Journal of American History* 66 (December 1979): 603–15; Page, *The Creative Destruction of Manhattan,* 108–9.

111. For some of this elite history, see Whitehill and Kennedy, *Boston,* chaps. 3 and 4; Jeffrey Klee, "Civic Order on Beacon Hill," *Buildings & Landscapes: Journal of the Vernacular Architecture Forum* 15 (Fall 2008): 43–57. For a discussion of its urban renewal, see Thomas H. O'Connor, *Building a New Boston: Politics and Urban Renewal, 1950–1970* (Boston: Northeastern University Press, 1993), chap. 5; Sean M. Fisher and Carolyn Hughes, eds., *The Last Tenement: Confronting Community and Urban Renewal in Boston's West End* (Boston: Bostonian Society, 1992). The remaining portions of the West End are now commonly referred to as the North Slope of Beacon Hill.

112. Much fine scholarship has been influenced by the work of Henri Lefebvre, *Production of Space,* trans. Donald Nicholas-Smith (New York: Wiley-Blackwell, 1992). For a discussion of the impact of these theories on architectural history, see Alice T. Friedman, "The Way You Do the Things You Do: Writing the History of Houses and Housing," *JSAH* 58, no. 3 (September 1999): 406–13.

113. Wright, *Building the Dream,* 114–19.

114. *Digest of Laws and Ordinances Relating to the Public Health and Tenement Buildings* (Boston, 1870), 16, as cited in Culver, "Tenement House Reform in Boston," 68.

115. Cromley, *Alone Together,* 52.

116. Literary historian David Flemming disagrees, arguing that the definition of tenement remained stable as a multifamily building that was "tall long and narrow." Fleming's analysis of the tenement as a literary trope is useful. David W. Fleming, "Restricted Spaces: The Urban Tenement and the American Literary Imagination" (PhD diss., Indiana University, 1994), introduction, chap. 1.

117. William Hazlet, "Of the Breed of Buddensiek," *Charities and the Commons* 17 (1906): 74–76.

118. Herter, "How to Invest," 764. King's handbook of New York of 1892 put the number at the slightly higher $300 a year, under which point "a flat rapidly degenerates into a tenement." Moses King, *King's Guidebook of New York* (Boston: Moses King, 1895), 218.

119. Peter B. Hales, *Silver Cities: Photographing American Urbanization, 1839–1939* (Philadelphia: Temple University Press, 1985), 221–76; Bonnie Yochelson and Daniel Czitrom, *Rediscovering Jacob Riis: Exposure Journalism and Photography in Turn-of-the-Century New York* (Chicago: University of Chicago Press, 2007); Amy E. Johnson, "Crooked and Narrow Streets: Photography and Urban Visual Identities in Early Twentieth-Century Boston," *Winterthur Portfolio* 47, no. 1 (Spring 2013): 35–64.

120. For a New Deal–era reformer explicitly employing verbal and visual tropes dating to the nineteenth century, see Langdon Post, *The Challenge of Housing* (New York: Farrar and Rinehart, 1938). Post was a commissioner of the New York Tenement House Department and later chairman

of the New York City Housing Authority, where he oversaw the construction of some of the first public housing projects. He boasted of overseeing the demolition of nine linear miles of tenements (xv). For a case study in photography's implication in clearance, see Mike Christenson, "The Photographic Construction of Urban Renewal in Fargo, North Dakota," *Buildings & Landscapes: Journal of the Vernacular Architecture Forum* 23, no. 2 (2016): 116–28.

121. For instance, photographs chosen for Jared Day's *Urban Castles* depict only old-law tenements from the rear or, more startling, after parts of the facade have been removed in construction. Day, *Urban Castles,* 30–31.

1. Dens, Rookeries, and Hovels

1. For further discussion of representations of the spaces of urban poverty in the pictorial press of this period, see Joshua Brown, *Beyond the Lines: Pictorial Reporting, Everyday Life, and the Crisis of the Gilded Age* (Berkeley: University of California Press, 2002), 87–98, 188–96; Christopher Mele, "Different and Inferior: The Ghetto at the Turn of the Century," chap. 2 in *Selling the Lower East Side: Culture, Real Estate, and Resistance in New York City* (Minneapolis: University of Minnesota Press, 2000), 31–78.

2. Schuyler, as quoted in Robert A. M. Stern, *New York 1880* (New York: Monacelli Press, 1999), 576. Stern, following convention, reproduces Hale's frontispiece in his discussion of the Stewart House.

3. "Sketches from the Life School: Number Five. The Old Brewery and the New Mission," *New York Times,* October 7, 1852, 2. "Dead-house" is an obsolete term for a building used to temporarily store corpses awaiting burial.

4. "Sketches from the Life School," 2.

5. The illustrator likely drew upon earlier depictions made when the building was standing.

6. For a history of the economic obsolescence of building, a concept that came about with the nineteenth century as part of capitalism's rising demands on the built environment, see Daniel M. Abramson, *Obsolescence: An Architectural History* (Chicago: University of Chicago Press, 2016), 1–37. The problem of the slum, however, was buildings that failed to be replaced long after they outlived their usefulness, rather than the converse.

7. For a discussion of the portrayal of the city as a wilderness, based in part on the name of Robert Woods's 1898 study of Boston's South End, see Steven Conn, *Americans against the City: Anti-urbanism in the Twentieth Century* (Oxford: Oxford University Press, 2014), 42–43.

8. Indeed, Dickens himself found the Five Points slum "squalid," "miserable," and "leaporous." Richard Plunz, *History of Housing in New York* (New York: Columbia University Press, 1990), 51. In literature, David Fine notes, such sentimental portals trace their roots to the eighteenth century, in the works of Defore and Field. David Fine, *The City, The Immigrant, and American Fiction, 1880–1920* (Metuchen, N.J.: Scarecrow Press, 1977), vii.

9. Alan Mayne, *The Imagined Slum: Newspaper Representation in Three Cities, 1870–1914* (Leicester: Leicester University Press, 1994), 3.

10. See, for instance, Carol Groneman Pernicone, "The 'Bloody Ould Sixth': A Social Analysis of a New York City Working-Class Community in the Mid-Nineteenth Century" (PhD diss., University of Rochester, 1973). Pernicone demonstrates that the social disintegration and family breakdown portrayed in the slum image were largely a fantasy.

11. For a discussion of slumming, see Chad Heap, *Slumming: Sexual and Racial Encounters in American Nightlife, 1885–1940* (Chicago: University of Chicago Press, 2005), chap. 1. For slumming as representation, see Ludwig Maria Vogl-Bienek, "Turning the Social Problem into Performance: Slumming and Screen Culture in Victorian Lantern Shows," in *Beyond the Screen: Institutions, Networks, and Publics of Early Cinema,* ed. Marta Braun et al. (Indianapolis: John Libby Publishing, Indiana University Press, 2016), 315–24.

12. For a discussion of early nineteenth-century developments here, see Nina Rolick Meyer,

"Building Early America: Architectural and Social Developments in Boston's North End, 1826–1850" (PhD diss., Boston University, 1986).

13. For a background on urban housing types in the early nineteenth century, see Bernard L. Herman, *Town House: Architecture and Material Life in the Early American City, 1780–1839* (Chapel Hill: University of North Carolina Press, 2005); Bernard L. Herman, "The Smaller House of the North Shore, 1630–1830," *Perspectives in Vernacular Architecture* 10 (2005): 3–14; Richard Candee, ed., *Building Portsmouth: The Neighborhoods and Architecture of New Hampshire's Oldest City* (Portsmouth, N.H.: Portsmouth Advocates, 1992); Laura Baker Driemeyer, "Rising from the Ashes: The Transformation of Nineteenth-Century Building Culture in Charlestown, Massachusetts" (PhD diss.: Boston University, 2006); Elizabeth Blackmar, "Re-walking the 'Walking City': Housing and Property Relations in New York, 1780–1840," *Radical History Review* 21 (Fall 1979): 131–48; Gwendolyn Wright, *Building the Dream: A Social History of Housing in America* (Cambridge, Mass.: MIT Press, 1981), chap. 2; Charles Lockwood, *Manhattan Moves Uptown: An Illustrated History* (New York: Barnes and Noble Books, 1976), 1–62. For a background on the visual culture of this environment, see Amy E. Johnson, "Crooked and Narrow Streets: Photography and Urban Visual Identities in Early Twentieth-Century Boston," *Winterthur Portfolio* 47, no. 1 (Spring 2013): 35–64.

14. Kenneth T. Jackson, *The Crabgrass Frontier: The Suburbanization of the United States* (Oxford: Oxford University Press, 1985), chap. 2; Stuart Blumin, "Explaining the Metropolis: Perception, Depiction, and Analysis in Mid-Nineteenth Century New York," *Journal of Urban History* 11 (November 1984): 9–38; Lockwood, *Manhattan Moves Uptown,* 1–57.

15. For a description of such buildings in the Five Points neighborhood, see Tyler Anbinder, *Five Points: The 19th-Century Neighborhood That Invented Tap Dance, Stole Elections, and Became the World's Most Notorious Slum* (New York: Free Press, 2001), 72–74. See also Blackmar, "Re-Walking the 'Walking City.'" For an excellent study of a related building type in London, see Peter Guillery, *The Small House in Eighteenth-Century London: A Social and Architectural History* (New Haven, Conn.: Yale University Press, 2004).

16. Jackson, *The Crabgrass Frontier,* chap. 2; Lockwood, *Manhattan Moves Uptown,* chaps. 5–7.

17. For a background on the emergence of distinctive working-class culture, see Lawrence W. Levine, *Highbrow/Lowbrow: The Emergence of Cultural Hierarchy in America* (Cambridge, Mass.: Harvard University Press, 1988); Sean Wilentz, *Chants Democratic: New York City and the Rise of the American Working Class, 1788–1850* (Oxford: Oxford University Press, 1984). For its manifestation in one New York neighborhood, see Anbinder, *Five Points,* chaps. 1 and 6. See also Kathy Peiss, *Cheap Amusements: Working Women and Leisure in Turn-of-the-Century New York* (Philadelphia: Temple University Press, 1986; David Ward, *Poverty, Ethnicity and the American City, 1840–1926: Changing Conceptions of the Slum and Ghetto* (Cambridge: Cambridge University Press, 1989); Oscar Handlin, *Boston's Immigrants: A Study in Acculturation,* expanded and enlarged ed. (Cambridge, Mass.: Harvard University Press, 1969); John Bodnar, *The Transplanted: A History of Immigrants in the United States* (Bloomington: Indiana University Press, 1985). This greater separation and freedom was applicable only to free workers in northern cities. In the slave cities of the South, many enslaved workers were still subjected to elaborate forms of surveillance. See Bernard Herman, "The Embedded Landscapes of the Charleston Single House, 1780–1820," *Perspectives in Vernacular Architecture, Exploring Everyday Landscapes* 7 (1997): 41–57.

18. For a general discussion of the introduction of stoves for heating and cooking, see James L. Garvin, *A Building History of Northern New England* (Hanover, N.H.: University of New England Press, 2001), 158; Priscilla J. Brewer, "'We Have Got a Very Good Cooking Stove': Advertising, Design, and Consumer Response to the Cookstove, 1815–1880," *Winterthur Portfolio* 25 (Spring 1990): 35–54.

19. I am grateful to Jeffrey Klee for sharing unpublished material on this topic with me before the completion of his recent dissertation. See Jeffrey Klee, "Building Order on Beacon Hill, 1790–1850" (PhD diss., University of Delaware, 2016), especially 219–25 and 309–42. For a related discussion, see Jeffrey Klee, "Civic Order on Beacon Hill," *Buildings & Landscapes: Journal of the Vernacular Architecture Forum* 15 (2008): 43–57.

20. For a history of the boardinghouse, see Wendy Gamber, *The Boardinghouse in Nineteenth-Century America* (Baltimore: Johns Hopkins University Press, 2007).

21. For a discussion of the role of the boardinghouse in the life of middle-class urban residents, see Elizabeth Collins Cromley, *Alone Together: A History of New York's Early Apartments* (Ithaca, N.Y.: Cornell University Press, 1990), chap. 1. For a study of a wide range of mostly purpose-built boardinghouses, see Paul Groth, *Living Downtown: The History of Residential Hotels in the United States* (Berkeley: University of California Press, 1994), particularly 56–163. For a classic period study of the transition of Boston's South End from an elite single-family neighborhood into a neighborhood of boardinghouses, see Albert Wolf, *The Lodging House Problem in Boston* (Boston: Houghton Mifflin and Company, 1906).

22. Harold Kelsey Estabrook, *Some Slums in Boston* (Boston: Twentieth Century Club, 1898), 15.

23. Traci L. Roloff, "Adequate Light and Proper Ventilation: The Multifamily Housing of the North End, 1883–1910" (master's project, Boston University, 2004), 52–55.

24. Nathaniel Hawthorne, *The Blithedale Romance*, 1852, in *Hawthorne's Works,* Illustrated Library Edition (Boston: James R. Osgood, 1872), 215.

25. For a background on Hutchinson's house, see Abbott Lowell Cummings, "The Beginnings of the Provincial Renaissance Architecture in Boston, 1690–1725," *Journal of the Society of Architectural Historians (JSAH)* 42, no.1 (March 1983): 43–53.

26. Edward Bellamy, *Looking Backwards, 1887–2000* (1888; repr., New York: Signet, 2000), 15.

27. Jacob Riis, *How the Other Half Lives: Studies among the Tenements of New York* (New York: Charles Scribner's Sons, 1890), 29.

28. Samuel Adams Drake, *Our Old Colonial Homes* (Boston: Lee and Shepard Publishers, 1894), 19–20. See also William D. DeMarco, "Ethnics and Enclaves: Boston's Italian North End" (PhD diss.: Boston College, 1980), 59–60. For a discussion of concern about the effects of immigration on the New England landscape and the perceived threat to Yankee identity, see Joseph Conforti, *Imagining New England: Explorations of Regional Identity from the Pilgrims to the Mid-Twentieth Century* (Chapel Hill: University of North Carolina Press, 2001), 208–11. Drake, as quoted in Conforti, *Imagining New England,* 209.

29. Michael Holleran, *Boston's "Changeful Times": Origins of Preservation and Planning in America* (Baltimore: Johns Hopkins University Press, 1998), 216.

30. Riis, *How the Other Half Lives,* 29.

31. Montgomery Schuyler, "The Small House in New York City," *Architectural Record* 8, no. 4 (April-June 1899): 372. The replacement building at 24 St. Mark's Place was built in 1903 by the firm of Braverman, Silverson and Loudon to the designs of Sass & Smallheiser. New York New Building Permit (NB) 395–03.

32. For a discussion of this system in New York, see Elizabeth Blackmar, *Manhattan for Rent, 1785–1850* (Ithaca, N.Y.: Cornell University Press, 1989), chap. 1. For a description of a similar system in Boston, see Handlin, *Boston's Immigrants,* 101.

33. "Tenant Houses: Conclusion of the Investigation on Rotten Row and Soap-Fat Alley," *New York Daily Times,* March 31, 1856, 1.

34. Bennett's record books and photographs of his properties are preserved in the collections of the Bostonian Society. Joshua Bennett Real Estate Book, 1886–1923, MS0090.

35. Harold K. Estabrook, *Some Slums in Boston,* as quoted in Maura Fitzpatrick, "From Template Tenements to Beaux-Arts Boulevards: The Architecture of Fred A. Norcross" (master's thesis, Boston University, 1993), 14.

36. "Unchristian Corporations," *Puck* 36, no. 930 (January 2, 1895): 343.

37. "Trinity Gives Reasons," *New York Daily Times,* December 8, 1894, 3. Under pressure, the church eventually improved the conditions in its building in the early twentieth century.

38. Lawrence Veiller, *Condensed Report: Trinity's Tenements* (New York: Charity Organization Society, 1909), 17. Industrial uses cover much of Trinity's former holdings.

39. For a background on this community, see James Oliver Horton and Lois E. Horton, *Black*

Bostonians: Daily Life and Community Struggle in the Antebellum North, rev. ed. (New York: Holmes and Meir, 1999). For its architectural manifestations, see Klee, "Building Order," 332–41.

40. While this feature would become rare in the urban tenement districts, it persisted in many manufacturing communities in the Northeast into the twentieth century.

41. These buildings are now known only through a set of drawings in the collection of Historic New England. See James F. O'Gorman, ed., *Drawing toward Home: Designs for Domestic Architecture from Historic New England* (Boston: Historic New England, 2010), 77–79.

42. Barrack blocks make frequent appearances in period representations of the slum landscape. Though more common in Boston, some seem to have been built in New York. One appears on page 45 of Riis, *How the Other Half Lives.*

43. Edward Everett Hale, *Workingmen's Homes: Essays and Stories* (Boston: James Osgood and Company, 1875), 171; Amy Johnson "Model Housing for the Poor—Turn of the Century Tenement Reform and the Boston Cooperative Building Company" (PhD diss., University of Delaware, 2004), chap. 1.

44. Phillips Street at the time was known as Southac Street.

45. Thomas Jefferson, from *Notes on the State of Virginia,* 1784, as quoted in Conn, *Americans against the City,* 11. "With the Opium Smokers: A Walk through the Chinese Quarter," *New York Daily Times,* March 22, 1880, 2. Also quoted in part in Anbinder, *Five Points,* 81.

46. Lillian Betts, *The Leaven in a Great City* (New York: Dodd, Mead and Company, 1902), 44.

2. The Better Sort of Tenement

1. James Ford, *Slums and Housing, with Special Reference to New York City* (Cambridge, Mass.: Harvard University Press, 1936), 95. While the 1824 date for this building has been traditional since the time of the 1856 Assembly Committee report, later quoted in the *Plumber and Sanitary Engineer* in 1879, there is some doubt about its veracity. While James Hardie's census of buildings built in 1824 notes the construction of eighteen buildings on Mott Street that year, none was over two stories in height. Tax records show it in its current configuration as early as 1855. See James Hardie, *A Census of the New Buildings Erected in This City, in the Year 1824* (New York: Printed by S. Marks, 1825), 10. "Wart" comment from "With the Opium Smokers: A Walk through the Chinese Quarter," *New York Times,* March 22, 1880, 2. Also quoted in Tyler Anbinder, *Five Points: The 19th-Century New York City Neighborhood That Invented Tap Dance, Stole Elections, and Became the World's Most Notorious Slum* (New York: Free Press, 2001), 81.

2. "Tenant Houses: Conclusion of the Investigation on Rotten Row and Soap-Fat Alley," *New York Daily Times,* March 31, 1856, 1.

3. Elizabeth Blackmar, *Manhattan for Rent, 1785–1850* (Ithaca, N.Y.: Cornell University Press, 1989), 20.

4. The family's house at 320 East 18th Street is extant. *Trow's New York City Directory, 1867–1868* (New York: John F. Trow, 1868), 1084; 1880 U.S. Census.

5. "Martin Ficken," *A Souvenir of New York's Liquor Interests* (New York: American Publishing and Engraving Company, 1893), 167. New York New Building Permit Number (NB) 46–75.

6. NB 638–87.

7. NB 170–07.

8. On mobility, see Donna Gabaccia, *From Sicily to Elizabeth Street: Housing and Social Change among Italian Immigrants, 1880–1930* (Albany: State University of New York Press, 1984), 77–79.

9. On immigrants' interest in the public sphere, see, for instance, Hadassa Kosak, *Cultures of Opposition: Jewish Immigrant Workers, New York City, 1881–1905* (Albany: State University of New York Press, 2004), 82–84.

10. "Tenement Floor Plans Compared," *Real Estate Record and Builders' Guide (RERBG)* 62 (October 7, 1899): 500.

11. Ernest Flagg, "A Profitable Tenement: Plans, Suggestions and Criticism," *RERBG* 65 (May 19,

1900): 865–68; [Peter Herter], "The Critic Criticized: Are Mr. Flagg's Plans Practicable?," *RERBG* 65 (May 26, 1900): 915.

12. For a background on housing reform laws, see Andrew Dolkart, *Biography of a Tenement House in New York City: An Architectural History of 97 Orchard Stree*t (Santa Fe, N.Mex.: Center for American Places, 2006), chap. 4; Richard Plunz, *A History of Housing in New York City: Dwelling Type and Social Change in the American Metropolis* (New York: Columbia University Press, 1990), chap. 2; Anthony T. Jackson, *A Place Called Home: A History of Low-Cost Housing in Manhattan* (Cambridge, Mass.: MIT Press, 1976), chaps. 2 and 3.

13. Lee M. Friedman, *Pilgrims in a New Land* (Philadelphia: Jewish Publication Society of America, 1948), 307.

14. For descriptions of this earlier housing standard in a variety of house types in London, see Peter Guillery, *The Small House in Eighteenth-Century London: A Social and Architectural History* (New Haven, Conn.: Yale University Press, 2004), chap. 1. For Paris, see François Loyer, *Paris: Nineteenth Century Architecture and Urbanism,* trans. Charles Lynn Clark (New York: Abbeville Press, 1988), 26–57. For Berlin, see Dietrich Worbs, "The Berlin Mietskaserne and Its Reforms" in *Berlin/ New York: Like and Unlike: Essays on Art and Architecture from 1870 to the Present,* ed. Josef Paul Kleihues and Christina Rathgeber (New York: Rizzoli, 1993), 145–59; and Rolf Kuck, "Palace Prison Mietskaserne, Myer's Hof: Misery vs. Utopia," ExploreLab Research Paper #8, Delft University of Technology, 2010 (http://preservedstories.com/wp-content/uploads/2013/01/Mietskaserne-1.pdf). For Amsterdam, Nancy Stieber, *Housing Design and Society in Amsterdam: Reconfiguring Urban Order and Identity, 1900–1920* (Chicago: Chicago University Press, 1998), 15–47, 73–97. For Philadelphia, Sam Bass Warner Jr., *The Private City: Philadelphia in Three Periods of Its Growth* (University of Pennsylvania Press: Philadelphia, 1968), 52. For the colonial-era South, see Cary Carson et al., "Impermanent Architecture in Southern American Colonies," *Winterthur Portfolio* 16 (1981): 135–96; Lee Soltow, "Egalitarian America and Its Inegalitarian Housing in the Federal Period," *Social Science History* 9, no. 2 (1985): 199–213; for New England in the same period, Michael Steinitz, "Rethinking Geographical Approaches to the Common House: The Evidence from Eighteenth-Century Massachusetts," *Perspectives in Vernacular Architecture* 3 (1989): 16–26. For a standard that remained persistent until a later period, see Thomas C. Hubka and Judith T. Kenney, "The Polish Workers' Cottage in Milwaukee's Polish Community: Housing and the Process of Americanization, 1870–1920," *Perspectives in Vernacular Architecture* 8 (2000): 33–52; A. K. Sandoval-Strausz, "Homes for a World of Strangers: Hospitality and the Origins of Multiple Dwellings in Urban America," *Journal of Urban History* 33, no. 6 (September 2007): 933–37. For a synthetic view, see Martin J. Daunton, ed., *Housing the Workers, 1850–1914: A Comparative Perspective* (London: Leicester University Press, 1990).

15. Thomas Hubka, *Houses without Names: Architectural Nomenclature and the Classification of America's Common Houses* (Knoxville: University of Tennessee Press, 2013), 63–68.

16. Gabaccia presents a detailed, comparative analysis of housing standards of Sicilian immigrants in New York tenements and their native rural agro-towns. While the urban buildings did not meet all of their ideals, particularly around ownership, she posits they were not especially shocked by the lack of air, privacy, or sanitary features. Gabaccia, *From Sicily to Elizabeth Street,* 11–34, 65–100. Though it focuses mostly on the reform of the farmhouse, some sense of housing in rural American can be gained from Sally McMurry, *Families and Farmhouses: Vernacular Designs and Social Change* (Knoxville: University of Tennessee Press, 1997); and Thomas Hubka, *Big House, Little House, Back House, Barn: The Connected Farm Buildings of New England* (Hanover, N.H.: University Press of New England, 1984).

17. Jacob Riis, *How the Other Half Lives: Studies among the Tenements of New York* (New York: Charles Scribner's Sons, 1890), 265.

18. For context of these changes, see Thomas Schlereth, "Conduits and Conduct: Home Utilities in Victorian America, 1876–1915," in *American Home Life, 1880–1930: A History of Spaces and Services,* ed. Jessica Foy and Thomas Schlereth (Knoxville: University of Tennessee Press, 1992), 225–42.

19. Peter Herter, "How to Invest in Tenement Property," *RERBG* 65 (May 5, 1900): 766.

20. Herter, "How to Invest," 764.

21. Lillian Betts, "Italian Peasants in a New Law Tenement," *Harper's Bazaar* 38 (1904): 802–5.

22. Herter, "How to Invest," 764.

23. For a history of public sanitary infrastructure, see Martin V. Melosi, *The Sanitary City: Environmental Services in Urban America from Colonial Times to the Present* (Pittsburgh: University of Pittsburgh Press, 2008), 1–7, 40–49.

24. For a discussion of the role and architecture of public baths in New York, see Andrea Renner, "A Nation That Bathes Together: New York City's Progressive Era Public Baths," *Journal of the Society of Architectural Historians (JSAH)* 67 (2008): 504–31.

25. "Out Among the Builders," *RERBG* 43, no. 1110 (June 22, 1889): 878.

26. For a discussion of how three fixture baths became standard, see Thomas Hubka and Judith T. Kenney, "Examining the American Dream: Housing Standards and the Emergence of a National Housing Culture, 1900–1930," *Perspectives in Vernacular Architecture* 13 (2006): 57; *First Report of the Tenement House Department of the City of New York* (New York: Tenement House Department, 1903), 154.

27. Friedman, *Pilgrims in a New Land,* 303.

28. "How to Build Tenements: Committee Receives 4700 Answers to Its Questions," *New York Times,* October 12, 1900, 11.

29. Herter, "How to Invest," 765. These buildings, Herter notes infelicitously, were occupied by "good American tenants."

30. Herbert Gans noted, as late as the 1950s, that residents of the West End of Boston often preferred to control the heat of their units by stoves rather than be dependent "on the landlords and their often miserly thermostats." Herbert Gans, *The Urban Villagers: Group and Class in the Life of Italian-Americans* (New York: Free Press, 1962), 13. On adding central heat, see Leo Grebler, *Housing Market Behavior in a Declining Area* (New York: Columbia University Press, 1952).

31. Herter, "The Critic Criticized," 916.

32. Gabaccia, *From Sicily to Elizabeth Street,* 76.

33. Gabaccia, *From Sicily to Elizabeth Street,* chap. 3; Elizabeth Ewen, *Immigrant Women in the Land of Dollars: Life and Culture on the Lower East Side, 1890–1925* (New York: Monthly Review Press, 1985), chap. 1.

34. The 500-square-foot figure is based on a standard New York dumbbell apartment, which contained a parlor and kitchen of about 12 by 15 feet each, and two bedrooms of about 8 by 8 feet, for a total of 488 square feet. Few tenement apartments in New York were larger than this. Boston apartments were only slightly larger, on average. Period accounts are full of descriptions of crowding in these spaces. Sampling of census returns seems to bear that out. At 59 Mott Street, a highly decorated dumbbell tenement, for example, ninety-seven people lived in the building's seventeen three- or four-room apartments. At least three of these seventeen households of Italian and Russian Jewish immigrants had a dozen or more members.

35. For a discussion of the removal of production from the home, see Mary P. Ryan, *The Cradle of the Middle Class: The Family in Oneida County, New York, 1790–1865* (Cambridge: Cambridge University Press, 1981), chaps. 4 and 5; Blackmar, *Manhattan for Rent,* chap. 4.

36. For a reformer discussing cooperative alternatives to such arrangements, see Lucia True Ames, "At Home in the Tenement-House," *New England Magazine* 7 (1893): 595–99. For the context of this, see Dolores Hayden, *The Grand Domestic Revolution: A History of Feminist Designs for American Homes, Neighborhoods, and Cities* (Cambridge, Mass.: MIT Press, 1982), chaps. 4 and 8; Stuart Blumin, *The Emergence of the Middle Class: Social Experience in the American City, 1760–1900* (New York: Cambridge University Press, 1989), 11–12, 138–91.

37. Andrew Heinze, *Adapting to Abundance: Jewish Immigrants, Mass Consumption and the Search for American Identity* (New York: Columbia University Press, 1990), chap. 10.

38. One *Boston Globe* reporter, accompanying a city health inspector in the tenement districts, noted with horror the story of an Italian fruit seller whose bedroom was stacked high with boxes of apples and pears awaiting sale at his pushcart. "Half the World: How It Lives in Boston Tenement Houses," *Boston Daily Globe,* August 6, 1893, 2.

39. New York State Court of Appeals, *Henry A. Conolly against Rosalie Hyams: Case and Exceptions on Appeal.* no. 483 (New York: Evening Post Job Printing, 1903), 115.

40. Elizabeth Collins Cromley, *The Food Axis: Cooking, Eating and the Architecture of American Houses* (Charlottesville: University of Virginia Press, 2011), 109; Sandoval-Strausz, "Homes for a World of Strangers."

41. Cromley, *The Food Axis,* 95.

42. For the effects of the evolution of domestic technology on women in the home, see Ruth Schwartz Cowan, *More Work for Mother* (New York: Basic Books, 1993).

43. Paul Groth, *Living Downtown: The History of Residential Hotels in the United States* (Berkeley: University of California Press, 1994), 84–86; Lizabeth Cohen, "Embellishing a Life of Labor: An Interpretation of Material Culture of American Working-Class Homes, 1885–1915," in *Common Places: Readings in American Vernacular Architecture,* ed. Dell Upton and John Michael Vlach (Athens: University of Georgia Press, 1986), 763; Cromley, *The Food Axis,* 135–37.

44. Gabaccia, *From Sicily to Elizabeth Street,* 90.

45. Mary Antin, *The Promised Land* (Boston: Houghton Mifflin Company, 1911), 337. Also quoted in Cohen, "Embellishing a Life of Labor," 763.

46. Blumin, *Emergence of the Middle Class,* 189; Christine Stansell, *City of Women: Sex and Class in New York, 1789–1860* (Chicago: University of Illinois Press, 1982), chap. 3.

47. Heinze, *Adapting to Abundance,* 133.

48. Katherine C. Grier, *Culture and Comfort: Parlor Making and Middle-Class Identity, 1850–1930* (Washington, D.C.: Smithsonian Institution Press, 1997); Collen McDannell, "Parlor Piety: The Home as Sacred Space in Protestant America," in *American Home Life,* ed. Foy and Schlreth, 162–90; Gwendolyn Wright, *Building the Dream: The Social History of American Housing* (Cambridge, Mass.: MIT Press, 1981), chap. 6.

49. Richard Bushman, *The Refinement of America: Persons, Houses, Cities* (New York: Vintage Books, 1992), 273.

50. Anzia Yezierska, *Bread Givers: A Novel* (1925; reprint, New York: Persea Books, 2003), 8, 13. For background on Yezierska, see Ken Koltun-Fromm, *Material Culture and Jewish Thought in America,* chap. 5; and Katherine Stubbs, "Reading Material: Contextualizing Clothing in the Work of Anzia Yezierska," *Melus* 23 no. 2 (1998): 157–72.

51. Herter, "How to Invest," 764.

52. Elizabeth Collins Cromley, "A History of Beds and Bedrooms," *Perspectives in Vernacular Architecture* 4 (1991): 177–86.

53. Ewen, *Immigrant Women in the Land of Dollars,* 153. Kingston Heath talks about closing the cold outer bedrooms of New Bedford, Massachusetts, three-deckers. See Kingston Heath, *The Patina of Place: The Cultural Weathering of a New England Landscape* (Knoxville: University of Tennessee Press, 2001), 18–24. Cohen also noted the tendency of residents to huddle in the kitchen or parlor for warmth. Cohen, "Embellishing a Life of Labor," 763.

54. Cromley, "A History of Beds and Bedrooms," 181.

55. For background on the global phenomenon of hybrid shop/house spaces, see Howard Davis, *Living over the Store: Architecture and Local Urban Life* (London: Routledge, 2012), particularly 68–84, 111–14.

56. Kathy Peiss, *Cheap Amusements: Working Women and Leisure in Turn-of-the-Century New York.* (Philadelphia: Temple University Press, 1986), 15–29, 88–115.

57. Cecil C. Evers, *The Commercial Problem in Building: A Discussion of the Economic and*

Structural Essentials of Profitable Building, and the Basis for Valuation of Improved Real Estate (New York: Record and Guide Co., 1914), 65.

58. Robert DeForest and Lawrence Veiller, *The Tenement House Problem: Including the Report of the New York State Tenement House Commission of 1900,* vol. 2 (New York: MacMillian, 1093), 439–49.

59. Herter, "How to Invest," 765. Howard Davis suggests that commercial rents accounted for at least a third of a tenement owner's income. Davis, *Living over the Store,* 194.

60. While *double-decker* is a period term for this type of arrangement, the use of the word *flat* was highly variable in the nineteenth century. It does most commonly refer to the plan type described here but is often also used generically for any type of respectable apartment. The double-decker is sometimes colloquially called a "railroad" apartment, or even a railroad flat, although this term is frequently applied to any unit with pass-through rooms, regardless of the floor plan. For terminology, see Christine Hunter, *Ranches, Rowhouses, and Railroad Flats: American Homes: How They Shape Our Landscapes and Neighborhoods* (New York: W. W. Norton, 1999), 225–32.

61. In upper Manhattan and in Brooklyn, double-decker apartments span the depth of the building, creating long, deep apartments with numerous dark interior rooms.

62. In an 1870 building by architect William E. Waring for developer S. W. Asheim. See New York Tenement House Department Inspection Card (I-Card), New York Department of Housing Preservation and Development, 19 and 21 Mott Street. NB-589–70. Waring's relationship to sanitary engineer George E. Waring, who was deeply interested in the conditions of New York tenements, is unknown.

63. On hall bedrooms, see Daphne Spain, *How Women Saved the City* (Minneapolis: University of Minnesota Press, 2001), 43–46.

64. While the physical evidence of markedly improved tenements in the 1890s is quite compelling, scattered evidence also exists in the documentary record. See, for instance, "Changes on the Lower East Side," *New York Times,* July 9, 1899, 14. Sources speaking to this "old law" improvement, however, have often been summarily dismissed, even in modern scholarship. Historian Nicholas Dagen Bloom, for instance, in noting a letter to the editor of the *New York Times* describing the high quality of the tenements built in this period (while also opposing proposals for public housing), suggested that it revealed "the callousness of the city's landlords." Nicholas Dagen Bloom, *Public Housing That Worked: New York in the Twentieth Century* (Philadelphia: University of Pennsylvania Press, 2009), 23. See Edward P. Doyle, "The High Cost of Housing," letter to the editor, *New York Times,* March 27, 1937, 14.

65. NB 857–01.

66. "Tenement Floor Plans Compared," 500.

67. Plunz, *A History of Housing,* 49.

68. "Tenement House Reform," *New York Times,* October 5, 1903, 2.

69. *Apartment Houses of the Metropolis* (New York: G. C. Hesselgren Publishing, 1908), 292.

3. Fantastic Shapes and Unfamiliar Profiles

1. "Architectural Criticism—No. 2," *Real Estate Record and Builders' Guide (RERBG)* 3, no. 15 (June 26, 1869): 1.

2. The *Record and Guide* complained frequently about the architecture on the Upper West Side. "Bits of Street Architecture," *RERBG* 40 (July 9, 1887): 920. For background on the neighborhood's development, see M. Christine Boyer, *Manhattan Manners: Architecture and Style, 1850–1900* (New York: Rizzoli International, 1985), 193–221.

3. "The Boquart and Monfort Apartment Houses," *RERBG* 39 (April 23, 1887): 549.

4. New York New Building Permit (NB) 203–89.

5. For background on Gellis and the Eldridge Street commission, see Annie Polland, *Landmark of the Spirit: The Eldridge Street Synagogue* (New Haven, Conn.: Yale University Press, 2009), especially 1–32 and 90–114. This is discussed in more detail in chapter 4.

6. Jacob Riis, *How the Other Half Lives: Studies among the Tenements of New York* (New York: Charles Scribner's Sons, 1890), 42.

7. William T. Elsing, "Life in New York Tenement-Houses as Seen by a City Missionary," *Scribner's* 11 (1892): 703.

8. For one of the many studies on the development of these ideas, see Leslie Topp, *Architecture and Truth in Fin-de-Siècle Vienna* (Cambridge: Cambridge University Press, 2004), 6–23, 132–69.

9. Adolf Loos as quoted in Eve Blau, *The Architecture of Red Vienna, 1919–1934* (Cambridge, Mass.: MIT Press, 1999), 67; Thorstein Veblen, *The Theory of the Leisure Class: An Economic Study of Institutions* (New York: Macmillian Company, 1912), 154.

10. For background on urban aesthetics in this period, see Donald J. Olsen, *The City as a Work of Art: London, Paris, Vienna* (New Haven, Conn.: Yale University Press, 1986). See also Roland Barthes, "Semiology and the Urban," in *Rethinking Architecture: A Reader in Critical Theory*, ed. Leil Leach (London: Routledge, 1997), 166–72. See also Roland Barthes, "The Eiffel Tower," in *Rethinking Architecture*, ed. Leach, 172–80; Rebecca Zurier, *Picturing the City: Urban Vision and the Ashcan School* (Berkeley: University of California Press, 2006), 1–23, 45–86; Richard Sennett, *The Conscience of the Eye: The Design and Social Life of Cities* (New York: Norton, 1990); David M. Scobey, "Anatomy of the Promenade: The Politics of Bourgeois Sociability in Nineteenth-Century New York," *Journal of Social History* 17, no. 2 (May 1992): 203–27; William Leach, *Land of Desire: Merchants, Power, and the Rise of a New American Culture* (New York: Pantheon, 1993); Thomas Bender and William R. Taylor, "Culture and Architecture: Some Aesthetic Tensions in Shaping Modern New York City," in *Visions of the Modern City: Essays in History, Art, and Literature,* ed. William Sharpe and Leonard Wallock (Baltimore: Johns Hopkins University Press, 1987), 189–217.

11. Henrik Reeh, *Ornaments of the Metropolis: Siegfried Kracauer and Modern Urban Culture* (Cambridge, Mass.: MIT Press, 2004); John F. Kasson, *Rudeness and Civility: Manners in Nineteenth-Century Urban America* (New York: Hill and Wang, 1990), 69–111; John F. Kasson, *Civilizing the Machine: Technology and Republican Values in America, 1776–1900* (New York: Penguin Books, 1977), 139–80.

12. Kasson, *Civilizing the Machine,* 161.

13. For discussion of middle-class priorities, see Karen Haltunnen, *Confidence Men and Painted Women: A Study in Middle-Class Culture in America, 1830–1870* (New Haven, Conn.: Yale University Press, 1982); Mary P. Ryan, *Cradle of the Middle Class: The Family in Oneida County, New York, 1790–1865* (Cambridge: Cambridge University Press, 1981); Stuart M. Blumin, "The Hypothesis of Middle-Class Formation in Nineteenth-Century America: A Critique and Some Proposals," *American Historical Review* 90, no. 2 (1985): 299–338; Robert K. Fitts, "The Archaeology of Middle-Class Domesticity and Gentility in Victorian Brooklyn," *Historical Archaeology* 33, no. 1 (1999): 39–62.

14. On historicism, see Mitchell Schwarzer, *German Architectural Theory and the Search for Modern Identity* (Cambridge: Cambridge University Press, 1995), 9–11, 102–12. On simplicity, see Dell Upton, *Another City: Urban Life and Urban Spaces in the New American Republic* (New Haven, Conn.: Yale University Press, 2008), 1–41.

15. On New York as the "image capital" in another context, see Zurier, *Picturing the City,* 49–51. For a background on New York architecture in this period, see Dell Upton, "Inventing the Metropolis: Civilization and Urbanity in Antebellum New York," in *Art and the Empire City: New York, 1825–1861,* ed. Catherine Hoover Voorsanger and John Howat (New Haven, Conn.: Yale University Press, 2000), 3–45. See also Morrison H. Heckscher, "Building the Empire City: Architects and Architecture," in *Art and the Empire City,* ed. Voorsanger and Howat, 169–89.

16. For a background of middle-class residential architecture in New York in this period, see Charles Lockwood, *Bricks and Brownstone: The New York Row House, 1783–1929* (New York: Abbeville, 1972), 125–227.

17. Exterior cast-iron ornament used on Boston buildings tended to be a high-status feature compared to their New York counterparts, as in the heavily foliated window caps on otherwise

brick row houses of Union Park in the South End. A small number of cast-iron facades were also built, mostly in the 1850s. For a discussion of the limited use of cast iron in Boston commercial architecture, see Douglass Shand-Tucci, *Built in Boston: City and Suburb, 1800–2000,* rev. ed. (Amherst: University of Massachusetts Press, 1999), 25.

18. "Municipal Architecture," *RERBG* 33, no. 835 (March 15, 1884): 260. Also quoted in part in Robert A. M. Stern, *New York 1880: Architecture and Urbanism in the Gilded Age* (New York: Monacelli Press, 1999), 139.

19. For representations of difference in the urban landscape of this period, see Carrie Tirado Bramen, "The Urban Picturesque and the Spectacle of Americanization," *American Quarterly* 52, no. 3 (September 2000): 444–77.

20. Schwarzer, *German Architectural Theory,* 7.

21. NB 572–85.

22. While the original permit for the building was not located, its construction was noted in "Building Intelligence," *American Architect and Building News,* March 21, 1885, 143.

23. NB 355–86.

24. NB 926–86.

25. NB 552–77.

26. NB 591–83.

27. On piers in factory construction, see Sara E. Wermiel, "Heavy Timber Framing in Late-Nineteenth-Century Commercial and Industrial Buildings," *APT Bulletin* 35, no. 1 (2004): 55–60.

28. NB 1502–89.

29. For a history of architectural terra-cotta in New York, see James Taylor, "A Review of Architectural Terra Cotta," in *A History of Real Estate, Building and Architecture in New York During the Last Quarter Century* (New York: Record and Guide, 1898), 509–29.

30. "The Bogart and Monfort Apartment Houses," *RERBG* 39, no. 997 (April 23, 1887): 549.

31. Stern, *New York 1880,* 642–64.

32. Margot Gayle and Carol Gayle, *Cast-Iron Architecture in America: The Significance of James Bogardus* (New York: W. W. Norton, 1998), 75–77.

33. For a discussion of the meaning of these figures, see Lady Raglan, "The 'Green Man' in Church Architecture," *Folklore* 50, no. 1 (March 1939): 45–57; and Kathleen Basford, *The Green Man* (Ipswich, Eng.: D. S. Brewer, 1978), 9–24.

34. Much of the well-known British green man sculpture from the thirteenth century varies significantly from those seen on the tenement, however, which are more closely related to more finely modeled classical forms. See Tina Negas, "Medieval Foliate Heads: A Photographic Study of Green Men and Green Beasts in Britain," *Folklore* 111, no. 2 (August 2003): 247–61.

35. Basford, *The Green Man,* 9–11. Basford suggests that the introduction of the figure into church architecture resulted from the chance survival of late Roman structures that became the Trier Cathedral in Germany. These were rediscovered in the nineteenth century. Trier, incidentally, was about a hundred miles from Peter Herter's Bonn birthplace.

36. Gayle and Gayle, *Cast Iron Architecture in America,* 75–77.

37. Pamela Simpson, *Cheap, Quick, and Easy: Imitative Architectural Materials, 1870–1930* (Knoxville: University of Tennessee Press, 1999), 40, quoting the 1887 catalog of the Bakewell and Mullins Company.

38. For example, a pair of Brooklyn tenements, built in 1884 by L. Levy to designs of Thomas Engelhardt, had a facade fully clad in galvanized iron panels. The resulting facade was quite elaborate, similar in appearance to many cast-iron loft buildings. One of the Levy buildings is extant at 844 Broadway. Its sheet-metal facade has since been clad in vinyl siding, although its ornate cornice remains. See "Out among the Builders," *RERBG* 33, no. 847 (June 7, 1884): 617. A somewhat later tenement on the nearby corner of Locus Street and Broadway retains most of its sheet-metal facade.

39. For Paris, see François Loyer, *Paris Nineteenth Century: Architecture and Urbanism,* trans. Charles Lynn Clark (New York: Abbeville Press, 1988), 388–96.

40. Colleen McDannell, *The Christian Home in Victorian America, 1840–1900* (Bloomington: Indiana University Press, 1986), 20–51; Colleen McDannell, "Parlor Piety: The Home as Sacred Space in Protestant America," in *American Home Life, 1880–1930,* ed. Jessica Foy and Thomas Schlereth (Knoxville: University of Tennessee Press, 1992), 162–90.

41. Albert J. Kennedy and Robert A. Woods, *The Zone of Emergence: Observations of the Lower and Upper Working Class Communities of Boston, 1905–1914* (Cambridge, Mass.: MIT Press, 1962), 63.

42. Peter Herter, "How to Invest in Tenement Property," *RERBG* 65 (May 5, 1900): 764.

43. Saskia Coenen Snyder, *Building a Public Judaism: Synagogues and Identity in Nineteenth-Century Europe* (Cambridge, Mass.: Harvard University Press, 2013), 25–44. After their successful use of neo-Islamic motifs on the Eldridge Street Synagogue, the Herter brothers would employ the same style in a smaller but even more elaborate synagogue on Henry Street two years later. That synagogue stood at 30 Henry Street. "Out among the Builders," *RERBG* (October 22, 1887): 1332.

44. Andrew Dolkart, *Central Synagogue and Its Changing Neighborhood* (New York: Central Synagogue, 2001).

45. Samuel Gruber, "Arnold Brunner and the New Classical Synagogue in America," *Jewish History* 25, no. 1, Special Issue on Synagogue Architecture in Context, 69–102.

46. Carol Herselle Krinsky, *Synagogues of Europe: Architecture, History, Meaning* (Cambridge, Mass.: MIT Press, 1985), 72–85. This issue is a fraught topic in the history of synagogue architecture in the nineteenth century. Krinsky has the most complete survey and analysis of the issue. For a discussion of one New York building, see Olga Bush, "The Architecture of Jewish Identity: The Neo-Islamic Central Synagogue of New York," *Journal of the Society of Architectural Historians (JSAH)* 63, no. 2 (June 2004): 180–201; Ivan Davidson Kalmar, "Moorish Style: Orientalism, the Jews, and Synagogue Architecture," *Jewish Social Studies,* New Series, 7, no. 3 (spring-summer 2001), 68–101; Anthony Alofsin, *When Buildings Speak: Architecture as Language in the Habsburg Empire and Its Aftermath, 1867–1933* (Chicago: University of Chicago Press, 2006), 43–52.

47. Carl Gottlieb Wilhelm Bötticher, "The Principles of Hellenic and Germanic Ways of Building with Regard to Their Application to Our Present Way of Building," in *In What Style Should We Build: The German Debate on Architecture,* trans. Wolfgang Herrmann (1846; Santa Monica, Calif.: Getty Center Publications Program, 1992), 153. Also quoted in part in Snyder, *Building a Public Judaism,* 38.

48. The elaborate pavilion of publisher Oswald Ottendorfer, overlooking the Hudson River with its elaborate Moorish dome, designed in 1879 by William Schickel, is one of the better examples of the period. See Stern, *New York 1880,* 837–39.

49. Stern, *New York 1880,* 674–76. The same architects designed an apartment house at 80–92 Perry Street with horseshoe arches in 1887. See Joy Kestenbaum and Jill Cowen, "Notable New York Buildings with Islamic Influence," *Middle East Studies Association Bulletin* 14, no. 2 (December 1980): 30–32. After the turn of the twentieth century, Moorish and other neo-Islamic forms were widely used by Shriner's masonic temples. See William D. Moore, *Masonic Temples: Freemasonry, Ritual Architecture, and Masculine Archetypes* (Knoxville: University of Tennessee Press, 2006), 93–117. For other uses of neo-Islamic architecture, see Zeynep Çelik, *Displaying the Orient: Architecture of Islam at Nineteenth-Century World's Fairs* (Berkeley: University of California Press, 1992), 95–153.

50. For Jewish clients' relationship within the nationalist framework of historicist architecture in the context of economic emancipation, see Fredric Bedoire, *The Jewish Contribution to Modern Architecture, 1830–1930,* trans. Robert Tanner (Jersey City, N.J.: KATV publishing), 15–20.

51. "St. Elizabeth Church," *RERBG* (February 2, 1889): 139; Sara Lowenburg, "Timothy Greenfield-Sanders Opens the Doors of His Historic Home," *Eldridge Street Synagogue* (blog), http://www.eldridgestreet.org/timothy-greenfield-sanders-opens-the-doors-of-his-historic-home-2, accessed August 21, 2016. The Herter brothers were Catholic.

52. Krinsky, *Synagogues of Europe,* 83.

53. Krinsky, *Synagogues of Europe,* 83.

54. In some ways these buildings, even those that do not directly employ Moorish forms, can be interpreted as a manifestation of what art historians have identified as the Jewish Baroque—a mode thought to continue in eastern Europe through the nineteenth century. The characteristic of this mode, especially in flat art, has been identified as "naive and exuberant, but also disciplined in a haphazard way. It is decidedly baroque in its obvious appeal to the emotions, its fluidity of movement, its florid designs, freedom of line, and richness of motifs—all within a formalistic symmetrical composition." See Joseph and Yehudit Shadur, *Traditional Jewish Papercuts: An Inner World of Art and Symbol* (Hanover, N.H.: University Press of New England, 2002), 47.

55. Snyder, *Building a Public Judaism,* 40–41.

56. NB 377–01.

57. NB 445–01.

4. Skin Builders and Plan Mills

1. Peter Herter's biography can be reconstructed from a number of court cases in which he was involved. See "Apartment House Suit: History of Peter Herter, Builder of the Antoinettes," *New York Times,* December 30, 1902, 16; New York State Court of Appeals, *Henry A. Conolly against Rosalie Hyams: Case and Exceptions on Appeal,* no. 483 (New York: Evening Post Job Printing, 1903), 137–40; Appellate Division of the Supreme Court, First Department, *Martin Disken v. Maria Anna Herter Case on Appeal,* no. 551 (New York: William Siegrist, Law Printer, 1902), 103–4.

2. For background on Jarmulowsky, see Rebecca Kobrin, "Destructive Creators: Sender Jarmulowsky and Financial Failure in the Annals of American Jewish History," *American Jewish History* 97, no. 2 (April 2013): 105–17; Jared Day, "Credit, Capital and Community: Informal Banking in Immigrant Communities in the United States, 1880–1924," *Financial History Review* 9, no. 1 (April 2002): 65–78; New York City Landmarks Commission, S. Jarmulowsky Bank, LP-2563, October 2009.

3. For a discussion of the Eldridge Street synagogue and the community that built it, see Annie Polland, *Landmark of the Spirit: The Eldridge Street Synagogue* (New Haven, Conn.: Yale University Press, 2009), especially 1–32 and 90–114.

4. Polland, *Landmark of the Spirit,* 19–22. For analysis of the use of synagogue architecture to project Jewish identity, see Saskia Coenen Snyder, *Building a Public Judaism: Synagogues and Identity in Nineteenth-Century Europe* (Cambridge, Mass.: Harvard University Press, 2013).

5. "Some Noteworthy Improved Tenements," *Real Estate Record and Builders' Guide (RERBG)* 49 (January 23, 1892): 131.

6. "Obituary: Ascher Weinstein," *RERBG* 52 (July 22, 1893): 104; "United States Census, 1880," index and images, FamilySearch (https://familysearch.org/pal:/MM9.1.1/MZ6Q-KM3, accessed 29 Dec 2013, Ascher Weinstein, New York, New York, United States; citing sheet 517B, family 0, NARA microfilm publication T9–0875.

7. *RERBG* 46, no. 1185 (November 29, 1890): 733. David Cohen became a prominent developer uptown after the turn of the century. His son Elias was later a major player in commercial real estate. "Elias A. Cohen, 72, Realty Operator," obituary, *New York Times,* July 3, 1952, 25. Jeffrey S. Gurock, *When Harlem Was Jewish: 1870–1930* (New York: Columbia University Press 1979), 47.

8. The architect as developer had a long history, especially in the realm of multifamily housing. For an examination of the motivations and methods of architect-developers in a later period, see Matthew Gordon Lasner, "Architect as Developer and the Postwar U.S. Apartment, 1945–1960," *Buildings and Landscapes* 20, no. 1 (Spring 2014): 27–55. Lasner argues that many architects who engaged in housing development in that period did so as "an extension of their professional commitment to educate the public about good design" and to undertake projects that others would not (49).

9. "Some Noteworthy Improved Tenements," 131.

10. For a framework for understanding the role of networks in immigrant entrepreneurship,

see Ivan Light, Parminder Bhachu, and Stavros Karageorgis, "Migration Networks and Immigrant Entrepreneurship," in *Immigration and Entrepreneurship: Culture, Capital, and Ethnic Networks,* ed. Ivan Light and Parminder Bhachu (New Brunswick, N.J.: Transaction Publishers, 1993), 25–51. For a study of the economic mobility of immigrants, see Thomas Kessner, *The Golden Door: Italian and Jewish Immigrant Mobility in New York City, 1880–1915* (New York: Oxford University Press, 1977); John Bodnar, *The Transplanted: A History of Immigrants in Urban America* (Bloomington: Indiana University Press, 1985), 117–42; Irving Howe, *World of Our Fathers: The Journey of the East European Jews to America and the Life They Found and Made* (New York: Touchstone Books, 1976), 148–63. For a background on community life in general, see Arthur A. Goren, *New York Jews and the Quest for Community: The Kehillah Experiment, 1908–1922* (New York: Columbia University Press, 1970), 1–24.

11. Polland, *Landmark of the Spirit,* 64–66.

12. Sara Stevens, *Developing Expertise: Architecture and Real Estate in Metropolitan America* (New Haven, Conn.: Yale University Press, 2016), 5–9.

13. See Donna Rilling, *Making Houses, Crafting Capitalism* (Cambridge, Mass.: Harvard University Press, 2001).

14. Jared N. Day, *Urban Castles: Tenement Housing and Landlord Activism in New York City, 1890–1943* (New York: Columbia University Press, 1999), 31.

15. Margaret Garb, *City of American Dreams: A History of Home Ownership and Housing Reform in Chicago, 1871–1919* (Chicago: University of Chicago Press, 2005), 2–19.

16. M. J. Daunton, *Housing the Workers, 1850–1914: A Comparative Perspective* (London: Leicester University Press, 1990), chaps. 1 and 7.

17. For a survey of the types of housing common to the working class in cities across America at the turn of the century, see Robert DeForest and Lawrence Veiller, *The Tenement House Problem: Including the Report of the New York State Tenement House Commission of 1900,* vol. 1 (New York: MacMillian, 1903), 130–56. These reformers found that few cities outside New York and Boston had tenements.

18. Although, as Joseph Bigott points out, the common two- and three-family houses of Chicago were also frequently owner occupied. Joseph C. Bigott, *From Cottage to Bungalow: Houses and the Working Class in Metropolitan Chicago, 1869–1929* (Chicago: University of Chicago Press, 2001), 109–45.

19. Abraham Schepper, "Jews as Builders of New York," *American Hebrew and Jewish Messenger,* July 4, 1913, 257.

20. Lee M. Friedman, *Pilgrims in a New Land* (Philadelphia: Jewish Publication Society of America, 1948), 306.

21. Day, *Urban Castles,* 32–33; Andrew Dolkart, "From the Rag Trade to Riches: Abraham E. Lefcourt and the Development of New York's Garment District," in *Chosen Capital: The Jewish Encounter with American Capitalism,* ed. Rebecca Kobrin (New York: Rutgers University Press, 2012), 62–92.

22. Herbert S. Goldstein, ed., and Harry Fischel, *Harry Fischel Pioneer of Jewish Philanthropy: Forty Years of Struggle for a Principle and the Years Beyond,* augmented ed. (Jersey City, N.J.: KTAV Publishing, 2012).

23. The permits for the building at 168 Clinton Street, now demolished, were filed in the name of Fischel and Margowitz, recording the name of a partner not mentioned in Fischel's account of the incident. Also not mentioned, F. A. Minuth was listed as the architect of record for the project. Fischel's relationship to Minuth, who has no surviving tenements on the Lower East Side, is unknown. New York New Building Permit (NB) 307–90.

24. By the time of the completion of the Clinton Street building, numerous tenements had been completed by Jewish builders. Fischel would go on, however, to have greater success than most of them.

25. Goldstein and Fischel, *Harry Fischel,* 32.

26. For background on Yiddish theater, see Howe, *World of Our Fathers,* 467–92.

27. Goldstein and Fischel, *Harry Fischel,* 33. As Deborah Dash Moore has noted, immigrant success stories such as Fischel's, particularly related to Jewish builders, became exceedingly common in a slightly later period, in which "Jewish builder success stories cluttered the desk of metropolitan newspaper editors." Deborah Dash Moore, *At Home in America: Second Generation New York Jews* (New York: Columbia University Press, 1981), 43.

28. Clarence Stein, "Housing Crisis," *The Survey,* September 1, 1920, 661, as quoted in Day, *Urban Castles,* 43.

29. Abraham Cahan, *The Rise of David Levinsky* (1917; New York: Harper Brothers, 1960), 464–68. The particular developments described by Cahan were taking place in Brownsville, Brooklyn, a peripheral neighborhood that experienced a boom in tenement construction after the turn of the twentieth century.

30. Friedman, *Pilgrims in a New Land,* 302.

31. Rilling, *Making Houses, Crafting Capitalism,* 39–90.

32. James A. Jacobs, *Detached America: Building Houses in Postwar Suburbia* (Charlottesville: University of Virginia Press, 2015), 30–36.

33. Rilling, *Making Houses, Crafting Capitalism,* chap. 1.

34. Cahan, *Rise of David Levinsky,* 464.

35. Maura Fitzpatrick, "From Template Tenements to Beaux-Arts Boulevards: The Architecture of Fred A. Norcross" (master's thesis, Boston University, 1993), 10.

36. "Their Creditors Satisfied: Herter Brothers Agree to Place All Their Property under Trust," *New York Times,* Aug 17, 1893, 16; "Liens against Architects Mechanics' Claims against Herter Brothers," *New York Times,* August 15, 1893, 9.

37. George Von Skal, *History of German Immigration in the United States and Successful German-Americans and Their Decedents* (New York: F. T. and J. C. Smiley, 1908), 271.

38. The Real Estate Record Association, *A History of Real Estate, Building and Architecture in New York during the Last Quarter Century* (New York: Record and Guide, 1898), 234–35.

39. Friedman, *Pilgrims in a New Land,* 301.

40. The story about Rudnick's interest in becoming a builder is recounted in Fitzpatrick, "From Template Tenements," 8, based on oral history.

41. In 1907 another Russian Jewish immigrant, Jacob Brilliant, a shoe dealer by trade, would build a large decorated tenement with prominent sheet-metal oriels on a lot near the Rudnick's former residence. The building, at 98–102 Middle Street, was purportedly the largest apartment building in the state when it was complete.

42. William DeMarco, "Ethnics and Enclaves: The Italian Settlement in the North End of Boston" (PhD diss., Boston College, 1980), 50; William A. Braverman, "The Emergence of a Unified Community, 1880–1917," in *The Jews of Boston: Essays on the Occasion of the Centenary of the Combined Jewish Philanthropies of Greater Boston,* ed. Jonathan D. Sarna and Ellen Smith (Boston: Combined Jewish Philanthropies, 1995), 71–84.

43. 1880 U.S. Manuscript Census, Boston, Suffolk County, Enumeration District 613, page 22. For Haffenreffer, see 142–146 Paul Gore Street, 1892.

44. "Many Big Tenement Houses Built with Little Capital," *New York Times,* September 13, 1903, 30.

45. Friedman, *Pilgrims in a New Land,* 303.

46. Lawrence Veiller suggested that the construction costs filed on city building permits were routinely inflated by speculative builders, seeking to provide evidence to prospective purchasers of the value of their building. He claims that while the average tenement in 1900 was reported to have cost $20,000 to $25,000, actual costs of these buildings could be as low as $16,000 to $18,000. See DeForest and Veiller, *The Tenement House Problem,* 373. For purposes of this study, only the reported construction costs could be used.

47. DeMarco, "Ethnics and Enclaves," 163–65.

48. Day, *Urban Castles,* 35.

49. For Boston-specific Information, see Fitzpatrick, "From Template Tenements," 44–47; and Friedman, *Pilgrims in a New Land,* 301.

50. William Hazlet, "Of the Breed of Buddensiek," *Charities and the Commons* 17 (1906): 75.

51. DeForest and Veiller, *Tenement House Problem,* 376.

52. Fitzpatrick, "From Template Tenements," 44–45.

53. For a discussion of this in a later context, see Stevens, *Developing Expertise,* 152–58.

54. Peter Herter, "The Critic Criticized: Are Mr. Flagg's Plans Practicable?" *RERBG* 65 (May 26, 1900): 918.

55. *The Jewish Messenger,* April 20, 1888, 7.

56. *Apartment Houses of the Metropolis* (New York: G. C. Hesselgren, 1908), 49.

57. "Their Creditors Satisfied: Herter Brothers Agree to Place All Their Property under Trust," 16; "Liens against Architects Mechanics' Claims against Herter Brothers," 9; Peter Herter, "How to Invest in Tenement Property," *RERBG* 65 (May 5, 1900): 764.

58. *Apartment Houses of the Metropolis,* 64, 201, 278.

59. For a history of premade architectural products, see Pamela Simpson, *Quick, Cheap, and Easy: Imitative Architectural Materials* (Knoxville: University of Tennessee Press, 1999).

60. For profiles of a number of important New York building materials firms, see Record and Guide, *Building and Architecture in New York,* 417–54.

61. Record and Guide, *Building and Architecture in New York,* 448.

62. Record and Guide, *Building and Architecture in New York,* 529–32.

63. Jacob Broschardt and William A. Braun, *Architectural Sheet Metal Ornaments* (New York, 1900).

64. *Perth Amboy Architectural Terra Cotta Company* (Perth Amboy, N.J.: 1887), 1.

65. New York Architectural Terra Cotta Company, Walter Geer, President, *New York Architectural Terra Cotta Company 1888 Catalog* (New York: Lowe and Company, 1888), 7–21.

66. Fine's relationship to Harris Fine, a prominent tenement builder is unclear.

67. *RERBG,* June 16, 1894, 974.

68. "Recovery of Insurance," *RERBG,* June 30, 1900, 1184.

69. Herter, "How to Invest," 764.

70. DeForest and Veiller, *Tenement House Problem,* 439–45. While Veiller presents a detailed study of rents of one Lower East Side block, it is difficult to correlate the figures he presents with specific building types, as he presents only footprints, and the block was demolished in 1930 for the construction of Sarah Roosevelt Park.

71. Estelle M. Stewart, *History of Wages in the United States from Colonial Times to 1928, Bulletin of the United States Bureau of Labor Statistics,* no. 499 (Washington, D.C.: Government Printing Office, 1929), 154–56, 219–21.

72. Assuming a three-room unit for the two-dollars-a-day worker, and a five-room unit for the four-dollars-a-day bricklayer.

73. "Many Big Tenement Houses Built with Little Capital," 30.

74. "Changes on the Lower East Side," *New York Times,* July 9, 1899, 14.

75. Cecil C. Evers, *The Commercial Problem in Building: A Discussion of the Economic and Structural Essentials of Profitable Buildings, and the Basis for Valuation of Improved Real Estate* (New York: Record and Guide Co., 1914), 55.

76. Herter, "How to Invest," 916.

77. Elizabeth Ewen, *Immigrant Women in the Land of Dollars: Life and Culture on the Lower East Side, 1890–1925* (New York: Monthly Review Press, 1985), 154.

5. Destroying the Rookeries

1. Max Shoolman would later become one of the most prominent real estate developers in New England, a theater owner, and a major philanthropist. "Max Shoolman, Philanthropist, Dies at 75,"

Daily Boston Globe, August 4, 1950, 20; 1900 U.S. Manuscript Census, Boston Ward Three, District 11984, page 24.

2. The specifications in their entirety read: "Building for Joseph Shoolman, to be erected at #112 Salem St. cor. of Carroll Place, Ward 6. Excavate to solid bottom for all walls, pier, etc and cellar to conform with plans; Foundation of block grant [*sic*] laid in 1/2 cement mortar; drain from 10 ft outside building and glazed [clay?] pipe joined in cement. Front Brick of even color facade laid in 1/2 cement mortar, backing up and pair brick to be good merchantable hard brick, laid in 1/3 cement mortar. Provide and set all constructional Iron Work and all wall ties and anchors; Indiana Limestone trimmings; chimneys laid; Cornice and skylights gal. iron. Pave sidewalks, build Cesspool etc. Make fire stop. Frame in a thorough and mechanical manner using stick shown on plans; Space under floors and roof matched; stud wall 2x3 and 2x4, bridged once; Build clothes dryer on roof in usual manner; Head house to have tinned door; Window frames box pattern; 1 1/2" pine sash, second quality plate glass; Wooden stairs of hard pine, halls, posts, rails and balusters; Iron starts with apron front. 3x5", angle iron posts, wrought iron balusters. Plaster three coats on metal lath, wall to wall and floor to ceiling. Make fire stops according to law. Pipe for gas as shown on plans, separate fit for each tenant. Three ply composition roofs. Interior finish N.C. pine, painted three coats; upper floors Gee & N.C. pine, laid over salamander papers. Apply usual hardware. Open plumbing." Boston Building Inspection Report, Boston Public Library (BIR), vol. 159, page 30.

3. Catherine Bishir, "Good and Sufficient Language for Building," *Perspectives in Vernacular Architecture* 4 (1991): 44–52.

4. "Real Estate Matters," *Daily Boston Globe,* October 12, 1901, 9.

5. The troubled Varrick Street building was demolished for street widening in the 1920s. Its twin at 49–53 Grove Street at Bleecker Street is extant, though missing its cornice. See New York Landmarks Commission, "Greenwich Village Historic District Designation Report" (New York, 1969), 235. On slums, see "Real Estate Owned by Trinity," *New York Times,* December 11, 1894, 3.

6. New York State Court of Appeals, *Henry A. Conolly against Rosalie Hyams: Case and Exceptions on Appeal.* no. 483 (New York: Evening Post Job Printing, 1903), passim. For a map of Trinity property, see *New York Times,* December 31, 1894; also reproduced in Jared Day, *Urban Castles: Tenement Housing and Landlord Activism in New York, 1890–1943* (New York: Columbia University Press, 1999), 53.

7. *Connolly v. Hyams,* 42.

8. Historian Elizabeth Blackmar traces the origins of the contract system in New York construction to the first decades of the nineteenth century. See Elizabeth Blackmar, *Manhattan for Rent, 1785–1850* (Ithaca, N.Y.: Cornell University Press, 1989), 188–91.

9. For the professionalization of architects, see Mary N. Woods, *From Craft to Profession: The Practice of Architecture in Nineteenth-Century America.* (Berkeley: University of California Press, 1999).

10. Bainbridge Bunting notes that the monotony of the row house development in Boston's South End neighborhood was a factor in that neighborhood's failure to achieve the elite status of the nearly contemporaneous Back Bay, where the streetscape featured a greater variety and individuality. Bainbridge Bunting, *Houses of Boston's Back Bay: An Architectural History, 1840–1917* (Cambridge, Mass.: Belknap Press, 1967), chap. 5.

11. For background on this competition and its relationship to building laws, see Richard Plunz, *History of Housing in New York* (New York: Columbia University Press, 1990), 24–29.

12. William B. Tuthill, *The City Residence: Its Design and Construction* (New York: William T. Comstock, 1890).

13. For a discussion of vernacular design methods, see Thomas Hubka, "Just Folks Designing: Vernacular Designers and the Generation of Form," in *Common Places: Readings in American Vernacular Architecture,* ed. Dell Upton and John Michael Vlach (Athens: University of Georgia Press, 1986), 427–46.

14. Abraham Cahan, *The Rise of David Levinsky* (1917; New York: Harper Brothers, 1960), 345.

15. "Application for Permit to Build," 32 Prince Street, 7/22/1895, #334; "Application for Permit to Build," 26 Prince Street, 3/2/1906, #733.

16. New York New Building Permit (NB) 333–86 and 531–86. For a biography of Schnugg, see Michael C. Harrison, ed., *New York State's Prominent and Progressive Men: An Encyclopedia of Contemporaneous Biography,* vol. 3 (New York: New York Tribune, 1902), 293–94.

17. See "Out Among the Builders," *Real Estate Record and Builders' Guide (RERBG)* 38 (October 30, 1886): 1331.

18. See New York City Landmarks Commission, "Ridgewood South Historic District Designation Report" (New York, October 2010).

19. William Hazlet, "Of the Breed of Buddensiek," *Charities and the Commons* 17 (1906): 74.

20. Robert DeForest and Lawrence Veiller, *The Tenement House Problem: Including the Report of the New York State Tenement House Commission of 1900,* vol. 1 (New York: MacMillian, 1903), 372.

21. For a discussion of the rise of the architectural profession, standards, and fees, see Diana Balmori, "George B. Post: The Process of Design and the New American Architectural Office (1868–1913)," *Journal of the Society of Architectural Historians (JSAH)* 46, no. 4 (December 1987): 342–55. See particularly page 348 for a discussion of fees. Woods, *From Craft to Profession;* Carl M. Sapers and Penny Pittman Merliss, "The Liability of Architects and Engineers in Nineteenth-Century America," *Journal of Architectural Education* 41, no. 2 (Winter 1988): 39–45; Mary Alice Molloy, "Richardson's Web: A Client's Assessment of the Architect's Home and Studio," *JSAH* 54, no. 1 (March 1995): 8–23. For an architect's view of the importance of architects in residential commissions, see E. C. Gardner, *Homes, and How to Make Them* (Boston: James R. Osgood, 1875), 15–33.

22. "Municipal Architecture," *RERBG* 33, no. 835 (March 15, 1884): 260.

23. Aline May Lewis Goldstone and Harmon H. Goldstone, *Lafayette A. Goldstone: A Career in Architecture* (New York, 1964), 50–51.

24. Goldstone and Goldstone, *Lafayette A. Goldstone,* 50–51.

25. "Buddensiek's Record," *New York Times,* April 15, 1885, 2.

26. New York Supreme Court, *The People of the State of New York against Charles A. Buddensiek,* case on appeal (New York: C. S. Hamilton & Co, printers, 1886), 437.

27. For a discussion of architectural office practice in this period, see Woods, *Craft to Profession,* 138–66.

28. For background on Snook, see Mary Ann Clegg Smith, "The Commercial Architecture of John Butler Snook" (PhD diss.: Pennsylvania State University, 1974), especially 5–21 and 134–62. The first known collaboration between Snook and the Korn brothers was for an 1867 tenement at 82–84 Attorney Street; see Smith, "The Commercial Architecture of John Butler Snook," 238.

29. Finding Aid, John B. Snook Collection, 1843–1948, PR 64, New-York Historical Society, 2012.

30. NB 916–91; see Smith, "The Commercial Architecture of John Butler Snook," 248.

31. New York architectural historian Andrew Dolkart asserts that the presence of brownstone lintels and an acanthus cornice at 97 Orchard Street "does not reflect an effort on the part of the tenement builder to create a fashionable, architecturally distinguished structure. Rather, cornices with this design were stock items in the 1860s, widely available from builders' yards." Andrew Dolkart, *Biography of a Tenement House in New York City: An Architectural History* (Santa Fe, N.Mex.: Center for American Places, 2006), 27.

32. The 1940 Department of Finance tax photo of the building, taken shortly before its demolition, shows the Neo-Grec caps and cornice. Otherwise, Snook's scheme seems to have been followed exactly.

33. Smith, "The Commercial Architecture of John Butler Snook," 5–8.

34. Maura Fitzpatrick, "From Template Tenements to Beaux-Arts Boulevards: The Architecture of Fred A. Norcross" (master's thesis: Boston University, 1993), 4–7.

35. Smith, "The Commercial Architecture of John Butler Snook," chap. 1.

36. "Silverman Engineering Company," *Jewish Advocate,* August 13, 1909, 6; "Necrology: Nathaniel Silverman," *Harvard Alumni Bulletin* 21, no. 1 (June 1918): 576.

37. Goldstone and Goldstone, *Lafayette A. Goldstone,* 57.

38. For a background on European architectural education, see Turpin Bannister, ed., *The Architect and Mid-Century: Evolution and Achievement,* vol. 1 (New York: Reinhold Publishing Co., 1954), 82–93.

39. Historical Publishing Company, *Finance and Industry: The New York Stock Exchange: Banks, Bankers, Business Houses, and Moneyed Institutions: The Great Metropolis of the United States* (New York: Historical Publishing Company, 1886), 133.

40. Appellate Division of the Supreme Court [New York], First Department, *Martin Disken v. Maria Anna Herter,* case on appeal (New York: William Siegrist, Law Printer, 1902), 103–4. The story of Peter Herter's troubles as a young man in Germany was told, somewhat inconsistently, in a number of places. See "Apartment House Suit: History of Peter Herter, Builder of the Antoinettes," *New York Times,* December 30, 1902, 16; *Conolly v. Hyams,* 137–40; *Martin Disken v. Maria Anna Herter,* 103–4.

41. New York Landmarks Commission, "So-Ho Cast Iron District Designation Report, " 178–79; "Obituary—Henry Fernbach," *New York Times,* November 13, 1883, 2; "Henry Fernbach," *Universal Jewish Encyclopedia,* vol. 4 (1969), 279.

42. For a background on Bauakademie theory and practice, see Mitchell Schwarzer, *German Architectural Theory and the Search for Modern Identity* (Cambridge: Cambridge University Press, 1995). See also Roula Geraniotis, "The University of Illinois and German Architectural Education," *Journal of Architectural Education* 38, no. 4 (Summer 1985): 15–21. For the influence of German architects on Chicago architecture, particularly on commercial buildings, see Roula Mouroudellis Geraniotis, "German Architectural Theory and Practice in Chicago, 1850–1900," *Winterthur Portfolio* 21, no. 4 (Winter 1986): 293–306. See also Paul Zucker, "Architectural Education in Nineteenth Century German," *JSAH* 2, no. 3 (July 1942): 6–13. The influence of German ideas on American architecture of a slightly earlier period is discussed by Kathleen Curran, "The German Rundbogenstil and Reflections on the American Round-Arch Style," *JSAH* 47, no. 4 (December 1988): 351–73.

43. Józef Sisa, "The Role of the Berlin Bauakademie in the Training of Ödön Lechner and Other Hungarian Architects, and the Limitations and Opportunities of Historicism," in *Ödön Lechner in Context: Studies of the International Conference on the Occasion of the 100th Anniversary of Ödön Lechner's Death,* ed. Zsombor Jékely (Budapest: Museum of Fine Arts, 2015), 167–76.

44. Schwarzer, *German Architectural Theory,* 120. For a discussion of the rise of the commercial consumption of cultural products in Germany, see Michael North, *Material Delight and the Joy of Living: Cultural Consumption in the Age of Enlightenment in Germany,* trans. Pamela Selwyn (London: Ashgate, 2008).

45. Pamela H. Simpson, *Cheap, Quick, and Easy: Imitative Architectural Materials, 1870–1930* (Knoxville: University of Tennessee Press, 1999), 136–64.

46. For background on the acceptance of Ruskin, see Roger B. Stein, *John Ruskin and Aesthetic Thought in America, 1840–1900* (Cambridge, Mass.: Harvard University Press, 1967), 57–101, 186–255.

47. David Shi, *The Simple Life: Plain Living and High Thinking in American Culture* (New York: Oxford University Press, 1985).

48. For background on the industrialization of this region, see Daniel R. Bower, *The Russian City between Tradition and Modernity, 1850–1900* (Berkeley: University of California Press, 1990), 7–91.

49. For background on the industrial and cultural history of Lodz, see Frederic Bedoire, *The Jewish Contribution to Modern Architecture, 1830–1930,* trans. Robert Tanner (Jersey City, N.J.: KATV publishing), 401–19; Irena Popławska and Stefan Muthesius, "Poland's Manchester: 19th-Century Industrial and Domestic Architecture in Lodz," *JSAH* 45, no. 2 (June 1986): 148–60.

50. Reymont, as quoted in Bedoire, *The Jewish Contribution to Modern Architecture,* 401–2.

51. On the role of Vienna, see Donald J. Olsen, *The City as a Work of Art: London, Paris, Vienna* (New Haven, Conn.: Yale University Press, 1986), 58–89 and 235–51. For Berlin, see Dietrich Worbs, "The Berlin Mietskaserne and Its Reforms," in *Berlin/New York: Like and Unlike: Essays on Art and Architecture from 1870 to the Present,* ed. Josef Paul Kleihues and Christina Rathgeber (New York: Rizzoli, 1993), 145–59; Brian Ladd, *The Ghosts of Berlin: Confronting German History in the Urban Landscape* (Chicago: University of Chicago Press, 1997), 96–125. For a discussion of the twentieth-century history of these buildings in East Berlin, see Florian Urban, *Neo-Historical East Berlin: Architecture and Urban Design in the German Democratic Republic, 1970–1990* (Burlington, Vt.: Ashgate, 2009), 1–67, 143–81. Urban notes the disdain in which these buildings were held in the twentieth century, when "stucco ornaments and back buildings came to be a cipher for social misery and political oppression" (12).

52. Rolf Kuck, "Palace Prison Mietskaserne, Myer's Hof: Misery vs. Utopia," ExploreLab Research Paper #8 Delft University of Technology, 2010, http://preservedstories.com/wp-content /uploads/2013/01/Mietskaserne-1.pdf, 6. For interior arrangement of multifamily housing, see Douglas Mark Klahr, "Luxury Apartments with a Tenement Heart: The Kurfürstendam and the Berliner Zimmer," *JSAH* 70, no. 3 (September 2011): 290–307.

53. Eve Blau, *The Architecture of Red Vienna, 1919–1934* (Cambridge, Mass.: MIT Press, 1999), 69. Blau also notes in an endnote that those Viennese manufacturers who built tenements for their own workers did so in a manner that differed little from speculatively built houses except that "they tended . . . to dispense with typical facade embellishments" (421). Just as in Lodz and in the mill towns of the United States, ornamented tenements in Vienna seem to be the product only of speculative builders.

54. Blau, *Architecture of Red Vienna,* 67.

55. For a history of the impact of German architects on the architecture of Chicago, see Geraniotis, "German Architectural Theory and Practice in Chicago," 293–306.

56. Paris's influence on American architecture in the nineteenth century has been a preoccupation of many historians. The lack of recognition of the role of the cities of east and central Europe may be due to the destruction of many buildings and records during World War II and the subsequent closing of much of the region behind the Iron Curtain during the Cold War.

57. "Many Big Tenement Houses Built with Little Capital," *New York Times,* September 13, 1903, 30.

58. Cecil C. Evers, *The Commercial Problem in Building: A Discussion of the Economic and Structural Essentials of Profitable Buildings, and the Basis for Valuation of Improved Real Estate* (New York: Record and Guide Co., 1914), 54.

59. "Tear Down House in Which Man Is Ill: Widow Claims That a Real Estate Firm Caused Her Husband's Death," *New-York Daily Tribune,* February 21, 1901, 7.

60. "Exposed to View: Old Galloupe House on Hull Street Shows Its Face to Passers-by for the First Time in Nearly a Century—New Building Will Soon Overshadow It," *Boston Daily Globe,* January 22, 1906, 20.

61. "Around and about Copps Hill—Old Wooden Landmarks of the North End Are Being Rapidly Replaced by Modern Brick Tenements," *Boston Globe,* June 23, 1907, SM 12.

62. "Many Big Tenement Houses Built with Little Capital," 30.

63. *Conolly v. Hyams,* 36.

64. New York Supreme Court, Appellate Division-First Judicial Department, *Edward R. Poerschke against Philip Horowitz, Meyer Horowitz, Hannah R. Simon, and Morris Garfinkel,* case on appeal, no. 542 (New York: Appeal Printing Co, 1903), 45–78.

65. The prevalence of such modifications is hard to document systematically. See, for instance, "Application for Permit for Alterations," 38 Charter Street, Boston, April 26, 1894, #800. Examination of the interior structural fabric of a number of these buildings could reveal more concrete answers to these questions, but such examination has been outside the scope of this project.

66. Lee M. Friedman, *Pilgrims in a New Land* (Philadelphia: Jewish Publication Society of America, 1948), 301–2; Fitzpatrick, "From Template Tenements," 45.

67. For the importance of reuse in the clothing trade, see Adam Mendelsohn, *The Rag Race: How Jews Sewed Their Way to Success in America and the British Empire* (New York: New York University Press, 2015), 9–12. For a discussion of Jews in the secondhand materials trade in general, though not building materials specifically, see Jonathan Z. S. Pollack, "Success from Scrap and Secondhand Goods: Jewish Businessmen in the Midwest, 1890–1930," in *Chosen Capital: The Jewish Encounter with American Capitalism,* ed. Rebecca Kobrin (New Brunswick, N.J.: Rutgers University Press, 2012), 93–113.

68. *Poerschke v. Horowitz,* 87.

69. *Poerschke v. Horowitz,* 100.

70. *Poerschke v. Horowitz,* 105–7.

71. Hazlet, "Of the Breed of Buddensiek," 75.

72. "The New Buddensiek," *New York Times,* September 29, 1896.

73. Jacob Riis, *How the Other Half Lives: Studies among the Tenements of New York* (New York: Charles Scribner's Sons, 1890), 274.

74. Goldstone and Goldstone, *Lafayette A. Goldstone,* 50.

75. "Obituary: Ascher Weinstein," *RERBG* 52 (July 22, 1893): 104.

76. DeForest and Veiller, *Tenement House Problem,* 372; Manhattan New Building Docket Books, 1868–1900.

77. Goldstone and Goldstone, *Lafayette A. Goldstone,* 50–52.

6. A New Style of Poverty

1. *The Brickbuilder* 1, no. 7 (July 1892), 49–50.

2. New York New Building Permit (NB) 1425–90; *Real Estate Record and Builders' Guide (RERBG)* 46, no. 1170 (August 16, 1890): 229; 1900, 1910 U.S. Census. Frohne's most important, and relevant, building is the German-American Shooting Society Club House, 12 St. Mark's Place, of 1889, which also featured overscaled terra-cotta ornament. See New York City Landmarks Commission Designation Report, 12 St. Mark's Place, LP-2094, June 26, 2001.

3. William T. Elsing, "Life in New York Tenement-Houses as Seen by a City Missionary," *Scribner's* 11 (1892): 701. The building was demolished in the 1940s for a housing project. See New York Department of Finance Tax Photo, 1940, Block 326, Lot 47. A second photo of the building is also erroneously filed under Block 336, Lot 47.

4. *The Brickbuilder,* 50.

5. For a framework for understanding demand, based in an earlier period, see Cary Carson, "The Consumer Revolution in Colonial British America: Why Demand?," in *Of Consuming Interests: The Style of Life in the Eighteenth Century* (Charlottesville: University of Virginia Press, 1994), 483–697.

6. The most important study of the impact of industrial production on ornament is Pamela Simpson, *Cheap, Quick, and Easy: Imitative Architectural Materials, 1870–1930* (Knoxville: University of Tennessee Press 1999). For more context on this period, see Leo Marx, *The Machine in the Garden: Technology and the Pastoral Idea in America* (New York: Oxford University Press, 1964); and Howard Mumford Jones, *The Age of Energy: Varieties of American Experience, 1865–1915* (New York: Viking Press, 1971), chap. 3.

7. Thorstein Veblen, *The Theory of the Leisure Class: An Economic Study of Institutions* (New York: Macmillian Company, 1912), 154.

8. Andrew Heinze, *Adapting to Abundance: Jewish Immigrants, Mass Consumption, and the Search for American Identity* (New York: Columbia University Press, 1990), chaps. 6 and 8. Lizabeth A. Cohen, "Embellishing a Life of Labor: An Interpretation of the Material Culture of American Working-Class Homes, 1885–1915," *Journal of American Culture* 3, no. 4 (Winter 1980):

752–75; Lizabeth Cohen, "Respectability at $50: Furnishing a Working-Class Home," in *Victorian Furniture: Essays from a Victorian Society Autumn Symposium,* ed. Kenneth Ames (Philadelphia: The Victorian Society in America, 1983), 231–43; Jenna Weissman Joselit, *The Wonders of America: Reinventing Jewish Culture, 1880–1950* (New York: Henry Holt, 1994); Elizabeth Ewen, *Immigrant Women in the Land of Dollars: Life and Culture on the Lower East Side, 1890–1925* (New York: Monthly Review Press, 1985), 147–64, 65–97; Kathy Peiss, *Cheap Amusements: Working Women and Leisure in Turn-of-the-Century New York* (Philadelphia: Temple University Press, 1986); Nan Enstad, *Ladies of Labor, Girls of Adventure: Working Women, Popular Culture, and Labor Politics at the Turn of the Twentieth Century* (New York: Columbia University Press, 1999), 48–84. For a similar analysis in a different context, see Leora Auslander, *Taste and Power: Furnishing Modern France* (Berkeley: University of California Press, 1996), especially 1–26. For a discussion of the way in which art was democratized among tenement residents, see Katherine Martinez, "At Home with Mona Lisa: Consumers and Commercial Visual Culture, 1880–1920," in *Seeing High and Low: Representing Social Conflict in American Visual Culture,* ed. Patricia Johnson (Berkeley: University of California Press, 2006), 160–76.

9. For a case study in varieties of taste, see Elizabeth Collins Cromley, "Modernizing: or 'You Never See a Screen Door on Affluent Homes,'" *Journal of American Culture* 5, no. 2 (Summer 1982): 71–80.

10. Enstad, *Ladies of Labor,* 61.

11. Henry James, *The American Scene* (London: Chapman and Hall, 1907), 132–36. James's vivid material descriptions of Rutgers Square stand in contrast to his vividly racist and anti-Semitic descriptions in this work and elsewhere. For a discussion of James's racism, see Matthew Frye Jacobson, *Whiteness of a Different Color: European Immigrants and the Alchemy of Race* (Cambridge, Mass.: Harvard University Press, 1998), 172–73.

12. "Keeping in Style," *New York Tribune,* July 3, 1898, as reprinted in Allon Shoener, ed., *Portal to America: The Lower East Side, 1870–1925* (New York, 1967). Also quoted in Ewen, *Immigrant Women in the Land of Dollars,* 26; Enstad, *Ladies of Labor,* 65–83. For a similar quotation, see Enstad, *Ladies of Labor,* 66.

13. Rebecca Yamin, "Introduction: Becoming New York: The Five Points Neighborhood," *Historical Archaeology,* 35, no. 3 (2001): 1–5; Stephen A. Brighton, "Prices That Suit the Times: Shopping for Ceramics at the Five Points," in *Historical Archaeology* 35, no. 3 (2001): 16–30; and Alan Mayne and Tim Murray, eds., *The Archaeology of Urban Landscapes: Explorations in Slumland* (Cambridge: Cambridge University Press, 2001).

14. Brighton, "Prices That Suit the Times," 28.

15. Albert J. Kennedy and Robert A. Woods, *The Zone of Emergence: Observations of the Lower Middle and Upper Working Class Communities of Boston, 1905–1914* (Cambridge, Mass.: MIT Press, 1962), 64.

16. Lillian Betts, another settlement house worker, lived for a period on the Lower East Side as part of her work and described her life there in a number of books and articles. See Lillian Betts, *The Leaven in a Great City* (New York: Dodd, Mead and Company, 1902); *The Story of an East Side Family* (New York: Dodd, Mead and Company, 1903); "Italian Peasants in a New Law Tenement," *Harper's Bazaar* 38 (1904): 802–5.

17. New York State Court of Appeals, *Henry A. Conolly against Rosalie Hyams: Case and Exceptions on Appeal,* no. 483 (New York: Evening Post Job Printing, 1903), 332.

18. *Conolly v. Hyams,* 194.

19. "Hardwood Burns Slowly," *The American Hebrew,* June 9, 1899, 186.

20. For a history of the ornamental iron trade, see William J. Freyer, "A Review of Ornamental Iron Work," in *A History of Real Estate, Building and Architecture in New York during the Last Quarter Century* (New York: Record and Guide, 1898), 489–502.

21. Robert A. Woods, *The City Wilderness: A Settlement Study* (Boston: Houghton Mifflin and Company, 1898), 34. Woods was describing a purpose-built tenement in Boston's South End.

22. *Conolly v. Hyams,* 261.

23. *Conolly v. Hyams,* 57, 67.

24. Cohen, "Embellishing a Life of Labor."

25. Martinez, "At Home with Mona Lisa," 176.

26. Robert A. Woods, *Americans in Progress: A Settlement Study by the Residents and Associates of the South End House* (Boston: Houghton Mifflin Company, 1903), 143.

27. Peiss, *Cheap Amusements,* 11–15. For a discussion of the social importance of the saloon in working-class culture, see Madelon Powers, *Faces along the Bar: Lore and Order in the Workingman's Saloon, 1870–1920* (Chicago: University of Chicago Press, 1998); Perry R. Duis, *The Saloon: Public Drinking in Chicago and Boston, 1880–1920* (Urbana: University of Illinois Press, 1983). For Jewish immigrants' involvement with the saloon and liquor trade, see Marni Davis, *Jews and Booze: Becoming American in the Age of Prohibition* (New York: New York University Press, 2012).

28. Peiss, *Cheap Amusements,* 141.

29. Paul Boyer, *Urban Masses and Moral Order in America, 1820–1920* (Cambridge, Mass.: Harvard University Press, 1978), 191–218.

30. This phenomenon is discussed in detail in the context of a western boomtown saloon in Kelley K. Dixon, *Boomtown Saloons: Archaeology and History in Virginia City* (Reno: University of Nevada Press, 2005), 55–72.

31. Moses King, *King's Handbook of New York City: An Outline History and Description of the American Metropolis* (Boston: Moses King, 1892), 216.

32. Marcus T. Reynolds, *Housing the Poor in American Cities* (Baltimore: American Economic Association, 1892), 33.

33. Robert DeForest and Lawrence Veiller, *The Tenement House Problem: Including the Report of the New York State Tenement House Commission of 1900,* vol. 1 (New York: MacMillian, 1903), 373.

34. The prices cited in this section, and used in computing the ornament costs for all buildings, are based on the catalog list price of each item. While these manufactures advertised that these prices were "subject to discount," the amount of this discount in each case cannot, of course, be ascertained.

35. This description is based on 42–48 Eldridge Street, New York, 1895; Weil & Mayer, builders; Schneider & Herter, architects.

36. This description is based on 17 Mulberry Street, New York, 1889; John P. White, builder; Schneider & Herter, architects.

37. "Municipal Architecture," *RERBG,* 33, no. 835 (March 15, 1884): 261.

38. Ransom E. Wilcox, "Management of Apartment and Tenement Property," in *Practical Real Estate Methods for Broker, Operator, Owner by Thirty Real Estate Experts,* ed. Francis E. Ward (New York: West Side Young Men's Christian Association, 1909), 52.

39. Cecil C. Evers, *The Commercial Problem in Building: A Discussion of the Economic and Structural Essentials of Profitable Building, and the Basis for Valuation of Improved Real Estate* (New York: Record and Guide Company, 1912), passim.

40. Evers, *Commercial Problem,* 113–14.

41. Evers, *Commercial Problem,* 109.

42. Evers, *Commercial Problem,* 149.

43. Evers, *Commercial Problem,* 175.

44. "Death of William Cruickshank," *New York Times,* September 22, 1894.

45. Real Estate Record Association, *A History of Real Estate, Building and Architecture in New York during the Last Quarter Century* (New York: Record and Guide, 1898), 173.

46. A few years earlier, Post had submitted a design for a mostly unornamented "colony of tenements" to the *Plumber and Sanitary Engineer*'s 1879 competition to design a more thoroughly

ventilated and plumbed building. That building, unlike the Third Street building, did at least pro-pose label moldings on the windows and a modest cornice. *Plumber and Sanitary Engineer* 2 (April 1879): 124.

47. Sarah Bradford Landau, *George B. Post, Architect: Picturesque Designer and Determined Realist* (New York: Monacelli Press, 1998), 40–42. For a more recent and more thorough analysis of this building, see Abigail Van Slyck, "The Spatial Practices of Privilege," *Journal of the Society of Architectural Historians (JSAH)* 70, no. 2 (2011): 210–39; Robert A. M. Stern, *New York 1880: Architecture and Urbanism in the Gilded Age* (New York: Monacelli Press, 1999), 596–601.

48. Landau, *George B. Post,* 67.

49. Lori Zabar, *Historic American Buildings Survey, Written Historical and Descriptive Data, 142–144 Beekman Street (Ellen S. Auchmuty Building).* HABS no. NY-5674 (1976).

50. New York City Landmarks Commission, "South Street Seaport Historic District Designation Report" (1977), 8.

51. See, for instance, Andrew Dolkart, "The Fabric of New York City's Garment District: Development in an Urban Cultural Landscape," *Buildings and Landscapes* 18, no. 1 (Spring 2011): 14–42.

52. New York City Landmarks Commission, "So-Ho Cast Iron Historic District Designation Report" (New York, 1973), vol. 2, 61.

53. For analysis of a similar building by an elite architect, see Cynthia Zaitzevsky, "A New Richardson Building," *JSAH* 32, no. 2 (May 1973): 164–66.

54. "Up-to-Date Buildings for Mercantile Purposes," *RERBG* 53 (January 6, 1894): 7.

55. A. K. Sandoval-Strauz, "Homes for a World of Strangers: Hospitality and the Origins of Multiple Dwellings in Urban America," *Journal of Urban History* 33, no. 6 (September 2007): 933–64.

56. Elizabeth Collins Cromley, *Alone Together: A History of New York's Early Apartments* (Ithaca, N.Y.: Cornell University Press, 1990), 41; Matthew Gordon Lasner, *High Life: Condo Living in the Suburban Century* (New Haven, Conn.: Yale University Press, 2012), chap. 1.

57. DeForest and Veiller, *The Tenement House Problem,* xxviii.

58. Palmer E. Lewis, "The Day's Work of a 'New Law' Tenement Inspector," *Charities and the Commons,* October 6, 1906, 82.

59. Julius Henri Browne, "The Problem of Living in New York," *Harpers Monthly Magazine* 65, no. 300 (November 1892): 920.

60. One important trade catalog for architectural terra-cotta also includes a history of the traditions and meanings surrounding it. See New York Architectural Terra Cotta Company, Walter Greer, president, *New York Architectural Terra Cotta Company 1888 Catalog* (New York: Lowe and Company, 1888), 7–21. See also James Taylor, "The History of Terra Cotta in New York City," *Architectural Record* 2 (July 1892): 137–48. See Landau, *George B. Post.*

61. Browne, "The Problem of Living in New York," 920.

62. For a discussion of this firm's important work in early cooperative housing experiments, see Lasner, *High Life,* 27–54. Lasner also discusses the context for Browne's critiques of the apartment house discussed below.

63. Hubert, Pirsson, and Hoddick, "New York Flats and French Flats," *Architectural Record* 2, no. 1 (1892–93): 55–64.

64. Hubert, Pirsson, and Hoddick, "New York Flats and French Flats," 63.

7. A Heartless Irony

1. Citizens' Association of New York, *Report by the Council of Hygiene and Public Health of the Citizens' Association of New York upon the Sanitary Conditions of the City* (New York: D. Appleton, 1865), 135; "The Health Department—Important Proceedings" *New York Times,* July 9, 1873; Richard Plunz, *History of Housing in New York* (New York: Columbia University Press, 1990), 15.

2. Manhattan Board of Assessors' Records, 15th Ward, 1838–1891. Martin's 1826 immigration

and passenger list indicate he was a stonemason. The 1850, 1870, and 1880 censuses list his occupation as none.

3. "Prices in an Old District," *Real Estate Record and Builders' Guide (RERBG),* June 6, 1889, 942.

4. Manhattan Alterations Docket Book 1888, Alteration 1614. The alterations raised the assessed value of each of the six lots by $1,500.

5. Riis's accompanying photo of the naked children on the roof, their mother in the process of hanging laundry, now in the collection of the Museum of the City of New York, is also seldom reproduced. In this image she is carrying a washtub. For an image of the rear yard, see Jacob Riis, *The Battle with the Slum* (New York: Macmillan, 1902), 121.

6. Elizabeth Klimasmith, *At Home in the City: Urban Domesticity in American Literature and Culture, 1850–1930* (Dover, N.H.: University Press of New England, 2005), 97.

7. "Mulberry Bend Park Proceedings," *RERBG,* October 22, 1892, 503; "Rear Tenements—Powers of the Board of Health," *RERBG,* October 23, 1897, 589; "Rear Tenement Nuances," *New York Times,* February 19, 1897, 3; "Rear Tenements Must Go," *New York Times,* Jan 24, 1897, 3; "The Razing of Tenements," *New York Times,* October 16, 1897, 16; Manhattan Board of Assessors' Records, 15th Ward, 1896–1899.

8. Jacob Riis, *The Making of an American* (New York: Macmillan, 1901), 348–51.

9. New York New Building Permit (NB) 786–01.

10. Jacob Riis, *How the Other Half Lives: Studies among the Tenements of New York* (New York: Charles Scribner's Sons, 1890), 19.

11. William Hazlett, "Of the Breed of Buddensiek," *Charities and the Commons* 17 (1906): 76.

12. Riis, *The Battle with the Slum,* 105. Like many nineteenth-century observers, Riis had a simplistic notion of the causes of variation in the death rate, many of which had more to do with demographics and ethnicity than housing. See David Ward, *Cities and Immigrants* (New York: Oxford University Press, 1971), 109–10, 115.

13. For an excellent overview of reformers' view of slum residents in general, see Yoosun Park and Susan P. Kemp, "'Little Alien Colonies': Representation of Immigrants and Their Neighborhoods in Social Work Discourse, 1875–1924," *Social Service Review* 80, no. 4 (December 2006): 705–35.

14. Alfred T. White, *Improved Dwellings for the Laboring Classes: The Need and the Way to Meet It on Strict Commercial Principles, in New York and Other Cities* (New York: Putnam's, 1879), 41; also quoted in James Ford, *Slums and Housing, with Special Reference to New York City* (Cambridge, Mass.: Harvard University Press, 1936), 66.

15. For a more synthetic view of the topic, see Richard Dennis, *Cities in Modernity: Representations and Productions of Metropolitan Space, 1840–1930* (Cambridge: Cambridge University Press, 2008).

16. Riis, *The Battle with the Slum,* 106.

17. Riis, *How the Other Half Lives*, 42.

18. Riis, *The Battle with the Slum,* 22.

19. "Buddensiek Pinned Down," *New York Times,* April 16, 1885, 2. New York Supreme Court, *The People of the State of New York against Charles A. Buddensiek,* case on appeal (New York: C. S. Hamilton & Co, printers, 1886).

20. Period reports list Buddensiek's address as 249 East Seventy-Seventh Street, an early 1880s tenement similar to many of the builder's other buildings.

21. "Buddensiek's Record," *New York Times,* April 15, 1885, 2.

22. These buildings were mentioned explicitly by Dudley in court testimony. Determining the builder's other properties is difficult because, as he admitted, he consistently filed deeds and building permits in the names of (sometimes fictitious) straw purchasers in an attempt to avoid creditors. The Third Avenue buildings were filed in the name of Samuel Simons. See *New York v. Buddensiek*, 491; NB 786–91.

23. *New York v. Buddensiek,* 438. "Buddensiek on His Mortar," *New York Tribune,* June 17, 1885, 5.

24. "The Conviction of Buddensiek," *New York Tribune,* June 20, 1885, 4; "Charles A. Buddensiek Sues," *New York Times,* January 27, 1898, 1.

25. Riis, *The Battle with the Slum,* 20.

26. "A Month of Building Disasters," *Inland Architect* 26 (September 1893): 1.

27. Hazlett, "Of the Breed of Buddensiek," 74–76.

28. "The Buddensiek Revival," *New York Times,* March 12, 1905, 10; "Built of Poor Materials: The Collapse of a 'Buddensiek' Building in a Massachusetts Town," *New York Times,* July 16, 1885, 1. "Buddensiek in Hartford," *New York Times,* February 22, 1896, 4; "Convicts as Architects," *Inland Architects* 24 (February 1897): 1.

29. "The New Buddensiek," *New York Times,* September 29, 1896.

30. "New York Topics: More Bribery Revealed: The Case of Buddensiek, the 'Skin Builder,'" *Boston Evening Transcript,* May 29, 1886, b7.

31. "Big Tenement Caves In: Eight Workingmen Injured, Two May Die," *New York Times,* September 18, 1903, 14. See NB 441–03.

32. "Eight Dead, 13 Injured, Workmen Buried by Collapse of Wall," *Boston Daily Globe,* August 26, 1908, 1–3.

33. Bernstein was born in Russia in 1867 and immigrated in 1876. U.S. Federal Census, 1910. He lived with his wife, Margaret, in Washington Heights.

34. Manhattan New Building Docket Books, December 1899, New York City Municipal Archives.

35. "Tenement Law Violated," *New York Tribune,* July 23, 1901, 1.

36. "Mr. Bernstein's Reply: Denies Charge That He Evaded Tenement Law," *New York Tribune,* July 24, 1901, 7.

37. "Tenement House Plans Questioned," *RERBG* 68 (July 27, 1901): 111.

38. Extant buildings include 54 Eldridge Street for P. and J. Horowitz; 169–171 Allen Street, two seven-story buildings for N. Greenberg; 211 East Broadway for H. D. Haber; 241 E. Thirteenth for Jacob Prenowitz; and 111 Eldridge Street for Herman Silberman.

39. "Tenement Law Evaded Says Mr. DeForest," *New York Times,* July 23, 1901; "Attempted Evasion of the New Tenement-House Law," *Charities and the Commons* 7 (July 27, 1901): 77–83.

40. "Mr. Bernstein's Reply," 7. Bernstein called the investigation a "libel."

41. *Father Knickerbocker Adrift: Greater New York Government, 1902–1903* (New York: Fusion Record Publishing Company, 1903), 71–73.

42. Henry Moskowitz, "Jews in Tenement House Department," letter to the editor, *New York Times,* October 25, 1903, 25.

43. "Tammany's Falsehoods: The Tenement House Department," *The American Hebrew and Jewish Messenger,* October 23, 1903, 733.

44. Grosvenor Atterbury, "The Phipps Model Tenement Houses," *Charities and the Commons* 17 (October 6, 1906): 57. For a general history of the project, see Christopher Gray, "Streetscapes: Henry Phipps and Phipps Houses; Millionaire's Effort to Improve Housing for the Poor," *New York Times,* November 23, 2003.

45. Atterbury, "The Phipps Model Tenement Houses," 57.

46. For a background on housing reform movements in England, from which many Americans drew inspiration, see, for instance, Jerry White, *Rothschild Buildings: Life in an East Side Tenement Block, 1887–1920* (London: Routledge and Kegan, 1980). For a view of reformers' interest in asserting power over tenement residents, see Robert Bremner, "'An Iron Scepter Twined with Roses': The Octavia Hill System of Housing Management," *Social Service Review* 39, no. 2 (June 1965): 222–31; Gareth Stedman Jones, *Outcast London: A Study in the Relationship between Classes in Victorian Society* (Oxford: Clarendon Press, 1971), 179–96. For a discussion of the New England background of later housing reformers, see Susan Marie Wirka, "The City Social Movement: Progressive Women Reformers and Early Social Planners," in *Planning the Twentieth-Century American City,* ed. Mary Corbin Sies and Christopher Silver (Baltimore: Johns Hopkins University Press, 1996), 55–76.

47. Gustavus A. Weber, "Improved Tenement Homes for American Cities," *Municipal Affairs* 1 (1897): 755.

48. Cynthia Zaitzevsky, "Housing Boston's Poor: The First Philanthropic Experiments," *Journal of the Society of Architectural Historians (JSAH)* 42, no. 2 (May 1983): 157–67.

49. [Charles Eliot Norton], "Model Lodging-Houses in Boston," *Atlantic Monthly* 5 no. 6 (June 1860): 678. Also cited in Zaitzevsky, "Housing Boston's Poor," 161; Zaitzevsky attributes the unsigned article to Norton.

50. Peter C. Hoffer, "Charles Eliot Norton: Aesthetic Reformer in an Unaesthetic Age," *Journal of Aesthetic Education* 8, no. 3 (July 1974): 19–31.

51. Zaitzevsky, "Housing Boston's Poor," 163.

52. Amy Johnson, "Model Housing for the Poor—Turn of the Century Tenement Reform and the Boston Cooperative Building Company" (PhD diss., University of Delaware, 2004), 258.

53. Johnson, "Model Housing for the Poor," 260, citing Margaret Henderson Floyd, *Architecture after Richardson: Regionalism before Modernism* (Chicago: University of Chicago Press, 1994), 377. For a discussion of the Portland buildings, see Martin Dibner, ed., *Portland* (Portland: Greater Portland Landmarks, 1972), 120–25.

54. Plunz, *History of Housing*, 5; Citizens' Association of New York, *Report by the Council of Hygiene and Public Health*, 50. For a history of the Workingman's Home, later dubbed the "big flat," see Robert H. Bremner, "The Big Flat: History of a New York Tenement House," *American Historical Review* 64, no. 1 (October, 1958): 54–62.

55. The key study of Flagg's work and career is Mardges Bacon, *Ernest Flagg: Beaux-Arts Architect and Urban Reformer* (New York : Architectural History Foundation ; Cambridge, Mass.: MIT Press, 1986), especially chap. 8. James Ford, *Slums and Housing, with Special Reference to New York City* (Cambridge, Mass.: Harvard University Press, 1936), 871; also cited in Bacon, *Ernest Flagg*, 234.

56. Which they rarely were in the study area of this project, where land was scarcer. Large blocks of tenements like this are more common on the Upper East Side and Harlem.

57. For a detailed (and highly critical) history of a City and Suburban Home Company development, albeit sponsored by a developer who was attempting to prevent landmarking in order to demolish the complex, see Gina Luria Walker Associates, ed., *The City and Suburban Home Company's York Avenue Estate: A Social and Architectural History* (New York: Kalikow 78/79, 1990). The document, in three volumes and nearly six inches in height, was authored in part by Roy Lubove, Robert Fogelson, and David P. Handlin. It lays out many of the cultural biases of the housing reform movement and makes an early argument for the significance of speculative working-class housing. The document also records a fascinating preservation controversy.

58. [Peter Herter], "The Critic Criticized: Are Mr. Flagg's Plans Practicable?," *RERBG* 65 (May 26, 1900): 916.

59. For important background on this topic, see Gwendolyn Wright, *Moralism and the Model Home: Domestic Architecture and Culture Conflict in Chicago, 1873–1913* (Chicago: University of Chicago Press, 1980), 105–254.

60. Bertha H. Smith, "The Gospel of Simplicity as Applied to Tenement Homes," *The Craftsman* 9 (1905): 84–95. For a discussion of art and social conflict, see Katherine Martinez, "At Home with Mona Lisa: Consumers and Commercial Visual Culture, 1880–1920," in *Seeing High and Low: Representing Social Conflict in American Visual Culture,* ed. Patricia Johnson (Berkeley: University of California Press, 2006), 160–76;

61. For a changing middle-class conception of the parlor, see Katherine C. Grier, "Decline of the Memory Palace: The Parlor after 1890," in *American Home Life, 1880–1930: A Social History of Spaces and Services,* ed. Jessica Foy and Thomas Schlereth (Knoxville: University of Tennessee Press, 1992); Sally McMurry, "City Parlor, County Living Room, Rural Vernacular Design and the American Parlor, 1840–1900," *Winterthur Portfolio* 20, no. 4 (Winter 1985): 261–80.

62. Smith, "Gospel of Simplicity," 85.

63. *Father Knickerbocker Adrift,* 72.

64. William B. Patterson, "The Religious Value of Proper Housing," *Annals of the American Academy of Political and Social Science* 51 (January 1914): 43.

65. See, for instance, "The Tenement Question," *Puck* 4, no. 104 (March 15, 1879): 3.

66. Marcus T. Reynolds, *Housing the Poor in American Cities* (Baltimore: American Economic Association, 1892), 109.

67. John Morrison, *Home Ownership versus Rented Houses: Moral Results* (Toronto: Williams Brigss, 1900), 5–7. For a study of reformers' interest in promoting the idealized nuclear family, see Laura L. Lovett, *Conceiving the Future: Pronatalism, Reproduction, and the Family in the United States, 1890–1938* (Chapel Hill: University of North Carolina Press, 2007).

68. "To Rid Boston of Slums," *New-York Daily Tribune,* May 17, 1903, 2.

69. Sam Bass Warner Jr., *Streetcar Suburbs: The Process of Growth in Boston,* 2nd ed. (Cambridge, Mass.: Harvard University Press, 1962), 101–6; Lawrence J. Vale, *From the Puritans to the Projects: Public Housing and Public Neighbors* (Cambridge, Mass.: Harvard University Press, 2000), 105–10; David P. Handlin, *The American Home: Architecture and Society, 1815–1915* (Boston: Little Brown and Company, 1979), 240–62. For period accounts, see Robert Treat Paine, "The Housing Conditions in Boston," *Annals of the American Academy of Political and Social Science* 20 (July 1902): 123–36; Robert Treat Paine, *Homes for the People* (Boston: Tolman and White, 1882); Edward Everett Hale, *Workingmen's Homes: Essays and Stories* (Boston: James R. Osgood, 1875).

70. Warner, *Streetcar Suburbs,* 103–5; Clifford Edward Clark, *The American Family Home, 1800–1960* (Chapel Hill: University of North Carolina Press, 1986), 252.

71. Margaret Crawford, *Building the Workingman's Paradise: The Design of American Company Towns* (London: Verso, 1995), 74–76; Susan L. Klaus, *A Modern Arcadia: Frederick Law Olmsted, Jr. and the Plan for Forest Hills Gardens* (Amherst: University of Massachusetts Press, 2002); Richard Candee and Greer Hardwicke, "Early Twentieth-Century Reform Housing by Kilham and Hopkins, Architects of Boston," *Winterthur Portfolio* 22, no. 1 (Spring 1987): 47–80. For a period source on Atterbury's work in this regard, see C. Matlack Price, "The Development of a National Architecture: The Work of Grosvenor Atterbury," *Arts and Decoration* 2, no. 5 (March 1912): 176–79.

72. The same ornamentation strategy was not employed by Paine at his earlier brick row-house developments near Madison Park in Lower Roxbury. These two-story houses were ornamented in a manner quite similar to the utilitarian tenement. The far more urban location, compared to the suburban tract for Sunnyside, and the masonry construction probably account for the difference in ornamentation.

Epilogue

1. The failure of the bank is described in Rebecca Kobrin, "Destructive Creators: Sender Jarmulowsky and Financial Failure in the Annals of American Jewish History," *American Jewish History* 97, no. 2 (April 2013): 105–17.

2. Belle Court's address was 395 Fort Washington Avenue. See New York New Building Permit (NB), 209–9.

3. Segel lived in one of a series of buildings he built at the corner of Georgia and Hartwell Streets in Roxbury. 1910 U.S. Census, Boston Ward 21, District 1590, page 46. Application for Permit to Build, 8 Hartwell Street, April 3, 1907. Permit filed in the name of Simon Dobkins, a frequent partner of Segel. Segel owned the property by the time of the 1915 Bromley Atlas.

4. Lee M. Friedman, *Pilgrims in a New Land* (Philadelphia: Jewish Publication Society of America, 1948), 305.

5. This period has elicited significant interest. It is covered most thoroughly in Deborah Dash More, *At Home in America: Second Generation New York Jews* (New York: Columbia University Press, 1981), chap. 2. See also Gerald M. Gamm, "In Search of Suburbs: Boston's Jewish Districts, 1843–1994," in *The Jews of Boston: Essays on the Occasion of the Centenary of the Combined Jewish*

Philanthropies of Greater Boston, ed. Jonathan Sarna and Ellen Smith (Boston: Combined Jewish Philanthropies of Greater Boston, 1995); Jeffrey S. Gurock, *When Harlem Was Jewish, 1870–1930* (New York: Columbia University Press, 1979); Deborah Dash Moore, "On the Fringes of the City: Jewish Neighborhoods in Three Boroughs," in *The Landscape of Modernity: Essays on New York City, 1900–1940,* ed. David Ward and Oliver Zunz (New York: Russell Sage Foundation, 1997), 252–73; Mindy Rhindress, "The End of the Line: The Relationship between New York City's Subway System and Residential Class Structure" (PhD diss.: City University of New York, 2007). For some sense of this discrimination, see "Boston Jews Being Forced into Ghettos: Objection to Jewish Tenants Has Spread through Brookline, Alston and Brighton," *Jewish Advocate,* August 5, 1910, 1.

6. 61 Hester Street, designed by Charles Straub in a manner more typical of buildings built a decade earlier. See NB 129–13.

7. See 18 Doyers Street for Mon Hing, NB 134–28; 26 Mott Street for Walter Foonpoos, NB 270–25. For a context on Chinatown architecture focusing on the West Coast, see Christopher L. Yip, "Association, Residence, and Shop: An Appropriation of Commercial Blocks in North American Chinatowns," in *Gender, Class, and Shelter: Perspectives in Vernacular Architecture, V,* ed. Elizabeth Collins Cromley and Carter L. Hudgins (Knoxville: University of Tennessee Press, 1995), 109–18. Christopher L. Yip, "San Francisco's Chinatown: An Architectural and Urban History" (PhD diss.: University of California: Berkeley, 1985).

8. On the background of rent regulation, see Robert M. Fogelson, *The Great Rent Wars: New York, 1917–1929* (New Haven, Conn.: Yale University Press, 2013), especially 109–96. For a later period, see Michael Lipsky, *Protest in City Politics: Rent Strikes, Housing, and the Power of the Poor* (Chicago: Rand McNally and Company, 1970).

9. Leo Grebler, *Housing Market Behavior in a Declining Area* (New York: Columbia University Press, 1952); chapter 3 discusses many of the financial motives for the abandonment of tenements in the 1930s and 1940s. Andrew Dolkart, *Biography of a Tenement: An Architectural History of 97 Orchard Street* (Santa Fe, N.Mex.: Center for American Places, 2006), 112, discusses the particular conditions that led to the abandonment of the building that later became the Lower East Side Tenement Museum.

10. Fogelson, *The Great Rent Wars,* 17–85.

11. Ernest Flagg, "The New York Tenement-House Evil and Its Cure," *Scribner's Magazine* (1894): 116.

12. Jacob Riis, *The Ten Years War: An Account of the Battle with the Slum in New York* (Boston: Houghton Mifflin Company, 1900), chap. 6.

13. Max Page, *The Creative Destruction of Manhattan, 1900–1940* (Chicago: University of Chicago Press, 1999), chap. 3.

14. Helen Hall, *A Dutchman's Farm: Three Hundred and One Years at Corlears Hook, 1638–1939* (New York: Henry Street Settlement, 1939), 33–34.

15. Page, *The Creative Destruction of Manhattan,* 69–109.

16. For obsolescence of housing standards, with a focus on the West End, see Daniel M. Abramson, *Obsolescence: An Architectural History* (Chicago: University of Chicago Press, 2016), 38–60.

17. For a discussion of the clearance efforts in Boston, see Thomas O'Connor, *Building a New Boston: Politics and Urban Renewal, 1950–1970* (Boston: Northeastern University Press, 1993), especially chap. 5; Lawrence J. Vale, *From the Puritans to the Projects: Public Housing and Public Neighborhoods* (Cambridge: Harvard University Press, 2000), chaps. 3 and 4; Sean M. Fisher, *The Last Tenement: Confronting Community and Urban Renewal in Boston's West End* (Boston: Bostonian Society, 1992). For New York, see Richard Plunz, *A History of Housing in New York City* (New York: Columbia University Press, 1990), chaps. 6–8; Nicholas Dagen Bloom and Matthew Gordon Lasner, eds., *Affordable Housing in New York: The People, Places, and Policies That Transformed a City* (Princeton, N.J.: Princeton University Press, 2016), 75–139.

18. Even those public housing projects created before the widespread influence of European

modernism demonstrate a concerted avoidance of ornament. See the New York Housing Authority's First Houses on Avenue A and East Third Street between Avenue A and First Avenue. These were designed in 1935 by Frederik L. Ackerman. Norval White and Elliot Willensky, eds., *AIA Guide to New York City,* 4th ed. (New York: Three Rivers Press, 2000), 177.

19. There have been many excellent recent studies on the design of the single-family suburban home of this period and the industry that supported it. See particularly James A. Jacobs, *Detached America: Building Houses in Postwar Suburbia* (Charlottesville: University of Virginia Press, 2015); Barbara Lane, *Houses for a New World: Builders and Buyers in American Suburbs, 1945–1965* (Princeton, N.J.: Princeton University Press, 2015); Dianne Harris, *Little White Houses: How the Postwar Home Constructed Race in America* (Minneapolis: University of Minnesota Press, 2013).

20. Aline May Lewis Goldstone and Harmon H. Goldstone, *Lafayette A. Goldstone: A Career in Architecture* (New York, 1964), 85.

21. Shoolman was joined by S. Pierre Bonan, a New York financier as well as attorney, and planner Jerome Rappaport. See O'Connor, *Building a New Boston,* 132.

22. "Theodore J. Shoolman, 86; Developed Charles River Park," obituary, *Boston Globe,* October 17, 2005; O'Connor, *Building a New Boston,* 131–32.

23. Herbert Gans, *The Urban Villagers: Group and Class in the Life of Italian Americans,* updated and expanded ed. (New York: Free Press, 1962), introduction. Slightly earlier, William Foote Whyte examined the social structure of the North End. See William Foote Whyte, *Street Corner Society: The Social Structure of an Italian Slum* (Chicago: University of Chicago Press, 1955).

24. Jane Jacobs, *The Death and Life of Great American Cities* (New York: Vintage Books, 1961), passim. Jacobs discussed the "unslumming" of the North End in great detail in chapter 15. There she notes that residents of that area, redlined out of credit and long the target of city planners, were slowly reforming the housing conditions on their own. This unslumming was due in large measure to the reduction in the crowded conditions that had previously marked that neighborhood.

25. Plunz, *A History of Housing,* chap. 9. For an analysis of competing ideas about housing in a tenement landscape, see Nathan Glazer, *From a Cause to a Style: Modernist Architecture's Encounter with the American City* (Princeton, N.J.: Princeton University Press, 2007), 165–91.

26. For a description of the process of housing abandonment, see Peter D. Salins, *The Ecology of Housing Destruction* (New York: New York University Press, 1980).

27. For a discussion of the abandonment of tenements in New York, see Christopher Mele, *Selling the Lower East Side: Culture, Real Estate and Resistance in New York City* (Minneapolis: University of Minnesota Press, 2000), chap. 6.

28. Ed Boland Jr., "F.Y.I.," *New York Times,* September 8, 2002.

29. Randall Wolff, correspondence with author, summer 2016. Wolff's story can be found in his memoir: *The Gargoyler of Greenwich Village* (self-published). For a fictional portrayal of the same phenomenon, see John Freeman Gill, *The Gargoyle Hunters: A Novel* (New York: Knopf, 2017).

30. *Batteries Not Included,* directed by Steven Spielberg (1987; Universal City, Calif.: Universal City Studios, 2003), DVD.

31. "Speculation Moves to Chinatown," *City Limits Magazine,* September 1981, 2–3; John Wang, "Developers Readying Three Towers in Chinatown," *New York Times,* September 20, 1981, R1.

32. Frank P. Braconi, "In Re *In Rem*: Innovation and Expediency in New York's Housing Policy," in *Housing and Community Development in New York City: Facing the Future,* ed. Michael H. Schill (Albany: State University of New York Press, 1999), 93–118. For a critique of the program, see Peter D. Salins and Gerard C. S. Mildner, *Scarcity by Design: The Legacy of New York City's Housing Policies* (Cambridge, Mass.: Harvard University Press, 1992), 100–4. See also Bloom and Lasner, *Affordable Housing in New York,* 258–80.

33. Dolores Hayden, *Redesigning the American Dream: The Future of Housing, Work, and Family Life* (New York: W. W. Norton, 1984), 155–58.

34. For one of the many excellent studies of the new ethnic dynamics in New York, see Roger

Sanjeck, *The Future of Us All: Race and Neighborhood Politics in New York* (Ithaca, N.Y.: Cornell University Press, 1998).

35. Bloom and Lasner, *Affordable Housing in New York,* 245–89.

36. For a context on this kind of gentrification, see Mele, *Selling the Lower East Side,* especially chaps. 7–9; Amy Zimmer, "From Peddlers to Panini: The Anatomy of Orchard Street," in *The Suburbanization of New York: Is the World's Greatest City Becoming Just Another Town?,* ed. Jerliou Hammett and Kingsley Hammett (New York: Princeton Architectural Press, 2007), 53–63.

37. The process, which involved evicting rent-stabilized tenants, took over five years. Jen Chung "47 East 3rd Conversion Explained," *Gothamist,* March 9, 2009, http://gothamist.com/2007/03/09/east_village_te.php; Dennis Hevesi, "Everybody Out," *New York Times,* June 26, 2005, http://www.nytimes.com/2005/06/26/realestate/everybody-out; Marc Santora, "Landlord's Dream Confronts Rent Stabilized Lives," *New York Times,* June 15, 2008, http://www.nytimes.com/2008/06/15/nyregion/15evict.html. Exact renovation costs for the project are not publicly available, although cost affidavits filed with the Department of Buildings (which routinely underestimates costs) for some portions of the multiphase project show at least $1.2 million in work.

38. While the economic effects of these laws are often debated, usually by interested parties from the real estate industry, their historical and cultural contingencies are less well understood. See, for instance, Salins and Mildner, *Scarcity by Design.* For a political history of zoning in New York, see S. J. Makielski Jr., *The Politics of Zoning: The New York Experience* (New York: Columbia University Press, 1966). The best discussion of the social aspects of these laws is found in F. Duncan Case, "Hidden Social Agendas and Housing Standards: The New York Tenement House Code of 1901," *Housing and Society* 8, no. 1 (1981): 3–17.

39. Christopher Cameron, "Rabsky, Greenfield Accuse Critics of Broadway Triangle Development of Anti-Semitism," *The Real Deal,* October 24, 2017, therealdeal.com/2017/10/24/rabsky-greenfield-accuse-critics-of-broadway-triangle-development-of-anti-semitism; Tanay Warerkar, "Pfizer Rezoning Brings Simmering Community Tensions to a Boil at City Council Hearing," *Curbed New York,* October 11, 2017, ny.curbed.com/2017/10/11/16454150/pfizer-rezoning-williamsburg-rabsky-city-council; Ari Feldman, "Angry Brooklyn Protesters Disrupt Hearing on Broadway Triangle Rezoning," *Forward,* July 27, 2017, forward.com/news/378234/angry-brooklyn-protesters-disrupt-hearing-on-broadway-triangle-rezoning.

40. For a discussion of the Tenement Museum and its program, see Ruth J. Abram, "Kitchen Conversations: Democracy in Action at the Lower East Side Tenement Museum," *The Public Historian* 29, no. 1 (Winter 2007): 59–76; Zoe Watnik, "Rebuilding the Past: A Critical Examination of the International and U.S. Frameworks Guiding the Reconstructions of Historic Properties" (master's thesis, Rutgers University, 2013), chap. 4.

41. It is used as the background cover photo for a recent edition of Anzia Yezierska's classic 1925 immigrant novel *Bread Givers* (Persa Books, 2003). It also appears as the default photo on the Wikipedia entry "tenement," under the New York section, http://en.wikipedia.org/wiki/Tenement, accessed December 10, 2013.

Index

Zachary J. Violette is an architectural and social historian. He has taught at Parsons/ The New School for Design and the Art Institute of Boston at Lesley University.